Impresario: Paul Taylor, The Melbourne Years, 1981–1984

Impresario: Paul Taylor, The Melbourne Years, 1981–1984

Edited by Helen Hughes & Nicholas Croggon

Surpllus / MUMA

In memory of Paul Taylor

Contents

Preface

Paul would have liked this book. Not just that it's about him or that the peacock in him is recorded in his tartan jacket, his fur coat and his purple trousers. He was keen in his last days that his work, which he unembarrassedly knew was important, would be talked about and remembered. Here in the book, and not as in life, so many of his disparate and broad range of friends, colleagues, admirers, mentors and critics, who had rarely been permitted to, are able to assemble. In life, Paul kept us apart, dashing between groups and continents. In these pages, we've joined to celebrate an impressive, admired and loved young man and brother.

Greg and Janice Taylor, and Philip Taylor-Bartels, 2013

Foreword

The art scene that Paul Taylor came to (briefly) dominate in the early 1980s was undergoing such swift and extensive change, it seemed the culture was being remade before our eyes. While Taylor's interests were national, Melbourne, where he was based and where *Art & Text* was produced, provided the focus for his activities and defined aspects of these cultural shifts. Taylor, arguably more prescient than any other Australian critic, understood, intersected with and engineered some of those shifts. While in retrospect the situation was more complex, Taylor emerged as the harbinger of an era. He marshalled the energies of two groups of artists, critics and curators: an older, more established group that included Judy Annear, Juan Davila, Lyndal Jones, John Nixon, Imants Tillers, Peter Tyndall, Jenny Watson and myself, and a younger crowd numbering Philip Brophy, Maria Kozic, Vivienne Shark LeWitt and Adrian Martin.

In the process of befriending us and drawing us together, Paul built dynamic networks and alliances. His project was both cultural and personal. Not only did the friendships form the core group of contributors and supporters of *Art & Text*, but also incorporated several of the artists whom Taylor selected for two key exhibitions: 'POPISM' and 'Tall Poppies'. Paul brought a brash new professionalism to the art world. As the curator for 'POPISM', he argued for and won payment for the participating artists. It was perhaps the first time a curator had fought for artists' interests in that way. Taylor's engagement with art's commercial side, underpinned by his entrepreneurial flair, meant he was prepared to strenuously promote the artists he favoured. As a critic and freelance curator in the same period, I was wary of such transactions, feeling that the artist's agent was a role more properly suited to a gallery dealer.

Elsewhere, I have characterised the cultural shift in the early '80s as a split between the idealistic, politicised, left-wing scene of the 1970s and a cooler, apolitical, theory-based approach to practice and criticism.[1] However, after the symposium on Taylor, which I co-convened with Adrian Martin at Monash University in September 2012, titled 'Impresario: Paul Taylor / *Art & Text* / POPISM', it seemed that some of Paul's ideas and strategies were more indebted to the 1970s than I'd realised. References to the '70s – its art, styles, ideologies and personalities – flowed through the daylong symposium. The comments were not merely nostalgic – though the symposium, the first devoted to Taylor, was a deeply moving event, especially for those who had been close to him. Rather, the references formed a historical frame to Taylor's enterprise.

In the introduction to *Anything Goes: Art in Australia 1970–1980* (1984), Taylor asked 'Can ... the Seventies ever be the subject of genuine history if we agree that history was problematised and archaeologies of culture mobilised in those years? The Seventies are too complex and varied, too *present*, to support a critical analysis of their outcome now.'[2] *Anything Goes* is the only anthology, and thus the only major, one-off publication, that Taylor produced focusing on Australian art. In 1984, he was twenty-seven, poised between the two generations of practitioners whose alliances he sought and whose work he admired. He was closer in age to the younger group, yet he chose not to concentrate on them. Why?

The '70s witnessed a collectivisation of contemporary culture. Projects such as journals, exhibitions, even the production of artworks, were often conceived of and enacted as group endeavours. While 'impresario' refers to the flamboyant style of Taylor's cultural strategies, it is worth noting that he was not an overbearing personality. Though he was a combative intellectual whose tone as a critic could range from candid to fierce, Taylor's modus operandi was encouraging, inclusive and generous. Taylor chose milieu over singularity and communality over isolated individualistic pursuit. The parties he hosted at Beverley Hills, the glamorous Art Deco apartment block where he lived in South Yarra, were certainly fun but they also provided a social context, designed by Paul, for brokering deals, negotiations and introductions. Taylor's approach to cultural change was collaborative. On a personal level, he could be difficult at times, even rather sharp-tongued, but loyalty was valued. Arguments were usually followed by reconciliations, heated words by a touch of humour. 'Am I off your Christmas card list?', Paul asked me after one disagreement.

The final essay in *Anything Goes*, Taylor's 'Australian "New Wave" and the "Second Degree"' (1981), positions him as a new authority who closes one decade while announcing another, an heir to the critics whose endeavours he respected and who, by their inclusion, he deemed to be shaping forces. Taylor took the long view and it is to his credit that he included some, such as Memory Holloway, with whom he'd previously sparred.[3] *Anything Goes* also gave Taylor the opportunity to document recent critical voices, an absence he believed undermined Australian art history. While *Art & Text* was often regarded as narrowly focused on 'fashionable' theorists such as Baudrillard, Barthes, Derrida and Lacan, and their apologists, a study of *Art & Text*'s contributors reveals an editorial net cast wider than the poststructuralist enterprise. That is not to diminish Taylor's goal: to foreground theory and to link Australian visual culture with international discourses. With *Anything Goes*, Taylor chose the '70s as the frame for his Australian endeavours. It is only now that the periodisation of '70s and '80s Australian visual culture has commenced that the significance of *Anything Goes* is being examined. If Paul had wanted to blow his own trumpet, he could have produced an anthology of *Art & Text*.

There is also a perception that *Art & Text* was an anti-feminist boys' club. On one level, it seemed a clash of cultures: '70s (feminism) versus '80s (conservatism). Money was also an issue. Taylor, the new boy on the block, had secured a level of government funding for *Art & Text* that the feminist arts journal *Lip* never received. In 1981, Taylor took *Lip* to task for its lack of critical bite.[4] His suggestion that *Lip* should incorporate a variety of theoretical perspectives—Lacan, Derrida and Kristeva were mentioned—was timely and apposite. But his assertion that feminism had not extricated itself from 'sociology' was the same reactionary response that had greeted the emerging field of feminist studies in the early '70s. In the next issue of *Lip*, collective members Annette Blonski and Jeannette Fenelon reviewed 'POPISM'. They argued that Taylor's catalogue essay misrepresented several artists, notably Maria Kozic, by placing their works within the fabricated and largely irrelevant theoretical frame of 'popism'.[5] Taylor hit back, accusing Blonksi and Fenelon of focusing on his essay at the expense of the art.[6] In the small but vociferous avant-garde of the early '80s, positions for cultural influence and ascendancy—and funding—were hotly contested: *Lip* and *Art & Text* were rivals. On another level, *Lip* had an argument to make about the lacks and omissions in the dominant culture; so did *Art & Text*. But cultural shifts and loyalties, while seismic, are layered. Taylor's ongoing friendships with feminists and their contributions to *Art & Text* indicate that he was not averse to feminist perspectives.[7] This should not distract from the dismal gender imbalance in *Art & Text*'s contributor figures. From the first issue in 1981 until the eleventh in 1983, there were one hundred contributors: twenty-four were women. Was that why, in *Anything Goes*, Taylor's farewell to Australia, he made sure that eight of the sixteen essays were by women?

The largely negative reception of 'POPISM' was bruising for Taylor: it marked a turning point and Taylor told friends it was a reason for leaving Australia. It was a curious aspect of Paul's personality that while he seemed to relish the role of *agent provocateur*, he was sometimes ill-equipped to deal with its consequences. *Art & a Texta* is a case in point. A parody of *Art & Text*, it was co-edited by several authors including Stan Anson, a tutor in political theory at La Trobe University, and published in December 1982 by Ted Hopkins's Backyard Press.[8] The essays in *Art & a Texta*, some of which are amusing and elegantly written, mocked *Art & Text*'s emphasis on French theory and popular culture. But *Art & a Texta* was no Ern Malley hoax, as was played on the editors of *Angry Penguins* in 1944.[9] It did not set out to deceive: it was clearly a spoof. Yet there are parallels with *Angry Penguins*: *Art & Text* was viewed as pretentious, cliquey and ripe for satire. Taylor was furious and initiated legal proceedings against Hopkins in the Supreme Court of Victoria. On the eve of the hearing, the case was settled out of court.[10] Members of Paul's circle will recall his anger together with the impossibility of persuading him to let the matter drop.

The fate of avant-gardes is to fracture almost as soon as they cohere, and that of the early 1980s was no different. The brief period that *Impresario* documents indicates how rapidly cultural change occurred and the extraordinary level of energy Paul brought to it. When I came up with the idea for the symposium in 2011 and shared it with Monash colleague Adrian Martin, it was because a vibrant, complex and fecund era in which I'd participated—together with many contributors to this book—seemed all but forgotten. How to reclaim it? How to interrogate it? How to contextualise it within a contemporary frame? Towards the end of that year, when Russell Walsh contacted several people, including Max Delany, alerting them that 2012 marked twenty years since Paul's death and thirty years since 'POPISM', it was the necessary spur: Martin and I, with Delany's enthusiastic support, immediately began planning the symposium. The warmth and alacrity that greeted its announcement from friends and colleagues, both old and new, revealed how opportune it was.

I believe Paul would be pleased, honoured and amused by this book. He would regard it, as he should, as his due. No doubt the New York years will be the subject of future research. But *Impresario* signals that the investigation of this era has begun in earnest.

Janine Burke, 2013

Introduction: Paul Taylor, presente

Helen Hughes & Nicholas Croggon

This book offers a constellation of texts orbiting around Paul Taylor, the Australian editor, writer, curator and impresario, and in particular his important and influential early years in Melbourne, between 1981 and 1984.

The dates of the texts included span some thirty years and take a variety of different forms – critical essays, reviews, short reflective texts, interviews, and transcriptions of lectures – the combination of which necessarily amount to a disjunctive, interdisciplinary, and parallactic take on Taylor and his work. Many of the texts, but not all, stem from the symposium 'Impresario: Paul Taylor / *Art & Text* / POPISM', convened by Janine Burke and Adrian Martin and held at Monash University, Melbourne, in September 2012, which marked thirty years since this period of Taylor's life, and the twenty-year anniversary of his untimely death in 1992.

As can be seen from the numerous accounts included here, and from the multiple terms required to describe him, Taylor has meant a great many different things to a great number of different people. In his obituary for Taylor, written in 1992 (and reproduced in this book), the artist Peter Tyndall said:

> I recently saw on TV an Argentinian remembrance ceremony in which, as the names of the dead were read out, those who had known them in life answered, 'presente'.
>
> Those who knew Paul personally will, at this time, be similarly holding him 'presente' in a great number of colourful recollections.[1]

With these words, Tyndall introduces with characteristic elegance the multiple complexities involved in the act of remembering – and, we suggest, the act of making history. In saying 'presente', Tyndall suggests, we not only attempt the difficult task of bringing the irrevocably past into the present, but to do this in way that invokes plurality. We seek to place the passed person back into circulation with the multiple people and places of the present, but we also acknowledge that this making present occurs through multiple people, resulting in a past with multiple different presents.

Today, Tyndall's moving words bear an even stronger resonance, as we occupy a time of the 'contemporary'—a time preoccupied with its own multiple presents, and with the multiple presents of the past.

In this introduction, we will briefly introduce Taylor's multiple presents, both as they manifested during his life, and as they are accounted for in the structure of this book. (The act of 'presenting' is, after all, as Edward Colless suggests in his self-admittedly perverse essay 'Ecce Homo', the task of the director, or the impresario himself.) But, moreover, we will also seek to justify why this act of making Taylor present is an historical and memorial task that is entirely suited to our own present.

Paul Taylor: 1957–1992

Paul Taylor was born in Melbourne on the 10th of September 1957. In 1979, he graduated from Monash University with a Bachelor of Arts (Honours), with a thesis on American Minimalist sculpture of the 1960s and the viewer's perceptual relationship to it (notably, the original version submitted to Monash had a reflective mirror glued to the front cover).[2] After a brief stint teaching art history in Hobart at the Tasmanian School of Art in 1979 and 1980, Taylor returned to Melbourne and, in quick succession, produced a series of publications and exhibitions that would become touchstones of Australian art history.

In 1981, he founded the art journal *Art & Text*, and in the first issue published his essay 'Australian "New Wave" and the "Second Degree"', which has become synonymous with both the agenda of early *Art & Text* and, more broadly, the application of poststructuralist and postmodern theory to the interpretation of Australian art. In 1982, at the age of twenty-four, he curated the exhibition 'POPISM' at the National Gallery of Victoria, which was accompanied by an extensive essay (and an extensive bibliography) on appropriation or, as he put it, 'photo rhetoric'. 'POPISM', the exhibition and catalogue, was shortly followed by his most important essay 'Popism: The Art of White Aborigines', commissioned for *Flash Art International* then published in Sydney art journal *On the Beach* in 1983. Also in this year, he curated the smaller exhibition 'Tall Poppies', an 'exhibition of five pictures', at the Melbourne University Art Gallery. In 1984, he edited and published an anthology of writing on Australian art from the 1970s, titled *Anything Goes: Art in Australia 1970–1980*. Soon after, Taylor departed Melbourne for New York, where he remained for approximately eight years, writing art journalism and conducting interviews for publications like *Vanity Fair*, *The Village Voice* and *The New York Times*. In 1992, Taylor returned to Melbourne, extremely ill from AIDS-related lymphoma, where he passed away a week after his thirty-fifth birthday, on the 17th of September.

Taylor's substantial influence on 1980s Australian visual art and art writing has been duly registered in multiple publications. His place within the broader picture of 1980s Australian art and its surrounding discourses of antipodean postmodernity has been surveyed most comprehensively in Rex Butler's books *An Uncertain Smile: Australian Art in the '90s* (1996) and more completely in *What is Appropriation? An Anthology of Writings on Australian Art in the 1980s & 1990s* (also 1996), as well as in Charles Green's critical history of postmodern and contemporary Australian art, *Peripheral Vision: Contemporary Australian Art 1970–1994* (1995).[3]

More specifically focused on Taylor's own writing, there is the posthumously released anthology of his New York–based writings, *After Andy: SoHo in the Eighties*, published in 1995 by Schwartz City in Melbourne and edited by Paul Foss.[4] The 44th issue of *Art & Text* (1993), also edited by Foss, featured a collection of obituaries for Taylor by Adrian Martin, Vivienne Shark LeWitt, Gregory Taylor, Thomas Sokolowski, Leo Castelli, Richard Prince, Carol Squires and Allan Schwartzman, which registered his impact, by this stage internationally, on the art world.[5] Heather Barker's PhD dissertation, 'A Critical History of Writing on Australian Art, 1960–1988', submitted in 2005, includes a significant section that analyses Taylor's writing in relation to the nationalist tradition of Australian art criticism inaugurated, she argues, by Bernard Smith's 1962 book *Australian Painting: 1788–1960*.[6] And in 2009, the Melbourne-born and now New York–based artist Rob McKenzie instigated the book *The &-Files: Art & Text 1981–2002* with Paul Foss, Ross Chambers, Rex Butler and Simon Rees, jointly published by the Institute of Modern Art in Brisbane and Whale & Star in Florida. Mainly comprising interviews with Foss, the second and long-lasting editor of *Art & Text*, this book focuses on Foss's editorship of the journal from 1984 until its final issue in 2002, leaving the early years under Taylor's editorship wanting further attention.[7]

Finally, in 2012, marking the twenty-year anniversary of Taylor's death, art historian Janine Burke and cinema historian and critic Adrian Martin (though their work frequently and radically exceeds these disciplines), both friends of Taylor's, as well as key figures in his art historical and theoretical milieu, convened the conference 'Impresario: Paul Taylor / *Art & Text* / POPISM', which led, with the support of Max Delany and the Monash University Museum of Art, as well as Taylor's family, to the publication of this book.

This book: Paul Taylor's pasts presented

The ripples from the period framed by Taylor's time in Melbourne in the early 1980s are today felt in multiple ways. On the one hand, his cultural achievements during this time – especially the establishment of *Art & Text* and the exhibition 'POPISM' – constitute key landmarks in the formation and theorisation of Australian art history. On the other hand, Taylor's role as a key player in the social and cultural arena of Melbourne in the early 1980s is still felt keenly in the memories of those who experienced it with him.

Accordingly, this book is divided into four parts. Part I, 'Paul Taylor: in context', comprises essays that introduce Taylor (Adrian Martin's 'Return Waltz'), then introduce the influential forces and intersections of music (Chris McAuliffe), theorisations of Aboriginality (Ian McLean), arts publishing (Ashley Crawford), fashion (Merryn Gates), gay history (Graham Willett), and – for want of a less timeworn description – 'pop culture' (Philip Brophy) that shaped Taylor's thinking in Melbourne in the early 1980s.

Part II, 'Paul Taylor: in action', looks at Taylor's key activities in Melbourne between 1981 and 1984, with essays that canvas his time spent in Hobart planning issue 1 of *Art & Text* (Jonathan Holmes), the subsequent and enduring critical legacies of the establishment of *Art & Text* (Charles Green & Heather Barker, and Adrian Martin), previously unpublished lectures on the exhibition 'POPISM' from 1982 (Philip Brophy and Adrian Martin), plus Robert Rooney's famous review of the exhibition for *The Age*, which subsequently got him fired.[8] This section also includes an essay by Judy Annear that, by contrast to 'POPISM', concentrates on the underanalysed 1983 exhibition curated by Taylor, 'Tall Poppies'. Part II closes with Rex Butler and Susan Rothnie's essay 'Paul Taylor's 1970s', which expands on Taylor's gesture, in 1984, of editing and publishing his *Anything Goes* anthology, making the argument that, for Taylor, the 1970s were the 'vanishing mediator' that made possible his totalising theory of Australian art in the 1980s.

The second half of the book shifts from a contextual and critical account of Taylor's time between 1981 and 1984 to provide an archive of source materials. Part III comprises interviews with individuals close to Taylor or who can shed new light on his work – Patrick McCaughey, John Nixon, David Chesworth, Janine Burke, Lyndal Jones, Imants Tillers, Juan Davila, Jenny Watson and David Pestorius. Part IV contains reflections on Taylor, by friends and colleagues—Vivienne Shark LeWitt, Ralph Traviati, Sue Cramer, Maria Kozic, Denise Robinson, Peter Tyndall, Paul Foss and Edward Colless.

To those of us not present in Melbourne in the early 1980s, it is clear that Taylor's significance arose, in part, from a particular knot of artistic, cultural, social, musical and political intensity—a series of 'moments', Adrian Martin explains, which today are defined as much by their intensity as their evanescence. Through the meticulous accounts of Janine Burke, Adrian Martin, Chris McAuliffe, Ashley Crawford and Jonathan Holmes, and the series of reflections in Parts III and IV, this book seeks to help us to remember these moments, which may have been forgotten.

Looking back through the lens of art history, Taylor's legacy might at first sight seem to have already been *over*-remembered. That is to say, there is something about the period of the early 1980s, and Taylor's work in particular, that transfixes us, compelling us to constantly glance back at it (even as the rest of the world resolutely ignores it), to always position contemporary art and critical practices in Australia in relation to it. This transfixing power stems, we would argue, from Taylor's presiding role over Australia's reception, and internalisation, of the logic of postmodernism.

In the early 1980s, Taylor, both in his writing and in his editorial and curatorial choices, promoted and analysed a new strain of Australian art known as 'appropriation art', embodied in the work of artists such as Imants Tillers, Juan Davila, Robert Rooney, Jenny Watson, Howard Arkley and Maria Kozic, amongst others. As is explained in more detail in the texts that follow, Taylor—in 'Australian "New Wave" and the "Second Degree"', published in *Art & Text* 1 and included as the closing entry of his anthology on Australian art of the 1970s, and in his 'POPISM' exhibition and catalogue of 1982—explained (with the assistance of Roland Barthes and Dick Hebdige) the way in which Australia's new 'appropriation artists' copied or quoted other artworks and presented them as new works, thus demonstrating the radical equivalency of all art, high and low, present and past.

Butler, Green, Barker, and McLean (in his essay 'Strategic Aboriginalism', included in this book) have each shown that *Art & Text*'s performance of this postmodern mode of thinking also allowed for the formation of a specifically national identity. The sequence of this next theoretical phase has been well-rehearsed. Paul Foss, in his influential 'Foreign Bodies' paper 'Theatrum

Nondum Cognitorium' of 1981, explained that 'Australia' is an image that precedes its own reality, an endlessly recursive series of maps and projections.[9] Tillers, in his *Art & Text* essay 'Locality Fails' of 1982, then argued that in a postmodern world there was no such thing as an original – that the original was in fact only the first copy.[10] Australia, then, as a place populated entirely by copies, and whose artistic styles were deemed to always be copies of other styles (along with the 'Australian experience' being one of 'simulation'), could be seen to be the paradigm of this postmodern world; that is, Australia was exceptional or authentic precisely in its unoriginality or its inauthenticity. In 1983, in 'Popism: The Art of White Aborigines', Taylor synthesised these streams, finally making the famous argument:

> A search for a regional Australian culture, ultimately a worthless pastime, reveals a centrifugal implosion wherein our art, like the mythopoeic Dreamtime of the aborigines, is the flak of an explosion not of our detonation. This art, born in mediation, has gestated within the camera where things are naturally upside down and is expressed in a carnivalesque array of copies, inversions and negatives. It is an ab-original, soulless, antipodal reflection and a name is written on every stone.[11]

In this way, the school of thinkers brought together by Taylor, as 'producer-*auteur*' of the early issues of *Art & Text*, negotiated a solution to Terry Smith's then-hegemonic 'Provincialism Problem' simply by inverting it – by showing that Australia was central in, and because of, its peripherality.

Under Taylor's deft guidance, the logic of postmodernism commenced its nationalistic unravelling and, as the contents of Butler's edited volume *What is Appropriation?* attest, continued in the late 1980s and 1990s to unravel in increasingly complex ways. In his trio of exhaustive analyses of postmodern logic in art criticism, art and finally art history (*An Uncertain Smile*, *What is Appropriation?*, and *Radical Revisionism*[12]), Butler recounts in immense detail the way in which Australian art and art criticism played out the endless folding and unfolding of postmodern logic, in which the original first precedes the copy (past precedes the present), then the copy precedes the original (present precedes the past) and, finally, both precede each other in an endless looping that ends by pointing to the condition of this looping itself – the writing of criticism and of history themselves.

In this way, Butler showed that the rhetoric of appropriation crystallised by Taylor comprised an endless paradoxical doubling in which the artwork is undecidably both an original and a copy, a collusion and a critique. Butler argued that even 1990s art and criticism, precisely in its attempt to move beyond this postmodern logic, gets caught up in the logic's process of framing and reframing, endlessly rehearsing the undecidability of the work's interpretation. Therefore, his important book on appropriation is named, formulated and played out as the question, '*what is appropriation?*', because this question is in principle, he notes, something that cannot be answered.[13] In this way, Butler's works themselves represent the final stage in the logic's unravelling – not as its refutation (which, as he explains, is always already anticipated, merely another reframing that can itself be reframed), but as its thorough explanation and, in this thoroughness, its exhaustion.

Paul Taylor's pasts in today's multiple presents

Today, over thirty years on from the first issue of *Art & Text* and 'POPISM', Australian art practice and history has left this postmodern logic of representation behind. Working under the sign of 'the contemporary', artists and theorists have partly abandoned the shaping discourses of nationalism to pursue an understanding of contemporary art as a global phenomenon, one which unfolds like a one-to-one map of the world, with biennales for every city, and contemporary art museums for every country. Today, the central question underpinning the most advanced art criticism is not how regional art expresses its regionalism, but rather how it moves beyond its putative borders to entangle itself more completely in the globalism of contemporary art. After, and perhaps only because of, Butler's explanation of the logic of postmodern appropriation's workings, contemporary artists, critics and historians no longer seem concerned to break from, perform or explain Taylor's postmodern logic, and its dynamic historical vaulting into the past and the future. Instead, as the philosopher Peter Osborne explains, the contemporary is a moment defined by a concern for the present and, in particular, its 'con-temporaneity' – the way in which the present is characterised by the coming together of 'different but equally "present" temporalities or "times"'.[14] This obsession with multiple presents also infects the past – we realise that what we once conceived of as the singular forward drive of modernity was, or is, in fact multiple modernities, the recuperation of which has been a major art historical paradigm since at least the publication of *Art Since 1900: Modernism, Antimodernism, Postmodernism* at the beginning of this millennium.[15]

It is at this crucial juncture – after the exhaustion of the postmodern, and the arrival of the contemporary – that this reevaluation of Taylor's work accrues a new significance.

By looking back at Taylor through the lens of the present, we can see that his achievement was not only to put in motion a hugely influential rhetoric of appropriation, but also to do so through an immense bringing together, by unifying the immense plurality of his own time and his immediate past – a reconciliation that occurred across the surface of his present. This book aims to show how well Taylor achieved this task: his incredible reconciliation of those short years of frenetic social and critical activity into a single, varnished surface – a sign of 'the sign' that enveloped and silenced the clamorous plurality of the 1970s, but which also, paradoxically, and as McLean brilliantly demonstrates through his analysis of Taylor and Tillers's early writings, briefly located Aboriginal art on the same moral and conceptual plane as other (white) contemporary art. As Rothnie and Butler point out in their essay, by looking back at Taylor today and analysing this activity, we thus not only see an important precursor for our contemporary attempts to think the plurality of the present, but also, perhaps for the first time, the plurality of the historical moment in which this occurred – the hinge that joins the plurality of the 1970s to the 1980s.

In other words, it is perhaps only in the contemporary moment, with its concerns not for a continuation of art history's mechanical surge into the future but for an exploration of the simultaneity of our multiple presents, that we can stop *performing* Taylor's legacy, and perhaps see it historically for the first time. It allows us to see Taylor's achievement as fragmented across his own life – his multiple roles and his multiple significances to different people – but also, hopefully, as it occurred against the plurality of different 'times' that comprised his historical present.

For these reasons, we have constructed this book in multiple, overlapping, even kaleidoscopic ways: as a sourcebook to fill gaps in the historical past, to reflect critically on specific cultural events, to reinvigorate particular moments – in all accounts, to do history, to make Taylor 'presente' in a way that is both historical and memorial, and in a way that we hope points to the singularity of his achievement, just as it gestures to the plurality of practices that constituted him, surrounded him, preceded him and followed him.

Part I
Paul Taylor: in context

The return waltz

Adrian Martin

All Things Must Pass

Modern historians have evolved many ways of trying to reconstruct the past on an almost day-to-day basis, to give a sense of ordinary lives and mundane activities: they go to the most banal office documentation, the official ledgers, the unglamorous record books... Such was Michel Foucault's ambition, for instance, when he and his collaborators in the late 1970s assembled the documents that he introduced under the title 'The Life of Infamous Men'.[1] Researchers of all stripes pore over the pages of daily newspapers, one by one, on microfilm or CD-ROM or in yellowing, physical versions, to relive, somehow, the same sort of daily succession or unfolding of a past reality. Artists, too, have been caught by the bug: the carefully preserved archive of Stanley Kubrick shows that, for his never-made film project on Napoleon, he attempted to establish a detailed card for each day, each moment, of his subject's life.

Of course, it is an impossible goal, virtually a dream of time travel: to relive the past, in imaginative, reconstructed retrospect, exactly as it was once lived, forward, unfolding day to day. A trick of perspective; a ridiculous ambition. Also a scholarly psychosis: who has that many lives to spare, that they can seriously seek to relive another biography in another time and place, when they should be getting on with living their own?

Andy Warhol—whom Paul Taylor greatly admired, and somewhat modelled himself on—had a particularly novel way of negotiating this psychosis (for him, a celebrity ego-psychosis, a wish to write himself into history), and of preserving the past: already with an eye to its future reconstruction. Whenever his desk got full of all the crap he had collected or received, the lot would be unceremoniously swept off into a box that was then duly labelled, sealed up and stored. Today, Warhol exhibitions are made from the strange pleasures of peering into, or meticulously laying out and annotating, the contents of these self-historicising boxes.

I was once a hoarder, I confess. It was the early 1980s, the *Art & Text* era. I had the madness of the opportunity (i.e., secondhand) shop in me—in my 'POPISM' lecture, I referred to the 'fabulous op shops of our minds'[2]—and I think I, too, had some shade of a

Warholian ambition: to curate, collect my own Museum of Ephemera. Flyers, program notes, small magazines that never got beyond one or two issues, letters, catalogues, notes, newspaper cuttings, invitations to exhibitions and performances, birthday card collages, plus odd types of paperbacks (movie novelisations, sexological volumes, lurid Z-grade pulp fictions) – it got to be quite a mountain, much to the chagrin of my parents or anyone who subsequently shared a house with me. The dream went kaput on me, not too many years down this track: at a certain moment, quite literally, the smell of op shops began to physically, viscerally revolt me – as they still do, to this day. Something inside must have been telling me, like in the George Harrison song, that *all things must pass away*.

But, like Andy, I stored the stuff in boxes, and then I stored the boxes. For the better part of twenty years! And finally – on the day of reckoning, when I actually needed and wanted to lighten my life – I yanked this (sometimes mouldering) deposit out of the storage facility that had made a small fortune out of me, and began working through the bits and pieces. And what I had before me was – with necessary acts of reconstruction and speculation – something like a day-to-day chronicle of the early 1980s in the art/culture/writing/film scene of Melbourne.

I am writing this far away, in Frankfurt, Germany; I have two laptop computers and a few suitcases. I have at last thrown out what was unrecoverable from my impossible Museum of Ephemera; some scraps will go to interested libraries and researchers. I have scanned some (not many) documents to keep. Basically, I am through with it, I must move on. But from it, in the cleanup, I have extracted the materials and memories that prompt this tribute to *Art & Text* editor Paul Taylor: my waltz of return (since all waltzes involve returning to an original spot, a point of departure). I once literally wrote a 'Return Waltz', when I was all of twenty-two; Paul provided the voice for the recording, which I have duly digitised and preserved.

I mentioned Foucault. I refer to one of his earliest texts, from the time of his PhD, about the writing of history – because working on the slim output of someone like Paul, who died young, orients you to the very particular charm and force of early writings (or 'juvenilia', as they are sometimes unkindly called). Foucault refused, up front, to provide a summary or *exegesis*, as he calls it, of the text he was introducing, Ludwig Binswanger's *Dream and Existence*, declaring: 'Original forms of thought are their own introduction'[3] – wise words, indeed. He suggests, instead, that there are two things that are proper when considering an historical object, such as a person's oeuvre or career. He says, first, that you can trace its *history* (its initial context, its origin) because that is 'the only kind of exegesis they permit'.[4] Second, you should attend to its *destiny* (its subsequent legacy, what is made of it and done with it). And this latter task always demands not a simple tribute, but a *critique*.

What follows is more history than critique. It is a story of Paul Taylor and of what he did with *Art & Text*, not a detailed consideration of the contents of each issue.[5] It is not especially my personal, subjective story, but it is certainly the story that came out of those old storage boxes of mine. What did Iggy Pop sing in 'Five Foot One'? *'Til I'm losing my head / I'm checkin' it twice / I'm gonna find out who's naughty and nice.*

Whole cloth

What I am engaged in here is not nostalgia. I am not, in fact, a nostalgic guy, and I actually prefer being in my early fifties now to being twenty-two in 1982. Many things I disliked about Australian culture then, I dislike even more vehemently now. The exposé that Mark Davis was ridiculed for, by the literary/cultural establishment, when he first published *Gangland: Cultural Elites and the New Generationalism* (1997), remains stolidly, depressingly the case: the public culture I entered as a teenager, with a Philip Adams, a Les Murray, a Germaine Greer or a Bob Ellis mouthing off on every possible political or artistic topic, reigns supreme, seemingly until Kingdom Come. There's *Quadrant* and *Australian Book Review*: same as they ever were. Newspapers – especially so-called quality newspapers – are far worse that they ever were. Art magazines have either stayed more or less the same (*Art Monthly*, *Art & Australia*), or become glossy, cheesy, tie-in promotional brochures for the art market (*Australian Art Collector*). A former Popist like me, still standing somewhere in this public arena, has to ask: did Paul Taylor and *Art & Text* change anything in this culture, anything at all? Even if the fault lines are no longer etched so visibly on the surface of the earth, his intervention did indeed cut a breach into the history of Australian writing and publishing. It is a breach worth remembering, re-inventing and restoring.

Going through the boxes gave me a way to chart, in depth, and also with a certain emotional distance, the detailed context of those years 1980–84. Whether or not you think Melbourne in the early '80s was a rich or vibrant cultural space, it was certainly *full*: a lot was going on, all at once, in many directions, and always opposed to at least two or three other things in the vicinity. This is what I want to give you a sense, and a reminder, of.

Why do we need to reclaim, in 2013, Paul Taylor, *Art & Text* and the Melbourne art scene that whirled around him in the early '80s—apart from the fact that, as Neil Young once sang, *all our changes were there*? One good reason: in the only official, book-length account of the history of *Art & Text* magazine, largely written (or spoken) by its second, long-lasting editor, Paul Foss, little is said or indicated about the first four years of its existence, or about the 'POPISM' exhibition, beyond a brief introduction by Foss's obliging interviewer. Foss claims that, in his Sydney arts/culture/theory scene of the early '80s, he had never even heard of *Art & Text*. Moreover, he tells us that he came to perceive Paul, whom he describes as 'a kid', as merely someone who angled the publication so as to 'broker his way into the New York critical scene'.[6] (*Art & Text*'s own later destiny in the 1990s, under Foss's guidance, was to become centred in Los Angeles, until its demise.) It is sad and irritating to see the same old 'careerist' scuttlebutt that dogged Paul while he was alive still surface, long after his death—and from the mouth of his successor.

Foss adds that, in contrast to himself as editor, 'I don't know the extent to which Paul could be said to have crafted these early issues out of whole cloth ... he never discussed his editorial philosophy'.[7] Well, Foss wasn't there, but I was. I can tell you that Paul Taylor *did* craft the first fifteen issues of *Art & Text* out of whole cloth (meaning: there was nothing like it in Australia before he brought it into being), and he *did* have an editorial philosophy. Does this indicate that he meticulously sub-edited—to the point of frequent rewriting, as was Foss's exacting method—every sentence he published? Probably not, but he did select, order, shape and guide every piece that appeared under his editorial watch. He was intimately involved in every aspect: typing, designing, marking-up proof pages. In fact, production of the magazine seemed frequently to be a one-man show, with Paul going back and forth to the printer; he had no regular assistants, paid or otherwise.

The curious case of Paul Taylor

As personal reminiscences of Paul's life and times often tend to slip and slide two, three, even five years out of whack, it is worth orienting ourselves with a few basic facts and dates. Particular acknowledgement, in this quest, must go to his old friend and colleague Jonathan Holmes, who found, perfectly preserved in the archived files of the Tasmanian School of Art, Paul's job application and CV from 1978 – which is both good bureaucracy and a rare instance of fully functioning corporate/institutional memory. (These things are scarce in twenty-first-century Australia.)

Paul from ages seventeen to nineteen: undergraduate years in Arts at Monash, from 1975 to 1977. His fellow students included Jan Minchin and Jenepher Duncan; the teaching staff in Monash Arts included Memory Holloway, John Gregory and David Hannan, under the progressive leadership of Patrick McCaughey. Paul works as a Monash Gallery assistant in '75; he travels to USA in '75–6 and works on window displays in San Francisco. In '76, he works part time at the Australian Opera Company. During his undergraduate years, he serves as 'arts reviews' editor and frequent contributor for the Monash student newspaper *Lot's Wife* – these are texts that we need to dig up from the archive, one day.[8]

In 1976, he exhibits a 'mixed-media sculpture' in *The Money Show* at George Paton Gallery – one of only a few artworks I am able to credit to Paul, alongside his production of *Play* (more on this later), and some fleeting involvements with the musical experiments by the Art Projects group, on a Melbourne–Brisbane axis. In 1978 – his Honours year – he co-ordinates a retrospective of Bill Fontana's 'Sound Sculpture' at the National Gallery of Victoria, and writes his required thesis on 'Sculpture and the Spectator 1962–1967'. Also in this year comes a significant displacement away from the arts culture of Monash, and towards the University of Melbourne: it is here, taking advantage of a cross-enrolment opportunity enabled by McCaughey, that Paul immerses himself in Margaret Plant's elective 'The Influence of Marcel Duchamp'. Every piece of evidence suggests that this was *the* major, formative turning point for Paul, a move in his intellectual orientation from *Artforum* in its transitional 1960s/'70s phase (the very end of the Clement Greenberg legacy, still the dominant note of his Honours thesis), to the full-blooded theoretical investigations of the *October* set (Rosalind Krauss, Douglas Crimp, Annette Michelson, and so on). *October* magazine had begun publication in the USA in 1976, during Paul's undergraduate years. As has frequently been noted, the very look of *Art & Text* – especially the stark, white cover of its inaugural issue – is an unambiguous homage to it.

During 1979 and '80, Paul works as a tutor at the Tasmanian
2 School of Art. A snapshot from a school yearbook of the period shows a fur-wearing Paul identified only as an anonymous 'friend' next to Howard Arkley and Elizabeth Gower at a gallery opening. One of his students here is the artist later known as Vivienne Shark LeWitt – who bonded with him, and spurred him on to read

Roland Barthes; once relocated to Melbourne, she would quickly become a key figure on the *Art & Text* scene, and in the pages of the magazine. Near the end of his commitments in Tasmania (September 1980), Paul curates the exhibition 'Recent Tasmanian Sculpture and Three Dimensional Art' – still bearing traces of his Honours work. 1980 also marks his move back to Melbourne, where he gets hold of an office at the Prahran School of Art, and plots his application to the Visual Arts Board for the birth of *Art & Text*.

1981, the first issue of *Art & Text*: Paul is twenty-three. (It is around this time, late in 1980 or early in '81, that I first met him.) June 1982: 'POPISM', and he's twenty-four. I need hardly underline what remarkable achievements these were for one so incredibly young. Not many have, in comparative terms, matched this level of precocious brilliance before or since – beyond, say, Orson Welles, or a few pop musicians! In April 1983, Paul curates the 'Tall Poppies' exhibition, which was already a more subdued, less splashy and controversial affair than 'POPISM' – less conceptual, because the 'return of painting' was in the air, internationally, and Paul wanted to play that game, however ironically or critically. By mid 1984 – which is where my documents on Taylor start to dribble out – Paul Foss is taking the reins of the magazine in Melbourne, and Taylor is beginning the process of relocating his career in art and writing to New York. Paul's American writing will later be gathered and published in Australia, after his death, as *After Andy: SoHo in the Eighties* (1995), but not as he wished it to appear: Foss, silently wielding his editorial hand behind the scenes, made the executive decision to reprint the highly transformed publication versions, not Paul's preserved, original manuscripts.

Paul's major writings? My selection would be: among his first post-student pieces in 1980, an interview with Clement Greenberg (Paul would prove himself to be a wily, excellent, sometimes combative interviewer – as I discovered when he interviewed Kim Beissel and I after the first performance of The Connotations in early 1981, a text that has been lost because the magazine *New Music* folded before it could appear there). 1981, *Art & Text*, No. 1, the veritable manifesto: 'Australian "New Wave" and the "Second Degree"' – mind the quotation marks in that title, please! 1982, *Art & Text*, No. 7: 'Angst in My Pants' – among my favourite articles (and article titles) by Paul, inspired by a Sparks song. 1983: 'Popism: the Art of White Aborigines', which appeared in both *Flash Art* (Milan) and *On the Beach* (Sydney). Also '83, *Art & Text*, No. 12/13: 'The Instrumentality of Dick Watkins'. All along the 1981–4 period: various editorials and article introductions – Paul was a master at these quick, 'occasional', framing pieces, where he got in some of his best, polemical jabs.

His first such editorial, 'On Criticism',[9] is worth recalling for its stated critical/editorial principles: by adopting an 'avoidance of extensive interviewing, [exhibition] reviewing, and lavish illustrations', he dealt a blow to the usual artist/gallery-centred coverage that reigned (then as now) in *Art & Australia* or *Art Monthly*; by attacking what he termed *impressionistic* writing (exemplars: Sandra McGrath in *The Australian*, Gary Catalano) and *list-making* (Suzanne Spunner), he sought to alienate both journalistic types and some left/feminist writers; and by announcing that *Art & Text* would provide 'a forum for experimentation' and launch 'enquiries into the relationships between the several arts', he broke new ground in Australian publishing – although, as we shall see, his proclaimed ambition in these regards would eventually generate a backlash from other local quarters.

This entire period is capped-off in an odd way, by the editing in 1984 of the book *Anything Goes: Art in Australia 1970–1980*: an ambiguous project in Paul's trajectory, I feel, since it is a gesture of respect towards the 1970s and all it represented for him – but, in many ways, Paul came to have, throughout the early '80s, a difficult and fractious relationship with the '70s, literally so in relation to some of his mentors, such as *The Age*'s art critic of the time, Memory Holloway.

With reference to Paul's relation to the Clifton Hill Community Music Centre (CHCMC) – he attended quite often, as I recall, far more so than many local artists – we come upon a mystery: a performance event that few people, including at least one person who was actually in it, can today recall. But I was there in the crowd; I saw it and remember it well: *Play-Reading*, a version of a Samuel Beckett piece staged by Paul on March 29, 1982 at 8:30pm. Three people – Philip Brophy, Lyndal Jones and Vivienne Shark LeWitt – sat on a stage and read their lines, from a screen projected in front of them – a transparent screen, so the audience could also see and follow it. Conceptual, simple, ephemeral. Art is easy! The performance with which this was advertised, David Chesworth's far more elaborate *Industry and Leisure*, was later incorporated into the events program of 'POPISM'.

The combo of Paul and Beckett strikes me as intriguing – a subject for further research. And the mystery goes deeper. Paul put an enigmatic date for the work on the invitation to *Play-Reading*: 1979 to 1982. Three years to work up this performance? In 1982, there also appears an important essay by Paul in *Art & Text*, No. 5:

'Self and Theatricality: Samuel Beckett and Vito Acconci'. The note on the bottom informs us that it was written in 1979 – perhaps while Paul lived in Tasmania. This essay was clearly personally significant to Paul, because he allowed it to be reprinted in 1987, in the prestigious American journal devoted to experimental writing, *Review of Contemporary Fiction*, at a point when it would have meant nothing to his high-flying journalistic career in the US – it was probably solicited by the guest editor of this Beckett issue, Nicholas Zurbrugg (died 2001), who had worked in Australia and contributed to *Art & Text* under both of its main editors.

One day at Monash

1 The date is September 29, 1982. I kept the Monash *Daily News* handout from this day, and it is evident that a great deal was going on, most of the time, in the public life of this university. Fourth item from the top: a musical performance billed as 'Post POPISM' by The Connotations, touted as 'Monash's musical event of the year' with four exclamation marks. I was in that band – but I didn't write that blurb, believe me. The concert was not in the Music Department (god forbid), but the Exhibition Gallery of the Visual Arts section on the seventh floor of the Menzies Building – a stone's throw from where my office is today. Naturally, the show's title refers to Taylor's curated exhibition at the National Gallery of Victoria that year, 'POPISM', and the fallout from it, the arguments that followed. However, by September of '82, it seems we in the 'scene' already considered our selves post-Popist – or, at least, it seemed humorous to declare such a thing. Things moved quickly, back then.

Look, for the deep context of the Melbourne scene, at what else was happening on the Monash Clayton campus that day, amidst the usual sports, health and religious groups. The Women's Network is screening German feminist films. There is a meeting of a Filmmakers Collective. The Department of History is publicly debating a television documentary on the history of the SS. And one of Australia's greatest literary theorists and analysts, Marie Maclean (died 1994), is presenting a lecture on 'Recent Developments in the Theory and Teaching of Speculative Fiction'. There is no longer, in 2013, a 'daily news' sheet resembling anything like this at Monash – or, I suspect, any other Australian university.

And that was the just the tip of the general Australian arts/culture/ideas iceberg in the early '80s. It would take a separate book to give the full flavour of all that was happening in the same moment. There were adventurous academic conferences such as

9 'Foreign Bodies' at the University of Sydney, which I believe Paul
visited, as the roster of New South Wales-based writers he
solicited for the magazine match almost exactly the list of speakers: Meaghan Morris, George Alexander, Ted Colless, Paul Foss,
Terence Blake, the Zerox Dreamflesh collective... There was a
constant procession of intellectual and art stars visiting from other
countries, including Umberto Eco, Keith Haring, Abramović &
Ulay, Daniel Buren, Félix Guattari (for an anti-psychiatry conference), Frederic Jameson, Jody Berland and Krzysztof Wodiczko,
Raymond Bellour, Peter Wollen and Ursula Le Guin. Paul hob-
nobbed with at least a few of them!

There were the Melbourne events of the Fashion Design
Council (Robert Pearce, who also died tragically young, was a sort
of social twin to Paul), and the punk-oriented annual 'Festival of
Surrealisms', which lasted a couple of years; among the available
publications, there were lively student newspapers, the design
magazine *Crowd* guided by Michael Trudgeon and his crew, Philip
4 Brophy's loose-leaf *Stuff*, Sydney's art-philosophical, hand-made
11 *Frogger* edited by Rex Butler and David Messer, and the artist-
slanted coverage of the local experimental film scene in *Cantrills*
12 *Filmnotes*; sound/music-wise, there was Bruce Milne's *Fast Forward*
cassette magazine and Sydney's similar (but more anarchistic/
Deleuzean) *La La Sequence Bruit*; there was the burgeoning field of
experimental dance (never forget Paul's early interest in dance as
an art form—as well as a social form!), and hybrid performance/
cabaret presentations such as *Television Works* by →↑→ in 1981 at
the mainstream nightclub venue of The Met. Not to mention
Melbourne radio station 3RRR in its heyday of proliferating
programs on film, fashion, art music... Paul was very aware of, and
made a point of dipping into, all these realms of activity. He knew
about *everything* that was happening.

A crucial aspect of Paul Taylor, something I can testify to, is how he would recruit people—both artists and critics—from everywhere; I was one of those recruits, at the age of twenty-one. (Paul had a ferocious faith in youth!) He had read my arts reviews in an RMIT student magazine in late 1980, and in *Cinema Papers*; he came to see the first performance of The Connotations at CHCMC in early 1981. He assembled a new community—a loose one, putting very diverse people together—from many different groupings; he was particularly adept at picking up on deeply, secretly dissatisfied people who were just on the cusp of moving out of their previous social-ideological set. And so Paul scooped up many renegades, recoiling from their experience (often a passionately political one) of the 1970s: people who were on a 'line of flight', as we Deleuzeans said at the time, away from left-wing art practices, or feminism, or hard-line film theory... Janine Burke and William Routt were two such renegades, exploring what was, for them, new fields and styles of writing in the early '80s.

Paul's particular style of *montage* – or *bricolage*, as he preferred to call it – also extended to acts of writing collaboration: our work together on a piece about Fassbinder's film *Querelle* (which appeared in both *Tension* and Rosetta Brooks' London/New York-based *ZG*, thanks to his clever marketing of it) was swiftly achieved with his revisions over my handwriting, scissors and glue, and a nearby typewriter to transcribe the finished result. Text is easy!

Enjoyable lessons

Paul was often called a provocateur – and this is true, but also overly solemn, because his provocative acts also expressed an irrepressibly boyish, cheeky side. For instance, Paul never hid where he lived in South Yarra, a glamorous block called Beverley Hills. He placed it on his various calling cards; and he published an article about it in *Art & Text*, 'Hooray for Hollywood' by Robyn McKenzie. In an image accompanying this article, we see how intricately Paul interrelated – *networked*, we would say today – his home life, his friends, artists and critics, and the activities of all the interesting people around him: it is a publicity shot for a cult 3RRR radio show of the time about style and culture, *Bedlam*, hosted by Merryn Gates and Julie Purvis, and the four suitors-paparazzi in the picture are various writers, musicians, broadcasters and general presences in and around the scene at the time: Philip Brophy, Dean Richards, Peter Lawrence, and my Connotations band mate, Kim Beissel.

A particular tale, in relation to issue 2 of Spring 1983, returns to me now. It's the issue with a gorgeous, Rococo, full-colour cover: François Boucher's *The Enjoyable Lesson* (1748). I happened to visit Paul's place just as he received in the post a generous cache of colour transparencies (pre-digital technology, of course) from the NGV; 'They're free!', he enthusiastically exclaimed. But, I naively asked, what article was this diverse set of pretty, crystal-clear images meant to illustrate? The imp of Paul's perversity was ready to pounce: the images would appear, apart from the cover, on every second page of the English translation of Jean Baudrillard's 'The Precession of Simulacra' – to which they bore absolutely no relation! And thus did Sloop Jean B, in this sensational text of his that meant the most to my generation, come to fill forty-four glorious pages of *Art & Text*!

But there is an undeniably odd undercurrent to this story. A recurring theme in Paul's work is what could be called the 'hyperconformist posture of complicity' (as Baudrillard described such gestures of the time), an ironic capitulation to the *status quo*, the perceived *zeitgeist*, the order of things, the hierarchy of established values. Naturally, this posture changed, at regular intervals, with the winds of cultural and intellectual fashion: Paul was never afraid of this game, which he approached with a smirk. In '81, in his first major essay, he declared: we are in a culture of the second-hand, the cover version, the happily inauthentic and unoriginal. 'POPISM' in '82: the arts are now ruled by the rhetoric of photography, which flattens and equalises images. '83 and 'Tall Poppies': five 'pictures' (by Dale Frank, Mike Parr, etc.) that were 'selected by non-Australian curators to exhibit abroad', and hence a self-conscious display of 'acquiescence' to this art world power structure. 1984: we must dance, dance, dance until 'the onset of power-failure' – that year, the talk was all about burnout, endgame, imminent apocalypse; AIDS had begun to cast its dark shadow on the carefree culture of 'anything goes'.

This posture of complicity made many observers of Paul – as well as some of his fellow travelers – uneasy. It triggers the more general question of Paul's relation to politics – and exactly what political values he held. The *Meanjin* critique by Stan Anson, 'The Conservatism of *Art & Text*', was (according to what Paul told me) originally titled 'The Conservatism of Paul Taylor', and was changed at his insistence – a measure of how intensely personalised these art debates became in the '80s. In this intriguing and intelligent text (Anson came from a solid background in socio-political theory, and later wrote the book *Hawke: An Emotional Life*), the accusation is made that Paul (and his magazine) engaged in 'public-schoolboy Futurism', i.e., not the deadly/dangerous/full-out Fascist type, in fact rather 'attenuated and effete' – but irresponsible, all the same, in the type of provocations it enjoys making. According to this account, Paul was essentially a right-wing figure, 'acquiescing' in the dominant games of power – even if he would never have described himself as being on the right.[10]

In the recent book *Camera Historica: The Century in Cinema* by the film critic and social historian Antoine de Baecque, we find a useful reflection on these issues, bearing on another time and place altogether. There is, after all, a striking continuity or similarity between Paul's favourite sort of rhetoric and what de Baecque describes as the public tone of the French *Nouvelle Vague* filmmakers in the early '60s: 'a penchant for polemics, political disengagement and elitism, through a defense of style, dandyism, neoformalism, mysticism, nonconformism and provocation'.[11] De Baecque's thorny question is: what, precisely, were the politics of the *Nouvelle Vague* crowd? There were many links between these budding directors (Truffaut, Rohmer, Chabrol, etc.) and various right-wing celebrities of the time, especially a bunch of writers known collectively as the 'hussars'. And *Cahiers du cinéma*, the flagship magazine of the *Nouvelle Vague*, was very far from being a left-wing journal in any sense, at least for the first twelve years or so of its long life (the radical-socialist counterpart to *Cahiers*, in that '50s/'60s period, was *Positif*). De Baecque sums up the appeal and the position of the hussars:

> The hussars took pleasure in [...] incisive phrases, brilliant conclusions, elegant formulations, a vigorous style with stimulating narrative, a fascination for bodies and feminine beauty, the despair of vanity, the pleasures of seduction, the sad intoxication of depression – all these were turned against the utilitarian logorrhea of militant discourse.[12]

Paul, himself in some sense in flight from the 'utilitarian' 1970s, undoubtedly offered a colourfully gay variation on this system of style and values – for better and for worse. A story I have never publicly told, until now, reveals how far he was willing to take his particular brand of provocation: he and I, a good fourteen years before the famous Sokal Affair that damaged the reputation of the journal *Social Text*, cooked up a plan to write a fake article of feminist art criticism and submit it to *Lip*, under a joint, female name. Although we didn't plot the consequences in any realistic detail, we knew that – if all went well – we had the ace up our sleeve of, eventually, publicly exposing the hoax (which was exactly what Alan Sokal went on to do). Our aim, for what it was worth, had an hussar-like justification: to point up the rigidity of a certain social/semiotic theory that was being wielded upon artworks, in a handy 'illustration' of (what seemed to us) sometimes repressive, inhibited, moralising strictures – this was a time when many things (narrative, pleasure, spectacle) were being ceremoniously 'outlawed' in one manifesto after another. (Now, I see better that it is a typical rhetorical move to imagine that your opponent is a humourless, policing bore, while *you*, of course, are the life of every theory-party.) As it happened, we didn't have the time, the energy or the nerve to go through with the idea. In retrospect, I am rather glad that we did not demonise ourselves into the history books as the perpetrators of such a hoax! But a part of Paul was certainly up for it...

All the same: Paul constantly militated for the professional rights of artists and writers, including their right to payment for the use of their works in 'POPISM'. His 'anything goes' code did not license wholesale piracy or violation of copyright. His magazine projected, on various levels, a progressive gay/queer culture with which many, at the time and since, cheerfully identified. And, whatever problems he had with the category of 'women's art' (and its expression in *Lip* magazine),[13] he undoubtedly supported many individual women artists and critics.

Nouveau mondo

The backlash against 'POPISM' and *Art & Text* became pretty fierce in the latter half of 1982, and for some years to come. There is no doubt that what Paul perceived as a backlash against what he had instigated, on so many levels, was a major factor in him seeking to relocate his career beyond Australia. Ominous events – going well beyond the Michael Leunig cartoon that I masochistically noted for posterity in 'Before and After *Art & Text*' – abounded in the aftermath of 'POPISM': Robert Rooney lost his post as art critic at *The Age* for reviewing (humorously) the exhibition; Memory Holloway in *Art Network* asked of it: 'What is the political point?' Lengthy essays of critique devoted to demystifying or debunking the '*Art & Text* scene' appeared in *Lip* and *Local Consumption*,[14] as well as *Meanjin* – drawing Paul's return fire that the 'opportunities to use POPISM with a view to research and a subsequent approach to Postmodernism evaded those it could interest most, i.e., the left, which is instead too preoccupied with licking its own wounds'.[15] By 1983, the legacy of 'POPISM' was being pitted – a rather banal, straw-man contest, in my opinion – against the so-called neo-Expressionist 'return to painting' at ROAR gallery in Fitzroy. (Although I have tried to avoid it here, commentators of the time and since have loved to play the glib game of categorising artistic or intellectual groups by suburb: Fitzroy, Carlton, Northcote, South Yarra...)

Holloway's *Art Network* piece brought out those troopers who were still willing to identify themselves, at least for this moment of public combat, as Popists. On the always-funny Letters page of *Art Network*, under the title 'POPISM Transgresses', Davila let forth with the following pronouncement, a handy summation of several currents of rhetoric that Paul had cleverly joined to form his 'scene':

> The main strength of the Art discourse is that it can constitute itself in the field of what has not been established yet, and as such it is beyond the control of the traditional powers. Its impact and critical function on determined society lies here, a critique situated in a different field from political discussion, situated in the language and signs field. Its power of eruption, creation of possibilities of life, is situated in the interior of the codes that constitute language itself [...] It will be a critical transformation of our discourse in a space of life.[16]

Or, in less fancy words: Life is Art! For his part, Paul – as the *Art Network* editors gleefully tell us – 'instructed us to print the text of
19 this postcard' as his reply to Holloway:

> Greetings from Kassel! Documenta is still very busy, grand and getting a little grimy much like a Biennale of Sydney after 2 weeks. I'm very annoyed I didn't get the chance to reply to Memory's stupid review in the same issue it's full of mistakes and possibly libellous, it's very unfair at the least to make me wait X months to try to set the record straight, and it's the 1st character assassination you've published. NO THANKS, Paul.[17]

The invocation of law turned out to be a kind of curse, or maybe a self-fulfilling prophecy: the *Art & a Texta* episode was on its way. I will not rehearse here the details of this case; it is intriguing that Paul's main antagonist in the incident, ex-football star, poet, publisher, and most recently sports-predictive statistical wizard Ted Hopkins, says absolutely nothing about it in his autobiography *The Stats Revolution* (2011). But, suffice it to say, Hopkins's one-off project *Art & a Texta*, which he brainstormed with a group of like-minded writers and artists, was a genuinely 'grass roots', rebellious, perhaps slightly resentful response to the fame that had been quickly garnered by *Art & Text*. To appropriate the Hollow Way of Memory: 'What is the political point?' I would sum up the *Art & a Texta* critique in the following terms; consciously or not, they echo the
15 finely argued review that Mary Eagle did of the very first issue of *Art & Text* on the Arts page of *The Age* (impossible to imagine such a piece appearing there today!): as Eagle saw it, Paul and his assembled crew stood to have a hard time squaring their subcultural

desire for a 'secret society' with the more civic drive to make their secret art (and subversive ideas) known to and accepted by all.[18]

First, *Art & a Texta* accused (by its own counter-example) *Art & Text* of not being a truly populist magazine – despite its enthusiasm for the intellectually defined object 'popular culture' – which was evident in its lack of embrace of more quotidian, suburban, *daggy* forms of that culture. Second, and jumping to the other foot, as it were, it accused this avowedly avant-gardist or experimental publication of being *insufficiently* experimental, as it unmistakeably 'drew the line' at poetry and related new-literary forms beyond the *belles lettres* template (Roland Barthes-style) of the 'creative essay'. (The most radical forms of experimental writing have always generated a substantial underground scene in various Australian centres: Melbourne, Sydney, Perth, Adelaide.) Third: that, as a theoretical organ, *Art & Text* was narrowly (and fashionably) theoretical – and therefore its avant-gardism was elitist. And fourth: that it lacked humour, especially about itself. I said on the radio then (Hopkins transcribed and included my remarks in his documentation of the legal case, 'John and Betty Go to Court', in 1983) that there was some validity to these charges – and certainly an identifiably Aussie tradition of larrikinism behind the gesture of making them in satirical form. As for Paul's subsequent, successful legal action against *Art & a Texta,* he summed it up plainly in an *Art Network* interview: 'I responded by getting a certain amount out of them'.[19] And I believe he was in his rights to do so.

What my boxes show me of Paul's trajectory in 1984 and into 1985 is that he was in a process of withdrawing from the local scene – not just withdrawing himself physically (going elsewhere), but also withdrawing his emotional and intellectual *investment* in the very idea of such a scene: it was his requiem for a dream. The art world's uptake on the artistic and cultural postmodernism he had so deftly helped introduce to Australia – in particular, the near-rapturous reception accorded to Jean Baudrillard on these
16 shores, as part of Sydney's epochal 'Futur*Fall' conference – happens largely without Paul. Meanwhile, there was a funding battle taking place, mainly via the entreaties of *Art Network* to the Visual Arts Board – a special, polemical target of which was the 'rather specialised discourse' of *Art & Text*. The atmospheric change that would lead, by June 1987, to the existence of the arch-conservative *Art Monthly Australia* under the Brit-invasion influence of Peter Townsend (not of The Who) was already in the air.

And there were unaccomplished, abandoned projects that might have left Paul frustrated or bitter: a mooted exhibition (planned in collaboration with Denise Robinson) for an exhibition called 'Critics' Choice' at George Paton Gallery, designed to push/provoke further the debate about the hierarchy of art and criticism, a sore point for many at the time – eventually 'cancelled due to the non-involvement of the critics themselves' (I was one of the few critics invited who replied enthusiastically to Paul's invitation); and a special catalogue/book on Robert Mapplethorpe at the end of 1985, for which galley proofs exist, but no publication.

Paul was not entirely displeased – but he must have been a little annoyed, and confirmed in his worst conclusions about Australia by this time – that he became (even without the *Lip* hoax!) an Art Demon; he continued to be blamed for the general disintegration of the art scene (into theory-mania, intellectual pretentiousness, superficiality, mere glamour, etc.) long after he had absented himself from it. Case in point: issue 18 of *Art & Text* in July 1985, devoted to the art and philosophy of Pierre Klossowski. Although he insisted his name appear as co-editor (alongside Foss and US art critic Allen Weiss) of this special (and remarkable) issue, Paul had little, or nothing, to do with the assembly of it. But in *The National Times* of September 20, 1985 – over *three years* after 'POPISM' – we encounter this wild spray of invective, from the pen of either resident arts journalist Tom Thompson, rising reactionary art critic John McDonald, or both:

> ART & TEXT 18 ($6). Sub-titled Phantasm and Simulcra [sic], this is a homage to the work of Pierre Klossouski [sic], the European pornographer. It is amusing to note that in the 1980s, thanks to "the pleasure of the gaze", our many male critics can now talk seriously about semi-naked women in stockings, bound by the wrist. In the 1970s, impossible. Look what they said about the work of Geiger ("necrophiliac") or Robbe-Grillet. Now it's just an "exorcism of the obsessions", these *femmes* in underwear with males "gazing".
>
> Edited in "New York" by Paul Taylor in Melbourne, the issue panders to current European tastes. With the absolute dearth of documentation on contemporary Australian artists, Taylor's choice of subject is peculiar, to say the least. Such choices take Taylor's reputation onward into the obsessive artistic cliques of the self-styled avant-garde, but would seem to be a blatant rip-off of the subsidy system which supports Art and Text [sic].[20]

What an agglomeration of horrors! Responsibility for the entire issue is freighted, in an irrational projection, onto Paul; the other two editors are not even noticed, or mentioned. In a spectacular display of nationalistic Aussie philistinism, 'Klossouski' is dubbed a 'European pornographer' — don't let the fact that he wrote a few dozen books get in the way of a good rant — and is apparently the acme of 'European tastes', while 'documentation on contemporary Australian artists' is going unwritten and unpublished! The old anti-intellectual two-step: 'male critics' now grubbily indulge the 'pleasure of the gaze' (this was the title of a post-'POPISM' exhibition in Western Australia in 1984 that drew much fire from McDonald, Bromfield, et al.) — but what about our forgotten, unfairly repressed '70s heroes like Geiger and Robbe-Grillet (favourites, clearly, of the *National Times* set)? Then it really gets good: *Art & Text* is 'edited in "New York" by Paul Taylor in Melbourne' (completely inaccurate in every way), and 'Taylor's reputation' — *cette mauvaise réputation*, as Guy Debord noted of himself[21] — marches 'onward into the obsessive artistic cliques of the self-styled avant-garde', clearly a terribly un-populist place to end up. All that's left to do is the time-honoured gesture worthy, today, of Andrew Bolt in the *Herald Sun*: to scream 'abuse of decent taxpayers' money' to fund such dastardly ventures as *Art & Text*. Wouldn't *you* want to leave Australia after those two paragraphs?

Repetition and difference

In 1982 I wrote and recorded — enlisting Paul as spoken-word performer — 'The Return Waltz'. A strictly DIY production typical of those days, made on primitive, domestic equipment, and with a toy organ moaning and wheezing in the background. It existed to be played-back once, during a show by The Connotations at CHCMC, and was never made available in any other form. It was one of the many things I found in a box of audiocassettes, thirty years after it was used, labelled and chucked in a pile. These are the words that Paul intones on the tape:

Returning, retaining, remaining the same.
Practice makes perfectly sure.
It's going to be just like starting over;
Return the tune to me.

Remember the moment our new world began?
I'm working my way back to then.
That was our song; I'm hearing it differently.
Retune the turn for me.

One two three, one two.
I'll keep changing partners
'Til I hold you once more.
One two three, one two.
Oh my darling, I will never change partners again.

Rewinding, re-finding, reviewing the scene
Which all of a sudden takes place.
Already inscribed, the trace of our history;
Re-set the stage for me.

Returning, retaining, remaining the same,
Playing me out to the end.
Wait for it now – the music delivers us.
Safely returned again.

What was this about, in 1982? As usual, it was a mangled quotation/appropriation of diverse things: John Lennon's awful Top 40 hit 'Starting Over' (we all hated Lennon, 'reactionary rocker' as Philip Brophy called him, and loved the much-reviled Yoko Ono); an old Bing Crosby song ('Changing Partners') that I fetishised for its forgotten, poetic strangeness (I wanted to put Super-8 images to the entire album, *Bing Sings*, a selection of Crosby recordings 1952–54 – and I still imagine doing this, with a digital camera, today); and the whole musical and cultural waltz-form itself, romantic and sentimental. At the same time, and by the same token, you can wonder in retrospect (I certainly do) whether the routine mocking of sentimentality and cliché that went with a Popist posture in fact offered a clever, functioning mask that, in truth, *allowed* us to be secretly sentimental – just a little bit.

I was also, in 1982, thinking about a body of films I worshipped, and studied – and have never ceased worshipping and studying: the cinema of Max Ophüls, so full of indelible scenes of waltzing. A waltz was never just a cliché or a convenience for him; the dancing, and all of the intense, ambivalent, complex emotion it contained, was the core of his immortal art. I was thinking about everything that a waltz is, in an Ophüls film: a circle, a return, a denial of passing (and tragic) time itself; but also a spectacle that dragged in, inevitably, traces of the real, of life's mundane other side, of ageing and disappointment, of 'changing partners' beyond the sublime forever-ness of an 'island of two', locked in their dance. Nowadays, I grasp better the properly psychoanalytic drama that is at the heart of Ophüls's bittersweet drama of the waltz, and of our tearing identification with it – a psychoanalytic drama that relates to the impossible preservation of time, memory and experience. And how uncanny, in 2013, that a film with a superb, explosive dance scene (*Io e te*) by a true disciple/inheritor of Ophüls (Bernardo Bertolucci) should marry that body-to-body drama of the *eternal moment* (this time, to the tune of a David Bowie ballad) with another, to which it becomes closely related: the storing and forgetting and retrieval of a family's memories in boxes in a basement, where the young hero flees to escape the world, but finds himself.

Already, in 1982, I was thinking about the intensity of *moments* – personal and cultural moments, 'scenes' as I have called them here – and also their evanescence. And thinking, now, about the passing of Paul himself, and *Art & Text* itself, into history; thinking about what that passing means, and what it means to retell this story today – thinking of all that, I return to a text I imbibed and annotated at the start of the 1980s, when I was twenty. It is a text, written by the great German critic Frieda Grafe, who said of Ophüls in 1968:

> Ophüls' films are historical films – not because they set out to reconstruct the past (this is precisely what they do *not* do), but in that they mediate between historical periods. It is not only the relationship between the present and the past of the characters that is fluid; even the past in which Ophüls' films appear to be set is open to the present of his audience. Ophüls encourages his audience to become aware of the present in the past, and to see that established practices have been subject to development. *His critique of the present is a critique of the past that has allowed the present to come about.*[22]

Why a record review in an art magazine?

Chris McAuliffe

The last time I encountered Paul Taylor was in 1990 at a nightclub in New York's meatpacking district when he loomed out of the crowd at a James Chance and the Contortions gig. The show itself had been a surprise; once a stalwart of the No Wave scene, Chance had fallen off the radar. ('He's still alive?', asked an East Village bartender when I mentioned where I was heading that night.) But bumping into Taylor in an out-of-the-way club wasn't unusual. It was like a flashback to the Melbourne of the 1980s, where art and music had been the cultural equivalent of a double A-side single, each resonating off the other, their precedence indeterminate.

The mutuality of art and popular music, especially punk and New Wave, is now congealing into one of the givens of art's recent history. Numerous exhibitions have plotted artists' activities, primarily along the familiar axes of London, Berlin and New York.[1] More than an updating of modernist bohemia, the union of art and alternative forms of popular music was heralded as the advent of postmodernism. 'What became clear, with the rise of the new wave', declared Bernard Gendron in his survey of the twentieth-century dialogue between the avant-garde and popular music, 'was that rock had decisively won over one of the key demographic constituents of highbrow culture, the young avant-garde painters and filmmakers making their way in New York'.[2] New Wave was identified as a kind of generational driver, shaping a redefinition of artistic experimentation; young artists preferred No Wave and New Wave bands to the now 'highbrow' efforts of Cage, Glass, Riley and Reich.

Speaking from a structural rather stylistic point of view, film theorist Peter Wollen observed in the mid 1980s that 'both the music industry and the avant-garde were forced to respond to the new popular music "from below" which followed the advent of rock'n'roll and which coincided with new electronic technology that transformed both performance and post-production'.[3] As a consequence, he concluded, 'The whole [modernist] apparatus of levels, standards, hierarchies, boundaries, limits, centres and sources needs to be re-thought'.[4]

Wollen's outline of this re-thinking delivered a sketch plan of what he termed postmodernism's 'adolescence'.[5] It could pass for a précis of the first dozen issues of *Art & Text*. There the phenomena that Wollen listed were manifested: the crossovers between art, mass media, subculture and electronic technologies; the tactics of 'appropriation, simulation and replication' or 'parody, pastiche and ... plagiarism'. There was 'reality' (now bracketed by quotation marks) superseded by representation (not, tellingly); there was the 'fashion event' hybridising performance and identity. And all of it propelled by the 'subversive new mode of *signifiance*'.[6]

As it happened, by the time Wollen got around to mapping that particular neck of the postmodern woods in 1986, Paul Taylor and a host of *Art & Text* authors had already worked over the territory.[7] Had in fact graduated from MTV-meets-subcultural-theory versions of postmodernism to more recondite explorations of hyperreality, desire and identity. But in the early 1980s, disco, punk, New Wave, noise, muzak and experimental music dominated *Art & Text*'s pages. This was not, however, a case of art being 'won over' by popular music, as Gendron envisaged it. The kinds of equivalence cited in relation to art and the New York No Wave were based in style (minimalism), geography (the downtown scene) or very broad art-like attributes (subversion, bohemianism). This kind of affective equivalence between art and popular music was rare in *Art & Text*. The tone was always manifesto-like; the meeting of art and music was a matter of strategy and discourse.

Taylor and his writers linked music and art as a prospectus for practice rather than as fans' notes. They were not so much seduced by punk and New Wave as fascinated by the idea of music as cultural discourse. The opening paragraph of Adrian Martin's 1981 review of a David Chesworth LP epitomised the approach, simultaneously redefining the role of an art magazine, the status of the record and the space of artistic practice:

> Why a record review in an art magazine? An opportunity, above all, to rescue an important work, a textual practice — David Chesworth's *Layer on Layer* — from the discourses of conventional rock criticism, from the predictable ready-made pronouncements that await it. More than ever today, we need a new space, another space in which to discuss music that involves itself with both popular culture and experimentation, and more specifically the products of that involvement — records.[8]

Popular music was identified as a key tactical element in an ambitious expansion of the field of artistic and critical practice. Paul Taylor's editorial for the inaugural issue of *Art & Text* endorsed critic Xavier de Ventos's demands that art 'transgress the boundaries which rigidly separate it from other social practices', 'redefine its relation with these practices' and enter domains 'considered external or improper'.[9] Art was to be taken out of the gallery and into the spaces of entertainment, political action, consumer goods and leisure activities. Vanguard priorities, too, were redefined. Taylor cited John Cage not as an epitome of musical experimentation but as an exemplar of Michel Foucault's model of a citational modernism. Cage, according to Taylor, 'produced works in a self-conscious relationship to earlier paintings and texts',[10] a conception of practice that dominated the fledgling journal.

This meant that music became the crucible for a properly contemporary avant-garde. Not an avant-garde that simply updated received tactics but one that abandoned modernist autonomy in favour of an expanded field, that was not oppositional in a classically agonistic sense, that cast experimentation as a meta-discursive reflection on cultural categories and histories. The kinds of music formally dubbed 'experimental' – Cage, Schoenberg, *musique concrète*, improvisation – received little attention in *Art & Text*. Taylor was responding primarily to recent developments in popular music; not so much to specific bands or songs as to emerging styles in the music video, performance, fashion and graphic design associated with punk and New Wave. To understand the character of his engagement, we need to review in more general terms what these kinds of popular music meant at the beginning of the 1980s and what artists were discovering in it.

Popular music had made a transition from rock'n'roll to rock in the late 1960s, primarily by invoking art-like concepts such as 'sophistication', 'auteurism' and 'depth'. And a self-conscious 'art' or 'progressive' rock was in place by the early 1970s. But the 'becoming art' of rock was less important than the ways in which rock's own internal upheavals began to generate discourses equivalent to those of contemporary art. That is, it was not a matter of one becoming the other, or of one leading the other, but more a matter of both converging in a critical space loosely described as 'underground', alternative or subversive.

More significant than stylistic borrowing was the fact that by the mid 1970s popular music was self-evidently an industry, a status increasingly lamented by critics, fans and performers alike. At the beginning of the decade, Australian rock journalist Lillian Roxon identified the hallmark of '70s rock as 'big business'.[11]

British musician and critic Mick Farren complained that rock'n'roll rebellion had become 'another mindless consumer product'.[12] David Bowie put it more bluntly to readers of Australia's *RAM* magazine: 'Rock and roll is dead... It's a toothless old woman. It's really embarrassing'.[13] This rhetoric – melding accusations of exhaustion and sell-out with longing for the halcyon days of teenage rebellion – became a staple of the emerging punk movement. From within the art scene, this attitude read as a visceral echo of attacks made by conceptual, feminist and community artists on art's commodification and institutionalisation.

At the same time, new media and modes of distribution threatened to destabilise a centralised and vertically-integrated music industry. The music industry was caught up in a cycle of crisis and recuperation; while the Sex Pistols rorted a succession of major record labels, the industry scrambled to package the more marketable angst of New Wave.[14] But channels such as university and community radio stations, music video, the cassette, the DIY label, mail order and fanzines – seemingly operating outside of that circuit – resolved disillusionment by recovering the idea of independence. With popular music being produced and distributed outside of the entertainment industry, the landscape seemed a more fluid terrain where style, media and channels of circulation could be strategically manipulated. Again, it was possible to see equivalences with practices in the art scene: the embrace of video technology, the rise of 'audio arts', the 'mail art' movement, and the 'alternative space'.

More directly, rock music trafficked in inherited versions of artistic discourse, especially bohemian and avant-garde values. Renato Poggioli's 1968 *Theory of the avant-garde*, considered somewhat dated in the art scene, still served as an accurate survey of punk and New Wave attitudes at the end of the 1970s. Poggioli's laundry list of avant-garde gestures – antagonism, hostility to tradition, nihilism, spiritual defeatism, provocation, scandal, youth, even the 'tough-guy act'[15] – could be found scattered throughout the literature of punk, as could allusions to Surrealism, Dada and Expressionism, the art styles embodying his theory. In structural terms, Simon Frith and Howard Horne later identified a pattern of cross-pollination between art schools and rock music throughout the period; a pattern so strong that an art school pedigree was commonplace (almost a pre-requisite) within punk and New Wave.[16]

More than ever, music was understood as a social space where identity was acted out in rituals of display and consumption. Sartorial style had always been a component of rock culture but, in successive waves over the course of the '70s, Glam, punk and New Wave had made fashion paramount for performers and fans. Increasingly the music press integrated fashion notes with music reporting, quizzed musicians about clothing, and meditated on the symbolic significance of short hair, leather jackets and safety pins. Among the efflorescence of independent music publications emerging in Australia in the late 1970s—*After work*, *Form 38*, *Virgin Press*, *Roadrunner*, *Vox*—fashion was covered as a topic in its own right. 'Melbourne's New Wave scene', it was suggested, was 'dominated by an ethos of fashionability and an excessive dedication to style'.[17] As punks re-discovered the transgressive power of pointy shoes and narrow ties, artists found the concept of 'the presentation of the self', which had been so significant within performance and feminist art, rearticulated in youth culture. Significantly, by the mid 1970s, the emerging discipline of cultural studies turned its attention to the symbolic effects of youth fashion, establishing a bridge between social science, semiology and art.

So by the time that *Art & Text* commenced publication, it was not unusual for an artist to engage with popular music, to rediscover the agonistic rhetoric of the modernist avant-garde in punk, to see a style-conscious inner-city music scene as a platform for bohemian behaviour, or to equate punk's DIY spirit and 'indie' attitude with the development of 'alternative' spaces in the art scene. Punk revived tactics championed by the iconoclastic modernist movements; Dada's anti-institutional gestures were the frequently drawn parallel. Punk licensed a vitality and informality that the dominant -isms had drained from art. Dave Laing's canny identification of the nostalgia inherent in punk—it 'was less a musical transformation than a return to an imagined uncompromised and genuine past'[18]—could equally describe the attitude it engendered in many artists. Tim Johnson admired Sydney band Radio Birdman for 'taking their destiny in their own hands and working outside the system ... They were fiercely independent'.[19] Embracing Melbourne's punk scene as a student, Jon Cattapan recalled, 'That whole idea of the Neo-Expressionist moment—the return to painting—was, I think, for a lot of us, tied very strongly to the punk example of knowing three chords and having a go at it'.[20] And punk mapped a direct route towards transgression. Sydney's Slugfuckers—whose personnel included future *Art & Text* writers John Young and Terry Blake—may have combined art, science fiction, postructuralist theory, film and performance, but when they played at the Sydney College of Art their worth was measured in classically oppositional terms: 'they made the police come to campus, so they must be great, better than old folkies'.[21]

Paul Taylor took a very different position. There were none of the trappings of rock criticism in his engagement with popular music; he made few statements about specific bands, records or gigs.[22] The notion that punk might breathe new life into modernist transgression didn't appeal to Taylor; he dismissed the 'historicist' idea of contemporary art as 'a canonised version of the past' in his editorial for the first issue of *Art & Text*.[23] What interested Taylor was the way that popular music was redefining the meaning of style. No longer a simple taxonometric system (disco, reggae, punk, etc.), style, over the course of the 1970s, had come to refer to conventions, especially those consciously deployed by performers and consumers in a commercial context. In its industrial maturity, popular music was now seen as a 'highly synthetic art' in which 'everything is reduced to gesture and image'.[24] The social analysis of popular music focused on structures of behaviour and display, especially in England where the significance of youth fashion in rock'n'roll had received close attention from the outset.[25] And performers themselves admitted that performance was now a choreographed exercise rather than a moment of visceral authenticity; as Bowie, ever the oracle, put it in 1975, 'I've helped establish that Rock and Roll is a pose.'[26]

For those who still believed in rock's outsider mythology, 'pose' was a pejorative term. A rejection of the pose in favour of 'honesty' was a hallmark of New York's New Wave underground.[27] In Australia, *RAM* magazine championed what it called 'street punk': an 'honest and relevant' version of rock, unadulterated by corporate values.[28] Melbourne's New Wave scene was repeatedly dismissed in the rock press as the domain of the 'image-conscious',[29] populated by 'weekend trendies',[30] 'hairdressers and art school students'.[31]

But it was the pose that preoccupied Taylor. It registered the semiotic structures of popular music: the use of 'cultural codes and mainstream sign-systems' by disco, punk and New Wave subcultures.[32] It declared that popular music was a social formation, a pattern of consumer behaviour. Music, noise or muzak were 'idiomatic facts of our everyday lives', according to Taylor, 'the products of industrialisation, consumerism and the mass-media'.[33]

Most importantly, the pose suggested a redefinition of oppositional practice in an art world still dominated by the Left rhetoric of power and resistance. Popular music's industrial and conventional structures didn't make it a prison house of sound. There was space for cultural agency within the 'hegemonic community of sound'.[34] It was a space constructed through the inversion of avant-garde strategies: not opposition but embrace, not autonomy but immersion, not expression but citation, not difference but repetition.

This was how Taylor envisaged artistic practice in response to the demands of de Ventos. Engaging with a social practice (popular music), especially one entering a mannerist phase of self-conscious stylishness, would redefine the location and critical character of art. 'The possibilities of noise and muzak', he wrote, 'depend on an unorthodox artistic situation in which intervention and consumption are creative acts and where such classifications as "music by artists" are meaningless'.[35]

Taylor openly declared the foundations of this approach; Dick Hebdige's study of punk subculture and Roland Barthes's pursuit of the 'second degree' and the 'third meaning' in literary criticism were his touchstones. Hebdige identified punk as a 'spectacular subculture', anchored in the 'leisure sphere' and communicating through commodities whose meanings are 'purposefully distorted or overthrown'.[36] Transposing Barthesian semiotics in social analysis, Hebdige declared that the 'obviously fabricated' spectacular subcultures 'display their own codes ... or at least demonstrate that codes are there to be used and abused'.[37] In what was for Taylor and his peers the crucial section of Hebdige's text, style was characterised as a 'signifying practice', an exercise in 'polysemy' emphasising the '*position* of the speaking subject in discourse' and 'concerned with the *process* of meaning-construction rather than with the final product'.[38] The subcultural space that Hebdige identified was the one Taylor sought, one in which art and everyday social practice, intervention and consumption, were melded: 'subcultural styles do indeed qualify as art but as art in (and out of) particular contexts; not as timeless objects, judged by the immutable criteria of traditional aesthetics, but as "appropriations", "thefts", subversive transformations, as *movement*'.[39] Paired with Barthes (to whom Hebdige was himself indebted), subcultural style became an aesthetic, 'a way of life' propelled by 'parody, amphibology, surreptitious quotation'.[40]

Recognising Taylor's acknowledged debt to Hebdige and Barthes indicates one of the hallmarks of his writing: a determined effort to construct an alternate epistemology underwriting contemporary practice, as opposed to merely renovating the modernist tradition. The task Taylor set himself from the outset — to find a way beyond modernism and pluralism — was to be sustained by Hebdige, Barthes, Feyerabend, Eco and any other discourse that might rupture the 'well-assimilated vocabulary of 60s Modernism'.[41]

There's no doubt that such theorists helped Taylor to amp up his reading of New Wave. His 1980 article on Jenny Watson identified her interest in the 'cultural signals' of 'low-brow' pop music[42] as pivotal to her work but Taylor rather primly defined New Wave as 'naïve, optimistic, adolescent and even self-indulgent', and as a 'fad ... in impeccably good taste'.[43] Within a year, Taylor had elevated this 'fad' into the motivation for an emerging movement in Australian art. But more important was his approach to those sources, how he framed them. Put simply, Taylor identified the Hebdigean model as an aspect of artists' practice, not as a post-facto description of what they were doing. He made clear that what he dubbed Jenny Watson's 'Mod'ernism was symptomatic of a generation of artists who had grown up in the mass media environment of the '60s; it was 'quotation, operating on the level of personal association'.[44] The 'second degree' tactics Taylor found in Australian artists' work appeared as cultural practices of a Hebdigean order because the artists were already directly engaged with the practice of spectacular subcultures and were exploring the implications of these in their art.

Taylor identified and marshalled the momentum of artists and writers, capturing their excitement in where they were *taking* 'intervention and consumption as creative acts'. When Philip Brophy reviewed Hebdige's *Subculture* (again in the first issue of *Art & Text*, colours were clearly being nailed to the mast) he wasted no time on rating the author's thesis — 'a great book, go out and get it'[45] — and immediately latched onto its implications for current practice. Astutely identifying the Achilles' heel of Hebdige's analysis (plenty on the origins of subcultural style, nothing on its dissemination), Brophy pointed out that the latest stylish style (Blitz or the New Romantics) had already taken polysemy up a notch.

What Brophy and other artist-writers who Taylor recruited had in common was that they had lived through popular music's increasingly self-conscious manipulation of style, were already incorporating its implications in art and criticism, and were now ready to declare (or 'theorise', if you must) an accelerated program. All of this emerges from popular music but couldn't be sheeted home to any Damascene encounter with punk or New Wave.

It's more a case of seeing one's own, hitherto implicit, sensibility emerge into the open. (This seems to happen on-the-fly in Taylor's 1980 article on Jenny Watson: in a long footnote defining New Wave, the formal, vaguely Margaret Plant–Patrick McCaughey voice drops away, and the tone becomes energetic and enthusiastic.)

This is what Taylor looked for in contributors to *Art & Text*: a passionate and reflective engagement with popular music that sustained a meta-textual cultural practice. When Philip Brophy finds himself standing in front of a shop window on Lonsdale St, looking at a mosaic of LPs by Greek pop stars, he realises that what is wrong with them, what is nagging at him, is not their foreignness but that so many of them hold a microphone. Rather than ratifying their status as pop stars, this intrusion of show biz equipment collapses the effect: 'Their images are *too* real'.[46] The more convincing pop star, the pop star of music video, 'is now a posture of the real; a breathing body of emotionalism that surprises its audience (and itself) with the effect of emotions, for what was once the affecting of emotions is now the *effecting* of emotions'. Only a fan would dwell on the nuances of record covers and music videos in this way. And only a fan who cut his teeth on glam, on the stylisations of Bowie and Ferry, would discover so much in the business of 'assembling objects out of surfaces'. Baudrillard, Barthes and Hebdige are there too, but the text isn't about them. What it's about is finding the place (the pretext, the object, the voice) for the kind of critical experimentation that Taylor had called for.

Perhaps the simplest way to distinguish this meta-discursive sensibility from the more common affiliations of art and punk (neo-Dada, agonism, DIY) is this: Taylor expected artists and critics to develop their practice out of an involvement with popular music but not to posit music as the cause or the outcome of the practice. The 'second degree' was neither a direct effect nor a performance of New Wave music. The activities of the Connotations, a band consisting of a cluster of *Art & Text* contributors, were typical.[47] The Connotations' first performance, 'Rock journalism', April 29, 1981, was propelled by the claims that music was not an 'autonomous activity', nor 'low-brow "fun" or high-brow "experimentation"'.[48] Instead it was 'work and research', because 'music can only ever be apprehended through its place in a cultural discursive ensemble'. Therefore rock journalism was not about texts in rock magazines, 'it is the general process ... through which music *acts* in the social sphere'. The performance itself was something of a structuralist exercise, re-enactments of cultural forms identifying, quoting or perverting a series of genres and subgenres (rock, disco, singer-songwriter) and semantic dyads ('dirty' vs. 'clean', 'rigid' vs. 'spontaneous'). A pointed differentiation from the ecstatic version of art/punk – the DIY, anyone-can-form-a-band ethos – was made: '"Rock journalism" is not an excuse for us to "make music" – it is an attempt to make connections, to restore to musical gestures their history and culture'.[49]

The indirect participation of Sydney's Slugfuckers in Taylor's project shows that music making was not what he valued most. Formed in 1979, and fuelled by the DIY spirit, the Slugfuckers' records and performances lived up to the title of one of their songs, 'Cacophony'. A reviewer reported being 'repulsed' by their performances, which the band described as 'absolute disasters'.[50] The band's disregard for the formalities of popular music was evident in their first single, *Instant Classic* (October 1979), which was inadvertently mixed with only one channel; the band passed this off as a revolutionary new audio process. But behind this comedy of errors lay more serious ambitions. Actively involved in ideological ruptures within the University of Sydney's Department of General Philosophy, the band used songs, performances, fanzines and student publications to pit a Deleuzian schizo-revolution against the 'Althusserian hegemony'.[51] Baudrillard, Deleuze, Guattari and Feyeraband were threaded together in an alternate epistemology which appeared in *Art & Text* 2 as 'Some alternatives to the code', written by Terry Blake (the Slugfuckers' singer) and John Young (providing 'zine illustrations and live projections). The tabling of a complex and provocative alternative to orthodox Left criticality was more important to Taylor than the Slugfuckers' status as the nadir of Australian punk. If the Slugfuckers' graphic, textual and musical tactics were anarchic ('Your revolution is a piece of shit/ My revolution is a cosmic fit'), all the better; Taylor had already asserted that 'Extremity is in all cases humorous'.[52] That Taylor later adopted Feyerabend's catch-phrase 'anything goes' as a title for his own anthology on Australian art criticism of the 1970s indicates that, when it came to the meeting of art and music, the goal was discursive re-zoning rather than a big night out.

Regardless of contemporary mutterings about inner-city cliques, all of this activity was shaped by historical trajectories rather than a Svengali editor. Taylor himself flagged one: the presence of popular music in *Art & Text* arose from the work of a generation of artists and writers who had grown up listening to Glam, disco, punk and New Wave speak of music's entrenchment in a thoroughly mediated consumer culture.[53] Meaghan Morris – film critic, cultural theorist, *Art & Text* contributor – identified another: this period was marked by a transition from a context in which 'everything was, oppressively, Political' to one in which everything became, 'obscurely, Cultural'.[54] That is, a shift from a modernist pattern, involving 'taking politics [from social movements] *to* various cultural activities', to a postmodern field in which the 'radical professional' debated increasingly theorised issues within increasingly atomised cultural spheres.[55]

The reception of new musical styles in Australia embodied this shift in microcosm. Acceptance of the urban myth that English punk was a working-class movement led to hilarious efforts (especially in the old-school political context of student newspapers) to attach the Sex Pistols to class warfare and the 'Political'.[56] New Wave, alluding to art, theatre and film, and wrapped in the stylisations of fashion, design and new media, looked 'obscurely, Cultural', apolitical, reactionary. The effrontery of New Wave was of a piece with the effrontery of 'theory' in intellectual circles; both left behind politics derived directly from social movements in favour of the affect, surfaces and semiosis of subculture.

The passage, as Morris saw it, was one from the ossified politics of the mid 1970s to the fluid theoretical spaces of the mid 1980s. Taylor's peers lived this out in their artistic and intellectual development. In 1978, Vivienne Shark LeWitt, then a student at the Tasmanian School of Art, Hobart, railed against a stultifying art scene: 'Art is a quagmire of ideas. The whole scene is like a tepid bath full of dirty water and a clogged drain keeps everything in'.[57] As Shark LeWitt grasped for a new project, popular music seemed to offer a way out: 'I think something on punk rock art. Music art. I don't mind as long as it has nothing to do with real art and the art you read about in *Art & Australia*. I want something absolutely new, exciting, rebellious and futile'.[58] Three years later, writing in *Art & Text*, Shark LeWitt had at her disposal a 'punk avant-garde', a poststructuralist methodology and the capacity to recognise, outside of art, a subcultural field in which the deconstruction of 'predefined images and signs was such to shift the power wielded by society to suit the requirements of the individual'.[59]

Taylor's most fulsome engagement with punk and New Wave, his curating of a 1988 survey of the career of Malcolm McLaren at the New Museum of Contemporary Art in New York, was an acknowledgment of that historical trajectory. McLaren cut his teeth among the Leftist irregulars of the '60s, eventually transplanting their 'playpower' tactics into fashion and rock music. As a punk and New Wave impresario, his buccaneering tales of life in the culture industry delighted the art world. McLaren's disdain for the classically political and his advocacy of style-driven interventions must have seemed to Taylor the epitome of the 'improper' practices he had committed to at the beginning of the 1980s. For all that, the exhibition was atypical of Taylor's approach in focussing on a personality, a star, within the music industry. What I think motivated Taylor's engagement with music, and shaped his somewhat abstracted, 'second degree' approach was a recognition of the trajectory that Morris noted; a passage from an instrumental to a textual conception of culture and politics.

Writing in 1970, George Melly remarked that two armies marched under the banner of pop culture: 'One army are the sophisticated descendants of the crude volunteers of Rock'n'Roll; but the other army are the intellectuals who joined pop culture with cool deliberation'.[60] Paul Taylor's achievement lay in marshalling a third force, a battalion with a passion for both rock music and the new theoretical tools that promised a way out the 'quagmire' of inherited ideas. For Taylor, popular music was a point of leverage of the kind identified by Lawrence Grossberg, who was 'convinced that popular music studies could force the most radical demands of interdisciplinarity onto the agenda'.[61] It was interdisciplinarity that drove *Art & Text* and that made it so challenging; more than anything, it was music that brought this interdisciplinarity to the journal.

Strategic Aboriginalism: Paul Taylor, postmodernism, neo-Expressionism and Aboriginal art
Ian McLean

> I might perhaps call him a dandy, and I should have several good reasons for that; for the word 'dandy' implies a quintessence of character and a subtle understanding of the entire moral mechanism of this world.[1]
> — Charles Baudelaire

Paul Taylor thought his fifteen minutes came when he scored the last interview with Andy Warhol in 1987. The rest of us think it happened half a decade earlier, with 'POPISM' and the early Melbourne years of *Art & Text*.

The early 1980s was also when Western Desert painting first got a foot in the door of the contemporary art world. Is there a relationship between these simultaneous occurrences? Despite Bell's Theorem it would seem unlikely.[2] Taylor's fame rests on his leading role in the postmodern turn that shaped this period, not his advocacy of Aboriginal art—in which he had little interest. Yet, under the guiding hand of Taylor, the postmodern turn continuously bumped into Aboriginal art. By 1983, *Art & Text* had found a surreal albeit imaginary alliance with it.

In these early years, *Art & Text* was particularly open to different voices, as if Taylor gained some vicarious pleasure from their very heterogeneity. His genius was shaping them into a distinctive *Art & Text* sound. One constellation he drew together was the artist Imants Tillers, the writer Stephen Muecke, and Gilles Deleuze and Félix Guattari's ideas of nomadology, all of which found their way into *Art & Text* between 1983 and '85.[3] This mix of artist, postconceptualist, semiotician, fictocritic, philosopher, political activist, psychotherapist and militant, typical of the heterotopia Taylor fashioned in the journal, set the stage for *Art & Text*'s encounter with Aboriginal art. Tillers played the leading role.

If Taylor was the strategist, the mastermind, Tillers first sensed the importance of Aboriginal art to postmodernism. He too had been uninterested in Aboriginal art during the 1970s. This changed when he saw the three imposing abstract Western Desert paintings hanging with contemporary Australian art in the 1981 'Australian Perspecta' at the Art Gallery of New South Wales.[4] It was a turning point in Tillers's work. From that moment he took notice of the exhortations of his fellow postconceptualist Tim Johnson, who had become an enthusiastic advocate of Papunya Tula painting, and more so those of his Melbourne dealer at the time, Marianne Baillieu (to whom he was closer), who had first exhibited Papunya Tula painting at her Realities Gallery in 1977.

The mythmakers

While Tillers and Taylor were, in terms of temperament and taste, quite different people, they shared a deep interest in the mythic structure of art and its potential to articulate fictional histories. For Taylor, postmodernism was not a theory for understanding the existing world but a fiction for reshaping it into a new place. Seeking to impose not so much his taste but his world-view, Taylor was a self-conscious mythmaker. To make new myths, existing ones must either be destroyed or assimilated. This is why, Taylor claimed, 'it was crucial that the Popism exhibition take place within the museum', where 'Popism's hall of mirrors' could 'terrorise' the museum's 'sustaining fiction of history'.[5]

Myth is fashioned by rhetoric not reason, fiction not argument. Taylor's rhetoric was mainly bluff, as these things always are. From the beginning he assumed a moral authority, as if he, like St Peter, had the keys. His myth of contemporary art brought with it moral claims about the past, present and future of Australian art, and who was in and out. Thus Taylor was a self-conscious dealer in myths. He sought to change the very structure of how art and its criticism were thought in Australia. It would, he emphatically announced in *Art & Text*'s first editorial, not be business as usual.

Taylor inserted the new fiction of postmodernism into the discourse of Australian contemporary art by scapegoating competing fictions. At first, existing myths of modernism, Marxism and feminism were the fall guys, but the sudden appearance of neo-Expressionism galvanised his thinking between mid 1982 and his departure to New York two years later. For Taylor, the neo-Expressionists were the false prophets of his day.

The early '80s was a time for prophets and mythmaking. Like Taylor, the advocates of neo-Expressionism sensed an end to the pluralism that had reigned for the previous twenty years and a chance to make their mark.[6] Neo-Expressionism's arrival was confirmed in Rudi Fuch's Documenta 7 in 1982, and William Wright's Sydney Biennale of the same year. The rhetoric – the grand claims – that surrounded neo-Expressionism suggests a similarity between it and Taylor's ambitions: both were in the same game of mythmaking, of claiming the day.[7] Taylor, though, was the more self-conscious mythmaker, which gave him an edge. He did well, in this climate, to heed the writings of Roland Barthes, which taught him that myth was more a matter of form than content, style than substance. Barthes defined the structure of myth as 'the elaboration of a second-order semiological system'.[8] This is where Taylor got his first theoretical idea, what he called in 1981 'an erotic, an aesthetic of the second degree'.[9] He initially outlined it in his main essay in the first issue of *Art & Text* (in Autumn 1981), 'Australian "New Wave" and the "Second Degree"'. Published shortly after the conference 'Foreign Bodies: Semiotics in/and Australia' (held at the University of Sydney), which Taylor attended, his timing was pitched to capitalise on the new French theory beginning to percolate on the fringe of the Australian art world, where it was 'still open territory and outside institutions'.[10]

According to Barthes, myth did its work by taking as its object a pre-existing first-order language system – a picture or text – rather than a sensation of nature. Hence, second-degree art is already 'once removed from "nature"', as Taylor aptly described the painting that he would often reproduce as exemplary second-degree art: Jenny Watson's *A painted page No. 1: Twiggy by Richard Avedon (for Paul Taylor)* (1979).[11]

If Taylor's mythmaking was customised to the rhetoric of postmodernism, what could it offer Aboriginal art? Aboriginal art did not lack institutional support, which it increasingly secured throughout the decade, but *moral* legitimacy. Some did doubt its aesthetic credentials – that it was fine art – but most wondered how an art derived from tribal customs could take its place in a contemporary art scene geared to the logic of modernity, indeed the most advanced postmodernity.

Aboriginal art needed most of all to escape its suffocating reception as primitivism, i.e., the myth of Western modernism. *Art & Text* was also seeking to escape this same myth. In the first issue, Suzi Gablik spoke of the 'spiritual eclipse' of modernism, arguing that 'the current crisis in art is a *moral*, and not an *aesthetic*, one'.[12] Required for both Aboriginal and Western art was a new myth. At first it seemed unlikely that Taylor's myth of post-modernism would change the landscape for either. However, neo-Expressionism introduced a new element into the mix that made all the difference.

Neo-Expressionism

Barthes drew an opposition between the language of myth and poetry. Whereas myth elaborates pre-existing signs, poetry, says

Barthes, seeks to deconstruct or decompose the sign: it seeks 'not the meaning of words, but the meaning of things themselves ... in the hope of at last reaching something like the transcendent quality of the thing, its natural (not human) meaning'.[13] This hope, which is the mythical work of poetry, is very susceptible to fables of origin, presence, authenticity and primitivism. Neo-Expressionism and the growing interest in Aboriginality fuelled this hope in the first half of the 1980s. Reacting against it, Tillers penned his first article for *Art & Text*. It was written at the time of the 1982 Sydney Biennale, which as well as introducing neo-Expressionism to Australia also included the first example of an Aboriginal ground painting into the arena of contemporary art. This is the context of Tillers recalling the previous 1979 Biennale:

> Australian artists were often dismayed by the interest and knowledge shown by visiting artists and critics of Aboriginal culture and the almost aggressive indifference they displayed to the Australian urban environment and its [postmodern] culture. Some, like Marina Abramović and Ulay even returned later (under a Visual Arts Board grant) to seek out (with typical Germanic zeal and determination) the aboriginal influence for their own work.[14]

They had returned in the summer of 1980–81. While Taylor laboured on his plans for *Art & Text* that summer, they hunkered down in the heat with the Aborigines of central Australia.

No matter how uninterested Taylor was in Aboriginal art, he came onto the art scene at a time when it was of growing interest to many contemporary artists, critics and curators. This would become more the case as the '80s progressed. This interest grew, like neo-Expressionism, from the '70s' postconceptualist interest in the environment, the body, performance, feminism, politics and archaeology. This tendency would have been obvious to Taylor as he was preparing to launch the first issue of *Art & Text* during the summer of 1980–81, especially after he read Gablik's assessment of Australian art, published in the summer issue (January 1981) of *Art in America*. He had interviewed her nine months earlier when she was visiting Australia and commissioned an essay from her for the first issue.

As he read Gablik's report, Taylor must have felt on another planet. Gablik responded mostly to artists who dealt with the local landscape in a primitivist fashion: Tom Arthur's 'totemic landscapes',[15] John Davis's '"low-tech" ... materials of nature' that resembled 'aboriginal ceremonial sticks, shamanistic prayer arrows or healing wands' (which he gifts 'as a mark of homage to more primitive cultures in which gift exchange practices were an important part of social life'), and Peter Taylor's lyrical carvings that reminded her of 'American Indian totems'.[16] Little wonder that 'prior to speaking about any contemporary work', Gablik announced an anthropological digression – that she would 'change direction briefly to speak about the aboriginal tradition'.[17] Gablik, you see, had felt 'the aboriginal presence of the bush' during her visit to Australia:

> It was only when I touched the country – which hangs back aloof and unapproachable just beyond the cities – and encountered a landscape so fierce and primevally strange ... that I felt myself in the presence of something uniquely Australian, a stored power ... it certainly changed me forever.[18]

Gablik wasn't the only influential critic thinking along these lines. That same summer Bernice Murphy was preparing the first 'Australian Perspecta' Biennial of contemporary art for the Art Gallery of New South Wales, the exhibition that triggered Tillers's revelation about Aboriginal art. Unlike Taylor, she welcomed the pluralism and heterogeneity of the '70s, including 'the recent emergence of Aboriginal art expression in post-tribal forms'.[19]

If Murphy eschewed the universal, like Gablik she was seduced by the archetypal. She pointed to 'the recent concern in [Australian] art with the environment, archaeology and anthropology, and rehabilitation (though performance art) of a mythopoeic consciousness, personal symbols and a sense of generated ritual', including 'works which focus a ritualistic, tribal and sub-rationalistic connection with the environment'.[20]

Thus at the very moment that Taylor launched *Art & Text* there was a clear trend towards what Robert Lindsay, curator at the National Gallery of Victoria (NGV), called 'the authority and simplicity of our tribal past'.[21] Taylor's retro-'60s style, which combined pop art and a semiotic version of conceptualism, was out of step with this development. Moreover, his favoured second-degree artists were already being subsumed into the emerging expressionist style of painting. In 'Australian Perspecta' Murphy characterised the work of Jenny Watson and Howard Arkley as displaying 'a return to figuration, pattern and imagery' and 'a vitalistic immediacy of contact with the painted or constructed surface'.[22]

These metaphors suggest Murphy's awareness of the exhibition 'A New Spirit in Painting', which opened at London's Royal Academy that same summer in mid January 1981. While it received poor reviews (as neo-Expressionism would continue to do),[23] the future seemed with it. The brief catalogue essay introduced what would become the key themes of neo-Expressionism: it was against the dominance and teleology of American painting (i.e., Greenberg and abstract art) and conceptualism, and was for painting, figuration and a conspicuous individualised masculine vision.[24] These simple oppositions produced a clarity of conception that underwrote the rapid success of neo-Expressionism. This contrasted with the notions of postmodernism and Aboriginal contemporary art, which had challenging ontological implications that were not easily digested.

By 1982, the postconceptual primitivism celebrated by Gablik and Murphy the previous year had morphed into expressionist painting and what at the time seemed the first dominant art movement since abstract expressionism. As a style, the origins of neo-Expressionism can be traced to the early 1970s shift, especially in New York, away from the hard-edge minimalism of the 1960s and towards using paint 'expressively and splashily'.[25] Its *raison d'être*, however, descends directly from the romantic primitivism and especially new 'relaxed internationalism' of the '70s,[26] which freed artists from the hegemony of New York. The latter was its particular claim to fame. As the *New York Times* reviewer of 'A New Spirit in Painting' wrote:

> the [Royal] academy has demonstrated that contemporary art is no longer the exclusive domain of the United States. According to this exhibition, the current score of world-class artists is West Germany 11, the United States 9, Great Britain 8, the rest of the world 10.[27]

The rest of the world was France and Italy (unless one counted Matta as Chilean and Picasso as Spanish). Leaving aside the Eurocentrism of this tally, it signaled a newfound de-centred regionalism. Leavened by the neo-Expressionist yearning for unmediated experience that, as Tillers said (in *Art & Text*), stressed 'integrity and authenticity over [postmodern] irony and ambivalence',[28] this regionalism played into pre-existing myths of Australian identity. Murphy certainly fell for it. Our relationship to place, she said, is shadowed by the psychic presence of 'the outback ... where European culture cuts out and gives way to the wide horizon of Aboriginal Australia'.[29]

Thus the links between neo-Expressionist values and the growing interest in Aboriginal art were all too obvious. For example, James Mollison, the Director of the National Gallery of Australia, became a convert to Western Desert painting at much the same time that he became an enthusiastic supporter of the Melbourne ROAR collective, formed in mid 1982 by mainly young expressionist painters who were the same generation as Taylor. Along with the older Peter Booth, they were hailed as the new Angry Penguins, as if Australian neo-Expressionism was a genuinely regional art that emerged 'independently of such shifts occurring simultaneously in other countries' (Tillers).[30]

While the ROAR collective disdained such comparisons, and felt little affinity with either Booth or European neo-Expressionists, they were natural allies of Aboriginal art and artists. Gabrielle Pizzi had her first exhibition of Papunya Tula painting at ROAR Studios in 1983, through which ROAR artists got to know the art and some of the artists. Some of its key members, such as Wayne (Iggy) Eager, David Larwill and Marina Strocchi would develop very close ties to Aboriginal artists and the central Australian landscape. Strocchi was instrumental in establishing the art centre at Haast's Bluff and the women's painting movement of Papunya Tula. Eager also worked for Papunya Tula, and both to this day work closely with Aboriginal artists from their base in Alice Springs.

Not only did Taylor do none of this, he completely disdained the expressionist turn in Australian art. In 1984, as he prepared to jet off to New York forever, *Art & Text* contemptuously brushed the ROAR collective aside as if swatting an annoying fly.[31] Not only were Taylor's heart and sensibility elsewhere, but he had by then effectively seen-off the false prophets. He did this by brazenly retrofitting neo-Expressionism's signifiers of regionalism, authenticity and primitivism with the look and feel of postmodernism.

Aboriginal art in *Art & Text*: The early issues

While Taylor's sensibility makes it difficult to imagine that Aboriginal art was ever much, if at all, on his horizon, Aboriginal politics were impossible to avoid in the 1970s. This made the politics of engaging with Aboriginal art even more difficult to negotiate. Tillers explained why in an essay published during the 'POPISM' exhibition (Winter 1982). This first essay that *Art & Text* published on Aboriginal art made the case for the journal's lack of interest in it:

> The reluctance for a more explicit identification with the

> aborigines, for an authentic 'cultural convergence' can in part be explained by the deep guilt underlying Australian culture. For the history of white settlement in Australia in relation to the Aborigines is a story of homicide, rape, the forcible abduction of children from their parents and the methodical dispossession of the lands upon which their well-being, self-respect and survival have depended. 'Cultural convergence' is attractive as an idea because it offers a painless way to expiate our collective guilt of this history while simultaneously suggesting an easy solution to the more mundane but nevertheless pressing problem of finding a uniquely Australian content to our art in an international climate sympathetic to the notion of 'regional' art.[32]

Tillers thus provides a political justification for Taylor's cynicism towards Western primitivism and its Australian version, Aboriginalism. Indeed, one could be forgiven for thinking that during its first year *Art & Text* ignored Aboriginal art altogether. Yet from its first issue things Aboriginal (as opposed to Aboriginal art) knocked up against Taylor's main concerns of contemporary art. They appear like unannounced guests, in peripheral vision. Take the first issue. Presumably Taylor had attended the Adelaide Festival in March 1980 to see the legendary avant-gardist British theatre director Peter Brook's production of Alfred Jarry's *Ubu*, as he secured an essay from Brook for the first issue of *Art & Text*.[33] However, Brook wrote not on *Ubu* but another play that he had performed called *The Ik*, which was based on a dubious but popular anthropological study of a central African (supposedly) hunter-gatherer tribe, and employed Aboriginal children as actors. Brook's essay is a searing indictment of Australian colonialism that gives an account of his journeys in central Australia after meeting a group of Aborigines from the desert who had been brought to see *The Ik*, and whose children were presumably the actors in the play.

Brook made no mention of Aboriginal art or Western Desert painting (Papunya was not on the itinerary). The closest illustration of an indigenous artwork in the first issue is in an article on photography, 'The mirror without a memory', which reproduces a photograph of a tattooed Maori skull with the caption: 'A particular trade grew up in New Zealand: buying tattooed and smoked heads from Maoris and reselling them to museums and collectors in Europe'.[34] This illustration is a type of Baroque allegorical emblem so loved by Walter Benjamin, in which the image and its caption combine in disturbing rather than clarifying ways to suggest hidden divine meanings that call the viewer 'to inspect the world speculatively'.[35] A disturbing, uncanny thing lurking in the journal, this grotesque illustration was like some sulphuric poison eating away at its text. In this respect it recalled Brook's article and his play *The Ik*, which was an indigenous version of *Lord of the Flies* (Brook had directed the 1963 film to much acclaim). This is an early indication of the layered resonances that Taylor achieved in *Art & Text*.[36]

It is difficult to imagine that when Taylor initially conceived *Art & Text* he envisaged publishing a political essay on Australian colonialism in the first issue. Yet a continuing if offbeat fascination with colonial history and vaguely indigenous matters characterise the first year of *Art & Text*. Issue 3 covered Abramović and Ulay's Australian desert adventure, in which the indigene are pictured as indifferent alien gods to whom these European avant-gardists have made a pilgrimage to learn the esoteric art of telepathic communication. In issue 4, Juan Davila penned an abstruse postcolonial allegory that called on artists to repudiate the 'appropriation of foreign cultural data', proposing instead 'his own body as a sign of a passionate fight with the historical modes of productions of art and culture' in this country—here in drag as Spider Woman. The comic book text reads: 'With this ring I thee web ... Black lady I love you too, but ... I fire with hope the victims of cynical regard ... left alone in this sunburnt hole ... I cry out against the void ... my wet dream for this thirsty land ....'[37] On a more picturesque note, in issue 5 (Autumn 1982), Jill Graham reviewed Bonita Ely's artist book *Murray/Murundi*, which traced oral histories of the Murray River town Robinvale (in northern Victoria), drawing into conversation the presences of the river and local Aboriginal and settler cultures.

Such digressions, like spices added to the main fare, must be seen within the context of Taylor's larger culinary approach to editing. Take the interview with Abramović and Ulay, made just after their return from the desert. If in the summer of 1980–81 Taylor had discovered ways to articulate the provocations of inauthenticity by ironically quoting modernism's looks, i.e., an art of the second degree, Abramović and Ulay had re-discovered authenticity by completely abandoning the distant memory of modernism's conventions. Out there, said Abramović, 'I got the idea of how the art in the future can exist'.[38]

> We had for a long time the idea to go somewhere in the desert ... and I must say for myself I expect very much from the contact with Aborigines ... Knowing some things about their

> culture and knowing their culture is not a material one was a very important fact for me ... that actually what one man can have is the Dream.[39]

Afterwards they joked that 'Buddha, Jesus Christ, Moses and Mohammed all went to the desert as nobody and came back somebody'.[40]

There is nothing of the second degree in Abramović and Ulay's ambitions and performances. Why then did Taylor publish an interview with them?

A pattern of Taylor's editorship was the inclusion of articles that diverged from his position. For example, the first issue had essays by Gablik, Ian Burn and Janine Burke, even though Taylor claimed he was seeking to differentiate *Art & Text* from the prevailing modernist, Marxist and feminist criticism that these writers represented. Taylor's aim was a fragmented Benjaminesque text, a collage of different voices that suggest a hidden, dare I say, divine purpose. On one level, he was intent on provoking controversy. He relished discord and even published attacks on his approach,[41] all the while, as Baudelaire said of the well-practiced dandy, smiling 'like the Spartan boy under the fox's tooth'.[42] Taylor smiled because no matter how fierce the attack, as editor he was the puppeteer. He pulled the strings in a careful orchestration that was designed not so much to provide a platform for free speech but a model for a moral universe, an ethos in which his notion of right and wrong was finely calibrated.

Importantly, Taylor's method was not democratic inclusion but the dandy's ironic purloining of deconstruction. It enacted the subversive potential of appropriation as a discourse of the second degree. Quoting Abramović and Ulay verbatim was the first step in transforming their text into such a discourse and thereby opening it to deconstruction.

The very absurdity of Abramović and Ulay's claims, which read like a 'Waiting for Godot' experience, must have appealed to Taylor (who loved Beckett and understood the truth value of the absurd). If we read *Art & Text* as collaged fragments in which meaning lies in the interstices between them—which is how Taylor insisted that contemporary art and culture were experienced[43]—then the interview should be read not in its own autonomous terms but as just one element in Taylor's ironic neo-Baroque poetics. Here, meaning is an effect of colliding fragments, in this case the interview's juxtaposition with other pieces in the issue, for example: Philip Brophy's paean to the 'absence of a ... mystic norm of purity in disco music';[44] John Nixon's manifesto of Anti-Music, a collage of quotes and cryptic one liners, such as '(THEIR EARS WERE ON FIRE)', 'ANTI-MUSIC IS AN INDUSTRIAL FOLK MUSIC', and 'PRIMITIVE RACES ATTRIBUTED SOUND TO THE GODS; IT WAS CONSIDERED SACRED AND RESERVED FOR PRIESTS, WHO USED IT TO ENRICH THE MYSTERY OF THEIR RITES';[45] and Ted Colless and David Kelly's rave 'The Lost World', a poetic collage of diverse contemporary spectacles of 'the outer limits', 'panic in the year zero', 'body snatchers' and 'savage nakedness'.[46] In these colliding fragments, we can see why Taylor referred to his approach as 'anarchic, multi-directional, a cruel joke that vectorises the fragmented field of Australian art'.[47] Adrian Martin, who admired Taylor's 'often witty and subversive sense of bricolage', claimed that it produced 'some of *Art & Text*'s finest moments.'[48]

Strategic Aboriginalism: Against neo-Expressionism

In these particular collisions, Taylor cast a mocking glance over not Aboriginal art but the primitivism of contemporary art. His ironic bemusement changed when, by 1982, it had morphed into neo-Expressionism, which Taylor took as a much more serious threat to his plans. His tactical response to neo-Expressionism can be precisely tracked. His essay for the catalogue of the contemporary Australian art exhibition in London, 'Eureka!', which opened in March 1982, was aware of but not particularly alarmed by the tendency—what he described as the 'subjective and neo-romantic model' and its belief 'in "pure" experiences unmediated by theory, ideology and representation'.[49] As if confident of history's hand, Taylor condescendingly dismissed it as passé. He also had little to say about neo-Expressionism in his 'POPISM' exhibition, which opened in June, other than to assert in a rather enigmatic and condescending throwaway line that 'POPISM refutes this humanism (now revived in neo-Expressionism) and instead confronts its fictitious spectator with an anagram of fragments'.[50]

Taylor would later claim that his curatorial intention in 'POPISM' was a tactic to infuriate his neo-romantic opponents—'those who responded bitterly to the exhibition's depreciation of personal biography, originality and immediate social purpose'.[51] However, the first alarm sounds in spring 1982, after the impact of Documenta 7 and the Sydney Biennale had sunk in. In *Art & Text* he hysterically lampooned neo-Expressionism for 'inspiring all kinds of semi-relevant practices to be remembered, rediscovered and retrieved from the closets into which they were forced years ago'. Here, he complained, the art world's 'unrevised theoretical ineptitude has been most visible'.[52] Such 'attempts to forget the 'advanced' artistic work of the 1960s and 70s and ... the investment by the art world's most powerful institutions in the return of an Australian expressionism', he accused, 'seeks to falsify art history and marginalise the most productive of our recent and contemporary arts'.[53] Based on a teleological model of avant-gardism, his first salvos were off target especially since neo-Expressionism's success quickly positioned it as 'advanced' and 'avant-garde' (both terms then in Taylor's lexicon).

However, Taylor's brilliance quickly came to the fore in a deft strategic shift in the summer of 1982–83. Shameless in his tactics, he sought to distinguish between international and local neo-Expressionisms, and claim that the postmodernism of 'POPISM' was the authentic neo-Expressionism. The European neo-Expressionists, he argued, had a 'reflexive' attitude to the self that the Australians lacked.[54] On these grounds he dismissed Australian neo-Expressionism for missing the point, and instead claimed that 'POPISM' was the real neo-Expressionism because it took a 'reflexive' approach to regionalism, primitivism and self-expression. Henceforth this would become, in his mind, the *raison d'être* of Australian postmodernism. As if reaching for an allegory of his own ambition, he compared its artists to the rock group the Monkees: initially the fabrication of 'a conspiracy' (Paul Taylor inc.), they 'learned to play their instruments', i.e., to actually paint (Imants Tillers). Just as guitars and drums signify rock group, so 'paint is the medium that will not only most quickly make one an artist but, above all, be perceived as an artist.'

> And what better medium than painting predisposes us to be anti-'radical', post-experimental, hyper-real. Painting is a trace of ancient culture collected by young artists who have ceased believing in art ... empty of meaning, painting is now filled with all kinds of expression proper to pop-stars (irony, stereotypes, subjectivity, theatricality) ... It's flush with the surface of traditionalism.[55]

Taylor and Tillers were clearly in close dialogue at this point. Tillers was far more ambivalent about neo-Expressionism than Taylor. While selected for 'POPISM', he had felt uncomfortable with its thesis, and he was also, after Documenta 7, becoming deeply interested in some of the German neo-Expressionist painters.[56] This is first clearly evident in *Island of the Dead*, a charcoal drawing he made towards the end of 1982. He had first used the phrase the previous year in reference to *One Painting Cleaving* – a set of paintings of which one version was exhibited at Documenta 7. Here it referred to a 'triangle of doubt' created when triangulation fails to locate a 'point of certainty'. Tillers's fanciful triangulation of Duchamp, Arakawa and de Chirico was, he said, 'three lines of influence (moving in the direction of melancholy)' that converged on Böcklin's painting *The Island of the Dead*.[57] The next year Tillers expanded this metaphor to include references to another triangle of doubt (Postmodernism, Australian art, Aboriginal art) and its melancholy history. He suggested that Böcklin's painting might be an effect (as per Bell's Theorem) of the 'extermination of the Tasmanian aborigines by the white settlers.'[58]

One of Tillers's earliest canvasboards, *Island of the Dead*, is based on a photograph of a Quinkan country rock painting given to Tillers by Marianne Baillieu.[59] Its subject matter, use of charcoal, finger drawing and handprints epitomised a reflexive engagement with the signs of neo-Expressionism. *White Aborigines*, made shortly afterwards, in early 1983, was one of his first painted canvasboards and took its name from a recently published essay by Taylor (discussed below). Its enigmatic juxtaposition of image and text, exemplary of Benjamin's neo-Baroque emblem (discussed earlier), greatly appealed to Taylor, who included it in his second curatorial project, 'Tall Poppies', which opened in April 1983.

'Tall Poppies' was the first clear indication of Taylor's post-Popism approach, epitomised in his rebranding the art of the 'second degree' as the art of 'white Aborigines'. It 'announced', said Adrian Martin, 'a lightning switch from conceptualist "cool" to ambiguous neo-romanticism'.[60] Sue Cramer diagnosed this 'marked shift from Popism' as a détente with the current 'Zeitgeist' of neo-Expressionism, as if 'there is a desire not to be marginalised, to rigorously confront such art on an equal footing'. The title of Tillers's 'painterly and turbulent' *White Aborigines* (1983), she said, 'creates ... a seemingly irrational and nonsensical relationship between image and text'.[61] Taylor would similarly claim that *White Aborigines* 'participates in the anti-Rationalism of the present'.[62]

However, Cramer's reading of Taylor's catalogue essay as 'romantic' and 'endorsing the values of "greatness" and "uniqueness" in art',[63] misses its irony and its references to Douglas Crimp's 1977 'Pictures' exhibition that had inspired 'POPISM'.[64] Of *White Aborigines*, Taylor wrote, 'The image and obscure German text are traces of worlds in collision which have temporarily brought themselves to rest as this picture'. And, he added:

> Every work here is 'postconceptual' in ambition and critical attitude towards the act of picturing ... these artists deliberately inhabit the pictorial terrain to benefit from both painting's cultural privilege as bearer of significance and its reinscription as a field of ironic distance, artifice and subjectivity.[65]

Tillers's reflexive engagement with the new Zeitgeist was still second-degree art, its gestures geared in a self-conscious and ironic way to the signs and codes of neo-Expressionism. In short, its turn to the local overtly deconstructed the discourse of regionalism. Thus Taylor insisted in the catalogue of 'Tall Poppies': 'There is nothing especially Australian in the work of any of these artists',[66] upturning his earlier claim that 'POPISM' was 'a specifically Australian utterance' of second-degree art. In fact, he said rather glibly, he chose the artists in 'Tall Poppies' for the simple reason that 'they have been selected by non-Australian curators to show overseas'.[67] In typically high-rhetorical fashion, Taylor told an interviewer at the time of the exhibition:

> I refute the stupid notion that Australians are going to "naturally" use Aboriginal motifs and are going to draw on the cultures of South East Asia and this kind of rubbish. If Australians are going to be reflexive about their regional situation, it's going to be to understand the position of combative anti-modernist thought which is really the tradition of Australian art.[68]

What he meant by 'reflexive' was evident in John Dunkley-Smith's installation in 'Tall Poppies', *Interior No. 7 (University Gallery) Melbourne* (1983), which featured 'Aboriginal artefacts' hanging on a wall, and slide projections of them on the opposite wall. However, said Taylor somewhat disingenuously, 'they appear by default' as the passive objects of a camera's mechanical panning gaze, in which 'they are the references by which we compare the work's actual location with the changes undergone in the projected images'.[69] With these prompts, Cramer concluded in her review: 'there is little specifically Australian subject matter in Tall Poppies. Notions of a regional or national identity, a truly "aboriginal art" seem not to appear, viewed perhaps as an oversimplistic response to the questions of "place"'.[70]

However, the explicit Aboriginal references in two of the five paintings in the exhibition, and the very title of Tillers's painting,

White Aborigines, suggests that Cramer's conclusion is itself overly simplistic. In the spirit of Barthes, Taylor, like Tillers, had made the signs of neo-Expressionism – such as painterliness, regionalism and primitivism – the new signifiers of second-degree art. If earlier in the 'POPISM' catalogue Taylor had characterised second-degree art as the 'rhetoric of photography' (Walter Benjamin and Douglas Crimp were his references), now, in an essay written in the summer of 1982–83,[71] it had become 'the art of white Aborigines'.[72] Taylor purloined the evocative phrase from Norman Mailer's classic essay 'The white negro' (1957), which analysed a white subculture that adopted the signs of black culture. Thus 'Popism: the Art of White Aborigines' strikes a very different note from the 'POPISM' catalogue essay. Taylor reasoned in a typical Möebius-like logic:

> Popism, like the aboriginal nomads, can therefore find a metaphor for itself in its existence on the surface and edges of the existing landscape. It is not coincidental that Popism, like the Australian population, has forsaken an interior and clung to the outside, emptying itself continuously of its valuable resources.[73]

At one level, Taylor's notion of 'white Aborigines' ranks with the crassest Aboriginalism. At another level, Taylor had in effect discovered (perhaps after seeing *Island of the Dead*) a postmodernism embedded in Aboriginal art. Tillers's essay 'Fear of Texture', published in *Art & Text* in the Winter of 1983, is a brilliant and witty summation of Taylor's rhetoric to date. It is also the first time that *Art & Text* reproduced an Aboriginal artwork: Papunya Tula artist Mick Namarari's *Kangaroo story* (1982).

The essay begins with an amusing parody on neo-Expressionism: 'Australian art is about to get thicker. Miles and miles of canvas are to be unfurled and acres of thick impasto paint are to be scraped and scum bled by thousands of antipodean "Art Ants" galvanised into a frenzied collective action.'[74] And then came the cavalry:

> Fortunately, in Australian art there are still some tendencies to deviate from this prescribed textural norm and many of those artists willing to deviate have taken refuge in the *dematerialisation of texture* which the dot-screen permits – i.e., in the reproduction of the reproduction or in allied photographic processes.

While referring to the work of several artists associated with Taylor, Tillers argues: 'This "dot-screen" structure however is most apparent in the works of the artists of Central Australia and the Western Desert who form the Papunya school of painters'. Here, he says, 'it acts as an *image of dematerialisation*',[75] a claim that leads him to conclude:

> Papunya paintings have a very strong conceptual aspect and in several aspects can be identified with the dematerialised aspects of the Australian conceptual art of the early 70's [...] Considering that the first canvasboards were done in 1970–1, Papunya painting shares exactly the same historical period in Australia as conceptual art. Yet it was only in the latter part of this decade that these two eminently compatible artistic movements came together when Tim Johnson as a conceptualist became one of Papunya painting's chief publicists.[76]

'Fear of Texture' also sketches out one of the reasons why Tillers had the previous year embarked on his own neo-Expressionist style canvasboard project. Somewhat tongue-in-cheek, Tillers commented that 'it is comparatively easy for young Australian artists without an existing artistic history to now partake of this burgeoning "regional" tradition', for he too was partaking of such 'an unabashed display of opportunism',[77] as if he had 'already caught up with the local "zeitgeist"'.[78] However, Tillers's new expressionist canvasboards also took their cue from the logic of Papunya Tula painting. A work of art, he said,

> might be thought of not in terms of a finite object but as a property of a continuous surface existing in time ad infinitum [...] The truth of this proposition is clearly evident if we look at a room full of Papunya paintings. The initial impression that each individual canvas is literally a fragment cut from the same cloth is in fact so overwhelming that it is only with the familiarity that comes from concerted and extended study that we begin to detect a whole range of pertinent differences between paintings.[79]

Tillers concluded:

> while we are condemned to eternally subsist on the arid surface of this 'Island of the Dead', before we acquiesce to the apocalypse of 'impasto' and simulated expression we should

> reclaim the 'dot-screen' and restore this 'cut-out portion of the fabric' back within the 'body' of modern Australian art'.[80]

A year earlier, in his essay 'Locality Fails', Tillers had written that the Australian colonial simulation of European styles 'is bound to a comfortable mediocrity by its own tentativeness. We do not yet have a white artist who can declare with conviction: "I am aboriginal."'[81] But the next year, in 1983, he and Taylor were prepared to make this claim. 'There is a supreme irony', he said, in Papunya Tula painting being 'convergent with the art of "White Aborigines" – Australian "unexpressionists"' like himself.[82]

Tillers demonstrated what he meant by this revelation in his
21 final *n*-space exhibition, 'Waiting for Technology', which opened in late August 1983 at the Yuill/Crowley Gallery in Sydney, shortly after 'Fear of Texture' appeared. Here were juxtaposed four paintings by Tim Johnson that depicted Papunya Tula artists with their paintings, with the actual paintings. These eight works were thus promoted as a collaborative event that, in the spirit of postconceptualism, transparently revealed their mode of production as evidence of a process and system of inter-subjective exchange.

The reckless boldness of this cross-cultural exchange, which implicated the one in the other, contrasts with the introduction that Bernice Murphy wrote at this time for the Australian representation at the XVI Bienal de São Paulo that would open in October 1983. It featured all Aboriginal work from Papunya Tula and Ramingining, and an Aboriginal commissioner, the ceramicist Thancoupie. Emphasising the contemporary nature of the art, made 'in the maintenance of their culture', Murphy concluded:

> This remarkable record of cultural integrity and survival has recently pressed more strongly into contemporary art consciousness in Australia. It is a record to which many white artists and critics readily pay homage, while acknowledging that there is no possibility of appropriation of this culture's forms from outside. From a conceptual distance of different cultures, many white artists acknowledge the power of a culture that has projected a quite different set of values for thousands of years about this ancient continent.[83]

This approach, which prevails in many quarters to this day and maintains a separation between Aboriginal and Australian art, re-imposes the barrier between Aboriginal and contemporary art that characterises the ideology of modernity, sublimating its primitivism in the guise of a contemporary art that is contemporary in name only. However, Taylor and Tillers put these two traditions into intimate if surreal dialogue, insisting that both occupied the same postmodern terrain, indeed were each implicated in the other.

Tillers was not the first to suggest that Western Desert painting was postmodernist. Kenneth Coutts-Smith, a British/Canadian artist and writer who wrote on avant-garde and indigenous art,[84] and a close associate of the postcolonial artist, theorist and editor Rasheed Araeen, had written in *Art Network* in 1982 that Papunya Tula paintings 'do not appeal to Euro-American notions of "the primitive" ... rather they appear to lock into late-minimal and post-modernist art'.[85] However, Coutts-Smith had left his observation hanging. *Art & Text* was the first to provide a theory of Aboriginal postmodernism.

Conclusion

What was the legacy of Taylor's tactic to outflank neo-Expressionism through appropriating its signs to his scheme?

Taylor's tactic had no impact on the rise and rise of neo-Expressionism. In December 1983, 'Vox Pop, into the eighties', curated by Lindsay, opened at the NGV. It championed Booth as 'the prophet' of these times and positioned 'POPISM' as a small moment in neo-Expressionism.[86] If Taylor had argued for the continuity between contemporary art and the cool art of minimalism and conceptualism, Patrick McCaughey (Taylor's former professor) claimed that new art of the '80s 'could not be more different from the "cool" ideological stances and attitudes of the 1970s'.[87] Taylor's greatest disappointment must have been seeing Watson allied with Larwill, the leading ROAR painter. Larwill's 'tribal diagrams' and Watson's 'New Primitivism', said Lindsay, are examples of 'archetypal images'; the 'apparent crudeness of the image and its execution invests it with an emotional aggression ... [and] a new emotive calligraphy'.[88] Watson's assimilation into the ROAR ethos was not without evidence: she had grouped her works 'under a general title "Cave Paintings"',[89] but Lindsay had missed her ironic intent.

The triumph of neo-Expressionism in Australia had already been confirmed in the Paris exhibition, 'D'un autre continent: L'Australie le rêve et le reel', organised by the French curator Suzanne Pagé.[90] It had opened a few months earlier in October. Including work by many of the artists in 'Vox Pop' and also a

Warlpiri ground painting (inspired by the previous year's Sydney Biennale), the whole event was packaged in a primitivising manner but one that lauded the authenticity and truth of the ground painting over the superficiality of the Australian art. In the hands of the French curator, this was handled in a far cruder manner than anything witnessed in Australia. The French critics responded enthusiastically, as *Art & Text* reported in a forensic article.[91]

In Paris the Warlpiri and Australian works were exhibited in separate spaces and treated as opposed discourses. One of the Australian participants, Philip Brophy, who was close to Taylor, complained:

> I'm listening to French anthropologists (yawn) tell us about how Art functions differently in primitive tribal cultures from industrialised technological cultures. And I'm listening to Aborigines (sporting cowboy-shirts, dark glasses and 'Australia windcheaters') calmly tell us about the pragmatic considerations they have made in order to publically exhibit a sampling of their more private sacred ... activities.

While finding 'no real interest in any of this', Brophy did 'hope they [the Warlpiri] are being opportunistic in inserting themselves into the ... public domain ... as a means to their own ends'.[92]

For Tillers, in this neo-Expressionist context, the ground painting, unlike Papunya Tula painting, played into the myths of primitivism and exoticism[93] – in much the same way that it had in the 1982 Sydney Biennale. Taylor, who had wind of what was afoot in Paris, successfully lobbied Tillers to withdraw from the exhibition. Tillers would regret his decision, as he lost the opportunity to counter the thrust of an influential exhibition that he believed was the culmination of the 'artificial blending' of 'the exoticism of Aboriginal culture with certain manifestations of contemporary art'.[94] In other words, at this time there was a sense that the battle against neo-Expressionism was being lost.

While *Art & Text* would soon be vindicated, it wasn't Taylor's tactics that won the day. Rather, he happened, as he always believed, to be on the right side of history. By 1986 neo-Expressionism's star was fading fast and today it is so forgotten that recently one critic wondered why 'so much effort is expended to suppress an episode and its memory'.[95] Yet Taylor's deliberate repression of neo-Expressionism through its appropriation produced his most important insight: that Australia, not New York, was the privileged site of postmodernism. Lacking authenticity, Australia's 'profound and radical superficiality' is expressed in a 'carnivalesque array of copies, inversions and negatives', 'an ab-original, soulless, antipodal reflection'.[96] Taylor's claim for the priority of Australian art appropriated another sign of Australian neo-Expressionism, making it his own.

While the claim for postmodernism's regionalism was clearly rhetorical, it did contain a small pearl of wisdom that in the coming decades would grow into the rich globalism of current art world discourse. However, Tillers, not Aboriginal art, was to benefit most from this little pearl. It had minimal impact on the future criticism or reception of Aboriginal art. On the other hand, Tillers grasped its value. In 'Perpetual Mourning', an essay published in the summer 1984 issue of *Art & Text*, he wrote:

> Today, in 1984 [after the 'relentless provincialism' of the previous decades] we place our hope in what the English critic John Roberts has termed: "the re-emergence of a strong urban-based art, orientated towards mimicry and deconstruction of the codes and signs of consumerism" ... By employing strategies of mimicry, deconstruction and hyper-conformism, [provincialism's] "invisibility" and "powerlessness" can now be turned to our advantage.[97]

By 'our', Tillers meant a 'post-Aboriginal' Australia, i.e., one in which Aboriginal traditions are enmeshed in contemporary Australian art.[98]

In 1996, Rex Butler identified a reversal in Australian postmodern discourse from the 'iconoclasm' of second-degree art, which 'attempted to destroy the notions of originality', to an 'iconic' mode that sought to appropriate the aura of the original and of tradition for the contemporary. Butler dated this shift to 1985 – specifically to an exhibition curated by a frequent contributor to *Art & Text*, Edward Colless (though Butler admits that the explicit logic of the second is implicit in the first).[99]

However, this reversal can be traced earlier to the discourse of white Aborigines and Tillers's appropriations of Aboriginal art from late 1982. Indeed, his canvasboard project begun at that time, and the earlier *One Painting Cleaving*, don't seek to decode the original image but inhabit it, and inhabit it in poetic ways that restore the aura of the original to the copy. Firstly, appropriating current apocalyptic discourses associated with neo-Expressionism, he linked his poetic enterprise to that of Aboriginal art in content as well as form. 'When authority ceases to be representative beware the dispossessed lest they rise up in revolt against everything held sacred to the prevailing order and inherit the ruins of a shattered ideology.'[100]

Secondly, recalling Abramović and Ulay, Tillers compared his poetic intentions to Aboriginal magic, implying that his recent appropriation of Aboriginal art was a shamanistic impulse to bring back to life the Aboriginal Australia decimated in the colonial genocide. Like that of the 'piercing cry' of the white cockatoo, his mimicry (he implied) was a warning to the living of the presence of the spirits in the bush. Tillers concluded: 'In this sense our culture is an Island of the Dead and our paintings facilitate the Return of the Living Dead'.[101] In this text (which was aimed at an international audience),[102] and 'Fear of Texture' from the previous year, Tillers effectively laid out his program, to which he still adheres to this day.

For Taylor, however, the idea of 'white Aborigines' was a brief tactical episode that he quickly left behind. He had largely left it to Tillers to progress the argument in the pages of *Art & Text* during these years. His most telling text in this regard, 'Popism: the Art of White Aborigines', was not published in *Art & Text*. And while Taylor clearly played an important role in the discourse of white Aborigines, we must wonder how much he believed its rhetoric. If Australia really was the privileged site of postmodernism, he moved to New York as soon as he could and never looked back. 'Perpetual Mourning' appeared on the eve of Taylor's departure. In relocating permanently to New York, Taylor moved to another planet, where he pursued what Martin called 'a style of aggressive artworld fashion journalism'.[103] From that point on, Taylor hardly wrote on Australian art, and, when he did, he wrote poorly, as if disengaged.[104]

Once Taylor was in New York, Paul Foss played an increasingly active role as editor of *Art & Text*.[105] Tillers ceased contributing, and in 1987 Davila, in *Art & Text*, dismissed Tillers's position as a form of neo-colonialism.[106] However, that year and the next, *Art & Text* published four articles by the anthropologist Eric Michaels that, with great originality, brought the earlier arguments made by Taylor and Tillers to bear on the production of Western Desert painting. It was to little avail. Davila's view soon solidified into an art world truism and the very market success of Aboriginal art in the 1990s brought it back into the fold of modernism, where it was lauded as a sort of abstract version of neo-Expressionism. If this suited the market and the institutions, it quickly resulted in remote Aboriginal art losing its theoretical purchase for contemporary art. For example, the potential to imbricate it in the relational aesthetics of the '90s, the ground which Tillers and Taylor had prepared, was missed.

Taylor's last words on Aboriginal art appeared at the end of the decade, in an interview with Rover Thomas for *Interview* magazine in June 1990, and in a preview a year earlier, in the *New York Times*, in one of the few articles he wrote on Australian art after 1984. No doubt to his great surprise, Aboriginal painting followed him to New York, brought there by John Weber, a prominent dealer of conceptual and postconceptual art. Taylor's preview of Weber's exhibition revealed his superficial engagement with Aboriginal art – even the name of 'Geoff Barden' is misspelt. But, typical of his New York criticism, Taylor had plenty of insider information. The article was full of gossip; about the collector who felt she was 'just terribly lucky with these paintings that they turned into money', and of deals between collectors and museum directors, and the artists and their dealers.[107] Postmodernism was now a rapidly fading dream and Taylor's attention had shifted to celebrating fashion-savvy artists. This is what he admired about the Papunya Tula artists: 'Today they are earning small fortunes by converting their traditional imagery into a commodity.' Taylor was clearly bemused by what he called this 'new fad in a jaded art market'. 'Certainly, the new acrylic paintings can be appreciated as decorative objects dashed off for suburban living rooms and Western museums. They can also simply appreciate – financially.'

Taylor was impressed by this brazen indigenous assault on the art world, especially given that 'the civilization of these former nomads is in ruins'. This phrase echoes Hal Foster's damning indictment, in his seminal essay in *October*, of MoMA's 'Primitivism' exhibition five years earlier: 'Though presented as art, the tribal objects are manifestly the ruins of (mostly) dead cultures'.[108] If Taylor thus gestures towards the journal on which he had modelled *Art & Text* at the beginning of the decade, he does not buy Foster's argument. Taylor, like Baudelaire, recognises in the ruin rather than in Foster's puritan appeal to 'vital others', the defining frame of *modernité*. Perhaps Taylor had Baudelaire's bohemian lifestyle in mind when he depicted Papunya Tula artists as idiosyncratic consumers rather than victims of capitalism, as dandies who, 'even if they can't drive … like to own cars'. He certainly had in mind that other dandy devotee of decadence, Andy Warhol. Taylor gleefully announced: 'In a way inconceivable to anyone but Andy Warhol and his followers [in which Taylor included himself], for the aborigines painting has become a license to print money.'

Heather Barker and Charles Green point out that *Art & Text*'s vision was 'more or less illegible in New York'.[109] It had all come to nought, including, they said, his efforts to promote Tillers. They quoted Jane Rankin-Reid, who knew Taylor in New York: 'Paul felt strongly that he [Tillers] belonged profile-wise alongside rising stars Sherrie Levine and Richard Prince, etc. He went in to bat for Imants in a way that he rarely did for other artists.'[110] While this is neither Tillers's impression nor one borne out in articles Taylor wrote after 1984,[111] Taylor was clearly struck by the most unlikely success of Papunya Tula painting. After a decade of intense official promotion of Australian artists in New York, only Tillers had had some success and now, in 1989, it too seemed to have vanished. Then, out of the blue, Aboriginal artists were suddenly making it internationally. With drooling admiration, Taylor reported that Michael Jackson, Mick Jagger, Wim Wenders and Yoko Ono had purchased work for their collections, 'and in Hollywood last November, a star-studded party launched Caz Gallery, which is devoted entirely to aboriginal art'.

As ever, Taylor was on the hunt for a new angle. But it was too late. Institutional and market success is what ultimately defeated *Art & Text*'s remarkable, surreal vision of Aboriginal art in 1983 and '84. The reception of Western Desert painting was already becoming paralysed by the worn out rhetoric of modernism that Taylor had sought to vanquish.[112] The brief window that had opened in the pages of *Art & Text* closed as the institutions and their curators returned Aboriginal art to its former place as the other of the contemporary. No amount of saying otherwise will fool anyone.

Art & sex: Paul Taylor

Ashley Crawford

Paul Taylor made art sexy. Sometime circa 1980, artist Jenny Watson met the aspiring critic, who had been based for a time in Hobart, at a party and rapidly recognised his restless energy and playful intelligence. Watson was the social connector par excellence (the fledgling Nick Cave was another she rather forcefully introduced the art world to) and before long Taylor's red MG would be spotted outside galleries and parties all over Melbourne. Never wanting to miss out on the action, Taylor would politely excuse himself from whatever party or opening to shoot across town to attend the next function, managing three or four in an evening.

Taylor, a Monash Arts graduate, was the classic entrepreneur. His ambition was to start a new magazine, to fill an obvious gap between the hyper-feminist *Lip*, the rather generic *Art Network*, and the broader and more journalistic *Virgin Press*. Publishing was a power base and Taylor knew that connections would make his project work. That, and some hefty networking to secure government funding (he received $30,000 from the Australia Council in 1981), and he gave birth to the difficult, controversial and often cheeky *Art & Text*.

At the time, I was one of the editors at the poorly designed but highly energetic *The Virgin Press*, which, down the track, changed its name to *Tension*. Despite the eccentric and almost schizophrenic approach taken by the editors,[1] *The Virgin Press* began building a solid audience immediately. Writers attracted to the new forum included Mark Mordue, Kathy Bail, Adrian Martin and Philip Brophy. The ever-resourceful Paul Taylor saw an opportunity to spread his gospel through its pages. He simply rang and informed me that we *had* to do a feature on him.

In 1981, the sixth issue of the *VP* ran a double page feature on Taylor complete with photographs of the editor lounging in his South Yarra apartment dressed from head to tail in black leather. While Jenny Watson and Tony Clark may have been pushing the pseudo-punk fashion of their friend Nick Cave, Taylor was obsessed with the glitter and glam aspect of English New Wave and the bands that were dubbed the New Romantics.

'It was called *Art & Text* because it wasn't just a coffee table book', Taylor said to me against a soundtrack of the British 'new-wave' band Visage. He continued:

> It's tied in with the sorts of ideas that have been put forward by French theorists, the relationship between art and culture, particularly people like Foucault and Barthes, in which a work of art is not looked at necessarily as a completed object but as a text, and this can be a work of literature or a visual art work. Different ways of speaking, a number of different forms of representation, photographic, modernist representation. So the title was designed to cover those areas.
>
> Half the writers have been artists, which dispels the ideas of an artist being a stupid painter. One of the most prominent areas is the relationship between art and culture – disco and other forms of performance, experimental theatre, new music which is presented for instance at Clifton Hill and that's done in the context of experimental art or new art. It also goes into the dynamics of what is behind things like the mod revival and how disco can be seen in the context of an art magazine or other forms of new wave. One of the basic attitudes being put forward by some of the writers is that these things have a history, a surreptitious history I suppose you could say, and that these things are as important as the things being taught in art history, which is considered to be very separate to what's going on in culture.
>
> Art is *not* just going on in art galleries and art schools but all over the place. If you're to define art you have to think of that, the utility rather than by any kind of aspiration put upon it.[2]

Taylor, then twenty-four years of age, would prove his point by invading the National Gallery of Victoria with elements of whimsy, pop, experimentation and theory with 1982's 'POPISM' exhibition. Taylor unselfconsciously hounded the media and seized the opportunity of a high profile public relations coup, telling Martin Armiger in *The National Times* (July 11–17, 1982) that 'We're not scared of the gallery. We accept it as a museum of art. We inhabit it as would a terrorist, to make a specific historical and political point.'[3]

Most of the artists in 'POPISM' – such as Howard Arkley, Juan Davila, Maria Kozic, Robert Rooney, and Imants Tillers – had either written for, or featured in, the first six issues of *Art & Text*. Rooney, in a playful approach to his role as critic at *The Age*, included himself in his review of 'POPISM' for that newspaper. *The Age* failed to see the humour and Rooney was dismissed.

For all his irreverence, generosity and humour, Taylor could also be precious and proprietary. In 1982, a loosely formed and largely anonymous group dubbing themselves 'New Art A Magazine Collective' produced an amusing, but largely insignificant, parody of Taylor's magazine. *Art & a Texta* utilised Taylor's *Art & Text* logo, adding on their cover: 'This is not a Taylor-made product but something else.'

Taylor's response was apocalyptic. He initiated legal proceedings, putting his not inconsiderable energies wholeheartedly into bringing down the 'impostors'. Moreover, *Art & a Texta* had taken out an advertisement in *The Virgin Press*, so we were inevitably drawn into the fray by Taylor.

The issue was finally resolved out of court. But the collective, now dubbing themselves 'John and Betty', decided to collect the legal documents for distribution to a select mailing list on which I was included. Upon hearing of their intentions, Taylor lashed out, with the direct result that his letter graced the front page of the resulting document. Dated January 20, 1983, Taylor had written:

> Dear New Art A Magazine collective,
>
> Regarding your forthcoming publication, *John and Betty Go To Court*, I hope my following points merit inclusion.
>
> 1. The background to our dealings with one another which go back to Ted Hopkins' self-admittedly poor printing job on *Art & Text*, the rejection of a piece by Ted Hopkins under the pseudonym of Les Hopwood which later appeared in ART & A TEXTA, and my association with Peg McGuire should all be taken into consideration in any account of the beginnings of ART & A TEXTA and the eventual, very lenient settlement of my claims against it.
>
> 2. Your collective cannot presume to be fully aware of my reasons for instigating court proceedings against what was at that time an anonymous set of people, nor for settling as we have out of court.
>
> 3. The collective is not in possession of all documents which supported my case nor those which weakened and contradicted its case. Similarly, it has not obtained access to the opinions of the numerous individual supporters of my case. Such documents and opinions undoubtably would annul the thrust and assumptions of your forthcoming publication.

In the absence of this material, I am certain your so-called "resource" publication will not be much of a resource at all. It can only be erroneous, incomplete, unfair and ultimately worthless – and another glimpse of the egg on your face.

Faithfully yours,
Paul Taylor[4]

'John and Betty' wasted little time in responding and their letter of January 26, 1983 followed Taylor's in the resulting publication.

Dear Paul,

Regarding your letter of 20/1/83, there is no reason for you to go on a hunt for motives behind *Art and A Texta* and in particular isolate one or two individuals as 'leaders of the pack' since there is no evidence of ill will towards you, *Art & Text* or its contributors in *Art and A Texta*. On many counts, *Art and A Texta* scores favourably on criteria strongly promoted in *Art & Text*.

For example, *Art & Text* promotes the role of art and language in the examination of popular culture. There could be nothing more 'popular' than a Lipton's Tea Bag, Leave it to Beaver, John and Betty: Learning to Read, The Age Newspaper, Victorian opera and "wogs". *Art & Text* states a preference for creative texts. The articles in *Art and A Texta* place themselves at risk from start to finish, especially those of Mr. Darwin, Mr. Hopwood, Mr. Yobo, Mr. Greene, the Ethnic Avenger and Mr. Lysiotis. *Art and A Texta* is, as we will argue, commentary in its own right and as such is consistent with your intention to upgrade the status of commentator. *Art and a Texta* also attacks "the artist-as-prince syndrome" in the contributions of Mr. Yobo, in the adoption of anonymity, and by generally sending up anything that is pretentious in artists and commentators.

Importantly, *Art and a Texta* has not borrowed anything from *Art & Text* more than is necessary for promoting a healthy respect for second order art which has been strongly promoted in *Art & Text*. Apart from the Leave It To Beaver and Age Odd Spot articles, the contributions in *Art and a Texta* vary radically in approach and form to anything that is found in the first seven issues of *Art & Text* and, we imagine,

> differ vastly from the approach *Art & Text* would take if it were to parody itself. On this account alone it is not adequate to describe *Art and a Texta* as a "hostile parody" of *Art & Text*, but rather as 'Something Else'. If anything, *Art and a Texta* works through the notion of 'absence', something that is again promoted in *Art & Text*. *Art and a Texta* signals a sense of joy, irreverence, spontaneity, something 'other' that is at hand; and as one of the affidavits in support of *Art and a Texta* comments – "it is heartening to see our culture provide something definite for the satirist to parody".[5]

But Taylor was also a pragmatist. He knew that the *Art & a Texta* fiasco would bring much needed publicity for his own magazine. He was also strongly aware that for an alternative culture to prosper, it needed funding. It was one thing to galvanise and promote, it was another to see artists and writers paid properly. Where most of the projects up and running – whether it be galleries like Art Projects or magazines like *The Virgin Press* or *Fast Forward* – had survived on enthusiasm, that was not likely to last.

The relationship between *Art & Text* and *The Virgin Press* (and then *Tension*) had always been friendly. Despite Taylor's aspirations to cosmopolitan cool, financial necessity reduced the reality of producing magazines into a cottage industry and the duties of wrapping subscriptions for both magazines would be shared on mutual lounge room floors.

In a burst of enthusiasm, in 1983 Taylor decided to take a hold of *The Virgin Press* and give it a solid shake. The magazine had moved from an intriguing melange of social issues, theatre, art and rock when it was established in 1980 until it began to concentrate largely on the 'alternative' art world circa 1981. By this stage, artists such as Howard Arkley, Juan Davila, John Nixon, Peter Tyndall and Jenny Watson were executing artists pages. Writers such as Taylor, Philip Brophy and Adrian Martin were even more conspicuous. It was beginning to look better under the design hand of Terence Hogan. However, if anything, the subject matter had gone from broad to chaotic. Jillian Burt wrote on tennis stars, Peter Lawrence on Clint Eastwood.

In mid 1983, an attempt was made to formalise the editorial structure with a board established, including this author in charge of rock music coverage, co-founder Robin Barden in charge of reviews, Peter Lawrence overseeing film coverage, John Nixon co-ordinating artists projects within the pages, and Paul Taylor sourcing criticism. In the first official minutes taken from an editorial board meeting (a first in the magazine's history), possible separate theme issues were listed as: DEATH, COMMERCIALISM and NOMADISM. The first issue of the revamped magazine was to appear in March 1983 with a cover conceived by Taylor of an upside-down map of the world.

Taylor organised a photo shoot of the new board with Jenny
Watson behind the camera. He strictly informed everyone to turn
up in severe black. Everyone complied except, of course, Taylor,
18 who arrived in a blazing white suit and cheeky grin.

As 1983 dawned, reality intervened. What was left of the original team was exhausted. Having produced twenty-two issues in two years on no money, even Taylor's boyish enthusiasm couldn't sustain the pressure of the printing bills. The mag stopped dead.

Ironically, as the following months went by, the advertising and distribution money finally flowed in and the bills were paid. Three months later, to everyone's astonishment, *The Virgin Press* had a profit of $3,000 (if one ignored the fact that wages and writers fees had never been paid). Even more astonishing was a letter informing the magazine it had received a Visual Arts Board Grant of another $3,000. After several glasses of wine, and considerable time spent pouring over the dictionary, the new name was decided. It seemed to sum up the travails and excitements of the new decade: *Tension*. As Hogan would immediately pun: 'A House Is Not A Home Without *Tension*'.

Taylor's enthusiasm had not abated. Nor had that of the small community of artists and writers behind the later version of *The Virgin Press*. Reinspired, the editors of *Tension* wanted to avoid too much influence from Taylor, Nixon, et al. However it was Taylor who suggested launching the magazine at the hippest spot in town — the newly revamped Inflation nightclub on King Street. The club had been redesigned by architecture's young turks Biltmoderne,[6] and rapidly became the haunt of a younger generation of artists and fashion designers. It was a sign of the times — 1983 — and rather than the peeling linoleum of Art Projects, which had seemed so bohemian just two years beforehand, hip now were the glass shards and smooth marble of Biltmoderne's design.

It was a publishing boom time. Michael Trudgeon (previously the designer for *Fast Forward*) and Jane Joyce started the fashion/art/music crossover, launching their new mag, *Crowd*, at the *other* hip nightclub, The Hardware Club in Hardware Lane. Robert Pearce, co-founder of the Fashion Design Council,[7] launched his short-lived, visuals-only, fashion magazine *Collection(s)*, while Philip Brophy, Adrian Martin and others launched the playful but theoretical *Stuff*.

Money remained an issue. The initial $6,000 that *Tension* had accrued went little distance to cover costs. It was a plight felt by many at the time. Art Projects was veering on bankruptcy, the George Paton Gallery, one of the most innovative spaces at the time, based at Melbourne University, was drastically underfunded, and *Art & Text* too was feeling the bite.

In another Taylor-initiated project, our two magazines (*Art & Text* and *Tension*) and the two galleries (Art Projects and the George Paton Gallery) joined forces to protest the lack of applied-for funding from the Victorian Ministry for the Arts. It is telling that Taylor, whose magazine *was* funded, took a stand alongside the less privileged organisations. Naturally, however, he had an agenda. In a letter to the director of the Ministry, Paul Clarkson, signed by Taylor as editor of *Art & Text*, Nixon as director of Art Projects, Denise Robinson as director of the George Paton, and this author as editor-in-chief of *Tension*, the following was sent:

> Dear Mr Clarkson,
>
> We are writing to you to express a grievance and hopefully to prompt a reconsideration of the Ministry's priorities. We wish to formally complain and have our applications for assistance in 1984 reassessed. We believe we are insufficiently understood and appreciated by the Ministry.
>
> In short, our separate contributions to the Australian visual arts are neglected by the Ministry, except in the case of *Art & Text*. Taken by what has taken place in major levels of contemporary visual art in Australia, in Australian exhibitions abroad and in overseas publications' coverage of Australia, *Art & Text*, Art Projects, the George Paton Gallery and *Tension* magazine (formerly *The Virgin Press*) have been the most influential groups of people in shaping the current young art scene in the whole of Australia.
>
> Although we have virtually nothing to show for it, we have brought so much of the national art imagination to focus on Melbourne, have shown or written about the majority of artists who are now receiving widespread critical and curatorial attention and we are trying to maintain our positions of attentiveness and initiative under difficulty. We have never before considered it necessary, but in the light of

the Ministry's recent decisions, we now wish to present a united front of protest and appeal.

Can we frankly ask whether those people considering our applications are sensitive to contemporary art and to the relevance of our work to the national and international art scenes in the '80s? The two magazines, for example, are considered by a literature panel which may not be acquainted with the material involved. We also strongly believe that the Ministry's commitments to an Australian Triennial and Centre for Contemporary Art should not preclude support for places like the George Paton Gallery and Art Projects which have been serving similar functions for years. The decisions of the Ministry seem little more than a provision for middle-of-the-road tastes. We believe that culture is the history of exceptional individuals, yet the Ministry's decision works against these people.

Of the four of us, only *Art & Text* magazine received assistance for 1984. It believes it received a low amount considering its potential for expansion, high profile and the particular realities of its institution in 1984. It is a totally independent production, yet is the only 'small' magazine in Australia to have substantial overseas readership, national influence, and which is entirely produced in Melbourne. The grant of $4,000 is effectively a substantial reduction of funds. The magazine has also been financially affected by the method of the Ministry's switch from financial-year to calendar-year funding.

Withdrawal of support to the George Paton Gallery necessitates severe cutbacks in its 1984 programme: cancellation of exhibitions and lectures, as well as forcing the gallery to close for longer periods between exhibitions. There is also the possibility that the funding of the Visual Arts Board will be reduced due to the Gallery's non-fulfilment of its stated programme. During recent years, George Paton Gallery has reinstated itself as a vital gallery attuned to emerging artists and it has also been instrumental in generating critical response. We do not believe the Centre for Contemporary Art will be duplicating this function. The withdrawal of support from the Ministry has greater than economic effect: the gallery's position with the Union Board of the University of Melbourne – always problematic – now becomes dangerously insecure as it can no longer cite Victorian Government support.

Of Australia's culture magazines, *Tension* is the only wide-circulation magazine concerned with the crossover between different areas of the contemporary arts. For three years, *The Virgin Press*, and now *Tension*, have survived without government support. In its attempt to upgrade the quality of the publication, provide more venues for writers and to continue its popular coverage of the arts, *Tension* is badly in need of support further than the $3,000 granted by the Visual Arts Board. *Tension* maintains a larger readership than other magazines which nevertheless receive assistance. Coverage of the young arts in Australia is not a commercial proposition. *Tension* is committed to new cultural forms but it cannot maintain this commitment without the Ministry's assistance.

Lastly, it seems both incongruous and unrealistic to withdraw the limited and only assistance to Art Projects when Art Projects' artists are included in every major Australian and overseas exhibition that includes Australian artists. For example, over the last couple of years, artists who exhibit at Art Projects have been chosen for POPISM, National Gallery of Victoria; Vox Pop, NGV; Tall Poppies, University of Melbourne; Australian Perspecta, Art Gallery of New South Wales; Australian artists at Kassel and Venice; 3rd, 4th & 5th Biennales of Sydney, AGNSW; Absence and Presence, Art Gallery of Western Australia; FORM–IMAGE–SIGN, AGWA; Minimalism, Institute of Modern Art, Brisbane; Recent Australian Painting, Art Gallery of South Australia; A Melbourne Mood, Australian National Gallery; The Paris Biennale, ARC, Paris; From Another Continent: Australia, ARC, Paris; Documenta 7, West Germany; EUREKA, Institute of Contemporary Art and Serpentine Gallery, London; Venice Biennale, Venice; New Work New York, Clocktown, New York; Continuum, Tokyo; Live to Air Audio Arts, Tate Gallery, London; and have been artists-in-residence at PS1, New York. Given all this, it is literally unbelievable that the Melbourne gallery which supports them possibly faces closure in its sixth year, 1984.

Unfortunately, the Ministry's lack of support for these enterprises is out of step with the current direction of Australian visual arts and the art in other countries, and is eroding the recent experimental and non-bureaucratic achievements of the Melbourne scene in favour of large, bureaucratically-inseminated ones.

It appears to us extremely short-sighted to decrease,

withdraw or deny funding to our endeavours in favour of such major assistance to the Meat Market, Heide, the Victorian Tapestry Workshop ... all of which will still be comfortably well-off even if each was granted, say, $5,000 less from the Ministry each year. They are undoubtedly worthwhile concerns, but surely not to the detriment of ours.

Can the four of us meet with the Ministry to hear our appeal and to discuss the practicalities of our continuation, *with* the Ministry's support?

Paul Taylor, Denise Robinson, Ashley Crawford, John Nixon[8]

The letter fell on deaf ears and no reply was forthcoming.

In January 1985, a sad notice was sent to Art Projects supporters and posted on the door in Nixon's distinctive, all capitals, type-written style:

NOTICE

1979–1984
ART PROJECTS, THE LEADING PRIVATE GALLERY DEDICATED TO THE AUSTRALIAN AVANT GARDE HAS CLOSED. I WISH TO THANK THE ARTISTS, CURATORS AND COLLECTORS WHO HAVE SUPPORTED THE GALLERY DURING THOSE 6 YEARS.

JOHN NIXON
DIRECTOR
JAN 1985

One gallery that did thrive, at least momentarily, was the ROAR collective. Despite being neighbours, *The Virgin Press* and ROAR groups saw little of each other. Having attended the raucous opening of the gallery, I returned some days later to see the work without the crowd and upon introductions was told bluntly by Mark Schaller that I was not welcome. The perception that *The Virgin Press* was in the 'conceptual camp' had spread. The situation had been galvanised by an essay in the Spring issue of *Art & Text* by Paul Taylor entitled 'Angst In My Pants',[9] in which he let fly at the expressionist movement, although not by name. Taylor was less subtle about expressing his distaste for the revivalist movement (and sounding pretentious) when asked by Martin Armiger of *The National Times* about ROAR in 1982:

> They are pre-occupied with an out-dated conception of self-hood. They think of us all as individuals, each with his own statement to make. A more useful view is that we are a series of surfaces upon whom is imprinted a set of cultural signs that can be read by anyone who takes the trouble. These romantics are simply using a set of known and privileged signals to further mystify their own egos.[10]

It was little wonder ROAR took a dislike to Taylor. As always, however, he could charm his enemies.

A year later, Paul Taylor threw a party at his lavish apartment in the Beverley Hills building in South Yarra. It was a highly gay and glamorous bash of fine clothes, champagne flutes and new wave dance music. By the window overlooking the Yarra and skyline of Melbourne was the only other person apart from myself drinking beer and gazing off into the distance. We began talking when socialite Jillian Burt wandered over. 'I wouldn't have imagined you two talking', she said. We hadn't been formally introduced and Burt did the formalities. 'You haven't met?', Burt said with mock horror. 'Mr Roar meet Mr Tension!' David Larwill recoiled in horror – 'You're the enemy!', he cried. 'You're at an *Art & Text* party!', was my rejoinder. Paul, looking on from a distance, smirked. We agreed to depart to the Toorak Inn to discuss matters over a cold beer.

Parties and socialising were lifeblood for Taylor. When such folk as Jean Baudrillard, Malcolm McLaren and Keith Haring came
5–8 to Australia, it was Paul who would throw the best parties for them. Paul, Jenny Watson and I had our only real falling out when I informed them that I would be the one interviewing McLaren for *Tension*, a gig that Paul, for reasons that would become later apparent, desperately wanted. (Paul would go on to edit *Impresario: Malcolm McLaren and the British New Wave*, MIT Press, 1988, and organise the accompanying show at the New Museum of Contemporary Art in SoHo, New York.)

Manhattan Inc.

Always a fan of the pop aesthetic, Paul Taylor had always wanted to meet Andy Warhol. He would succeed, indeed conducting the last interview with the infamous Popist before his death in 1987. 'I hope he says something interesting for once', quipped Taylor in a postcard before interviewing Warhol.[11]

In 1984, Taylor decided to tackle Manhattan and leave the strains of magazine editing behind him. For several months he worried about the task of appointing a new editor. Adrian Martin and Edward Colless were high on his list, but the mantle was eventually handed to Sydney academic Paul Foss.

At first, the relationship between *Art & Text* and *Tension* remained cosy. Indeed, with Taylor's prompting, Foss asked Terry Hogan to design the upcoming issue of the journal as well as the cover for a book on Juan Davila, *Hysterical Tears*. These projects had their own share of tears and histrionics, to Hogan's bemusement, but seemed to conclude well enough. However the relationship faltered badly when Taylor offered an interview with Robert Mapplethorpe to *Tension*. Foss penned an essay on Mapplethorpe's *Man In A Polyester Suit*, accompanied by a headless image of a suited man with his penis hanging from his zipper, for the same issue of *Tension*, but Foss's essay was rejected by the editorial board as being gratuitous. Foss responded by saying that the *Tension* editors were afraid of the image and were in fact homophobic. Taylor refused to be drawn into the fray. It was all fairly amusing at first, but the rift between the two editorial groups never really healed and Hogan wasn't approached to do any further work for *Art & Text*.

With his infectious charm, Taylor rapidly made a name for himself in Manhattan. For all his original derision of mainstream journalism, Taylor reinvented himself as a feature writer for *The New York Times*, *Vanity Fair*, *Interview*, *Vogue* and *Manhattan Inc.*

Taylor had continued to write for *Tension* during his New York years – largely reprints of his articles appearing in Manhattan magazines – leading to an ongoing correspondence between us (much of it screaming for overdue payments). Taylor had bragged about walking up to Robert Hughes in New York and informing the *Time* art critic that his days were over now that Paul was there. Excerpts from Taylor's correspondence (often on *Vanity Fair* letterheads) give an indication of the fun he was having and his tendency to drop names.

> 4 March, 1985
>
> I have just come from London where I had appointments every hour for one week and I am enjoying the rainy weekend in Paris. Next I go to Canary Islands, all First Class and courtesy Vanity Fair. (It'll be hot.) How goes ACCA? My best regards please to John Buckley. I'm dying to see Visual Torpor[12] – did you send me one yet? I'm also disappointed that you and Terry and Paul F. fell out – he can be temperamental. I agree Terry did a good design job, and I trust he's still designing Juan's book.

You shouldn't mind the arguments with Jenny [Watson].[13] As much as I love and admire her, she acts like a fox in a trap sometimes and loves getting a response – of any kind – from her friends. I used to just shrug my shoulders when she turned on me...

Australia seems very incestuous from afar – at least that's the impression gleaned from reading *Art Network* – which I try not to do...

Dale Frank leaves NY soon – to live in Milan. He doesn't like being obscure in USA and likes the celebrity he has in Europe – who blames him, except he does deprecate NY as a result, often without cause. NY is basically a city for hard working (which Dale is), extrovert (which Dale isn't) and mature strategists. Talent is a must, except there are millions of hangers-on with none, who do no more than clutter up the exhibition openings ...

Must go – I have an appointment with, of all people, Balthus. He's extremely difficult to see, but the words 'vanity fair' are like 'open sesame' to almost anyone. I am, however, discreet and self-effacing about it all, as it's only a fraction of my real desires – as you can imagine.

Paul[14]

June 3, 1985

I saw John Buckley last night and he invited me to work on the Mapplethorpe exhibition, on which there doesn't seem to be a lot I can do, except in the realm of the catalogue (maybe I too can have the pleasure of turning down Paul Foss's *Man In A Polyester Suit* essay), and also to 'curate' a show of my own at the Centre. I immediately said yes, even though we haven't discussed where, why, what, when, who, how and how much. But at least now as I'm going to Europe at the end of the week I will have another show to think up. I'm visiting Florence, Milan, Basel (for the wretched art fair), Cologne (maybe), Paris, London in the space of a few weeks. I'll see the Lowes [a reference to Geoff Lowe and Naomi Cass], and hopefully a few highs.

I read *On The Beach*[15] – that magazine is largely a review of metacriticism – endlessly discussing what other writers and thinkers are doing. I wish they would (or could) do something themselves, except for a glorified student rag. I did, however, chuckle to myself many times while reading Paul's, Juan's and Meaghan's essays.[16] But in the end – why bother? Why not write about things for a wide audience (see – the American mentality has already set in).

Tomorrow night I am taking Naomi [Cass] and John Kaldor out on the town ... Paul Foss's letters to me are becoming increasingly green with envy that I can scoot around town – he thinks it's costing the magazine a fortune, but everywhere is free, if you're on certain lists, I guess. And last night John Buckley and I had supper with Ross Bleckner (painter) which was a giggle. John embarrassed me with tales of my former existence down under.[17]

12 November, 1990

Did you read my interview with Mapplethorpe?[18] I have had some interesting times at his place lately, including a frisky argument with Susan Sontag ... Malcolm McLaren is buzzing around a lot these days – things are warming up for my show of his career. Currently I'm art advisor on one of his films, but you might have heard how CBS is possibly disbanding its film division, so M.McL will once again be out of a job. Nick [Waterlow] is trying to get him into the [Sydney] Biennale too, and he might visit, which would be good...

Years ago I suggested an article on AIDS. Do you think it might be a good idea yet? If yes I could possibly find a writer in NY to cover the NY scene for you – it's hairraising![19]

23 June, 1990

Your fax was awaiting me when I returned from Paris and Venice this weekend. I was in Paris with Lou Reed and John Cale et al for the one-song Velvet Underground reunion. (My article will be in the *Village Voice* soon.) In Venice I saw a rather lacklustre Biennale ... Juliana Engberg departs New York next week. Jillian Burt last week. Louise Neri is here in September to be *Parkett*'s New York editorial assistant ... I have been asked to apply for the 92 Biennale of Sydney. What do you think? ... I may be in Australia at the end of July or early August for Fiona Pratt's engagement party at Raheen...[20]

In 1992, the elite of the art world received an invitation from Anna Weis (later to become Schwartz) 'to a party in honour of Paul Taylor' at 9:00pm on Saturday, December 21. 'Dress Code: Up.'

Only a small number of people knew that this was Taylor's final party (I was, sadly, one of them). He had contracted AIDS in New York. It was speculated by some whether this was the high cost of his portrait by Robert Mapplethorpe. Taylor loved bragging about having his photo taken by Mapplethorpe. In 1989, Mapplethorpe had also died of AIDS.

Three entrepreneurs du chic

Merryn Gates

One of Melbourne-based fashion identity Robert Pearce's monikers was 'entrepreneur du chic'. 'Entrepreneur' is a good word that brings with it a wider context than the arts-oriented 'impresario', one that is particularly apt for the post-punk era (1978–84), acknowledging, as it does, the role of the risk-taking producer, a person who exercises inventiveness and initiative in their wide-ranging projects. In the phenomenon that was *Fashion 82* and *Fashion 83*,[1] there is a convergence of three individuals whose practices are indeed 'entrepreneurial' in scope: editor Paul Taylor, artist Maria Kozic, and stylist Robert Pearce.

Art & Text, launched by founding editor Paul Taylor in 1981, was a player in post-punk Melbourne as much as the man himself. The city was one of several notable sites around the world where the interdisciplinary nature of subculture was played out in the post-punk period. The journal looked to fellow publications *Semiotext(e)* (established in 1974), *October* (1976) and *ZG* (1980), whose editorial mixes marked a shift towards the emerging discipline of cultural studies and whose agendas were to 'expand the traditional scope of an art magazine, bringing together essays on music, fashion and politics'.[2] Taylor defuses the 'tall poppies' mindset from the start, positioning his journal, as he did the artists he championed within its pages, as 'not emulating overseas models but ... actually [being] contemporaneous to them'.[3] This was a bold recasting of the cultural landscape away from a centre–periphery model to a more nuanced and interconnected one. Fashion theory cut its teeth and earned its place in such publications, as the 'couture down' gave way to the 'from the streets to the catwalk' theory in the same period, while subcultural writers grappled with the implications. Like *Semiotext(e)* editor Sylvère Lotringer, Taylor grasped the theoretical moment of the late 1970s when cities in the grip of recession were 'cheap, fluid, and wide open', and 'Artists were living as a kind of tribe'.[4]

Speaking for this tribe in Melbourne, Taylor made the claim for fashion explicitly in his influential treatise 'Australian "New Wave" and the "Second Degree"' in the first issue of *Art & Text*. 'New Wave music, fashion and visual art comprise a newer subcultural style', he wrote. 'Its appeal, characteristic of the modes of pop-culture, is generated within an audience steeped in the vocabulary and information channels of the mass media'.[5] This approach was expanded in Philip Brophy's review of Dick Hebdige's *Subculture: the meaning of style* in the same issue. From within the very moment of an emerging subculture, Brophy perceived that Hebdige had already been overtaken, that it was now 'totally based on style – not *a* style, but *style* itself.'[6] Not surprisingly, fellow →↑→ (tsk tsk tsk) members were in evidence at *Fashion 82* (Maria Kozic with her *Kozico* take on packaging) and *Fashion 83* (Jane Stevenson with 'second degree' Butterick style).

The agency of fashion was very much to the fore in Taylor's proposed 'Impresario: Malcolm McLaren and the British New Wave' exhibition at the New Museum, New York, in 1988. Perhaps Melbourne's milieu, in which fashion events[7] and exhibitions comprised of new music[8] first appeared in alternative spaces, played a part in Taylor's concept for the exhibition. Fashion[9] and music[10] are now a regular, crowd-pleasing part of programming in major public galleries. The New Museum director, Marcia Tucker, recalled in her catalogue preface to *Impresario: Malcolm McLaren* that 'it was clear we were faced with a challenging proposal: an exhibition of pop artifacts (clothes, record covers, posters, music and video tapes, films, etc.) associated with an individual who, to many, is not an artist at all but a master manipulator...' Eventually, theory won the day and the decision to proceed was based on a recognition that such an exhibition 'made perfect sense' from the 'point of view of postmodernist theory and practice'.[11]

Maria Kozic was the subject of a substantial article by Adrian Martin in issue number 2 of *Art & Text*, Winter 1981, the first artist to be so featured. She was well represented in 'POPISM', Paul's 1982 exhibition at the National Gallery of Victoria, and also performed as a member of →↑→. Taylor said that 'POPISM' artists were from 'an area of intersection between late modern music, photography, fashion, advertising, comic strips, pornography, theory and painting'.[12] Kozic was in many ways the poster girl for the *Art & Text* and popist missions and, in one person, she embodied the mix celebrated by the journal.

From the outset, Kozic resisted being categorised as working with one medium. Of the first art school she attended, she bemoans:

> they kept pressuring me to choose one thing. Someone said, 'Oh you should be doing painting, sculpture or printmaking.' They were the three they were pushing at the time. I didn't

want to do that. I didn't understand why I had to do just one. I wanted to do it all at any time.[13]

Her move to Preston Institute of Technology in 1976 allowed her to work more freely, as evidenced in her 1979 show packed full of prints, floor to ceiling curtains, and sculptures.[14] Kozic's solo show at George Paton Gallery, the subject of Adrian Martin's article, increased her profile in 1981. The following year was a frenzy of activity: she made an impression at the 12th Adelaide Festival; the hugely successful seed packet 'Kozico' dresses were in *Fashion 82* and much featured in media coverage; a month later 'POPISM' opened at the National Gallery of Victoria and later that year an exhibition of her new work, 'Animal Vegetable Mineral', was held at Reconnaissance Gallery in Fitzroy. She recalls that 'Everything was happening at the same time – it was like a little explosion!'[15]

Kozic's work is often in multiples or series and encompasses painting, printing, sculpture, performance (she was a member of →↑→), film, video, music, zines (such as *Things*, *TITS* and *Dynamite*), acting, branding and merchandising. The dresses, modelled on seven different vegetable packets hand printed in an edition, were made in response to hearing that packet seeds were bred to be infertile. They tap into a recurring theme of clothes, from the 1979 pyjama prints to the many printed t-shirts seen in Kozic's exhibition 'MKart' at the Museum of Contemporary Art, Sydney, in 1992.[16] If we look at Kozic's process, alongside the photo-based silkscreen printing, there is a handmade quality that is unexpected. For multiple works – *500 fish* (1977–78), held in the collection of the National Gallery of Australia, Canberra, *Goatem poles* (1982), and *The Birds* (1981), held in the collection of the National Gallery of Victoria, and the *Kozico* dresses (1983) – the sewing machine is her tool. This was a natural process for her, as she remembers: 'when I was a teenager, I used to make stuff for myself just to wear for a couple of days. You know, I'd get material and make a bag, or temporary clothing that was just needed for an occasion or a couple of days.'[17] This is the other side of the coin to the 'second degree' knowingness of post-punk: the DIY ethos of the punk legacy that energised youth culture around the world. You want to 'rip it up and start again'?[18] Nowhere was this more evident than in the graphic design of the period.

Robert Pearce was the graphic designer and media frontman for *Fashion 82* and *Fashion 83*. He had worked as a much sought-after fashion illustrator for, among other magazines, *Rag Times*, before he co-founded the Fashion Design Council at the end of 1983,

building on the success of *Fashion 83*. He published the short-lived magazine *Collection(s)* (1984–85), and became an advocate for independent Australian fashion designers and more of an art director or stylist – a role that grew in influence during the postmodern 1980s. Like many of those connected to *Art & Text* and *Fashion 82* and *83*, Pearce was to be heard on 3RRR-FM, the community radio station that subcultural Melbourne listened to.
14 Pearce presented the fashion radio show *en masse*, Philip Brophy
and Bruce Milne did *eeek!* (with Maria Kozic as Mrs T on the
13 phones), and Julie Purvis, with this author, *Bedlam*. Pearce's graphic
design hails from a time when artwork was literally cut and paste: Letraset was used for text, figures free drawn with Rotring pens, coloured with professional felt-tip pens, and bromides scaled, printed and pasted in place, onto a blue grid that was adhered to or transgressed. His design for the *Fashion 83* brochure reveals how readily such processes embraced the *bricolage* so characteristic of the post-punk look.

Pearce, the 'entrepreneur de chic', interviewed glamorous arrivals as they entered the Seaview Ballroom for *Fashion 83* for his 3RRR-FM program, among them the 'impresario' Paul Taylor. Ironically, this archived fragment of outdated technology fails us, and we can't hear what these two notorious raconteurs are saying.

Paul Taylor's gay Melbournes

Graham Willett

In the course of the 1970s, Melbourne's homosexual world underwent a remarkable transformation, best summed up as a shift from 'camp' to 'gay'. Camp was a social scene, lived mostly through private parties, supplemented by a handful of hotels and cafes where, with a little discretion, homosexual women and men could gather in public. This subculture can be traced back to the 1920s and '30s, and if it was a little more visible by 1970 than it had been in the past, it was nonetheless a world that worked hard to keep itself safe from the public gaze. A decade later, at the end of the 1970s, this old world was being challenged by forces that celebrated themselves flamboyantly and very publicly as 'gay', demanding law reform and a change in public attitudes (when it wasn't calling for the overthrow of the entire sex/gender order) and carving out very different spaces in which to pursue new social and political ambitions. The seventies marked a period of transition – a time when these old and new worlds coexisted and in some ways competed. In his influential 1977 work, *Marxism and Literature*, New Left thinker Raymond Williams spoke of the need to recognise that all societies are profoundly divided and he argued that analysts needed to do their work looking at what he called emergent, dominant and residual elements in a society.[1] Williams was not interested in gay subcultures, but this attention to what was coming into being (emerging), what was strongest at any particular moment (dominant), and what elements and aspects were hangovers from the past (residual) is a useful way to think about homosexual Melbourne in the 1970s. For a young man like Paul Taylor, this was a city pregnant with possibilities and there is a project to be undertaken to explore how this Melbourne – or perhaps these Melbournes – shaped him. That, however, is not my task here. While I introduce a little-known incident that occurred on the pages of Monash University student paper *Lot's Wife* that involves the local attitudes towards gay issues and Taylor's earliest writings, an incident in which, perhaps, his future, more public figure can be discerned, I want to focus mainly on the world as it was – offering a wider context in which the terms of the variously invested exchanges in *Lot's Wife* occurred, but leaving the more detailed task of fitting Taylor into this world to those better able to tackle it.

Camp Melbourne

Since at least the 1930s, there had been a discernible homosexual subculture in Melbourne, although this is a history that is only now being seriously researched.[2] It centred on parties held in the flats and homes of homosexual women and men, and except for the tiny wealthy elite who always had access to privacy, this really only became widely possible with the availability of flats (apartments) in the inter-war years.[3] For a more public life, there were cafes whose owners and staff could be trusted to turn a blind eye to their more 'flamboyant' or 'theatrical' clientele, although with the exception of Val's, opened on Swanston Street in the early 1950s, most of these disappeared in the early post-World War II period (perhaps as a result of a police crackdown).[4] The most public places in which camp people gathered ('camp' being the term most widely used by homosexual women and men until the early 1970s) were the city hotels – the Australia, Phairs, the London, the Saracen's Head, the Graham. Going back as far as the 1930s in some cases, these venues offered a degree of acceptance of (or at least indifference to) small and not too boisterous groups of homosexuals.[5]

Finding your way into these worlds was often a matter of luck. But most camp women and men spent a good part of their day with one eye open, on the lookout for others of their kind, who could be found on the streets, at work, and – for men – in beats (parks and public toilets where men could pick each other up). In many ways, then, people might be said to have been making their own luck. Once one had established some kind of connection, doors were opened all over the city.

Private parties and pubs remained central until well into the 1970s, and, of course, people never really gave up hosting dinner parties. It is just that in the mid to late 1970s, new forms of socialising started to emerge.

Gay Melbourne

In 1975, Peter Langford visited Melbourne and wrote about his experiences in *Campaign*, the newly-founded Sydney-based national gay newspaper.[6] So impressed was he that he predicted that Melbourne would soon surpass Sydney as having the best gay scene in Australia, characterised as it was by 'vibrant, interesting venues', filled with 'lots of pretty faces' and crowds that were 'well dressed, well behaved'.

Three years later, in its ten-page 'Guide to Gayer Melbourne', *Campaign* revealed a scene that was larger, more diverse and more dispersed than ever.[7] Looking back over the Christmas–New Year period, Honey Bee reported that private parties of dozens or hundreds of people filled the calendar. Organisations such as Melbourne University's GaySoc hosted end-of-year events, while Acceptance (a group for gay Catholics) attended midnight mass together. Bars like the Union had special 2am licences to let the latecomers catch some of the fun as they dashed from event to event. Even outside the festive season, the scene had come on considerably since 1975. There was somewhere to go every night of the week now.

Meanwhile, for those who were not looking for a dance or for the inconvenience of conversation, but preferred to be out of Melbourne's famously capricious weather, there were the saunas. The Caulfield Sauna appealed greatly to *Campaign*'s Peter Langford. For a $4 entry charge, you got access to a pleasantly clean venue, better run and with a more attractive clientele than any sauna the much-travelled observer had seen anywhere in the world. It was, he said, 'highly recommended'.[8]

And then there was the Continental Baths, conveniently located opposite the Hotel Australia.[9] This sauna could trace its origins back to 1956, when a man called Michael came to Melbourne as a member of the Italian Olympic team and stayed on to run gyms and saunas for many years. Gay men were always welcome at the Continental Baths and, despite the mixed crowd, there was no need for bouncers and rarely any trouble between gay and straight clientele. Even the cops left Michael alone to get on with his business.

But, however fondly people remember this time in Melbourne's history, it was less than ideal. The dominant mode was the one-night-a-week, here-today-gone-tomorrow pattern that these places operated on, and in the absence of a regular gay press that people could use to keep themselves up to date, finding the venues was often a hit or miss affair.

Political Melbourne

This new gay scene of the mid to late 1970s can be seen as a development, an intensification, a coming to visibility of a world that had long existed underground and out of sight. The same could not, however, be said of gay politics, which was something entirely new.

In Australia, gay politics really begins with the formation of the Campaign Against Moral Persecution (CAMP) in Sydney in 1970, whose founders John Ware and Christabel Poll spoke openly as homosexuals, demanding an end to discrimination and persecution. In 1971, a Melbourne branch of the organisation was established with its first public activity taking place on March 17, 1971, when it participated in a Melbourne University Debating Union discussion on homosexuality, in front of several hundred people. In May 1971, the organisation launched itself even more decisively onto the public stage with an interview published in *The Age* and a television appearance. Within eighteen months, the committee was celebrating a membership of almost 600.[10]

The Melbourne branch was in some ways less outgoing than Sydney. Among other things it set aside the name CAMP in favour of the more closeted Society Five – referring to the five aims of the group and to the fact that homosexuals were thought to compose five per cent of the population. But, like the other branches around the country, Society Five's committee and its members were out to change the world, with all that that required in terms of activity. Working groups were set up to deal with legal issues, membership and public speaking, to manage the clubrooms and social events, to do publicity work, to run the library and to conduct research. There were politicians to be lobbied, churchmen to be talked to, and community groups (dozens of them, clamouring for speakers) to be addressed.

For the ordinary members, the Society's social life was perhaps the most important aspect of its activities: the wine and cheese tastings, treasure hunts, film nights, trash and treasure sales, mad hat dances, Christmas parties and other fancy-dress events, as well as regular Friday and Saturday night dances. It was the clubrooms that made much of this possible. Open four or five nights a week, at a time when gay friendly places were few and far between, the dances, the library and the coffee shop were a haven. Here members and their friends could gather, have a drink or a coffee, catch up on the gossip, and, on occasion, listen to speakers as diverse as Catholic priests, Humanists, lawyers and gay liberationists, all expounding versions of the idea that it was OK to be homosexual.

Over the course of the 1970s, Society Five played a prominent role in Melbourne's gay life, both social and political. Although often dismissed as conservative, too social and even closeted, as well as condemned for the predominance of men in its membership and on its committees, it did provide representatives to the various law reform bodies of that decade, played its part in lobbying and public education work, and attended and organised picnics and other public social events. Society Five lasted until about 1981, but as the new gay scene emerged to provide a richer and more diverse range of social life, and as more radical politics took up the struggles for equality and acceptance, it entered into a period of decline.

Gay Lib

Society Five did not have the stage to itself for long. In early 1972, a group of lesbians and gay men decided that the time had come to launch Gay Liberation – a more radical approach to gay politics – in Melbourne.[11]

The early meetings were held at Melbourne University and often attracted as many as fifty to sixty people a week, and they reflected the euphoria which so many felt during these heady days. All these gay people in one place: talking, working, meeting, cruising, debating, sharing, planning actions – or simply basking in the company of so many others.

On December 1, 1972, hundreds of lesbians, gay men and their friends took to the streets of the city in a brilliant and defiant celebration of homosexuality. 1973 saw the first ever national gay rights event: Gay Pride Week was staged in several cities around the country in September of that year. Melbourne had a week of activities including graffiti runs, talks to high school students and to parents of gays, a demo in the City Square – all culminating in a picnic in the Botanic Gardens that attracted 150 people. The years after 1973 saw the fragmentation of gay and lesbian politics along political, sex and operational lines. Radicalesbians and effeminist men rejected the sexism of radical gay men, just as Gay Lib had rejected the conservatism of Society Five. But many chose to stay away from these debates and to throw themselves into social or political activism in one of a variety of organisations from religious groups, election campaigns, law reform, radio collectives, the Gay Teachers and Students Group, regional gatherings in Central Victoria, Gay AA, Gayline's telephone help service and many more.[12] Universities were a convenient location for gay lib groups. They provided a variety of venues from meeting rooms that could accommodate scores of activists, to spaces for public meetings and dances of several hundred, to smaller rooms for the consciousness-raising and action groups and working parties – all free or cheap for student-union affiliated clubs. In 1974, Monash had been the venue for an important series of public lectures in which leading gay activists, gay men and lesbians from Melbourne and Sydney spoke on topics as various as the homosexual family, homosexuals in literature, psychology, religion, feminism, socialism, the US movement, sexism...[13]

By 1977, Monash GaySoc's 'informal, friendly and enthusiastic atmosphere' was attracting up to thirty people to its activities – weekly meetings, discussion groups, dinner nights, pub nights, theatre outings and parties.[14] Politics, too, caught the imagination of some. Access to state-of-the-art technology, such as gestetners, made the production of leaflets, even in quite large quantities, quick and easy. Similarly, the student press provided a platform for gay liberationists to reach wider audiences, and the first few years of activism were played out as much in the pages of the press as on the streets of the city.

At Monash University, *Lot's Wife* was one such forum. By the mid 1970s, it was publishing on a wide variety of gay and lesbian issues, from small announcements about meetings, to the Gay Liberation Group's attempts to avoid adopting a name that 're-enforces a tendency in our society to stereo type [sic] individuals', through letters, debates, and deeply felt and personal reflections, such as Andrew's 'Thinking a Bit About Things....'[15] In 1976, the sexuality section ran to some twelve pages.[16]

There was inevitably an air of provocation here – even talking about the topic was too much for some people, but articles like 'Hi Mum I'm a Poofta' were not soft-peddling on this.[17] Yet, Paul Taylor's review of *The Elocution of Benjamin Franklin*, a one-man play in which an aging transvestite (to use the language of the time) reflected upon his life, pushed beyond even these limits. Taylor conducted an inoffensive, indeed rather dull, interview with the author of the play, Steve J. Spears. But he opened his review declaring that 'Gordon Chater degrades himself by appearing' in the play. The world of the transvestite was shown as 'sordid, secretive, dishonest and unhappy', and the central character as 'effeminate, limp-wristed and flighty'. The whole thing is 'unabashed depravity and unchecked indecency shoved down the throats of the public'. The polemic escalated: Chater's nauseating nakedness, the need to protect teenage children, the recommendation that transvestites ought to seek help from the local police station...[18]

Not surprisingly the result of this review was outrage. In the following issue, Gordon Balfour wondered whether Taylor was being 'tongue-in-cheek or ... indulging in unashamed poofter-bashing'.[19] Stephen McLardie took the entire review at face value and systematically demolished its claims.[20] In response to letters and complaints, the editors printed Taylor's rejoinder. He begins by declaring that it is 'irrelevant whether or not I was serious in what I wrote'; and then quickly explains himself. The 'collection of cliches, ravings, outcries and hysterical misrepresentations' that he had written was intended to 'stimulate thought on the subject if not argument'. Having elicited the response that he had, he 'therefore considered the review to be successful'. The problem was his readers who were 'in possession of an underdeveloped and narrow sense of humour'. He had been trying, apparently, to overcome the problem of 'the general familiarity with the homosexuality debate' as a precondition for 'informed and sensible discussion'.[21] Bebe Loft and Virginia Johnson probably got it right when they declared that 'If Paul Taylor does not actually believe the thing that is strongly conveyed ... we should prefer to read that, and not the sort of thing that was present last week'.[22]

The Australian Union of Students

Beyond the individual universities, the gay movement was supported by the national student union – the Australian Union of Students (AUS), whose office was for a long time located in a fine old terrace in Drummond Street, Carlton. In the 1970s, AUS had been influenced by the radicalisation of its student membership, taking on issues beyond the narrow sphere of campus life and drawing radical students into leadership roles. Among these radicals and activists were lesbian and gay students. In early 1975, a caucus of homosexual AUS members was set up to prepare for the organisation's annual conference. This caucus drafted, argued for and won a majority vote for a policy which opposed 'all discrimination – legal, economic and social – against homosexuals', endorsed the 'struggles of lesbians and homosexual men against heterosexist oppression', and offered active support to campaigns aimed at achieving liberation. The union recognised the 'validity of homosexual relationships' and committed itself to 'publicly advocate the positive and healthy nature of those relationships'.[23]

In addition to this policy statement, the 1975 conference also adopted a more targeted set of motions that called on education departments, teachers, trainee-teachers and teacher unions to examine curricula in order to identify biases in favour of 'heterosexual nuclear family-oriented lifestyle in texts, songs, library facilities and general course disposition etc.'; and called on AUS officers to mobilise resources to challenge the exclusively heterosexual nature of teacher training and to prepare a submission to the federal government's Schools Commission on this matter. These motions went well beyond the then widely accepted calls for decriminalisation and tolerance. At the initiative of the homosexual caucus, the conference decided to submit these motions for ratification by union members at affiliated campuses. Ron Thiele, of Monash University and a member of the caucus, explains that this approach was designed to take the issue beyond the core activists of the AUS conference and out into the wider student community, the belief being that the benefits of having the debate outweighed the risk of losing the vote.[24]

At Monash, the motions were submitted to a meeting of the student assembly on May 7, 1975. The week before, *Lot's Wife* published a number of letters addressing the vote and the issues surrounding it. The Women's Liberation Group strongly endorsed a yes vote, arguing that an affirmation of homosexuality was a contribution to the broader struggle for the freedom of women: 'Women's Liberation wants freedom for everyone and the elimination of sex casting on both sides ... completely rejecting imposed definitions upon our humanity'.[25] Ross Moor was less enthusiastic, noting unhappily that such motions rested on the idea that 'the validity [of homosexuality] could be discussed publicly and even voted on ... a crying example of exactly the kind of oppression that we undergo'. He nonetheless urged a yes vote.[26] Excerpts from the debate, published in *Lot's Wife* after the vote, give some of the flavour: on the one hand 'homosexuality is just as valid an alternative and natural a lifestyle as heterosexuality'; on the other, there were references to sadism, mass rape, pigs (for some reason), the corruption of children, the innateness or otherwise of homosexuality, and who education was for and what it should do. In the end, a 'large general meeting' passed the motions 'with a solid majority'.[27]

Perhaps AUS's most important contribution to the movement was its organisation of the National Homosexual Conference at Melbourne University on August 16 and 17, 1975, in what proved to be the first of an annual series that lasted into the mid 1980s, moving from city to city as activists could be found to take on the task of hosting. The 1975 conference was organised in Melbourne by a collective of lesbians and gay men, and funded by AUS, and brought together gay and lesbian activists to share ideas, to develop strategies, to debate and argue, and to pick each other up. It was expressly not a Gay Liberation conference, being open to a wide range of participants – 'from Christian homosexuals to feminist lesbians, from society five [sic] to effeminists ... homosexual activists of many years, and homosexuals for whom the Conference was first contact'.[28] In the end, some six hundred people attended from as far away as Perth and Townsville. The effect, according to Phil's report in *Lot's Wife*, was a 'mood of militancy [which] encouraged confidence, openness and frankness [and] a feeling of solidarity that had not previously existed...'.[29]

Community

When we think of homosexual Melbourne these days, we think most commonly of a social field that encompasses a diversity of sexual identities expressed in labels such as gay, lesbian, bisexual, transgender, intersex – all conveniently grouped under the label 'queer'. We think, too, of 'community', a real entity served by gathering places such as bars, community centres, bookshops, cafes and restaurants; a media including newspapers and magazines, radio stations/programs and TV shows; a literature which aims to express, describe and develop queer identities and experiences; hobby and interest groups; lobby groups and spokespeople; and festivals such as Mardi Gras and Midsumma and the film festival – and, binding these, a consciousness of being gay, lesbian, bisexual, transgender, intersex, queer.[30]

The coming into being of this community began to be most visible in the late 1970s. Before this time, Melbourne's homosexual world was characterised by a deep estrangement between the social scene and the political movement. For the most part, the early movement did not really approve of the scene – it seemed altogether too cautious ('closeted' was the word used most), lacking in pride and dependent upon to the exploitative practices of bar-owners and entrepreneurs. The scene, in turn, was likely to see activists as trouble-makers, threatening the safety that had long been guaranteed by not drawing attention to themselves.

By the late 1970s, however, a new, larger and more confident commercial scene was emerging and political activism was waning somewhat.[31] The balance between the two worlds was shifting and something was going to have to give. And so it did: in 1980 a debate suddenly erupted among gay and lesbian activists in Melbourne about how to respond to a disturbing new development – the Clone, a name given to (and adopted by) a newly assertive masculine gay man, characterised by a particular style: short hair and moustache, jeans and flannel shirts and work boots, and by a mode of self-presentation that even in the discos (which were full of them) was visible: 'Little smiling, little moving, lots of muscles, no free-form dancing, thumbs in the loops of belts, beer in hand … An aping of all the best traditions of the ocker male', as one (sympathetic) observer put it.[32]

For many gay activists, deeply influenced by 1970s feminism, this 'new masculinity', as it was dubbed, was a problem. It was seen not as some interesting new style, but rather as reflecting an unthinking misogyny or, at best, an attempt to ride out the gathering right-wing backlash (which most activists saw all around them in the late 1970s) by concealing homosexuality behind approved models of real male behaviour.

But the discussion of the Clone *style* was actually something of a distraction from the central issue. Those who defended the new look did so because they saw the Clone as the bearer of a new gay political consciousness and the expression of a new gay radicalisation. The macho Clone, by adopting so visible a look, which was essentially a uniform, was proclaiming himself publicly, expressing his confidence and pride and reflecting 'a growing gay consciousness and a positive assertion of sexual identity'. The Clone was the new (male) homosexual and taken to be the agent of a new homosexual politics.

Developed first by Tim Carrigan and John Lee in Adelaide in about 1977, and taken up in Sydney by Craig Johnson among others, this political analysis became the focus of a hot debate in Melbourne in 1980, where the older political model endured most strongly and was fought out in particular in the pages of *Gay Community News*, an activist magazine established in 1979.[33] Taylor's style owed nothing to any of this, but his interest in style as political expression, and in the subcultures that it represented, is very much of his time.

Theoretical drag and textual disco: I was a drummer in *Art & Text* (2012)
Philip Brophy

My intention was to get here just in time to talk so that I wouldn't have to think about anything at all. Unfortunately, I did just see Lyndal and Juan talk. And I actually spoke to some of you.

No one has asked me anything about this era, I think, for thirty years. So, off the top of my head: what will I talk about, Philip?

Well, I guess because I'm here as an artist, even though in *Art & Text* I was a writer, I'll attempt to talk about what it was like to blur those two categories back then, but, more importantly, what it means to blur those categories now.

22 In terms of how I first encountered Paul, I don't think it was through art, I think it was through disco. Paul contacted me after Judy [Annear] and Aleks [Danko] at the George Paton Gallery invited me through →↑→ to present something at the gallery. By that stage, →↑→ ... this is probably the first time I've ever had to publically say →↑→ rather than make those clicking sounds. So, you know, if you're a dickhead then, you've gotta wear it now. I figured it would be other people's problem, not my problem.

Anyway, the →↑→ group had probably been going for three years. My vague recollection of the energy of that time was basically that it was a mess. There were no definitions, no guidelines. If anything – and I don't want to lionise the whole punk era because that was so small and insular, and really quite boring in many respects – there was just this vague thing, like anything goes, you know. It wasn't really a big deal; there was just a lot of trial and error and experimentation. I also think it related to a term that was used vaguely around the time, but then very quickly wasn't used much at all, which is 'pluralism': the idea that there could be multiple things happening, and that that would be healthy for art.

My first recollection of Lyndal was in her underwear, doing a performance outside at La Trobe University. A completely amazing performance. At the time, I was just discovering the *nouveau roman* cinema – particularly Robbe-Grillet, Alain Resnais, Marguerite Duras. I remember it was clear to me that Lyndal was referencing that particular type of French textuality, that kind of approach to fiction.

These were the kinds of things that were happening around

the time. I happened to be discovering those experimental areas, their backgrounds and their artistic influences. But I have to say, none of them were in art. They were in cinema, they were in music. I'd like to pretend and say that they were in literature, but I don't read books, so I wouldn't know.

I was more into cinema and music. →↑→ was definitely a kind of entity that used film and music as its material basis, as well as its cultural basis. I was informed about the history of cinema and music in all sorts of ways, in every way possible. It was the George Paton Gallery in its openness that allowed something like that exhibition ['What is this thing called "Disco"?', 1980] to enter the gallery space.

There was the Clifton Hill Community Music Centre, which was a very small place where very few people went. It had an open door policy, and lots of people just tried out different things there. There was no strategising, no professionalism, no career aspect to it.

The ease of just being able to try things out – to manipulate things, coalesce things, make different types of cross-references – is also what set up things for Paul. Paul essentially 'tried out' at a theoretical level. (I don't know how he found the time to read the books he was meant to read, frankly ... I remember we used to talk about that. 'How does he read all these books? Was he up all hours?') Anyway, Paul 'tried out' in terms of critical discourse and in terms of social engagement – by connecting different scenes, and stuff like that.

Paul must have got my number through Judy and contacted me. He ended up coming around one day when Maria Kozic and I were in Northcote (that would have been late Septemberish, 1980). What we mostly talked about was disco. The interesting thing was that I was coming to disco from the post-punk angle, like the Bowie/Iggy Pop collaboration *The Idiot* in 1977, which is kind of like the start of all post-punk flirtations with disco and dance culture. Paul had come from a gay subcultural disco background, and so a lot of the stuff that he liked I just hated. But we met at this point just when Grace Jones was kind of crossing over with *Warm Leatherette*. Paul kept saying, 'you should have said more about Grace Jones in your essay!' Still to this day, I think it is the Grace Jones from *Warm Leatherette* that is more interesting – more than the sort of queeny, black, post-Stonewally kind of like gay-gay disco before that.

Our discussions were always about movies and music: they were always about existing cultural forms. They were quite materialist discussions. That type of discussion was very good to have with Paul, because the discussion was still about the objects, but we would be talking at a deeper, more textual level about them.

Because I deliberately tried to come here today just in time to talk, I only just caught the end of yer little Barthes discussion there, and frankly I'm not sure what Paul's specific take on Barthes was. Yes, I know there was the second degree thing, but Paul just flipped it up in the air and tried it out. Barthes in particular stuck for a little bit, and it stuck because it went into the context of art.

The likes of French poststructuralist theory ended up like a strangling Isadora scarf wrapped around textual discourse. It did this first to film theory in the '70s, then to art in the '80s. It became a clinical discourse of some form, whereas Paul was just trying it on like a drag act more than anything. And frankly, I think he just as quickly disposed of it too.

The ideas of appropriation, quotation, second degree – they got stuck in history, that's the best way to describe it. In 1980, even three years before that, we weren't talking about quotation. In fact, I don't think there was much image content to that early discussion about textual theory, as such. I learnt all this through Sam Rohdie at La Trobe University, once he came to Melbourne after being at *Screen* magazine in the UK. So my sense of textuality was connected to '70s film theory more than anything else.

Back then, and still to this day, artists have the worst taste in movies imaginable. What they think is a good movie is deplorable. It's like, 'oh Philip, have you seen Tarkovsky?' And I'm like, 'no I fucking haven't. What am I going to watch *that* for?' I did end up watching some Tarkovsky, but only in the last decade. There was no reason to watch Tarkovsky before.

What I'm trying to outline here is that Paul connected to a fluid mix of different voices, of different critical perspectives, and, most importantly, he intersected theories with a form of practice. He discussed heavy concepts with practitioners and makers, materialists who were willing to listen.

In my head now, I have a sudden concept, an image, of ROAR studios in Brunswick Street. 1981, Brunswick Street was the most embarrassing fucking place to walk down, and it just got worse, and worse, and worse, and worse.

The idea that anything culturally interesting could happen there is beyond me. But ROAR, for those that don't know, were a group who wore cheap, farmers-type shirts, flannel shirts! They drank beer, they liked the footy, and they painted shit that looked like it belonged on Mambo t-shirts.

The work was utterly Australian and utterly anti-intellectual.

The thing is, at the time Paul revelled in connecting with anti-intellectualism, and I kind of did too. But Paul was more strategic about it. He knew there was a purpose in actually addressing some of these issues and platforming them.

23 To end on a sour note, this is what I found on the ground, crumpled, just last week. I thought, 'I'll use *this* for the Paul Taylor talk'. Names have been blacked out to protect the innocent, but you can make up anyone you like.

It's the middle section that really gave me the shits when I was reading it; the whole idea that "critical writing is a vital component of your arts practices, whether you go on to practice in the *real world* or choose postgraduate study, or both, good writing skills and the ability to articulate your practice, and the practices of those around you, are essential." That is such a lie! The idea that if you can articulate clearly what you're doing as an artist, as a practitioner, as a material maker ... I can't think of a more unfortunate outcome of Paul and *Art & Text* than this idea that critical theory in itself is somehow so important that it's rammed down the throats of young students who are having to think, 'yeah, I've got an idea, I kind of want to try something out, but I've got to articulate what it is'. That is so putting the cart before the horse. I'm like, 'dude, have you got a fucking good idea in the first place, or not?' Don't explain or justify yourself about whether you have a good idea or not, just deliver the goods! Just show me what it is that you're actually doing.

So when I think about that period of *Art & Text* and what Paul was doing (and it's only in thinking back that I would perceive this), I note there was a kind of willingness for artists to accept the uncomfortable fit of having to think critically about their work and then having to figure it out in some way; you know, figuring out whether it would impact on their work or detract from their work.

Then, unfortunately, what became more prevalent is that artists would think more strategically or competitively, as if critical discourse or critical thinking would become important tools to enable them to just make their art. And this is a problem that only happened in art: it didn't happen in music, and it didn't happen in cinema. It never tainted me because I didn't come from the art context, but I could gradually see it happening more and more with successive generations.

I'm only throwing this up to say: if you're going to celebrate the outcomes of this stuff, you have to remember that culture is a *germ*. You've got no control over it. If someone's going to play culture or intersect with it, or critique it or whatever, it just generates all sorts of shit that you cannot control. This is like a sickness, this idea.

When I say this, it's like I'm returning to a Patrick McCaughey-like anti-intellectualism. But what I'm really talking about is just keeping open the ways media practitioners—people who make stuff—engage with those who critique or discuss or talk about their work.

I was thinking about this only last year. I'm reading something supposedly about art, but I'm thinking, 'this essay has been written only because the person that wrote it studied sociology or anthropology, and they've got these ideas about society and what would be good or bad in society.' I have no fucking interest in that as a concept whatsoever. I never have. Society? You can all die; I don't fucking care. This idea that there's some kind of meta-life structure—a power system, whatever it is—that somehow exists and that you somehow connect with it and think about it—asking 'what are we going to do about this situation?'—and then you see a fucking painting, and then you write something that's got all your bad baggage about what you think's going on in the world and using this painting for this reason, that reason, whatever. So I'm looking at this writing and I'm thinking, 'well, I care about the sound of snare drums ... I don't care about the world ... I care about the sound of snare drums'. And I'm thinking, 'maybe that's why I write the way I write'. Because I'm writing from being *inside* the material objects. I'm not writing from the outside, about where the snare drum fits in the world, where the musician fits in the world. Where *anything* fits in the world. Because from my perspective, a snare drum *is* the world. That's why I'm a hyper-materialist. It's completely about what the thing is. When I engage with artworks, that's what I'm after. What's *your* snare drum? What is it materially that you've got happening that you have completely made in your own way?

And please, don't tell me what your political persuasion is; don't tell me your cultural background; don't even tell me anything ethical or moral about anything you think or believe in the world, because I don't care. I've come to see your art. I've come to see what it is you're doing. If I want that other shit, I'd enroll in a sociology course somewhere. Or I'd enroll in an art course, just like the one outlined on this crumpled piece of paper.

Transcript of talk delivered at 'Impresario: Paul Taylor / Art & Text */ POPISM', September 1, 2012, Monash University, Melbourne.*

Part II

Paul Taylor: in action, the Melbourne years, 1981–1984

A pink Moke, fur coat and the flying duck collection

Jonathan Holmes

Adrian Martin mentions that inimitable fur coat in his essay, 'The Return Waltz'. It's there in an unattributed photo captioned
2 'Elizabeth Gower, Howard Arkley (r) and a friend', which was probably taken at Easter time in 1979 at the opening of the 'European Dialogue, 3rd Biennale of Sydney'. Paul would have hated the caption, of course: never the shrinking violet, he was always *there*.

The pink Mini Moke, with the canopy folded away, arrived in Hobart sometime in late January 1979, from Devonport in north-west Tasmania with a rugged-up Paul Taylor at the wheel. Pretty well everything that he possessed was piled up in the open vehicle including a great collection of polychromed plaster flying ducks and a comprehensive collection of disco music. A by-then very bedraggled and rather motley assortment of pot plants, including a fading *monstera deliciosa*, came too, all of which immediately found their way into our greenhouse for a period of much-needed R&R after the open-air battering they had received on the way
24 from South Yarra in Melbourne. Paul had made it to Hobart just in time to begin teaching art history and theory as a tutor at the School of Art at the beginning of term.

In 2012, Adrian Martin asked me to give him some brief recollections about Paul's time in Hobart for the symposium 'Impresario: Paul Taylor / *Art & Text* / POPISM' held at Monash University on September 1, 2012 and much of what I had to say was retold there and captured in his essay in this publication. This essay, then, is prompted by two things: first, at the time, I hadn't been able to forage through the archive boxes stored away in the attic since the early 1980s. These held all my correspondence from the late 1970s and early 1980s, along with the agenda papers and minutes of over four years of membership on the Visual Arts Board of the Australia Council.[1] Secondly, there were a few scraps of memory that have come back to me since I wrote to Adrian.

Paul arrived at a time of very considerable change for the Tasmanian School of Art: we were in the throes of negotiating a complex deal for the School to become part of the University of Tasmania. It was in the aftermath of the recommendation in 1976 by Professor Peter Karmel that the relatively recently formed

Tasmanian College of Advanced Education be disestablished in Hobart and relocated to Launceston. It was a difficult and highly political campaign and pretty well everything was in the balance as we prepared to become a faculty of the University of Tasmania. It meant that everyone's future was uncertain as Geoff Parr and several other senior staff members negotiated with the University to secure the School's and the staff's position. This wasn't the only hiatus: several staff left after the Karmel Report was published, including the then-Head of School, Udo Sellbach, as we struggled to maintain a foothold in Hobart; also, in early 1978, my friend and colleague Bruce Campbell took his own life following an horrendous 'gay' bashing that had left him badly injured and deeply depressed for several months. His suicide left a big gap, not just in the teaching of history and theory at the School, but also because of the affection staff and students felt for a popular and influential teacher.

The renowned artist and academic, Robyn Stacey, took over Bruce Campbell's role for second semester in 1978 but had indicated at the outset that she would be moving on, and late in 1978 – fresh from Honours at Monash – Paul was appointed as a tutor at the School to commence duties on February 1 the following year. He plunged himself into a hectic teaching schedule when he arrived that year and, as well as taking over other art history units that were already in place, he developed along the way a new seminar unit that focused on the history of twentieth-century performance art. As he argues in a 1980 curriculum vitae, the unit was:

> the first history of performance-art to be taught in Australia and preceeded [*sic*] the publication of Roselee [*sic*] Goldberg's definitive history of performance art. The course embraced artists as stage designers, the theory of total theatre from Wagner to Gropius, cinema, environmental art and music, the new dance of the 1960's, the development of performance-art since Futurism and included a seminar on Performance in Australia.[2]

I recall him being a highly effective and extremely engaging teacher: he was only twenty-two years old at the time but had already built up an extensive and critical understanding of art of the twentieth century, very much influenced by his study under Professor Patrick McCaughey and Dr Memory Holloway at Monash and in a one-off honours unit on Duchamp that Professor Margaret Plant was running at Melbourne University in 1978. And despite the 'party-animal' persona he radiated when he was in Hobart, he was extremely well-read and well-prepared for teaching,

Apart from the profound structural changes that were occurring for the Art School in 1979, it was also a remarkable year for another reason. The photograph of Paul at the Sydney Biennale will always be a memory trigger because it marks one of the most extraordinary periods in the Art School's forty-year-long guest lecturer program – a program established by Bernice Murphy in 1972–73 and which I was overseeing, along with then-final year student and later artist, writer and curator, Grace Cochrane. During the space of about eight weeks over the Easter period that year, the international artists Hamish Fulton, Daniel Buren, Marina Abramović and Ulay, Mario Merz and Daniel Spoerri all spent brief periods in Hobart lecturing and talking to students as part of the Sydney Biennale Outreach program. All were memorable visits in one way or another and, of course, Paul was in his element:[3] others have reminisced with me about Paul's amazing tunnel-focus when he wanted to meet a new or strategically significant visual artist, critic, curator or arts administrator and, of course, the weekly guest lecturer program at the Art School was grist for his mill as a weekly flow of new visitors flew in to give lectures in Hobart. When Paul was 'on a mission' he seemed to be able to create an invisible and impenetrable forcefield in which he and the subject of his attention were contained. It was remarkable to watch in action – the intensity of his attention was palpable – and it yielded results.

During 1979, he honed his critical skills with a weekly interview program that was broadcast on the recently established Hobart FM Station founded by, among others, a remarkable broadcaster, music librarian and audiophile, John Stafford, who used his own extensive and very rare classical music collection as the mainstay of his programs. Hobart FM was based at the Tasmanian College of Advanced Education on Mt Nelson until that institution was disestablished in 1980, and so it was a relatively easy segue for Paul to gather up prospective interviewees in the aftermath of the weekly Art Forum programs that were held on Fridays and to interview them in the on-campus FM broadcasting studio. If my memory serves me correctly, the interviews were bookmarked with music drawn from Paul's own extensive disco and electronic music collection.

The skill with which Paul Taylor put together those early broadcasts is perhaps best exemplified in the engaging transcribed interview he conducted with Clement Greenberg in early November 1979, when the latter critic visited Sydney to deliver his now-famous William Dobell Memorial Lecture titled 'Modern and Postmodern' on October 31, 1979. Paul flew to Sydney to interview him: Clement Greenberg's essay was published in the journal *Arts* in February 1980 and was followed almost immediately by the publication of Paul Taylor's interview with the critic in the summer edition of *Art & Australia*.[4] Re-reading this interview, one is reminded of just how well Paul could construct an unfolding argument; in 1979, his technique was already formidable. Equally, one becomes aware of the careful preparation he always undertook to make the interview a success. The extensive background reading that underpins the Greenberg interview is carried lightly in the discussion as the doyen of modernist criticism spars and parries with his precocious and talented interlocutor. Because of that enormous amount of preparation Paul had undertaken in the lead-up to the meeting, however, he elicits some remarkable insights into the renowned critic's thinking and writing.

Towards the end of 1979, Paul moved into the mews annexe of a stately colonial house in Davey Street, South Hobart and proceeded to decorate his new lodgings with what seemed like an ever-expanding flock of flying ducks and an equally eclectic collection of carnival ware. He was also beginning to accumulate some iconic examples of 1950s and '60s furniture, and his music was the signature for a number of celebrated dance parties.

The initial teaching contract was for 1979 and he reapplied and was reappointed as a tutor in 1980. Paul and the new head of the Tasmanian School of Art, Geoff Parr, had some rather testy exchanges because the position continued to be advertised at the tutor level (which most certainly didn't square with Paul's opinion of his own worth) but the appointment at this level was very much due to the fact that the School was undergoing a dramatic structural change from late 1979 as the negotiations for the creation of a new faculty in the University were brokered. It wasn't just Paul's teaching position that was under review during this period, and later in 1980 (although Paul had, by then, decided to move on) Parr encouraged him to apply for the substantive lecturing position that was created in the move to the University.

Apart from teaching, Paul focused on two critical projects in 1980, both of which were to have a significant impact on his later
25 career. The Tasmanian School of Art Gallery had been established in 1978, and during 1979 it had begun to be known as the venue for a number of important locally generated and touring shows of contemporary Australian art; it was also the venue for one of the

Sydney Biennale international satellite exhibitions that year, 'Recent European Drawing', curated by Dr Wieland Schmied.

Towards the end of 1979, Paul proposed an ambitious exhibition titled 'Recent Tasmanian Sculpture and Three-Dimensional Art' that was developed during the early part of 1980 and shown jointly at the Tasmanian School of Art Gallery on the Mt Nelson campus of the College of Advanced Education and in the University of Tasmania's Fine Arts Gallery in September, travelling to the Queen Victoria Museum and Art Gallery during the following month.

The exhibition focus seemed to be a logical outcome of the work he had undertaken in his honours thesis eighteen months earlier, supervised by Patrick McCaughey and Memory Holloway, in which he had researched the work of Robert Morris and Anthony Caro in a project titled 'Sculpture and the Spectator, 1962–1967'. Furthermore, the exhibition was informed by an important essay, 'Sculpture in the Expanded Field' by Rosalind Krauss published in the journal *October* the previous year, an article that gave him a cue for the theme behind an exhibition that consisted of a very eclectic group of fourteen artists working at the time in Tasmania. Drawing on arguments presented by Rosalind Krauss and referring also to the writings of Graeme Sturgeon, Paul wrote in the catalogue:

> More adventurous critics are investigating recent art from the point of view of logical structures in which seemingly wide diversities are made connectable by recourse to a deeper social structure, namely that of language and signs. From this perspective, artistic categories such as 'theatre' and 'sculpture' become irrelevant.[5]

This argument underpinned his catalogue essay as he explored the work of artists such as the much-underrated sculptor, Peter Taylor, whose evocative huon and celery-top pine figurative sculptures would be seen in the 1984 Sydney Biennale, and the robust, modernist-influenced metal sculpture of Chris Beecroft and Stephen Walker. Sculptures by these artists were set beside works by Frances Joseph and Loretta Quinn, which drew their inspiration from the artists' association with the Tasmanian Puppet Theatre and which were created in a much more informal sculptural language. Towards the conclusion of the catalogue essay, which remains a remarkably insightful study of the sculpture of the period, Paul writes:

Further inroads to the pluralism of the '70's art have been proposed by artists whose autobiographical work, like Frances Joseph's, emphasises both the importance of personal artistic sources and a close relationship between the artwork and the life and emotions of the artists. Many, like Peter Taylor, stress the particular beauty of well-made objects, works whose value is not simply visual but tactile, sometimes functional and the result of great skill and care. Similarly the miniature fictions of Dusan Marek's paintings and Loretta Quinn's 'cages' demand a participation and concentration from the spectator — an involvement which is so often disregarded in favour of the flatly immediate, historicist and impersonal.[6]

Throughout the essay there are thoughtful and perceptive observations of individual works that remind us of Paul's emerging maturity as a critic. There's a great set of observations about the figurative sculptures of Ewa Pachucka, whose work had been the subject of a National Gallery of Victoria survey in 1978;[7] there are similar insights into the paintings of Dusan Marek who was living in Tasmania during the 1970s,[8] as well as timely critical appraisals of artists such as Paul Zika, Lorraine and Bob Jenyns and Lutz Presser.

Although Paul had been involved in assisting Bill Fontana when he produced his *Sound Sculpture* installation and performance with *Dance Exchange* at the National Gallery of Victoria in 1978, it is probably fair to say that the Tasmanian sculpture experience was his first significant individual foray into curatorial activities. He was successful in obtaining Tasmanian Arts Advisory Board funding to assist in mounting the exhibition, and during July and August he worked towards the completion of that project. The publication of the catalogue, like most of the catalogues produced by the Tasmanian School of Art from 1978 through to the present, was largely done 'in-house', with the typing and typesetting being carried out by an indefatigable School secretary, Penny Hawson, and with design assistance from the department of Graphic Design in the Tasmanian School. Mention is made of this because the approach, along with the hands-on experience that Paul had gained from working as Review Editor at the Monash University student newspaper, *Lot's Wife*, a couple of years earlier, gave him an insight into catalogue and journal publication that would stand him in great stead in the next phase of his career, both as publisher and as a curator.

In a letter in March 1980 to Visual Arts Board (VAB) Senior

Project Officer, Katrina Rumley, Paul inquired about the status of his application to travel to Washington, D.C. to attend the Eleventh International Sculpture Conference in June – an application that I recall was eventually unsuccessful. The letter is particularly noteworthy, however, for two other comments he makes. On the one hand he draws attention to the interview that had just been published in *Art & Australia* with Clement Greenberg, and on the other hand it asks the seemingly innocent but actually leading question: 'Has Bruce LeCompte been to Tasmania yet as planned? If so he must have been very quiet about it, but if not, please remind him to visit us here.' LeCompte, who was also a Senior Project Officer at the VAB, was the administrator of its extensive publications program, which, since the mid 1970s, had provided significant funding for a variety of journals, monographs and catalogues, mostly on contemporary Australian art. Paul, of course, would have been exceptionally keen to meet LeCompte because he would have been in the process of lodging his application for initial funding for *Art & Text* and wanting to underline the importance of the proposal to his potential sponsors.[9]

Paul had discussed his developing ideas about the proposed journal with me in the latter part of 1979 and in early 1980. In a fading photocopy of his hand-written draft of the eventual application for funding of *Art & Text*, which I have in my possession, he carefully outlines the strategy he was adopting to ensure the magazine's early success. As others have noted, applying for funding for an as-yet-untried and unpublished journal would later be a matter of great contention and the VAB received a number of letters of representation regarding the eventual decision to fund the journal – especially from supporters of the journals *Aspect*, *Art Network* and *Art & Australia*. Although all three of these journals were actually funded in 1980, *Aspect*'s funding was reduced, supporters of *Art Network* felt that it had already established its credentials whereas *Art & Text* had not, and *Art & Australia* was placed on notice that it would not receive further funding beyond 1980.

Paul's application included the development of a substantial rationale for the new magazine. It is written in a feisty tone with a lengthy section on 'defining the problem' in then-current Australian art criticism and art publishing, and then a switch to the 'suggestion of a solution' which, of course, involved the establishment of the new publication. He writes:

> A danger facing art in Australia at present is that the entire

> enterprise of criticism is being stifled. The inconsistent ambitions and achievements of existing art magazines, the incomprehension of a large section of our art world to new experimental art, and tightening of opportunities for younger writers and artists threatens the potential of new art in the coming years.[10]

Taylor was critical of *Art & Australia* in the application, describing it as 'inadequate as a representative forum for contemporary art and ideas', and he remarks that journals such as *Quadrant* and *Aspect* 'present very few articles and interviews on art', continuing by saying that *Aspect*'s editorial approach is inconsistent and uncritical and 'does nothing towards presenting an understanding of our new art'.

Later in the year, after it had been announced in the broadsheet *News from the Visual Arts Board* that *Art & Text* would be funded,[11] Paul McGillick, associate editor of *Aspect*, wrote to Nick Waterlow, the Director of the Visual Arts Board, to complain about the cut in *Aspect*'s funding and, along with pointed criticism levelled at the funding of *Art & Australia* and *Art Network*, he went on to say:

> In addition to this questionable distribution of largesse [to the above journals], it is reported that $15,000 is to be given to an unnamed magazine in Tasmania which is still to bring out its first issue. Given this fact and the additional reservation regarding the possibility of editing a truly national magazine from Hobart, one is intrigued as to the source of the VAB's confidence in this apocryphal journal.[12]

To be fair to Paul Taylor, the VAB did fund a number of other untried publications – particularly monographs – during the period and I do recall that by the time that the Board considered the applications for publications funding, he had already secured almost all of the copy for the first issue.

Returning briefly to the draft application, Paul's argument about why the new journal should be funded included the observation that several Australian critics were now beginning to focus on publishing overseas in an effort to overcome what was perceived to be the stagnant state of journal publication in Australia, and he goes on to say that the majority of then-recent articles on Australian art published in journals such as *Art International* were primarily on the work of painters. Then, returning to the Australian context, he continues by making the following observation of *Art & Australia*, which remained, at the time, the most popular visual arts journal with a circulation of several thousand copies:

> Not even *Art and Australia* is willing to publish critical articles on photographers, performance and film artists and those on the fringe of music, dance and video, let alone theoretical texts, which challenge conceptions about the structure of art, Australian art-culture and aesthetics. What is more crucial, and more disappointing, is that I don't believe any Australian art magazine exists which is able to discriminate and co-ordinate intelligent material relating to contemporary artistic issues.[13]

Only the feminist magazine *Lip* received Paul's relatively unqualified endorsement, with him arguing that:

> Only *Lip* magazine has gone any distance towards achieving this. Not only has *Lip* managed to clear the ground for a great deal of discussion and writing about women's art, criticism and history, but it has always been based in radical politics which has ensured its relevance to a considerable amount of recent art.[14]

Taylor points out, however, that its presence didn't rule out the need for a significant new critical voice because its focus meant that it didn't publish writing by male writers and didn't carry any articles about male artists.

In suggesting his solution, Paul points towards the success of *Artforum* in the decade 1965–1975, and goes on to say that of the new journals, '*October* is forging such a path, brilliantly tempering its American critical heritage with French structuralism, establishing, I believe, a model for art journals of the future.' There follows a long paragraph that deserves to be reproduced in full because in many ways it captures the intentions sitting behind Paul's first editorial essay in issue 1 of *Art & Text* in 1981:[15]

> The character of the proposed journal of new Australian art and criticism will primarily be serious and informed, comprising a small number of long articles. It will of necessity be a quarterly in 1981 but with ambitions to becoming a monthly in 1982. The content will not be exclusively Australian, and it will range from: art to ideas, environmental art, performance,

> photography and other media. The important, connecting sensibility between articles will be a desire for challenging work of considerable weight and purposes. This, I believe, will render both lavish illustrations and small news pieces irrelevant. As well as this, the journal will aim to present critical and informed documents about visitors to Australia. This could take the form of either an article by these visitors, or an intelligent (not the usual wide-eyed) interview. One can ask: which magazine approached, for instance, the recent Robert Cumming exhibition or the visits of Jack Burnham, Lucy Lippard, Clement Greenberg or Germano Celant? Who is prepared to criticise the forthcoming exhibitions of work by Vito Acconci and Richard Smith?

To this he adds, in the concluding paragraphs of the draft:

> As editor, my role would be to present the best ideas and writings put forth by contemporary writers on the arts. I will make no attempt to "present both sides" on an issue as I don't believe that impartiality encourages debate and growth of ideas. Nevertheless this does not mean that the magazine will not be pluralist in its outlook. I have no illusions of a mainstream in Australian art, nor will I discriminate against any article on contemporary art as long as it is well argued and to the point.

It is worthy of note that he was true to his word here and despite claims of *Art & Text*'s supposed elitism at the time, during the next five years the journal would publish the writings and work of over sixty writers and artists, and in the spirit of Baudelaire, *Art & Text* was robustly partial and political.

Although Paul wasn't notified that he had received initial funding for *Art & Text* until late September 1980, he had already made up his mind that he would be moving on from the Tasmanian School of Art at the end of the year (he tendered his resignation in June 1980 and gradually resigned from his other Hobart commitments over the next few months). As noted earlier, by mid-year he had already secured most of the content of the first issue of *Art & Text*. This would help to explain why the Visual Arts Board was prepared to fund what was an untried magazine that year. I do recall that the debate about the funding of publications was particularly 'robust' in 1980 and that opinions about how the funding should be distributed were divided amongst the Board.

On October 1, 1980, Paul wrote to Bruce LeCompte to thank the Board for funding the first two issues of *Art & Text* and shortly afterwards he requested leave of absence from the School of Art between the 17th and 21st of November 1980 in order to 'visit Melbourne galleries and printers'.[16] Much of the last month in Hobart was then spent continuing to prepare the first two issues of the journal, which, as Adrian Martin has pointed out, were largely singular efforts on Paul's part.

In many ways it was a remarkable two years and the excitement of the emergence of this new journal was palpable around the School of Art during the period – made so by the infectious enthusiasm, and single-minded and purposeful planning that Paul brought to its creation.

The next phase was, of course, the Melbourne story: not just Paul working on the journal out of the office made available by the Prahran College of Advanced Education, but the advocacy and the curatorial projects that framed the next period in Paul's life before he moved on to New York. The first issue of *Art & Text* was published on time in April 1981, with reviews of the journal coming out in *The Age*, *The Sydney Morning Herald* and *The Australian* during the first few months of its publication. Ever the planner, Taylor also secured its indexing in *Art Bibliographies Modern* and the *Australian Public Affairs Information System* database from the very first issue, and by the time that he applied for a second tranche of funding to carry *Art & Text* over the next four issues, he had already secured the articles for the mid-year issue of the journal from an extremely diverse range of writers and artists: John Young and Terry Blake, Adrian Martin, Patrick McCaughey, Terry Smith, Peter Tyndall, Judy Annear, John Nixon, Ian North, David Bromfield and Noel Hutchison. This pattern of diversity was to continue as the journal developed – a pattern that we had witnessed in Hobart during 1979 and 1980 as Paul Taylor began to reach maturity as a critic, curator and publisher.

Provincialism no more: *Art & Text*

Heather Barker & Charles Green

Introduction

This essay describes the writing and personalities surrounding the 1981 establishment of the Australian art magazine *Art & Text*, traces its progression under Paul Taylor's editorship up to his relocation to New York, and locates its programmatic art critical aspirations amidst the writing and publications of the period.[1] During this period, *Art & Text* published Taylor's own essays and, arguably more importantly, those of other writers and artists – Meaghan Morris, Paul Foss, Philip Brophy, Imants Tillers, Rex Butler, Edward Colless – all articulating a consistent and complex postmodern position. The magazine sought the niche and status of an antipodean *October*. The essay argues that the magazine's founder and editor, Paul Taylor, personified the shattering impact of postmodernism upon the Australian art world as well as postmodernism's severe limitations. Taylor facilitated a new theoretical framework for the discussion of Australian art, but one that no longer continues to shape the internationalist aspirations of Australian art writers. He produced a transiently convincing but spectacular solution to problems that earlier critics had wrestled with unsuccessfully, in particular the twin problems of provincialism and the relationship of Australian to international art.

Australian art writers and critics of the early 1980s used a methodology and a vocabulary that were new for writing on Australian art. Like good avant-gardists, they said that they were freeing themselves from traditional assumptions, relationships and strictures, questioning and deconstructing the unchanging truths to which their antecedents putatively subscribed. Instead of beginning with revelatory foundational models such as Marxism, young postmodern theorists in Melbourne and Sydney eclectically combined ideas from the new, still fluid canon of French poststructuralist philosophy. In particular, their art criticism often layered Jean Baudrillard's concepts of the simulacrum and the copy onto the idea of Australia, discarding both the privilege of artistic authenticity and the search for an artistic self-definition based on national uniqueness (their favourite theorist, Baudrillard was to visit Australia as an artist and exhibit his own travel photographs a decade later, at the tail end of this period). When 'truth' was removed from art, the nature of art changed, and so did its camp followers. In contrast to the engaged critics of the 1970s, the new Australian writers and artists of the 1980s were no longer true believers or ideologues. They were no longer political in the sense that the social activists of earlier magazines such as *Lip* or *Art Network* had been Australian Labour Party political. At the heart of this shift was the magazine *Art & Text*, and its flagship Melbourne-based editor, Paul Taylor. Taylor's years with *Art & Text* were an explosive combination of education, eclectic erudition, acuity, entrepreneurship and personal ambition. Taylor's achievement during this time was to popularise a combination of postmodern theory with the emergent theories of subculture, taken from the expanding university disciplines of cultural studies and visual studies, charting and interpreting a radical new contemporary art scene that incorporated visual art, punk and disco music, and New Wave fashion.

Before *Art & Text*

By the end of the 1970s, a mere three Australian art magazines were active, apart from a few special-interest publications that catered to miniscule audiences. The publications *Other Voices*, *Art Dialogue*, *The Great Divide* and *Arts Melbourne* had all folded. *Art & Australia* continued as it had begun in 1963, under its founding editor, Mervyn Horton. Despite the funding vicissitudes and committee burnout of the late 1970s, *Lip* was in a momentarily confident prime. *Art Network* had begun publication in 1979, full of pluralist optimism, hoping to draw on the support of a wide cross-section of art students and artists. *Lip* and *Art Network* were motivated by the collective politics of social and institutional reform. Unlike overseas journals such as *October*, *ZG*, *Critical Inquiry* and *Diacritics*, the two publications were focused on promoting and celebrating art from outside the commercial mainstream, but not overly concerned with publishing theoretically inclined writing, nor with the implications of postmodern theory for Australian art. Australian art writers who wished to explore complex theoretical issues were in effect left without a venue in which to publish.[2] For Paul Taylor, this was a gap to be filled.

Art & Text was the creation of Paul Taylor, even though he was to remain its editor for only a very short, though remarkable, period. Taylor was already very familiar with Australian art magazines and their politics and he wanted to publish an Australian art magazine that would become international and important.

To do that, he had to come up with a practical solution to the provincialism divide, a solution other than 'ignore it and it will go away'. The debate was already old. The terms of the argument had changed little since the Cold War-inflected stalemate of 1974, when Terry Smith had concluded that the centre (American artists and critics) had responsibilities to the periphery—'the most responsible kind of exhibition would be one that took as its aim, not the supposedly "neutral" presentation of selected art works, but the display of the very problematic which its own incursion into a provincial situation raises'.[3] Change was long overdue, with cracks widely noticed in the façade of America's political and economic hegemony from the Vietnam War and the 1973 OPEC Petrol Crisis onwards. New York had lost its reputation as a centre for innovation within, as opposed to the marketing of, international art. During the early 1970s, the Nova Scotia College of Art and Design (NSCAD) had gained prominence to the point that American conceptualist artist and critic Les Levine (who visited and exhibited in Australia during the 1970s) speculated that NSCAD might be the best art school in North America.[4] Los Angeles art schools, in particular CalArts, in suburban Valencia, had displaced East Coast studio schools in influence and their graduates would become the first generation of postmodern American artists. In other words, it had become increasingly obvious that New York's position as political, economic and cultural centre of the world no longer appeared unassailable.

In Australia, Taylor received a firm grounding in modernist art history at Monash University. Patrick McCaughey was the charismatic foundation Professor of Visual Arts, and it was from McCaughey's lectures that Taylor's predilection for applying the methodology of literary criticism to art criticism arose. Taylor graduated with a Bachelor of Arts (Hons) in 1979, majoring in Visual Arts, and almost immediately was appointed a tutor in Art History (Theory) at the Tasmanian School of Art in Hobart. The Tasmanian School of Art, under its Dean, Geoff Parr, had a reputation for hiring adventurous young staff from the mainland, and an ambitious and substantial weekly program of visitors to compensate for its isolation.

Taylor needed money to launch his new magazine. His application to the Australia Council for a grant to establish *Art & Text* was the culmination of a carefully developed strategy, exceptional in that funding was requested in advance of the first issue.[5] He had already organised the articles for the first issue and much of the second issue.[6] The timing of the application was important.

Of all the Australian art magazines that began in the 1970s, no clear alternative to *Art & Australia* had appeared, and certainly none that could be characterised as promoting emerging art. Taylor would have known (Jonathan Holmes recalled) that the Visual Arts Board (VAB) was making a 'concerted effort to lift critical discourse at the time'.[7] His proposal, coming as it did from a young writer properly trained in an art history department, was bound to be received favourably. Taylor's decision to apply from Tasmania, his place of employment, was deeply strategic: he correctly calculated that the VAB should be supportive of a regional application from a small, usually under-represented state.[8] In *Art & Australia* (Autumn 1993), curator Nick Waterlow recalled the VAB meeting that considered Paul Taylor's initial application for funding:

> Jon Holmes, the Tasmanian representative, spoke supportively but added it was a good thing Taylor was not present to plead his case as after having us eating out of his hands for the first ten minutes he would then have castigated the Board's entire value system and within half an hour we would have had him thrown out, with his application.[9]

Waterlow also remembered Taylor's tenacity, obdurateness, iconoclasm and 'highly tuned critical acumen'.[10] The application was approved and $15,000 was granted to Taylor for the 1980–81 financial year.[11]

The emerging shift in writing on art was by no means an exclusively Melbourne (and by extension Hobart) affair. Sydney-based writers were equally important, as were more isolated groups of artists and writers in Brisbane and Perth; both of the latter centres saw small publications emerge of a broadly similar but less programmatic nature at approximately the same time. Several magazines around the nation – specifically Ashley Crawford's *The Virgin Press*, Arthur and Corinne Cantrill's *Cantrills Filmnotes*, as well as *On the Beach*, *Slug*, *Frogger*, *New Music* and *Zerox* – covered musical and performance work, comics, fashion shows, Super-8 films, independent records, posters, and program notes. In 1980, a collective of recent young graduates, not all involved with art but with an intense enthusiasm for recent French philosophy, generated 'Foreign Bodies: Semiotics in/and Australia', a major international conference, which was to be held at the University of Sydney in February 1981. 'Foreign Bodies' was designed to address issues raised by the new 'Theory', the post-1960s wave of French structuralist and poststructuralist philosophers that included Louis Althusser, Roland Barthes, Jacques Derrida, Michel Foucault and Jean Baudrillard. New Theory was beginning to have an immense impact on the way Anglophone sociologists, historians, architects, art theorists and artists thought about culture. Sydney University's art history department – the Power Institute, where screen studies theorists like Alan Cholodenko had introduced Theory – was already teaching cinema theory, and it was far more open to new discursive shifts than Melbourne University's longer established and more conservative Department of Fine Arts, or Patrick McCaughey's Department of Visual Art at Monash University. The young organisers of the Sydney conference devoted an obsessive and excessive amount of time and care deciding on the invitations, negotiating with the speakers and publicising the event, which foregrounded the theme of the 'foreign' in relation to the already intense and, it was emerging, surprisingly positive Australian reception of Theory. We should note immediately that in the next decade, the trope of foreigner was to blur into the multicultural image of the exile; images and theories of diaspora, along with the associated phenomenon of globalisation, were to periodise and supplant postmodern Australian art.[12]

The conference was a watershed: it summed up the political and feminist discourses of the 1970s but also signalled the direction of the postmodern 1980s. The two key Australian speakers at the conference, Sydney cinema theorist Meaghan Morris and Faculty of Science-trained Paul Foss (later to succeed Paul Taylor as editor of *Art & Text*, upon Taylor's permanent relocation to the US), were familiar enough with this philosophy in the original French to have begun, in collaboration with philosopher Paul Patton, to translate it into English almost as it was published.[13] Some of those translations, most notably Jean Baudrillard's essay 'The Precession of Simulacra' by Paul Foss and Paul Patton, became the first published English translations.[14] Both Foss and Morris used Baudrillard's theories to turn upside-down questions surrounding Australian identity. Their conference papers were aimed squarely at Australian art writing.[15] 'Import Rhetoric: Semiotics in/and Australia', by Meaghan Morris and Anne Freadman, consisted of two parts, one by each author. The first part, Meaghan Morris's 'Catatonia', remains particularly important and it is worthwhile looking at it more closely. Morris's essay was of signal importance and, we might assert, its impact on Taylor's thinking was considerable. The point we make is that Taylor should not be retrospectively valorised through an emphasis on his putative exceptionalism. He was a key part of a complex, rapidly evolving network in which others, such as the far more prolific Morris, were of at least equal importance.

If the recurring complaint about Australian art writing by Donald Brook and Terry Smith had been that it had not kept up with current ideas,[16] then Morris now thoroughly diagnosed the hostile Australian response to 'foreign ideas', amongst which were now semiotics and poststructuralism. Morris began by referring to the 'silence of the stunned mullet', a colourful way to describe the betrayed, bewildered response to French Theory by older Australian critics and art historians, whose reaction was to denigrate the newer theories as 'fashionable' or as nothing more than 'the latest French knickers'.[17] Morris argued that established writers concentrated on an imagined 'problem' of cultural importation, simply failing to address or even read Theory itself. By that she meant that local writers assumed that Theory, derived not just from French philosophy but also from the pages of American art journal *October*, was simply the latest attempt of overseas influences to colonise Australian art. From there it was a small step to argue that theoretically literate art and criticism was un-Australian. In doing this, even writers as sophisticated as Ian Burn avoided any real engagement with Theory, failing to see the crucial application it could have to the Australian situation. Making that connection was to be *Art & Text*'s contribution to Australian art criticism.

Morris established her credentials by recounting the history of her own interest in 'import rhetoric'. As a student in the University of Sydney's French Department, reading semiotics in the original, she was 'increasingly mesmerised' by Anglophone references to 'Frenchness' and 'French ideas' as signifiers of extravagance, hysteria and instability. She tied Theory further into its Australian context, recalling a comment made by Joh Bjelke-Peterson, the Premier of Queensland from 1968 to 1987 and one of the most extreme right-wing figures in Australian politics. Outside Queensland, he was regarded as a near-fascist anachronism, the butt of countless leftist political cartoons and jokes. Bjelke-Peterson had famously asserted 'Just because a few wogs want their spicy tucker doesn't mean Australian health has to be put at risk', a comment with just the right tone of jingoistic racism to illustrate Morris's point for the almost exclusively anti-Bjelke-Peterson conference audience, who would have been, in latte-sipping Sydney, completely unsympathetic to the populist Queensland politician's Menzies-era view of the world. But her next example, from a source absolutely opposed to everything Bjelke-Peterson represented, was aimed closer to home. Speakers at the 1980 Art Workers Union forum, 'Should Australian Art Have a National Content?', had expressed similar views, though the subject was ideas not cuisine:

> [T]he notion that 'foreign' ideas are imported in exactly the same way as camembert was combined with hygiene metaphors (the tainting, contagion, infection and invasion threatening the health of local culture) to produce an overwhelming sense of impending foot and mouth disease.[18]

Morris was demonstrating that she came to Theory without prejudice. She was neatly distancing herself both from the Australian Right (Bjelke-Peterson) and the Left (Art Workers Union). She had created an image – Bjelke-Peterson, the rustic populist premier – to ridicule his narrow-mindedness, but then equated him with the Art Workers Union, and implicitly with neo-Marxist writers like Ian Burn and Ann Stephen. Morris's tactic was clever and deliberate. It was also frequently used by *Art & Text*'s editors and writers.

Her point was that 'semiotics' was characterised as something foreign, threatening and dangerous, unsuitable for use by Australian writers. The *importation* of foreign theory was clearly this putative problem. Morris distinguished two types of writing that constructed the so-called importation problem. The first was nationalist writing that appealed to three cultural tropes: to solidarity, locality and history. This national approach set up a simple opposition between home and foreigner:

> A 'we' is asserted as existing (perhaps as a type of political consciousness) while an 'us', an objective – that is the national culture in some sense – remains in the future or in the past and has to be fabricated and/or to be re-discovered.[19]

Morris might well have been describing Bernard Smith's *Australian Painting*, in which he constructed the narrative of a national school of Australian art for which the time-lag of knowledge transfer from the North Atlantic art centre to the Antipodes produced a distinctive culture, or his *Antipodean Manifesto* (1959), in which Smith unequivocally saw the influence of New York School abstract painters as an importation problem. A little later, in 1970, Terry Smith had imagined that an Australian avant-garde now existed, one that had modified the late modernist syntax of 'Color-Field' abstract painting (a cultural importation itself) to transcend local boundaries and take a place at the centre. But, by the time he wrote his 1974 article, 'The Provincialism Problem', Terry Smith had come to acknowledge the hegemonic, imperial power that regulated any model of centre and periphery, containing local art by reducing the regional to the provincial. The New York art establishment had the power to present itself as constituting international art, imposing the terms of success upon others who lived outside New York. Artists who wished to be successful had to simply adopt those standards, and by and large, within the wider but equally regulated field of centralised globalisation, they still do.[20]

So, for the Art Workers Union, and leftist writers and artists preoccupied with national self-definition in the face of imperial American power, wrote Meaghan Morris, 'location, in a sense, is the *a priori*'; there was no consideration of space beyond the assumed dichotomy of here and there.[21] History was superficially important in the accompanying dichotomy of now and then. But History was flawed because of what had been forgotten, lost or buried, and now had to be rehabilitated 'according to the needs of the future'.[22] Morris offered the debate surrounding 1930s Sydney modernist painter Margaret Preston as her example, but her biting criticism applied as much to the 1970s Australian feminists' project to rehabilitate women's art, and to the neo-Marxist sublimation of conceptual art into collectives that provided support material and posters for the union movement. Finally, the aspiration to an Australian art history was constricted by the same limiting perspective; her salutary arguments predate Rex Butler's important essays on unAustralian art by two decades.[23]

The second category of writing identified by Morris was concerned not with the issue of identity—of who we think we are—but with the issues of discourse—about 'how it can be spoken, how it should be spoken, and where it's spoken from and to whom and with what potential effect'.[24] In other words, its concerns were more abstract and conceptual than those of art writers of the left or the right. She summed this up, declaring that here were two types of catatonia:

> One is the problem of falling into a space where you no longer know who you are because you are spoken by something else; and the second is one of lapsing into an imaginary void where the problem *might* become that you don't know how to speak or what to speak it to.[25]

When Morris began to explain Type Two Catatonia, the examples she gave were not from art criticism, even though Type Two's symptoms can be found there from the 1970s onwards. One symptom was the ritual insistence on the need for accessibility and clarity in art writing. Even the editorials of early 1970s' *Other Voices* stumbled there. The most comprehensive demands for this were yet to come, in long reviews by *Sydney Morning Herald* art critic John McDonald from 1983 onwards, and finally in journalist Peter Timms's despairing, bleakly populist book, *What's Wrong with Contemporary Art* (2004).[26] Many writers, anticipating a hostile response from readers to any display of sophistication, constructed apologetic defences in advance: this was the pre-emptive 'discourse of self-protection'.[27] In most cases, of course, editors *knew* they would encounter opposition or hostility from readers because their magazines were founded to provide a venue for styles of writing that wouldn't be published elsewhere, and certainly not in the review columns of daily newspapers. *Other Voices*, *Art Dialogue*, *Lip*, and *The Great Divide* had been outstanding examples of such defensive art criticism, in part because they had been founded upon short-term, fractious alliances of many artist and writer constituencies, all with aspirations – or the rhetoric of such aspirations – to wider readership rather than to any intellectual program. Throughout her discussion of importation, Morris referred to the 'flagrant and flaunted pleasure in translating'.[28] The rhetoric of pleasure and overt pleasure in obscurity were to appear again and again during the 1980s, not least in the New Wave of *Art & Text*. The style was to be clever, confident and alert. The theorists amongst them were actual translators of Theory and, often as not, university academics or artists. They were the keepers of the keys to understanding difficult new, foreign material. They flaunted their association with Theory. It distinguished them from the suddenly quite old-fashioned, Leftist art establishment.

Morris wrote about Australian reactions to foreignness in relation to the endlessly discussed 'problem' of cultural importation: in other words, she was re-working the 'provincialism problem'. Her discussion centred on the inability to 'speak' – to culturally construct – Australia. This was caused, Morris suggested, by the ambiguity of the cultural space that Australia occupied. Morris ridiculed existing points of view, both the jingoistic right and the nationalism of the left, demonstrating in her encyclopaedic citations her own virtuoso cosmopolitanism and the 'flagrant and flaunted pleasure' of the rapidly emerging postmodern enterprise.[29] In his equally influential paper, 'Theatrum Nondum Cognitorum',

Paul Foss argued that the space that Australia occupied was a zone of representation hovering between the map created by European images of the Antipodes and the territory that their map purported to represent. Both papers, though not specifically about Australian art, were intensely preoccupied with visuality and nation. They indicated the direction that Australian art writing would take in the 1980s, employing the literary studies rhetoric that was to be adopted by later art writers such as Rex Butler. But from the above, it is clear that the process of evolving a theoretical framework was well under way by the time Taylor watched Foss deliver 'Theatrum Nondum Cognitorum' at the 'Foreign Bodies' conference.[30] As Foss recalled: 'Paul Taylor once told me that he attended the semiotics conference and that my paper gave him the inspiration for *Art & Text*. Though I think the notion is fanciful at best.'[31] Foss is correct, for *Art & Text* was already into production by February 1981. Foss and Morris had, however, confirmed Taylor in his inspiration that a new art-critical framework, constructing an international place for Australian art beyond that of a province, would exploit the concept of the unoriginal, the copy and the simulacrum, and it need make no apology—in fact it should flaunt—a cosmopolitan obscurity.

Art & Text 1

In retrospect, *Art & Text* was the logical development for Australian art writing, and this explains the powerful hold the myth of *Art & Text* exercised upon its contemporaries. Upon its publication in 1981, it appeared to be a controversial, even iconoclastic departure from the norm. But everything about *Art & Text* was carefully planned to be different. Taking the American journal *October* (founded in 1976) as its model, *Art & Text* was an art magazine visually dominated by text. This text was invariably complicated and difficult. Illustrations were few and were in grainy, modish black and white. The magazine sought the niche and status of an antipodean *October*. Most challenging of all, the magazine was extremely well funded, in advance of its first issue, by the Visual Arts Board of the Australia Council. The first issue of *Art & Text* appeared in March 1981. Paul Taylor, an Art History–trained but eclectic, intellectual bowerbird, was constructing a new and unique image for Australian art within the global landscape.[32] Taylor took English cultural studies theorist Dick Hebdige's idea of subculture to shift the site of contemporary art, expanding the signifiers available, discarding much else (except the art object) as old-fashioned. Taylor appropriated Foss's re-interpretation of

Baudrillard and his channelling of early Bernard Smith to describe a space in international art that only Australia could occupy, though, as we shall see, this exceptionalism was myopic. Other settler societies, notably in Brazil, had arrived there first, decades earlier. This neat reformulation meant that the model of centre versus periphery lost its power to marginalise. The antipodean position could only be held by uniquely unauthentic Australian art. *Art & Text* was the perfect venue for the promotion of this happily perverse new art. Not even an editorial board complicated the first issues, though Taylor drew on all his associates and former mentors for advice and copy. *Art & Text* was, above all, initially a one-man show.

The first *Art & Text* editorial explained the magazine's theoretical position and aims.[33] The title, 'Editorial: On Criticism', signalled that good writing was crucially important to the magazine. This was exceptional; for almost all other art magazines, writing was the means from which to project art. But this editor was projecting a sophisticated understanding of critical genres. In true essayist style, Taylor began with the statement that Australian art writing was 'underrated and neglected',[34] asserting that no healthy art critical forum existed in Australia. His view was that 'the continuing factionalisation of our writers is a direct result of Australia's involvement in internationalist art history and art politics.'[35] Australian criticism was shaped by two particular art histories that believed in the linear continuity of artistic styles and which were, therefore, as exclusive and reductive as they pretended not to be. Taylor cited Patrick McCaughey, Terry Smith and Janine Burke, tracing their indebtedness to Greenberg. He then packed them neatly away in the back of the Australian art criticism cupboard, quoting Monash University lecturer Margaret Plant (one of his younger mentors and McCaughey's successor at Monash University's Department of Visual Arts, she was a transitional figure in writing on Australian art), who had written that 'the critic passes with the style he espouses'.[36]

Taylor then moved on to discuss the term 'pluralism'. This, he wrote, was a reaction to the teleological historicisms defined above. But it had become all-inclusive and, in doing so, had lost any sort of intellectual rigour. A final pluralist method, he hissed, 'is barely criticism at all': this was what he rightly pilloried as 'list-making'. Here, the critic was a passive, non-judgemental 'onlooker and bookkeeper'.[37] His carefully chosen example was Suzanne Spunner, a member of the *Lip* collective, an academic and theatre critic. Implicitly, he was attacking older, much-loved writers such as Alan

McCulloch and, in Sydney, Elwyn Lynn (who of course was also the curator of the Power Institute's collection and who Donald Brook had often fiercely disagreed with). His assessment of Marxist criticism was that it was neither historicist nor pluralist because it was more concerned with sociology, with 'the premises of the contemporary art world' more than with contemporary art.[38] In other words, Marxist critics (by whom he meant Terry Smith, Ian Burn, Ann Stephen and Charles Merewether) were preoccupied with describing the power relationships between art institutions, especially galleries and artists, rather than art. It allowed this analysis to replace art. Taylor asserted that in reality the publishing opportunities for difficult, ambitious writers had been severely limited. *Art & Text* was going to provide a venue for such writing.

Taylor then carefully constructed an argument to support the journal's second ambition: to 'sustain a level of cultural critique in which the artist, more a "producer" (in Walter Benjamin's sense of the word) than a "performer", actively features'.[39] By invoking Walter Benjamin, who had been resurrected from obscurity in the US during the previous decade, he tied his editorial to intellectually impeccable avant-garde foundations. Taylor continued in the same vein, quoting Xavier de Ventos, whose *Heresies of Modern Art* (1980) called for the redefinition of art in relation to other cultural practices. He was justifying the relocation of visual art inside the field of mass cultural production. He cited John Cage on Beethoven, then wrote: 'As Michel Foucault writes of Flaubert and Manet, Cage too "produced works in a self-conscious relationship to earlier paintings or text ... erect[ing] art within the archive"'.[40] Taylor connected art to music, firmly grounding the New Wave practice of quotation in the past, and in particular within conceptualism's archival turn. He placed all this in the context of the new and difficult, but stylish and fashionable, Theory.

From here, Taylor deftly took up Roland Barthes's suggestion that 'the critic, too, will be an artist'.[41] Raising Robert Venturi's 1966 book, *Complexity and Contradiction in Architecture*, to legitimise quotation from past styles, Taylor declared, 'As an architect, Venturi himself manipulates signs and symbols from the existing architecture and (urban) landscape rather than seeking to innovate a building's form by means of technology'.[42] Finally, he tied this back again to Barthes: 'both Venturi and Barthes propose what could be called a "lateral" or trans-historical approach to form'.[43] This was the last stop in Taylor's argument. He had gathered impeccable sources (Benjamin, Foucault, Barthes and Venturi) to construct an academic model that placed mass culture, music and architecture firmly within the horizon of contemporary art. Taylor concluded with the following proclamation:

> [T]he counter-cultures of the early and mid-seventies, which espoused pluralism as an alternative, have themselves become an institution; their critical apparatus has become a block to analysis. In the form of alternative spaces, journals, collectives and so on, an 'alternative institution' has sprung up in which the artist's implicit role remains that of historical performer. As such, pluralism, and its related alternative institutions of power, compels the experimenter to transgress further boundaries.[44]

Taylor was insisting that although pluralism had been the necessary antidote to formalist hegemony during the early 1970s, it had become institutionalised. It was now an irrelevant idea. To reach this point, Taylor had relegated conservative art critics such as Patrick McCaughey, radical art critics such as Terry Smith, feminist art critics such as Janine Burke and Suzanne Spunner, newspaper art critics such as Sandra McGrath, and well-meaning poets such as Gary Catalano to the past. He had done this in the style of an academic, citing references that most in his list would not have known. Taylor had argued that these leading Australian art writers employed old art critical frameworks that had become irrelevant, in an excellent example of the rhetorical technique of declaring one's opposition irrelevant, boring and old-fashioned. It was another technique often used by *Art & Text* writers. Taylor's editorial ended with a statement of what the journal would include and what it would avoid. Essentially, *Art & Text* aimed to do what other Australian art magazines did not, and steered clear of existing models. *Art & Text* was going to publish reflective essays about art and visual culture, not lavishly illustrated reviews. The later introduction of reviews and feature articles on artists was a matter of careful deliberation by *Art & Text*'s second editor, Paul Foss and managing editor Jeff Gibson, who had begun working for the magazine in 1988 and who was crucial in its later, transnational incarnation and new-found visual elegance, the opposite of the determinedly worthy monochrome of Taylor's early issues.[45]

As well as setting out the magazine's editorial aims, *Art & Text*'s first issue included essays detailing what was to be the magazine's theoretical position: an article, 'Australian "New Wave" and the "Second Degree"', by Taylor and a book review of Dick Hebdige's *Subculture: The Meaning of Style* by artist-musician Philip

Brophy. Taylor's and Brophy's articles were effectively the journal's mission statements, but the issue also included articles by a surprisingly broad range of well-known writers, including *Lip* regular Janine Burke on artistic collaboration, US pluralist art critic Suzi Gablik on 'Modernism and Morality', and Australian artist-theorist Ian Burn on 1960s art. Although he was associated with an identifiable group of artists and writers, Taylor cleverly cultivated contributors from across the spectrum of the art-writing world, even if he had little regard for their intellectual positions.[46]

Taylor's first issue feature article considered the work of four artists within what he termed the 'realm of the second degree'.[47] This was a postmodern realm constructed from Hebdige's theory of subcultures and Barthes's concept of the 'second degree'.[48] Taylor adapted three concepts – subcultures, subversion and signs – to postulate the existence of a new New Wave. The proposition went like this. Subcultures such as the Mods, Beats, Gays and Punks had emerged in Western consumer society post-World War II. They had repositioned and reconceptualised mainstream cultural codes and sign systems inside small, exclusive subcultures. Recontextualisation subverted the mainstream's codes, new configurations appearing from the entropy of older elements. The body was a prime signifier, Taylor wrote, closely echoing Hebdige, so that 'clothing, hairstyles and accessories speak of the tastes and sensibilities of the wearer and, most crucially, identify him'.[49] These subcultural methods, which subverted conventional values and created new relationships, characterised a New Wave aesthetic. Adrian Martin remembered that *Art & Text* had to be seen in the context of a vibrant scene and a cultural life that was characterised by 'militant dilettantism' and 'cultural *amateurism*'.[50] Rejecting Terry Smith's accusation that this was 'anything goes silliness', Martin emphasised that 'anything goes' meant the 'free, open possibility of *experimentation*', not to '*do* anything' but to '*try* anything'.[51]

The fashion, music, and art of the New Wave were, Taylor argued, 'steeped in the vocabulary and information channels of the mass media'.[52] Its young audience and artists quoted from popular styles of the past, particularly from the 1960s, detaching them from their political and economic history: '[New Wave's] pleasure', wrote Taylor, 'exists in this very dislocation of memory'.[53] Again, we see the conjunction of pleasure and dislocation. Taylor's argument to this point was that subcultures now had a significant cultural presence. The New Wave artist would place cultural signs in new relationships, re-interpreting the history of Modernist art 'as a series of signs and as a style that can be quoted'.[54] This artist was a 'tinkerer (bricoleur)' who collected and combined fragments, 'a pure surface crossed by cultural flows'.[55] In other words, the artist was not a creator or a visionary but a 'producer' or a 'mixer' who 'originated nothing but tinkered furiously with pieces—pieces of thought or "theory" as much as aesthetic forms and mass cultural signs'.[56] We see this in Jenny Watson's painting, *Twiggy by Richard Avedon (for Paul Taylor)* (1979). The work is a crude rendering in oddly but consistently textured brushwork of a famous photographic portrait of the British model Twiggy set amidst the geometric fields of an abstract painting. As the title makes clear, Watson was quoting other art and making no attempt to look original. The work was dedicated to Paul Taylor, acknowledging that the world of fashion (which Taylor adored) was made up of quotations (the use of which he championed).

But the Australian New Wave remained within the dominant culture and was a cultural sensibility linked to the notion of subculture, not to an actual counterculture.[57] The distinction between the two was crucial to New Wave art, making it a very different product from the substantially countercultural—or alternative—political art of the 1970s. This distinction is crucial. It was the intellectual impetus that gave Taylor's identification of subculture with Australian popist postmodernism its power: a member of a subculture does not want mainstream membership, but the fashion-conscious mainstream (the art world) admires subcultures. Add to that the postcolonial spin possible upon the subculture's cannibalism of mainstream signifiers (here, of canonical North Atlantic art; a cannibalism already embraced by Brazilian artists decades before, as we shall see) and the equation was complete.

Who was inside the subculture and who was outside? Carol Squires later was to comment that, 'As Paul's friend you were the smartest, cleverest, funniest, most talented person around', suggesting how he was able to mediate a 'Melbourne alliance' of artists, musicians, writers and curators.[58] The significance of the term 'alliance' should not be underestimated. This was not a collective, a club or an association. It was a disparate collection of people who were brought together for projects or activities by the entrepreneurial intervention of Taylor. The alliance held together for about two years, long enough to become a recognisable presence in the Australian art world and beyond. This was also the reason for its reputation as an elitist clique, for it was a 'province of the white, urban leisure-class' whose obsessive consumption 'cut creative trails through a culture of objects both shiny-brand-new

(12 inch import records) and functionally obsolescent (op shop bric-à-brac)'.[59] There were two overlapping groups of *Art & Text* contributors: one was based around Art Projects, an important artist-run gallery orchestrated by John Nixon in Lonsdale Street; the other was centred at the Clifton Hill Community Music Centre. According to Adrian Martin, Paul Taylor—along with artists Juan Davila, Vivienne Shark LeWitt and curator Judy Annear—occupied 'a mediating position' between the two groups, though some artists spanned both. The artists showed or performed at Art Projects, the George Paton Gallery, the Clifton Hill Community Music Centre, and the Seaview Ballroom in St Kilda.

The relationship between New Wave music and visual art was particularly close. Taylor's friend, Philip Brophy, leader of the art-music group Tsk Tsk Tsk (→↑→), recalled in 2005 that 'Paul was a big fan of my *Asphyxiation* project of 1980—that's how he contacted me—as well as the work of Maria Kozic. He reprinted my catalogue essay to the exhibition "What is This Thing Called 'Disco'?" in the third issue [of *Art & Text*].'[60] *Asphyxiation* consisted of three separate performances and a month's installation at the George Paton Gallery. It dissected the world of disco: 'We broke it up into every part possible', said band member Ralph Traviato in a 1981 *Virgin Press* interview.[61] Taylor immediately grasped the similarity between appropriation art and disco and was soon to write, 'Disco's *modus operandi* is repetition within the fertile space of the cover version, the re-staging of an original in terms of a specific use-value (dance)'.[62] In 1977, artist Jenny Watson had documented her association with singer Nick Cave's band, The Boys Next Door, in a series of portraits of band members based on photographs.[63] As Chris McAuliffe explained, she first went to hear the group because Cave was one of her students at the Caulfield Institute of Technology.[64] In 1979, she had persuaded Cave to hold aloft her painting, *An Original Oil Painting (Black and White): For Nick Cave* (1979), while the band performed a song called 'Let's Talk About Art' at the Crystal Ballroom. The artwork became a prop within a three-minute performance. What McAuliffe called a 'telling symbiosis' between art and music is a little overstated, but his delineation of the importance of punk as community, citing the movement of musicians between bands and the blurring of boundaries between performer and audience, was accurate. The Melbourne New Wave, accompanied by Paul Taylor, invented itself according to this model, ostensibly rejecting established institutional values and putatively seeking a space like Watson's prop within a wider world than that of art. In fact, it made a space for itself inside the existing culture but immune from its criticism. If artists and musicians had already made the link between art and subcultural style, Paul Taylor took the notion across into the covertly structured culture of art writing and criticism through which artists were accredited.

Taylor's art critical method was clever and calculated – Adrian Martin later recalled that 'Paul revelled in this provocateur status'.[65] Vivienne Shark LeWitt remembered that, 'Paul could heap scathing, withering scorn and merciless contempt on anything or anyone he deemed "second-rate" or "know-nothing".'[66] Taylor's version of the New Wave, according to Adrian Martin, had a 'serious playful' relationship with history and politics, which manifested itself in 'an extra edge of irony, intractability, extremism or outrageousness' that marked Taylor's first issue of *Art & Text*.[67] Serious-minded critics later began to accuse Taylor and *Art & Text* writers of not understanding the theory they espoused.[68] Comments such as 'I write from a position of having nothing to say' and 'I'm very fond of contradicting myself', combined with constantly shifting argument and personal flamboyance, were calculated to induce near apoplexy in the magazine's buttoned-down, slightly older opponents.[69] Taylor's appropriation of subcultural theory could not be criticised for its lack of political and ideological commitment, because it did not assign the same commitment to codes and signals. Worse still for his feminist and Marxist precursors, his argument ignored or ridiculed everyone who disagreed. *Lip* writer Julie Ewington admonished feminists to beware. In her article 'Fragmentation and Feminism', published in *Art & Text*, No. 7 (Spring 1982), she explained that New Wavers believed that only those with a New Wave sensibility could understand the New World.[70] This was fairly accurate; the members of Taylor's circle dismissed anyone who hadn't 'caught up' with the 'pulse of hyperreality'.[71] In 1988, Adrian Martin remembered how *Art & Text* 'made short work of many "counter cultural" enemies' and 'revelled in an almost irrational, *de rigueur* disdain for "message" art, community art, artworkers' collectives', a disdain that certainly included *Art Network* and *Lip*.[72] It was Taylor as provocateur who featured in Adrian Martin's short memoir, 'Before and After *Art & Text*' (1988). With considerable affection, Martin described New Wavers as naughty children who meant no harm. The Lip collective and *Art Network* certainly would not have agreed that there was much about their relationship with *Art & Text* that was playful. Many of the rhetorical and critical wounds inflicted at the time were still raw and open while

Martin was walking down memory lane. He conceded that the New Wave campaign against *Lip* and *Art Network* had probably been a mistake: they were not the true enemies at all. The rhetorical gulf between worthy Marxism and feminism on one hand, and the 'wicked clever delights of New Wave' on the other, was greater than the actual divide. The true enemy was the Establishment, the almost unchanged institutions, and the 'echelons of high culture'. Nothing the New Wave did really impacted on that Establishment. 'But', Martin said, it was 'polemically necessary'.[73] Why? Because the New Wave was trying to establish a new and radical critique *against other publications*. It was a battle for discursive territory with contemporary Australian art as the prize. According to Martin's account, Taylor was trying to create a subculture. We disagree completely. What is surely significant here is that Paul Taylor identified and tapped into an *existing* art critical subculture. He didn't need to expand it because its sub-groups provided all the writers, artists and events that he needed in order to establish *Art & Text* as [in Martin's words] the 'public flagship of new writing, new theory, marginal culture'.[74]

Four paragraphs into 'Australian "New Wave" and the "Second Degree"', Taylor had already quoted essays by Umberto Eco, Hal Fischer, Val Hennessy, Dick Hebdige, and Susan Sontag. Two of these references (Fischer and Sontag) were essays on gay and camp subculture and two (Hebdige and Hennessy) were examinations of subculture. Developing the idea of 'pleasure in dislocation', Taylor introduced Roland Barthes's concept of the 'second degree':

> The second degree is [...] a way of life. All we need to do is change the focus of a remark, of a performance, of a body, in order to reverse altogether the enjoyment we might have given it.[75]

Barthes provided Taylor with the most memorable description of the New Wave's highly erotic aesthetic: 'As soon as it thinks itself, language becomes corrosive'.[76] Such an aesthetic would clearly distance itself, even whilst claiming descent from, conceptual art. Language literally constituted Art and Language's art; feminism's reform of language was a project in itself; arcane terminology was crucial to Marxist ideology. Taylor's eclectic New Wave was anti-literary but not anti-textual.

So, Taylor took sociology, cultural studies and semiotics – all emerging sub-specialisations in the academy, all new university disciplines that threatened enrolments in the only-recently established discipline of art history – to define New Wave art as a subculture, and to take advantage of this identification to give its appropriation a political – and geopolitical – spin. This was not necessarily obvious: Taylor's favoured artists, including Jenny Watson, Maria Kozic, John Lethbridge, Howard Arkley and the collective art-music group →↑→, were making relatively conventional artistic objects, though they were using popular culture as their major artistic source. Taylor wrote, 'immediate taste reactions are crucial to work's experience, and many such "gut reactions" – subversive, discriminatory and highly strung – are ultimately just as willing to embrace a good pair of shoes as a good painting'.[77] He was rhetorically assaulting the central assumptions of Australian art criticism. When he referred to Kant, to 'immediate taste reactions' and 'gut reactions', he was stealing the language of his art history training, at Monash, under formalist critic McCaughey, but dismissing its claims to competence. Instead of elevating mass culture to the level of art, Taylor – like visual culture theorists before him – had done the reverse: denying art any special, paradigmatic status, he relegated it to a lesser role, as one sign system amongst many. Taylor's condemnation of educated taste and its 'gut reaction' linked him powerfully to philosopher-theorist Donald Brook's earlier rejection of art history's pretensions to particular competencies, as well as his rejection not just of Greenberg's taste, but also his eye and nose. If the greatest Australian proponent of the art critic's 'gut reaction' had been the well-meaning but parochial critic and Director of the Art Gallery of New South Wales, Laurie Thomas, and if Thomas's taste had been closely related to Australian blood and soil, not footwear (unlike Taylor), then Taylor was in many ways Donald Brook's successor in rejecting both art history and art criticism.

Much of Taylor's writing that we have described was melodramatic and frankly silly. Paul Taylor was not unique. His rise to prominence as an art critic was very similar to that of Robert Hughes and Patrick McCaughey. They, too, were examples of the flamboyant *wunderkind* supported, even indulged, by the institutions and publications of the art world. There would have been no *Art & Text* without the institutional support from Taylor's established academic colleagues in Tasmania, the Visual Arts Board, and the Prahran College of Advanced Education (CAE), which, with astonishing generosity, provided *Art & Text* with free office space and a free phone and fax service; this was the result of sculptor John Davis's and painter Vic Majzner's support. Assisted by part-time lecturers, including the flamboyant, neo-bohemian Howard Arkley, the two were encouraging the most experimental approaches from their students. Prahran had an important artist-in-residence program, where famous English painter's painter John Walker first encountered Australia. Downstairs, Taylor's Art Projects friend John Nixon taught in the college's foundation year program, along with Tony Clark and Aleks Danko.

The response to *Art & Text*'s appearance was immediate. Taylor made sure himself that the arrival of *Art & Text* did not go unnoticed. After all, as Vivienne Shark LeWitt recalled in 1993, he was a consummate networker:

> He was not secretive or paranoid. He did not plot and scheme—but he was the first to know everything about what everyone else was doing and liked nothing better than to casually, and publicly if possible, expose those who did.[78]

Paul Taylor's associates remember that above all he was a great editor. Carol Squires recalled in 1993 that 'Paul was a born editor ... I think he valued writers above all'.[79] He could inspire people to produce the kind of writing he wanted. Ashley Crawford recalled that he was choosey, 'he recognised talent and placed it'.[80] Jane Rankin-Reid knew Taylor well, particularly just after he moved to New York. She commented in 2005 that he was particularly good at recognising 'new writers who've since emerged as major names in international criticism'.[81] His personal style was made up of candour, confidence, charm and hard work. He attended every exhibition opening and function. He handed out copies of the magazine at openings, collecting money for them later. Reactions were not slow in coming. *Art Network* was especially interested in *Art & Text*, assessing the new competitor in *Art Network* 3 & 4 (Winter/Spring 1981). That issue's editorial took *Art & Text* as an illustration of the disproportionate and erratic Visual Arts Board funding of magazines.[82] But the issue also contained a review of *Art & Text* by Judy Annear, an article specifically on the magazine's editorial by Richard McMillan, and even a more than passing comment on that editorial in Ian Burn's review of *The Years of Hope: Australian Art and Criticism 1959–1968*, by Gary Catalano.[83] Curator Judy Annear was impressed.[84] This is hardly surprising, for she was the director of the George Paton and Ewing Galleries between 1979 and 1982, and the gallery formed part of an avant-garde network with Clifton Hill Music Centre, Art Projects and *Art & Text*. →↑→'s *Asphyxiation* had been performed at the gallery in 1980 and, in July 1981, Annear was to curate the landmark exhibition, 'Art in the Age of Mechanical Reproduction' there. This title was inspired by Walter Benjamin's famous essay – in the early 1980s on every seminar reading list – and included works by Maria Kozic, Imants Tillers, Peter Tyndall and Jenny Watson, all friends of *Art & Text*. Annear declared that the 'advent of *Art & Text* is a milestone in Australian art writing', noting that it was the first Australian quarterly art journal with a full-time editor to be publicly funded, and that is was going to provide ample space for serious art writers. She accurately mapped the landscape that *Art & Text* would inhabit: *Art Network* was a source of information and a forum for social and political aspects of art; *Art & Australia* documented the status quo; *Lip* was a necessary venue for women in the arts; *Art & Text* would parallel the role of overseas journal, *October*.[85] *Art & Text* was 'solid and pertinent', but also 'nicely balanced: dry, academic, amusing, romantic, hard-headed, depressing, sane, reasonable, enthusiastic'.[86] All she found wrong with it were spelling mistakes and some technical problems. Richard McMillan and Ian Burn, however, were not so convinced.[87] McMillan compared Paul Taylor's 'Editorial: On Criticism' unfavourably with Paul McGillick's 1978 article in *Quadrant*, 'The Decline of the Australian Art Critic', on the rather odd grounds that McGillick's title was more meaningful and he buttressed his arguments with facts and figures.[88] McGillick's article had rehearsed the standard complaints about the decline of Australian art criticism: none of the good critics write anymore; art was not taken seriously; there was no 'concerned and informed discussion of art'. The best theory of criticism had been expressed by old-style populist Laurie Thomas when he said, 'Two things have never changed and I don't think they ever can change: the irreplaceability of the creative artist himself, and the quality of what he makes'.[89] McGillick defined the reasons for decline: inflation; the removal of postal concessions to small magazines in 1974; the questionable disbursement of funds by the Australia Council; low fees paid to writers; reduced space available in journals and newspapers (7,100 words in 1969 and 2,500 words in 1978); the 'meretricious style of arts reportage' in *The Australian*; and an 'enduring Australian anti-intellectualism' and lack of dialectical tradition.[90] McGillick concluded his article with a list of 'Ten Things Wrong With Australian Art Criticism', repeating the usual yearning for the good old days, a general lack of funding, and the absence of genuine intellectualism. But McMillan was right: McGillick supported his argument with statistics showing funding and word counts. McMillan accused Taylor's editorial of 'desperate insularity', implying that the spectacle of Sydney/Melbourne rivalry and the Antipodean Manifesto surfaced again in the pages of *Art & Text*. He criticised the magazine for not reviewing exhibitions and accused Taylor of condescending to artists. Ian Burn argued that Taylor's editorial failed to provide a genuine basis for developing any worthwhile analysis of art, depending on a too limited range of works: 'its blinkered form has allowed him to miss the major currents and tensions in art writing during the decade.'[91] Burn's complaint was, of course, that Taylor dismissed Marxist-inflected criticism as too concerned with power relationships in the contemporary art world rather than with art. For him, posters, murals and community art activities were as worthy of coverage as paintings and sculptures. Burn's response is less surprising than the presence, given his distaste for bohemianism, of his important revisionist article 'The Sixties: Crisis and Aftermath' in the first issue of *Art & Text*. On reflection, however, Burn's inclusion was not unexpected. Taylor was a pragmatist. He recognised good writing – Burn's was the piece with the most lasting significance in the issue – and, above all, Taylor wanted to edit and publish a successful art magazine. Burn was a major writer and even more strategic a player of the game to direct art history than Taylor. The intelligence of his interventions in Australian art history cannot be underestimated. McMillan's and Burn's reviews were the first but not the last to accuse Taylor of an inadequate cultural critique based on a 'few footnotes and selected quotations', of perpetrating a 'cheap formalist trick, even if dressed up in the latest French knickers'.[92] But the terms of their criticisms showed that both McMillan and Burn wilfully missed the point of 'Editorial: On Criticism'. The comparison between Taylor and McGillick was a gift to Taylor and *Art & Text*, illustrating how different *Art & Text* was to be from existing art journals and how successfully Taylor had instantly established that difference.

Bernard Smith soon wrote an appreciation of *Art & Text* under the title 'Critical Reformation' in *The Age Monthly Review* (March 1982).[93] Smith's review was very supportive; he approved of the magazine, arguing that its circulation of 3000 indicated that there was an audience in Australia for serious art criticism and theory. Smith commented favourably on Taylor's 'On Criticism', unexpectedly noting an (unlikely) 'appropriate editorial restraint'.[94] He approvingly singled out *Art & Text*'s writers' awareness of aesthetic and political theories from abroad, and their reviews of overseas publications that habitually 'receive scant attention from other Australian art journals'.[95] Predictably, he praised the articles by

David Bromfield, Janine Burke, Patrick McCaughey and Memory Holloway, but he also commented favourably on *Art & Text*'s more Theory-oriented articles: Mick Carter's 'The Re-education of Desire' and essays by Peter Tyndall, Edward Colless and David Kelly.[96] Smith welcomed the appearance of structuralist writing, saying, 'it has in my view far more important insights to offer into the functioning of art than ever the naïve formalists offered'.[97] He did suggest, though, that *Art & Text* 'declare a moratorium' on the 'pretentiously opaque language within which the new Australian converts to structuralism express themselves'. Much of his article was devoted to a defence of the discipline of art history, a common and recurring theme in Smith's writing. This was natural in the face of *Art & Text*, given art history as a discipline was under attack at the Power Institute, where Smith had been Director from 1967 until 1977; Carter and Colless were both a part of the Power's shift away from art history towards visual culture studies after Smith's departure. Overall, however, the review was a positive, surprisingly balanced assessment of *Art & Text*, demonstrating that, even in this early phase of his long retirement from academia, Smith remained intellectually engaged with the latest thinking on art even as it tilted against the discipline – Australian art history – that he had created.

Antipodality

In 1981, Patrick McCaughey was appointed the Director of the National Gallery of Victoria (NGV). He invited Taylor to curate a large exhibition of contemporary Australian art at the NGV as a freelance curator, a generous and almost unprecedented invitation – one that certainly sidelined the NGV's own curators who had been crucial in the definition of the art of the previous decade. This nevertheless left little time to create a major exhibition, for 'POPISM' opened on June 16, 1982. It featured twelve artists, including *Art & Text* contributors Juan Davila, Imants Tillers, Peter Tyndall and Richard Dunn, and two bands, one of which was →↑→. The exhibition catalogue essays were a loud and strong declaration of a break between past and present generations of artists and critics, and were clearly intended as part of the same campaign as the June 1982 issue of *Art & Text* (No. 6), which featured a special section comprising essays by artist Imants Tillers, Meaghan Morris and Paul Foss under the title, 'Antipodality'. This special section was closely linked to the direction underpinning 'POPISM', and in retrospect we notice New Wavery less than the reconfiguration of Australianness.[98]

The semi-standard Director's preface that McCaughey contributed to 'POPISM' carried a caveat: it warned visitors that contemporary art could be challenging, requiring 'an open mind as well as a critical one'.[99] Taylor's own essay set out to explain the challenge, the apparent amateurishness of the works he had chosen. It was crucial that the show's 'blatant excursions into amateurism' be understood and accepted before Taylor introduced the more complex argument in which he recapitulated the themes of New Wave.[100] For the works in the exhibition were apparently deliberately badly painted or badly photographed; they used everyday and popular culture images; they copied and were superficial; and they blurred the distinction between high and low culture. Perhaps just as disconcerting was that in conjunction with this de-skilling, the art wore its theory self-consciously and blatantly on its sleeve: it was unapologetically knowing. And theorists were central to the essay's next argument. Heavily indebted to Douglas Crimp's catalogue essay for the famous Artists Space exhibition, 'Pictures' (1977), which was reprinted in *October* in 1979, Taylor noted that the works in the show were all in some way indebted to photography, the medium of the indexical transmission of images and the postmodern theories surrounding photography. Further, the 'act of picturing in these works is the act of referencing and cross-referencing' pre-existing images or images 'borrowed' from an earlier source.[101] The images, he continued, could be seen as a palimpsest, a 'surface that has been written on, erased, and written on again', in the sense that images take on new and different, unintended meanings dependent on reader reception rather than artistic intention.[102] Taylor's essay adopted the terms 'quotation', 'assimilation' and 'appropriation', referring to 'an art which layers meanings on old meanings', and this catalogue essay, over-reliant upon Crimp, was in many ways a first draft for his next major piece of writing, written immediately after he completed 'POPISM', where he began to clearly depart from the reification of New York postmodern art's particular preoccupation with appropriation. In his new essay, 'Popism: the Art of White Aborigines', which appeared in a small Sydney journal not dissimilar to his own, *On the Beach*, Taylor developed the connection between a palimpsest and Australian national culture, with an attendant undercurrent of history, memory and trauma that marked his essay as diverging from Crimp's, which was already years or three more old.[103]

'Popism: the Art of White Aborigines' was written just after the catalogue essay for 'POPISM', but it appeared while the exhibition was still open. It is subtly different from Taylor's catalogue essay. He had modified his earlier, largely received, statements about unoriginality, understanding that originality now occurs as it does in disco, as variations of the original.[104] He had moved on slightly from Crimp. The most significant change, however, was the model he now constructed, heavily indebted to Foss, of Australia as palimpsest. There was, he suggested, no 'real' Australia, just images and representations, 'the flak of an explosion not of our detonation'.[105] That is, the search for a 'regional Australian culture' would always be futile because it does not exist. Australia is uniquely unoriginal and inauthentic because of the circumstances of its definition by others. This had been Paul Foss's argument in 'Theatrum Nondum Cognitorum', but now Taylor reasoned that recent Australian art was taking this world-view as a starting point for its particular quotation or appropriation of images. Australian art, according to 'Popism', was perfectly placed to use the practice of appropriation 'in a carnivalesque array of copies, inversions and negatives'.[106] By taking the idea of an Antipodes and reflecting it through Foss's prism of French theory, Taylor's argument appeared to prise Australian art from the centre/periphery bind. 'In this new scenario', triumphantly wrote Paul Taylor, 'Australian art can become the well-paid beneficiary of its timely, profound and radical superficiality'.[107]

This was an art critical moment when everything seemed to come together perfectly and coherently with powerful explanatory force. Taylor argued that Popist culture included visual art along with fashion and music. He had taken the ideas of subculture from Hebdige and the second degree from Barthes, locating the New Wave at the forefront of pop culture. Foss contributed the third idea, an image more than an argument, that Australia is Europe's complement, a simulacrum of the Great Southern Land. His suggestion that Australia is an idea, existing in a void between map and territory, allowed a corollary: that Australian identity is unauthentic and unoriginal. From there, it was a small step to argue that true unoriginality was uniquely Australian, making Australian appropriation art unique. In a masterly introduction—the best introduction to the Australian spin on theory ever published—for the anthology *What is Appropriation? An Anthology of Critical Writings on Australian Art in the '80s and '90s* (1996), Rex Butler explained that 'Popism' was the inauguration of appropriation in Australia.[108] Butler, himself intellectually shaped by these arguments and the period, noted that →↑→'s performance *Texts* (1979), and Judy Annear's exhibition 'Art in the Age of Mechanical

Reproduction' (1981), both predicated on an understanding of postmodern appropriation, pre-dated 'POPISM'. But, he correctly argued, Taylor was the first to 'give this practice of appropriation its rhetorical charge', making the connection between appropriation and Australian cultural identity.[109]

Taylor's introduction to 'Antipodality', the special section of *Art & Text*, No. 6 (Winter 1982) declared:

> Ours is a multinational, not an international art. The question of our artistic imagination is not a question of national and natural characteristics [...] Our specificity is undermined by our reproducibility, a condition of being nowhere in particular within the multinational image.[110]

Art & Text 6 and *On the Beach*, with Taylor's and his friends' redevelopment of the exhibition's thesis, were in circulation (in numbers that were of course not large) at the same moment as 'POPISM' was on the walls. Now, Taylor was concentrating on Australian identity and antipodality, emphasising that Australian art was *neither international nor national art*: it could stand in for art from anywhere (that is, it quoted from all art) and was therefore truly multinational. To support this claim, 'Antipodality' assembled essays by Imants Tillers, Meaghan Morris and Paul Foss, and photographs by Lynn Silverman, to argue that the problem of 'Australia' was not one of geography and origins, but one of texts and textuality.

The first essay in 'Antipodality' was by artist Imants Tillers.[111] In 'Locality Fails', a much-quoted essay, Tillers began by explaining how Australian artists and writers—and international visitors—had attempted to create an 'indigenous' Australian art by incorporating aspects of Aboriginal art and culture into their work. But the amnesia of late 1970s and 1980s Australian consumerism, heading towards the Bicentennial year, urgently demanded forms of collective memory that could both encompass the world beyond Australia and also the dispossession of Aboriginal people. White Australian works and theorists of the 1970s attempted to construct solutions to the provincial bind, identifying with an Aboriginal Dreaming—a landscape of traces—attempting cross-cultural image making and a link with aboriginality. Apart from Tim Johnson's paintings and Imants Tillers's early canvasboards, the best and most audacious examples were in film. Michael Glasheen's avant-garde video *Uluru: Mythology of the Dreamtime*, 1978, used time-lapse photography, superimpositions, video mixing and rapid montage in a layered, stratified, extravagantly psychedelic twenty-four minute portrayal of Uluru. The work was screened in art house cinemas in Melbourne and Sydney. On the other hand, overseas artists – German artist Nikolaus Lang and London artist collective The Boyle Family came to Australia for the 1979 Biennale of Sydney, visiting the Outback then and on repeat visits to record and painstakingly mimic the strata and textures of the red landscape, with more conventional results. Lang's works attracted negative criticism, Gary Catalano writing, 'his works trespass on the terrain of a host of other disciplines – among them geology, anthropology, geography and archaeology – and effectively trivialize both their objects of inquiry and their procedures'.[112]

Even when this tactic appeared to be successful – and even when it attracted a degree of international attention – it soon became clear that international interest was really going to turn to Aboriginal culture, not the culture of white Australia. Tillers went on to argue that white artists' incorporation of indigeneity could never succeed because 'locality fails'. He eccentrically based his argument against a local Australian art, especially one tied to a particular time and place, upon a scientific theory, Bell's Theorem (1964). Bell's Theorem emerges from the domain of quantum physics. It shows that either the statistical predictions of quantum theory or the principle of local causes is false.[113] The Clauser-Freedman Experiment (1972) confirms, in turn, that the statistical predictions of quantum theory are correct and, therefore, that the principle of local causes is false. Tillers then argued:

> The failure of the principle of local causes implies that there can be unexplained connectedness between events in different 'space-like separated' places and that this connectedness allows for example, an experimenter (e.g., an artist) in one place to affect the state of a system in another remote (apparently unconnected) place. Or this can happen in reverse.[114]

In other words, the development of a genuinely local art is not possible. Even where obvious contact has not taken place, provincial or regional art can be *seen* to be influenced by metropolitan art. Tillers's second point – that influence travels in two directions – was certainly not new. It had been the central premise of Bernard Smith's *European Vision and the South Pacific* (1960). But it was now very important. If accepted, Tillers's argument removed the pervasive taint of provincialism and put Australian art on an equal footing in the world of multinational art simultaneously posited by Taylor.

Taylor, Foss, Morris and Tillers were constructing a theoretical framework that supported an art practice that absorbed and processed existing images, producing new but unoriginal works. This is to say, in a fashion, that appropriation artists *ate* images, in particular those of the North Atlantic canon. *Art & Text*'s theories were an autonomous recapitulation of the Brazilian modernist Oswald de Andrade, who had attempted to orchestrate national identity by proposing in the 1928 'Manifesto da Antropofagia' ('Anthropophagite Manifesto') that all European culture be subsumed by Brazilians, in the same way that ritual cannibalism was a way of gaining strength through the consumption of the enemy's power.[115] Australian and Brazilian culture shared a colonial settler heritage that generated in settler artists a sense of subordinated status, unoriginality and an underlying inadequacy. Paul Taylor's promotion of Australian art as uniquely unauthentic introduced irony to the critical method, exactly as the adoption of cannibalism as a metaphor for cultural exchange had done in Brazil in the 1920s. So, although the eventual aim (the national independence of Australian and Brazilian culture) was always important, the process was not necessarily phrased through straightforwardly legible metaphors. Ridicule is a powerful weapon and, as we have seen, was a key New Wave tactic.

The second essay for 'Antipodality' was by Meaghan Morris, written to accompany photographs by Lynn Silverman.[116] Silverman was a photographer who worked in strict series, commenting on the environment. She had moved from New York to Australia in 1975, and by 1980 was teaching photography at Sydney College of the Arts.[117] Morris's essay starts with a hand-drawn map of Silverman's journey from Port Augusta across South Australia, through outback New South Wales via Bourke and Lightning Ridge to Sydney, and then back through Broken Hill and Tibooburra to Innamincka, Birdsville, Mara and Port Augusta.

The texts' photographs are printed four per page with two accompanying essays: one above the photographs and the other below them. The first essay is a reflection on the desert as a concept of generalised space. It picks up ideas of preconception and myth. Morris wrote, 'The desert is always a pre-existing pile of texts and documents, fantasies, legends, jokes and other people's memories.' She was explaining that the desert did not, and could not, exist apart from what had been read, heard and remembered.[118]

The essay's second idea was the desert as contrast: 'In urban imaginations, that space is *there*—immense, unique, invested with meaning, and rather expensive to tour'.[119] Instead of following the usual trope of characterising the desert as a threatening space, Morris noted the features that might have been threatening but in fact reduced the desert to a tourist destination. The third proposition was also reductive, designed to re-assert the postmodern view as well as to contain the idea of the desert: 'Documented, measured, mapped and crossed, the inland is viewed through a grid of pre-established procedures of possession'.[120] This owed much to Barthes and Baudrillard, but it neither cited nor referred to either; nor did the essay refer to the photographs. The photographs could just as well have been added as illustrations by the designer. The second essay was completely different, beginning with the statement: 'I see Lynn Silverman's photographs as a study in the construction of inland space', in an engaged and personal response to an artwork.

In summary, Tillers and Morris had adopted different approaches to the problem of Australia's place in relation to the rest of the world. Tillers used scientific theories to argue that there was no problem. Australian art was in an equal relationship with world art because 'locality fails' as a barrier. Morris argued, just as Foss had in 'Theatrum Nondum Cognitorum', and as Taylor did in 'Popism: the Art of White Aborigines', that Australia occupied a unique place, distinguished by its unauthenticity and its existence between territory and map. Both writers negated the centre/periphery problem by reconstructing the situation that produced it. These arguments had little in common with Bernard Smith's attempts in the 1950s to convince the scions of the UK art establishment that Australian art had matured and was now vigorous enough to revive flagging British art. Nor with Terry Smith's pleas in 1974 that it was America's responsibility, as the centre of world art, to support and nurture the provinces. Paul Taylor published 'Antipodality' as a defiant statement, as a new approach to the centre/periphery relationship. The approach posited a place for Australian art, and for Taylor, in a postmodern, globalised art world.

Secondary market art dealer and critic Jane Rankin-Reid had begun working in New York galleries in 1981. She was accustomed to assisting visiting Australian artists and art professionals. She met Taylor in Melbourne in 1984 and found that when he relocated to New York shortly afterwards, he was already very attuned to the New York and European art scenes. According to her, he clearly saw himself and was briefly seen as one of the new generation of Australian arts identities, but astutely added, 'Paul's "Australianness" was an unquantified or unquantifiable component for him, New Yorkers didn't care about our pioneering characteristics, they're pretty game themselves after all'.[121] Taylor set up meetings with prominent SoHo galleries for his chosen Australian artists but put considerable effort into promoting Imants Tillers:

> I would say that Paul's most significant contribution around in his first year in Manhattan was in inserting Imants Tillers' work and theories into the Manhattan Appropriation mix. Imants is very retiring but a brilliant thinker (or was, and importantly his work matched his intellectual insight beautifully at that time) and Paul felt strongly that he belonged profile-wise alongside rising stars Sherrie Levine and Richard Prince etc. He went in to bat for Imants in a way that he rarely did for other artists.[122]

Tillers had solo shows in 1984 and 1985 at the Bess Cutler Gallery in New York. Venerable American critic Donald Kuspit reviewed Tillers's work in *Art and America* (March 1985). The review began, 'Taken together, the paintings in this exhibition constitute a super-parody which reveals the limits of the parody: the joke may have been on the joker.'[123] Kuspit had read Tillers's artist's statement – he quoted it in his review – but he simply did not register the *Art & Text*-derived theoretical position – the combination of Second Degree and Antipodality – that it exemplified. In his book, *The Postmodern Art of Imants Tillers*, Graham Coulter-Smith attempts to explain away Kuspit's negative judgement, claiming that the critic confused Tillers's appropriation with a New York deconstructive appropriation to which he was unsympathetic.[124] However, this was not Kuspit's only review of Australian art in that issue of *Art and America*. A few pages earlier, he had written a review, 'Australian Drawings at CDS', an historical overview of Australian drawings curated by American academic resident in Australia, Memory Holloway. In the course of his review, Kuspit mused about what makes Australia so appealing to Americans, linking this to the 'great issues of cultural identity'. He also referred to Holloway's catalogue essay – certainly inflected by *Art & Text* criticism, given Holloway's teaching position at Monash University where Taylor had studied – suggesting that Australian self-analysis had led to 'the disavowal, presumably once and for all, of any clear and distinct meaning to being Australian'.[125] Kuspit thought Holloway's comment was important enough to quote in his review, but he quoted it as an unfortunate development, not as a stunning new approach to Australian art or as a new imperative for art theory. Not only was *Art & Text*'s Antipodality more or less illegible in New York, but locality had failed. Ironically, Tillers was shortly after to begin a long transition in his paintings from the juxtaposition of Aboriginal motifs with quotations from European and American contemporary art towards an unabashedly poetic, metaphoric landscape painting (upon his move to Cooma, near Canberra). These paintings were constructed from quotations from Aboriginal art; they now exemplified a white artist's sincere and heartfelt incorporation of Indigeneity; the Tillers of 1982 would never have accepted them because, still, 'locality fails'. Artist and writer Ian North was to later take up Tillers's revision of 'Locality Fails', suggesting another term again, 'postAboriginality', carefully rebutting the paternalism and essentialist implications of the older term, 'Aboriginalism'.[126] This word had, North explained, been used in literary criticism as a parallel to the idea of Orientalism in order to register a movement of fascination with Aboriginal culture and a denial of Aborigines' right to speak on their own behalf. But 'postAboriginality' still sounded like it implied historical closure. So North coined the word *starAboriginality*. This was an awkward idea, since white Australian art regarded Aboriginality as beyond the cultural pale, avoiding it out of a kind of courtesy while drawing deeply on the landscape's apparent presence and its colonised past. We are arguing that Taylor's writing was in intimate but unintended double dialogue with his historical moment: the Cold War and the looming issue of Indigenous reconciliation. Though there were the overt references to indigeneity and Aboriginality, there was no sense of a debt, a moral responsibility for the dispossession of Aboriginal people.

But through the same, innovative period of *Art & Text*'s appearance and emigration, from 1979 and 1983, Ian Burn, Nigel Lendon, Charles Merewether and Ann Stephen were writing a book that was belatedly published in 1988, *The Necessity of Australian Art: An Essay About Interpretation*.[127] Burn and his co-authors argued that existing interpretations failed to account for many recent developments in Australian art; this was what Donald Brook had been arguing since 1967. But they, unlike Brook, developed a political solution to the problem. They argued that although Bernard Smith's *Australian Painting* had expanded the understanding of Australian art, it had constructed Australian art history within a framework of dependency. That is, Smith's model, which Taylor had absorbed at Monash University, had pioneered the necessity of interpreting Australian art in terms of its dependency on English, European and American art. This 'inhibiting power of the interpretation' resulted in a 'process of cultural devaluation' that Burn and his co-authors set out to address.[128] In a carefully constructed, elaborate argument, they asserted that the dependency explanation was appropriate when it was written, at the early 1960s stage of Australian cultural development, but by the 1980s was no longer useful. They wanted attention to be paid to the often artistically conservative Australian landscape tradition, so that 'the idea of a regional tradition might be reclaimed, thus re-establishing a more complex and richer sense of cultural specificity'.[129] True to their neo-Marxist sympathies, the collective argued that Australian artistic practices should be interpreted 'in terms of a peripheral capitalist formation', and that the significant artistic traditions grew out of a relationship with the land.

In other words, the landscape tradition was fundamental because it reflected the Australian relationship with the land, moving from appropriation to a focus on imagining regional locations, and from there to a national symbolism that embodied a national cultural identity.[130] Their leftist solution continued the Australian Left's deeply conflicted Cold War attempt to reconcile nation with a cosmopolitan ideology. Burn, Lendon, Merewether and Stephen had developed a critical framework for contemporary Australian art that circumvented the centre-periphery dialectic, and in a way this uncannily doubled *Art & Text*'s appeal to subcultural self-sufficiency. But theirs was a historicist framework that was inherently irreconcilable with *Art & Text*'s postmodernist, opportunist Realpolitik, a politics defined and circumscribed by semiotic formalism that thought it understood, as Taylor thought he did, Burn's argument. *The Necessity of Australian Art* was to be influential in the 1990s, and it was a significant, if subliminal, part of sweeping aside the provincialism model that had been so powerfully codified and set in motion by Bernard Smith. It was ultimately more influential than Taylor's essays. But even this was to be subsumed by new understandings about Australian art history in the reception of another landscape tradition altogether, one with a confident conversation with modernity based on cultural equality and semiotic appropriation: the efflorescence of Western Desert painting and the reconsiderations its understanding was to force. This was to gather pace more or less from the 1988 Bicentennial onwards.

Expatriation

With *Art & Text*, an Australian art writer/editor—Taylor—was finally making a carefully calibrated bid to plausibly intervene with Australian-produced art in international art history on terms that rewrote international contemporary art. Whether this was to succeed at all is irrelevant. Rose-coloured recollections of the early 1980s emphasise the iconoclasm of Taylor's alliances. We think this perspective is marked by sentimentality, and underplays the audacity of Taylor's attempt—in collaboration with his friends, including Tillers—to rethink art history's historiography. *Art & Text* was more than a tool for promoting young artists and thumbing his nose at the art establishment. A magazine devoted to young, unknown Melbourne artists, however radical in Australia, was not going to attract international attention. Ashley Crawford remembered that Taylor saw publishing as a power base. From the start, Taylor planned and worked to establish *Art & Text* as an Australia-based but international magazine, to place Australian art and Australian art writing in an international context.[131] Ashley Crawford recalled that Taylor was fascinated by the international stage, always asking why Australia should be such a backwater; no chauvinism there.[132] Jane Rankin-Reid recalled similarly. Asked, in 2005, what *Art & Text* did for Taylor, her reply was instant, 'He developed and used it as his international calling card'.[133] He interviewed famous international theorists and critics including Clement Greenberg and Rosalind Krauss.[134] He co-published 'Double Trouble' with British journal *ZG* (*Art & Text*, No. 15 [Spring 1984] and *ZG* 11 [Summer 1984]).

And then, of course, Taylor moved to New York. The Summer 1984–85 issue, *Art & Text* 16, was co-edited by Paul Taylor and Paul Foss. *Art & Text* 17 listed Foss as the Melbourne-based editor with Taylor as the New York editor. *Art & Text* had applied to the Australia Council for $10,000 to establish a New York office during 1985–86.[135] The application letter reported on the magazine's management restructure: 'This last year has seen the setting up of a New York office and Paul Taylor's relocation, as well as the inauguration of Paul Foss as Melbourne editor and business manager'. The justification for the New York office was as follows:

> This move could be described as one concerning intercultural relations, to aid the dissemination and discussion of Australian art and art criticism in North America and by proximity Europe, and the reciprocal process, to increase the circulation of overseas work in the Australian context and therefore to

help expose in a more effective way the internationalist dialogue currently vitalising art everywhere.[136]

This was a capitulation, a recanting of the carefully constructed bracketing of national art that *Art & Text* had evolved. Worse, it was short-sighted, since at that moment the impact of globalisation was about to become very apparent in the form of contemporary Asian and, in particular, Chinese art to clever collectors, curators and biennale directors. Later in the letter, Foss referred to the 'Double Trouble' issue of *Art & Text* and *ZG*, noting that it gained a record total circulation of 14,000, demonstrating to Taylor and Foss that it was not enough to produce a good art magazine based in Melbourne: there had to be an editorial presence and distribution overseas. When Taylor wrote to Ross Wolfe, Director of the Visual Arts Board of the Australia Council, on April 1, 1985, he had been living in New York for more than six months and was writing for *Vanity Fair* magazine. He wrote that he rejected an 'extremely well-paid offer to be exclusive to the magazine, which pains a little but *Art & Text* comes first'.[137] He repeated this in a postcard from Stuttgart to Wolfe dated January 9, 1986, in which he wrote, 'Am now also working for *Vogue* and *Flash Art* but *A & T* is still #1'.[138] Was he anxious to reassure the VAB that he was committed to *Art & Text* so that they would continue to fund the magazine, including a New York office? Or was he sincerely committed to the magazine he had founded and developed?

The answer to both questions is yes. By *Art & Text* 23/24 (February 1987), Paul Foss was sole editor and the magazine had moved to Sydney. Its office was located at the College of Fine Arts, in inner city Paddington. Taylor continued to support *Tension*, a slightly more populist magazine founded by Ashley Crawford and others in Melbourne in July 1983. *Tension* survived until the 1990 recession, and never genuinely attempted any international reach (though Crawford's later magazine, *Art World*, did; it also attempted a double office – one in Melbourne, one in New York – before its publisher relocated the operation to Amsterdam, where it collapsed). Taylor remained generous with his time to Australian art world visitors to New York and supportive of projects, including *Peripheral Vision* (1995).[139] Although *Art & Text* continued to publish essays on Australian identity and provincialism, most importantly Tillers's 'In Perpetual Mourning' in issue 15 (Spring 1984), and Philip Brophy's 'A Face Without a Place: Identity in Australian Contemporary Art Since 1980' in issue 16 (Summer 1984–5), it was obvious by the later 1980s that the attempt to convince international audiences that Australian art was authentically unauthentic had failed and was already being abandoned, although that same formulation was to dominate Australian art criticism through the writings of Rex Butler and a host of revisionist art historians less significant than Butler through the 1990s; Butler was even to publish an anthology of such attempts at revisionist Australian art history based on white art's inauthenticity and its relationship to black indigeneity.[140] By then, end-of-century globalisation was overtaking the imperative to define art by national categories, even those that were defined by absence or negatives. The end of the Cold War flattened even the national self-definitions of artists in new, post–Cold War nations such as Russia, so that late 1980s Soviet dissident art disappeared from the international art scene, or redefined itself as retro-kitsch, or was rapidly redefined by others, as with Sots Art by luminaries Ilya and Emilia Kabakov and others who relocated to New York, as international art. The 1990s seemed to proceed from postcolonial redefinitions—seen in David Elliott's shows at the Museum of Modern Art in Oxford (UK) during the 1980s, to curator Jean-Hubert Martin's vast and unmistakably landmark survey of world art, *Magiciens de la terre* (Paris, 1989)—that relativised both artistic postmodernism and modernism, criticising attitudes of the West. But seeking to understand the power relationships, manipulations and misunderstandings that occur when regional art enters a Western forum, this art and theory also defined its place in art history through negatives and the absence of affect.

The 1980s wave of globalisation had enabled *Art & Text* to successfully establish a world presence from its base in Melbourne. In the 'anything goes' and 'anything's possible' exuberance of early 1980s boom-time Melbourne, Taylor and the New Wavers were ready to tackle the centre/periphery problem in a new way, through a quasi-postcolonial theory of appropriation. A postcolonial impulse (surfacing in Taylor's *Art & Text* as much as in Burn's and friends' *Necessity of Australian Art*), explains, in retrospect, *Art & Text*'s 1980s attempt to appropriate American and European themes and styles, thus highlighting cultural hybridity, cross-fertilisation and transformation. By 1998, these critical tropes were no longer confined to the periphery. They had become part of a globalised cultural consciousness. And in Australia, indigenous painters managed what Tillers and Davila could not.

The attempt to reconstruct the world-view of Australian art had been overtaken by globalisation. Appropriation as an art practice and the concomitant argument that Australian art was uniquely unoriginal were predicated around a centre/periphery model that had shifted from a Europe/Antipodes dichotomy to a Cold War binary of Left and Right — complicated by the appropriation of cosmopolitanism by the Right and of nation by the Left, and by the assumption that the Right stood for the mainstream and the Left stood for subculture — that was fading during the 1980s and destroyed by the fall of the Berlin Wall in November 1989. The public sentiment surrounding the 1988 Australian Bicentennial signalled a widespread resurgence of interest in mainstream Australian national identity precisely as this identity was validated by subcultural identity politics, both in terms of the appropriation of the images and icons of minority groups and their struggles, and by deviant, atavistic new nationalisms that did not attain any meaningful artistic expression.

For all this — and Paul Taylor's writing — was fatally compromised and weakened by the triumph of late-capitalist globalisation, which was able to contract cultural production out to the periphery so long as distribution was still regulated at the centre. In this sense, 1988 was the end, not the beginning, of the definition of Australian art through nation. This was reflected first in the efflorescence of identity and postcolonial art criticism, especially around indigenous art in the years following the Bicentenary, and in the triumph of indigenous art. We have seen that *Art & Text*'s theory was as much postcolonial as subcultural. Both were then swept aside or suborned by the inclusive meta-culture of globalising biennales. From the end of the Cold War, locality was less and more of an issue than Australians thought: a few hundred metres from one gallery to another in New York or London — the distance in Chelsea from Barbara Gladstone Gallery to Anina Nosei — equally described the distance between centre and periphery.

Before and after *Art & Text* (1988)

Adrian Martin

This is a version of a talk given May 4, 1988 at Theatre Works in the course of the series 'The Present and Recent Past of Australian Art Criticism'. It is dedicated to Philip Brophy.[1]

> Our gaze can fall, not without perversity, upon certain old and lovely things whose signified is out of date. It is a moment at once decadent and prophetic, a moment of gentle apocalypse.[2]
> — Roland Barthes

There can be no doubting that the arrival of *Art & Text* in 1981, under the editorship of Paul Taylor, marked a decisive moment around which everything else, in retrospect, seems to come before or after. Few people or institutions in the Australian art world of the late 1980s can make a move without somehow declaring their sympathy or antipathy towards *Art & Text*. It has become one of those amorphous cultural symbols, like the British journal *Screen* in the 1970s, that people can relate to with enormous certainty, even if they rarely — or never — read it. To smarmy columnists in *The Australian* or the now defunct *Times On Sunday* — swilling around the latest Kundera or Henson or Herzog on their oh-so-cultured palettes — *Art & Text* is always a handy scapegoat: it stands for French Theory, postmodernism, pop culture obsessions; for esoterism, elitism and avant-gardism.

In addition to the arguments that should be had out about the history and meaning of all these words and labels, the simple fact that the magazine is a very different fish today [1988] than it was seven years ago is often conveniently overlooked. So, I am going to concentrate on the first coherent phase of *Art & Text*, from the beginning of 1981 to around the end of 1983, in relation to a particular set of activities in Melbourne.

To me, *Art & Text* in its early days constitutes an 'old and lovely thing' — but, I hope, not too nostalgically. I have no wish to either indulge or disavow my contribution to that period, but I do want to get inside the dream that animated its sense of collective adventure. I prefer the risks of an inside critique to the smug 'I knew what was wrong all along' stance practiced by some prominent outsiders – those who never got their hands dirty or made their mistakes in public, and who like to reduce local specifics to global universals.

The period I am addressing has been called one of 'anything goes silliness'.[3] There is a neutral and culturally specific term for this: what Paul Taylor, in the first history-making article in the first issue of *Art & Text*, called Australian 'New Wave' (the quote marks are his, but I will henceforth drop them).[4] New Wave, perhaps most easily recognisable in its musical form (Blondie, Devo, Kraftwerk, etc.) as a cultural style growing out of and away from punk, is a beast with very particular markings. As a cultural *sensibility* (rather than simply a set of surface stylistic tics and tricks), New Wave is crucially linked to the notion of *subculture* – one of those ideas doomed, post-1983, to dreaded unfashionability. The once-vaunted subcultural resistance of gays, Mods or punks was a matter of their manipulation of cultural signs, their play with conventional and congealed meanings. Unlike some later cults of appropriation, New Wave sustained an open relation to both history and politics – a seriously playful relation.[5]

Taylor attempted a particular gambit with *Art & Text*, beginning with this seemingly innocent remark: 'New Wave music, fashion and visual art comprise a newer subcultural style'.[6] The sleight-of-hand in that sentence involves the smuggling of Art – 'visual art' – into a subcultural arena which is not, first and foremost, devoted to art, and is basically opposed to institutional frameworks like the art world. Subculture is one of the privileged places where people have tried to observe and theorise what Michel de Certeau calls the creative practices of everyday life, like gossip, jokes, dressing, walking around, and so on. New Wave, with its particular accent on flamboyant style, would seem to incorporate art as simply a natural extension of such everyday practices; indeed, it reawakens the dream of snatching artistic creativity back from its increasingly reified and autonomous state (i.e., Art is what is done by Artists from Art School). The artists and writers Taylor drew upon had already (sometimes intuitively) made the link between art and subcultural style in the late 1970s: the band/collective →↑→ played in the first official Melbourne punk events; Jenny Watson painted portraits of The Boys Next Door members.

The initial dream of *Art & Text*, it seems to me, was to *create* a specific subculture – a proud and exciting swell of activity in the *margin* of dominant culture, and of the art world institution. Taylor's singular and largely unprecedented intuition was that such a margin could be systematically pieced together from a large range of people and practices — that an alliance, however temporary and unstable, could be formed. It was a dream that indeed floated for a little, precious while. But one of the reasons it could not last forever, or indeed for very long, was that, from the start, *Art & Text* was haunted by the tension between two forces. On the one hand, the dream-force that was trying to pull Art back into Life, to fuse them into a living art, an art of life; and on the other, an institutionalising force that inexorably kept reducing everything that was going on to simply Art, i.e., paintings on gallery walls, government-funded publications, and suchlike.

It should never be overlooked what a ragtag of people were involved in this first phase of *Art & Text* — nor how, at its limits, the magazine could occasionally accommodate the contributions of those who would never be identified as *Art & Text* types (e.g., Patrick McCaughey, Donald Brook, Warren Burt, Julie Ewington). The ragtag included some (like Meaghan Morris and the subsequent editor of the magazine, Paul Foss) who were, and have basically remained, non-art in their orientation — a consistently irritating factor to art world purists of the *Art & Australia* ilk. The *Art & Text* alliance was formed under the sign of *bricolage* and experimentation — based more on the loose and shifting 'family resemblances' between different people and their interests (whether New Wave, film theory, Australian cultural studies, specific areas within French philosophy, or any combination thereof), than a hard and fast platform with its philosophical roots deep inside any one, particular tradition. Often pegged from a distance as academic, the magazine in fact boasted a remarkable range of writers from the model institutional academic (dogged, relatively well paid) to the non-, semi-, anti-, and disaffacted academic: to put this another way, it was the realm of the *freelance* (snobs prefer to say *public*) *intellectual*.

It was the goodwill of the members of this ragtag that allowed *Art & Text* to sail as the public flagship of new writing, new theory, marginal culture. It should always be remembered that in fact, probably for all these raggers (and perhaps particularly those with a foot in the New Wave project), the magazine was never really thought of as a *central* site for activity — just one site among very many. If it seems more central in retrospect than it was at the time, simply because it continues to float to the surface where other things have fallen to the ocean bed, we need to adjust our perspective accordingly. One cannot get the historical measure of *Art & Text*, or grasp its spirit, without properly surveying the whole scene of which it was a part—smaller magazines like *The Virgin Press* (later *Tension*), *Cantrills Filmnotes*, *Slug*, *New Music* and *Zerox*; musical and performance work at popular venues and specialised ones like the Clifton Hill Community Music Centre; mail art ventures; posters; fashion shows; program notes; Super-8 films; independent records ... *Art & Text* looks clean, it has lasted, continued and evolved; but, at the start, it lived in a dialectical relationship with all that other work which was often framed in a freeform, messy, ephemeral way.

Re-reading *Art & Text* today, detached from that general context, one can too easily miss what constitutes the veritable *episteme* of the early 1980s, at least for New Wavers: *bricolage*, experimentation, what Philip Brophy once called *militant dilettantism*. Hence the necessity for some of us, at the time, to try everything at once, several kinds of theory alongside several kinds of practice, as a way of radically refusing the ideology of specialisation, authority, professionalism. One cannot really overplay, even in retrospect, the liberating, 'dreams come true' force of this glorious moment of cultural *amateurism* for those who partook in it. The lessons and dreams of amateurism seem lost to us today, in these upwardly mobile, normalised times. At stake in militant dilettantism was precisely that tantalising fusion and revitalisation of those mutually Lost Worlds of Art and Life—an aspiration made abundantly clear in the wholly non-ironic 'Manifesto for a Renewed Art Practice 1980' by John Nixon, which appeared in the second issue of *Art & Text*:

> 'MUSEUMS ARE THE CEMETARIES OF DEAD ART'
>
> 'THE *REAL ART* OF THE 1980'S IS ADVERTISING, TV, MAGAZINES, FILM, RECORDS, CLOTHES, MUSAK, SUPERMARKETS, NEWSPAPERS, JETS, SPORT, DISCOS'
>
> 'DRINK IT ALL IN!'
>
> 'WE MUST BEGIN TO REFLECT OUR DAILY LIVES—THE HAPPINESS, THE SADNESS, THE JOY, THE PAIN, THE TURMOIL, THE HOPE, THE ANGUISH, THE ROMANTICISM'
>
> 'LIFE IS ART!'[7]

Before going any further with the dream of *Art & Text*, I want to lay down a few of the material parameters of the local New Wave moment – the personnel, the key sites. As I see it, the specific 'Melbourne alliance' organised by Taylor drew from two main groupings: an Art Projects grouping and a Clifton Hill one.[8] The first (named after Art Projects gallery) has its roots in the conceptual and minimalist art of the 1970s. Its protagonists include: John Nixon, Jenny Watson, Peter Tyndall, John Dunkley-Smith, Imants Tillers, Lyndal Jones, Ania Walwicz, Mike Parr, Tony Clark and Richard Dunn. The Clifton Hill grouping (named after the aforementioned Community Music Centre) includes: Philip Brophy, Maria Kozic, Ralph Traviato [later Traviati], Jane [later Jayne] Stevenson, David Chesworth, Andrew Preston, Rolando Caputo, Paul Fletcher, Ian Cox, Robert Goodge, Kim Beissel and myself. Each grouping had a central site for activity, plus a host of more ephemeral sites. As *Art & Text* emerged, and the two groupings began to mix or occasionally collaborate, other players came to share a mediating position alongside Taylor: among them, Juan Davila, Vivienne Shark LeWitt and George Paton Gallery director of that time, Judy Annear. (We must bracket off here a more social history of the Melbourne scene that would mention many lesser-known names – people who are no less central to the life and spirit of a cultural moment despite being less obviously 'productive' as artists or writers.)

It would be possible to chart, quite carefully, the rhizome of family resemblances which enabled these actants to enter into exchange: areas of concern that, pragmatically, provisionally, could immediately allow more similarity than difference – all for the sake of forming a necessary alliance against those hostile Others lurking everywhere else. Of course, internal differences became clearer later. But, for a while, the key terms of the program worked. Strategies of minimalism; a feverish interest in theorising popular culture; new possibilities for a radical art practice; the desire to marry theory and practice; an experience of subcultures – these ingredients went into the glue that held together, for the fleeting moments of their existence, assemblages like the 'POPISM' show at the National Gallery in 1982.

Despite the trying on of many ideas in passing, it is not hard to trace a fairly consistent and coherent system across Taylor's major editorial statements of what *Art & Text* was for and against. It was against the infamous Romantic notion of the artist as unique origin, bearer of a vision, a tormented soul. Of course, this was not news; all progressive currents in art thinking and practice dating from the 1960s and '70s (Marxist, feminist, conceptual, etc.) were similarly opposed to this hoary old myth – to the extent that one wonders how anybody, these days, would even want to be an Artist in that devalued sense anymore. Yet *Art & Text* took the opposition to expressive artwork of any sort even further. It adopted an extreme, carnivalesque response: in place of the artist as *creator*, suddenly the artist as *tinkerer* (*bricoleur*) was extolled, whose function is essentially that of collecting and combining different pre-given fragments. In place of the artist as pristine Self – who felt, reflected, struggled to express – stood the artist as invaded, divided, decentred self, a pure surface crossed by cultural flows, a mere effect of everything around him or her. Hence the proud, oft-derided, more-or-less poststructuralist slogan of the time: *I do not speak, I am spoken*.

Instead of the Artist, the New Wave cultural moment proposed (as much in disco music as in artwork) the principal figure of the *producer* or *mixer* who originated nothing, but tinkered furiously with pieces – pieces of thought or theory as much as aesthetic forms and mass-cultural signs. This is why it was quite natural and logical for Taylor – who endured much abuse as a careerist – to sometimes elevate the curator or the magazine editor above the Artist; for these producers did the really elaborate staging, whilst art was sometimes only a prop. And what is wrong with that?

Anything goes: the catchcry was adapted, by quite different agents simultaneously, from Paul Feyerabend's *Against Method* (1975) – a greatly misunderstood, almost already forgotten, but visionary book. (Taylor was proud to nab a long text by Feyerabend, 'Science as Art', for *Art & Text*, Nos 12/13.) The term conjured the idea of a great flux of materials from which one could pick, more or less, at will. And then came the combination of these fragments: the (far from smooth) mixing, superimposing, layering. This process formed (as we said at the time, with the words of Gilles Deleuze and Félix Guattari) machines, assemblages or multiplicities. Again, the idea of the ephemeral, the never settled, the provisional. Knowledge as a toolbox with variably workable bits and pieces; not the 'hard theory' which critics often projected onto the magazine (usually in order to then object, with disdainful academic superiority, that it finally was not hard *enough*, that it was theoretically incoherent).[9] The idea of anything goes, understood generously, meant the free, open possibility of *experimentation*: not the amoral, potentially unethical attitude of 'you can *do* anything', but the suspended, anticipatory cry of '*try* anything!' Of course, there was a limit to this dream, which we shall reach in due course, but it is important to remind ourselves of its attractiveness and force at particular historical moments or conjunctures.

The Art-is-Life stance of the New Wave sensibility presupposed a quite specific definition of the cultural space of the West: culture as a total environment, a fabulous array of surfaces to be worn, of moveable units, constellating in an eternal present. Mass produced, popular culture provided the terms for all cultural and intellectual experience: a matter of immediate consumption and dizzy turnover, of endless flow, mutation, self-regeneration. More than ever, culture became an autonomous realm, its variable and multiple effects ridiculing all bygone theories of economic or superstructural determinism (especially as derived from Marxist theory) – and the equally variable responses of the so-called masses seemed unknowably wild, diverse or perverse. New Wave revelled in the definition of popular culture as consisting of flat, artificial, plastic units easily lifted and combined: disco beat, comic strip, Polaroid photograph. This is the *photo-rhetoric* that, for Taylor as critic-curator, informed 'POPISM'.

It is useful to distinguish a few particular anything-goes practices. There was, first, a practice with its roots in the 1970s, dedicated to an analysis of power relations in the art institution and beyond, via the incisive *montage* of collected fragments: think of Peter Tyndall's vast oeuvre, Richard Dunn's use of seriality and juxtaposition, Lyndal Jones's multimedia *Prediction Pieces* or Juan Davila's quotational frescoes.[10] In relation to the more conventional political art of the 1970s, such work had an extra edge of irony, intractability, extremism or outrageousness. (It duly became, alas, more like the official political art of the late 1980s, taking care to distance itself from the directionlessness of a demonised anything-goes stance.)

Second, anything-goes with a pointedly irrational, overridingly poetic, sometimes quite mystical orientation: reveries of a new order of time and space, a world of alchemical (not historical) causalities floating free, fragments coming to rest on the multiple, superimposed layers of the picture frame. Hence Imants Tillers's and John Young's pictures of 'worlds in collision' where 'locality fails'. Terry (later Terence) Blake's magnificent writing is an important reference point here, with its eyes for both traditional Eastern philosophies and recent theories of our new world (Jean-François Lyotard, Deleuze and Guattari, Michel Serres).[11] Popular culture enters this swirling pool of floating particles in the collages of Zerox Dreamflesh (Tim Pigott, Will Soeterboek, George Alexander), and the films and writings of Mark Titmarsh. *Art & Text* incorporated only a fraction of this sensibility; it found a home mainly post-'83, in issues of *On the Beach*, *Limit of Maps*, *Tension* and the various Dreamflesh publications (*Zerox*, *Cargo*).

Third, and somewhere in between the first two, an anything-goes practice with a particular investment in popular culture – betting on the gains of theoretical experimentation, and yet resisting the pull into total cultural hyperspace. Thus, the work of →↑→ ('What Is This Thing Called Disco?'), or my own early writing, dances between a distanced analysis of the forms and protocols of popular culture – keeping open the possibility of charting a real history and steering a valid cultural politics – and pure, undetermined, resolutely individualist fascination, celebration.[12] This was perhaps the fine and risky dialectical tension which drove the New Wave sensibility in its moment of greatest glory – a dialectic which was to *give* (in the sense of the famous song lyric, 'Something's Gotta Give') in varied and interesting ways.

One should also note in passing a fourth voice in the early *Art & Text*, a steadily growing undertone destined for a later moment of glory: a nihilistic, anti-idealistic, witheringly critical voice, beyond the charms of both '70s-style radical politics and '80s-style anything-goes experimentation. Ted (later Edward) Colless and David Kelly's 'Lost World' series is the major expression of this sentiment, backed up by Jody Berland's 'Popular Music and the Post-Pop Avant-Garde'[13] – wearily exposing all dreams (popular culture, subculture, neo-avant-gardism, marginality) as so many historically induced shams ... I do not dream, I am dreamt, I am merely a symptom of the social! We shall return to this line of attack.

Jean Baudrillard once asked: 'Is Pop an art of consumption?'[14] Insofar as New Wave is self-professedly a continuation or restatement of the Pop Art impulse, the answer is unashamedly: yes. New Wave is characteristically the province of the white, urban leisure-class – not necessarily wealthy or even particularly comfortable, but drifting in that strange historical condition which is our own, in a country like this, where class and privilege seem to have disappeared (I stress *seem*, as in an optical illusion), and a democratic, consensus culture devolves its material benefits upon most (?) of us. New Wave goes the way of subculture, not counterculture. It assumes dominant or parent culture as the umbrella of reality, and it makes sport as best it can within that shadow. Consumption is not robotic but obsessive: it cuts creative trails through a culture of objects both shiny-brand-new (12-inch import records) and functionally obsolescent (op shop bric-à-brac), and the society of the spectacle (film, TV). New Wave rests, fundamentally, on the dream that the space of mass media experience can be expanded to infinity – that, for all intents and purposes, nothing else exists.

Allowing this rhetorical expansion is the intuition – a very powerful one – that a New Wave sensibility is necessary to come to terms with a New World, a world utterly and fabulously different from anything that has been comprehended before (particularly by media sociologists). The hunch gets a nod of assent from very high up: it is a key theme of Umberto Eco's book *Travels In Hyperreality* (also known as *Faith in Fakes* of 1986). The *Weltanschauung* of New Wave – elaborated subsequently (beginning in 1983) under the name of postmodernism – seizes on all that has become mad, hyperreal, undecidable and entirely relative; a New World of inscrutable appearances beyond truth. And also beyond the unity of a shared history or a common social formation: New Wave emphasises the diagnosis of social fragmentation to the point of declaring that every individual can constitute his or her own unique subculture.

One of the problems inherent in holding to a New World position is the eagerness with which one then sneers at and excludes from debate anyone who is judged as not yet having caught up with the pulse of hyperreality. It is as if, in declaring itself and its identity, any emerging cultural sensibility falls prey to grandiosity – an inevitable part of which is enemy-baiting. Very soon after the start, *Art & Text* and its 'scene' had two handy enemies pegged in its sights. The first enemy was, in retrospect, perhaps an unwise but a polemically necessary choice (it could not have happened any differently); the second enemy is still nasty and horrible and still at large.

Art & Text made short work of many countercultural enemies – among them magazines like *Art Network* and *Lip*. Cast off opportunistically into the Old World, and tainted with the brush of institutionalisation and dogmatism, was most '70s leftist art. 'Hard' semiotic cultural theory – considered hopelessly dim-witted, old-fashioned, puritanical and repressive – was similarly laughed at, creating a great divide between the Marxism and/or feminism of *Block*, *Screen* or *Local Consumption* and the wicked, clever delights of New Wave. *Art & Text*, underwritten by a massive dose of super-individualism, revelled in an almost irrational, *de rigueur* disdain for 'message' art, community art, artworkers' collectives ...

Inhabiting the Mad Western World projected by New Wave, Taylor reached the point of declaring that, since 'reference between the image and both the perceived world and social action is severed', then 'that which had previously been radical, the left-wing, is powerless'.[15]

Briefly, the situation panned out with the eventual realisation that there was more in common between these warring parties, and that the real enemy to be ganged up against was elsewhere: basically where it had always been, in the echelons of high culture. In some sense, the New World reverie blinded a few of us for a while to the fact that some things just never change—like *Art & Australia*, *Art Monthly* and *The Age Monthly Review*. Again and again, the various platforms of a deathlessly conservative high culture position are hammered into place in the pages of these publications: the at-arm's-length treatment of mass culture as the place par excellence of barbarism (as in the writing of Jacques Delaruelle and John McDonald); the suspicious treatment of almost any new art; the reduction of all Great Works to matters of the artist's biography and noble aesthetic emotions; utter cynicism displayed towards any form of *artspeak* (terrible term) that wavers for a single moment from the task of maintaining and flattering the institutions of Art, Artist and Art world.

In the brief period I am encircling with a story, the New Wave dream—the fusion of art and life in a mass media space expanded to infinity—eventually cracked up. It did so due to both internal tensions and external attacks. For such a fragile, provisional ensemble, this much was indeed inevitable, and not particularly lamentable. Let us begin with perhaps the most general factor. *Art & Text* was doomed from the start to reach the exhausted limit of its dominant New Wave tone: that of naughtiness, cheek, delinquency. One cannot live forever on irony, indirection, and a particularly ruthless and superior stance of playfulness (always more playful than the last gamesman); as Dick Hebdige wisely remarked on these fatal shores in 1987, 'irony is sometimes not enough; irony is sometimes what's wrong'.[16] The cheek surrounding the magazine—particularly in Taylor's more outrageous and provocative pronouncements—would take much space to document, and is perhaps better left to the ephemeral bittersweetness of personal recall; let me merely cite my personal favourite, the occasion when, upon being charged from the floor at yet another art forum to 'speak for himself', Paul replied, completely unfazed, that he would 'rather speak for everyone else'!

Six crack-up points beginning near the end of the 1983 period:

1. The anything-goes philosophy eventually slid — one of its potential in-built fate-lines — from buoyed-up experimentation to easy *indifference* — which became one of the keywords of the following Baudrillardian period (1984–7). The shrug of acquiescence, the 'who cares?' stance... This inflection of anything-goes took its cue from the Warholian tactic of *hyperconformism*: simulating, like a chameleon, whichever superpowers were in the vicinity — big business, the art world, the New Right, you name it. A decadent reflex took over: some let the call of tradition and convention seduce them (it was all such a game!), and that weird, undecidable hybrid *neo-classicism* (Tony Clark-style) rolled into the alternative art spaces. Paul Taylor, on the cutting edge of this bizarre conversion with the 'Tall Poppies' show of 1983, made quasi-Fascist jokes, on the fickle New Wave principle of 'if that's what they call me, then that's what I'll pretend to be'. Which is another of those games that cannot be played forever.

2. The interest in popular culture was appropriated in a few different directions. To some extent, it was simply co-opted as a cute, new novelty by the art world, which came no nearer to actually understanding it, or getting hands dirty in its deeply collective contradictions. Pop became — one more time — a superficial, optional ingredient in art school practice (note the reception accorded Keith Haring on Australian shores in 1982). To those who were popular culture's true connoisseurs, a more deeply felt contradiction emerged: the problem of maintaining oneself as a commentator on popular culture, somehow both inside and outside it, without simply turning it into a metaphor, *intellectualising* it beyond all recognition. Why not — another mode of indifference — just let the culture flow, and us flow into it, mutely? Baudrillard's argument about the sublime apathy of the silent majority made its mark here, for a while (with me, it resulted in a nine month writer's block).

3. From the start of the *Art & Text* moment, there was a tension in play between the figures of the amateur — the dilettante trying to get out of his or her pristine Self — and the canny producer or mixer who didn't have to travel very far to become a full-blown operator or entrepreneur. The amateur held on for as long as possible to both the romance and reality of marginality (living on the edge), whilst the operator was keen to get upwardly mobile. The New Wave obsession with style, and being stylish at all costs, naturally constituted a splitting point here: following the trail of creative consumption to the likes of the Fashion Design Council left a few dags like me floundering well behind; the op

shop lost its all-embracing power. When Jenny Watson remarked in early 1984 that the model 'mid-'80s artist' was at the same time 'poor' and 'fashionable', it was not yet a contradiction in terms.[17] But, as a popular TV ad of the time promised: *it won't happen overnight, but it will happen!*

4. Sneering at all rigidified orthodoxies, real or invented, in the vicinity, it was also inevitable that *Art & Text* would end up being pegged itself as no less rigid or orthodox. It is probably the fate of any magazine or event that receives a relatively generous subsidy in a small scene (everyone desperately wanting a piece of funding action) to be eventually or immediately labelled as part of the 'establishment'. *Art & Text* courted this charge through its immaculate cleanness as a publication, its comfortable cut-off points (boasting an editorial 'preference for creative texts', but publishing no fiction or poetry), and its general policy favouring a certain select group of artists (again, in a small scene, funded magazines are called upon to represent everyone else who can't get funding or exposure—a ridiculously unreasonable complaint that scarcely understands the flow of movements within marginal culture). This exclusivity on several fronts explains the need for gestures like the 1982 parody *Art & a Texta*—wilder and freer gestures than *Art & Text* could by that stage allow. In a less combative way, the loose-leaf *Stuff* (begun 1983) was a related attempt to return to the looseness, immediacy and ephemerality largely expunged from the pages of *Art & Text*.

5. There was always a sound leftist political critique of *Art & Text*[18]—but it was usually voiced with an ungenerous and only partial understanding of why the magazine's protagonists were driven to say what they said. (One should always try to understand the *forces* at play in a statement—another more or less poststructuralist lesson—alongside, or above, evaluating its ultimate truth-value.) On the plane of cultural theory, *Art & Text* was reacting badly to heavily determinist theories of ideology and subjectivity, such as those that derived from the Ayatollah Althusser. There was a perceived gap, on the part of those who took up arms against this determinism, between the postulated iron-clad structures of the social order and the messy, squiggly, heterogeneous explosions of everyday experiential reality (with which publications like *Screen*, well into the '80s, were still only fitfully catching up). The response was to go as far as possible in the opposite direction—total undetermination by history, politics, gender, class, money...—in order to describe, for the first time, so it seemed, potential *free spaces* in a hoped-for Utopia of everyday life.

All the favourite theorists of the time offered rapturous descriptions of ideal, dream states easily adaptable to this task—like the unfettered rhizomes and becomings of Deleuze and Guattari. The risks and limits of this move are much clearer in hindsight, of course; then, in the heat of it, we simply had to shove a few new items on the agenda of cultural analysis (I think we half succeeded). In this sense, the work of *Art & Text* in this period was less true than driven, symptomatic—but that may well be true of all work, all art, all cultural production and all writing.

6. From the dream of subculture, *Art & Text* drew a particular model of resistance—not armed or oppositional, but sly, evasive, *cool*. Indeed, we can speak of a big, powerful Myth of Cool—a well of resistance often undetected by society itself, but vitally known to its membership. Everyday cool comprises all those games we variously play in the shadow of the authorities, institutions and powers that be. In what is, for me, the finest and most significant article ever to appear in *Art & Text*, Bill (a.k.a. William D.) Routt gave perhaps the best description of this cool:

> It would seem that what I have called 'the aesthetic of the cool' proposes [...] a culture of evasion, privileging object over subject, moving over looking. In such a never-never land, aesthetic works would wear their souls on their sleeves. They would be garish and offensive. They would be evanescent, stroboscopic—everywhere and nowhere.[19]

Much of the New Wave sensibility is wonderfully encapsulated in these words, which make me proud to recall here what I was part of—even if it was a never-never land. Yet Routt's article induces a very troublesome, niggling self-doubt—for what he is describing is in fact *black* culture, not the tinkerings of those he curtly dubs the 'white avant-garde'. The New Wave fantasy has its good (Utopian) side, but also its bad side: it is in one sense a classically colonialist fantasy, a white boy's and girl's daydream of being dispossessed and oppressed, 'submerged and rioting',[20] and hence more fully, more stylishly *alive*. Not that this generation is more particularly disposed towards colonialist fantasies than any other; it is more that, having missed out on the spectacular politicisation afforded earlier artworkers by Vietnam or November 1975, there was nothing else to do but *invent* a state of oppression and resistance, and pose (with uneasy humour) as 'white aborigines'.

Before and after *Art & Text*: the story concerns not only the life and death of a special cultural moment, but the general state of art culture – the function of magazines, the role of theory, the use of expanded discussion lifting off from art. Personally, I would have to say that, if all *Art & Text* has achieved, then or now, is the furnishing of a few cute, novel ways to surround art with an aura in catalogue essays, then it has hardly been worth anyone's effort. So-called artspeak – the opportunistic attachment of a work of art to a proud, preening, purely fashionable display of 'in' buzzwords, saying only that the writer is very, very clever – is not the invention of *Art & Text*. Gushing aesthetes and moral ideologues practice artspeak in the pages of our most respected journals, as much as those bright young things out sometimes merely to dazzle in the smaller magazines. Doubtless there has always been, and always will be, bad writing, merely obscurantist or show-off prose – just as there will always be rarified Fine Arts or Lit Crit odes to Bill 'Lux et Nox' Henson, or whomever. If that is what constitutes artspeak, then I really could not care less about it.

But I do care about speaking – and thinking. There is never a shortage of important, serious matters to speak and think about out there in the real world. If art can be used any time to focus one of these issues, that is great – that is what criticism and theory are, or should be, in the first and last instance, all about. If *Art & Text* has succeeded in making this point loud and clear, and if it has provided a few working examples of expanded criticism (as I believe it has), then something has certainly been achieved. If not...

Art & Text has, inevitably, borne the brunt of the charge of initiating and spreading too-specialised, elitist languages for the discussion of art and further matters cultural. Again, such a charge rests on a few standard preposterous assumptions: that specialised languages have never previously ruled art culture (not to mention the sciences); and that there is some plain, common language readily available, if only critics would use it. Yet, if I learnt just one thing that was more reality than dream in the early *Art & Text* days – the days when one read about the Autonomia movements in Italy, listened to 3RRR, and watched the proliferation of youth subcultures outside the front door – it was simply this: that there are many languages, high and low, left and right; that they overlap and correspond with each other in strange and sometimes wonderful ways; that they chatter in a modern social space which is indeed an extremely fragmented one. The Mania of the All – the fantasy of One mass audience, of a single common language – belongs, in fact, to those who never want to get too serious or passionate about anything (not even Art), who would rather placidly unify us all around an illusory centre than enter into division over what might really be at stake at any given moment, or in any given gesture. The great film critic Serge Daney once said it so well: around an image, the role of the critic should be to divide, not to unite.

Something needs to be said here in defense of that much abused trope of recent critical discourse: *rhetoric*. If you ever want to damn any given piece of artspeak, try calling it 'mere rhetoric'; the applause will not be far behind. Rhetoric has been painted by many (such as plainspeaking David Bromfield) as a principle Bad Thing: it stands for empty, mystificatory word play, pure form without content, performance without substance ... as if there could be a kind of writing that touches directly the things of which it speaks, and engages in acts of pure communication. As for myself, I have always considered writing to be an extremely complex movement of references, effects, affects, rhythms and structures. When a piece of writing is pretending to (for instance) point at a painting, it is nothing *but* rhetorical: it tells stories, conjures scenes, creates relations, and generally engages in what Umberto Eco calls *effects of sense*.

This is why some of the best writing in *Art & Text* has enraged so many art-types; for it dares to *mobilise* art in the service of a work of rhetoric that is shooting for an altogether different (or more expansive) destination. Such is the gauntlet that the magazine has helped lay down: how to move *through* art, sometimes past it when necessary, to somewhere really significant. In this sense, *Art & Text* continues to say to art culture that anything goes ... and that everything remains to be spoken.

Let us pick up the *Art & Text* story just after the crack-up point of 1983. To where did the dreamers scatter? Where did their dreams go?

1. Upmarket, in the case of *The Virgin Press* become *Tension* — into the waiting embrace of the art world (Brett Whiteley on the cover of issue 11, 1987: 'I can no longer dismantle my art from my disease...'); or the pop music industry, as with Essendon Airport become I'm Talking. Overseas, in Paul Taylor's case, to pursue a style of aggressive art world fashion journalism (who's in, who's out in New York). Onto the funding merry-go-round for all those once-marginal artists all too easily (perhaps even against their will) co-opted and highlighted as the current art stars (the so-called and much pilloried *avant-garde academy*). In short: Yuppieville.

2. Downmarket, back to making gestures with no immediately apparent financial return or cultural response; cries in the

wilderness. *Stuff*, succeeded by *Stuffing*. A recovery from the momentary muteness induced by popular culture, and the researching of new ways to speak about it across the broken and overlapping lines of marginal cultures: in fanzines, on public radio, through teaching. In short: serious cultural action somewhere between Nowhereville and a terrain that is only slowly coming into existence.

3. Intellectually, a few lines-of-flight always lurking in the 1981–3 period streak forth: dandy-nihilism for some (the denizens of Sydney Super 8, for instance), taking only the world-weary tone without engaging the angry polemic of their fathers Baudrillard, Colless and Kelly; a quasi-religious art-mysticism for others (Parr, Nixon). After Sydney's 'Futur*Fall' conference in 1984, postmodernism muddles everything for at least five years to come, including any widely discernible difference between the former group's gestures of irony and the latter's gestures of faith (see them tangle in the pages of *On the Beach* circa 1987). An endless show of paradox slowly moving around the perimeter of a circle: Alphaville.

And what of *Art & Text* itself under the very different editorship of Paul Foss from late 1984 on? From the viewpoint of my narration of the story, the new picture appears both as a great resurgence and as what Barthes called a 'gentle apocalypse'. As to the gains, the magazine has effectively managed to re-tap the energy of marginal culture, in the form now of those subcultures considered unfashionably radical, with less box-office style appeal: gay, black, Latin American. Foss is more conscious of the political traps of acquiescence and indifference, and avoids them. He draws in what is, without doubt, the best writing being done in this country, true models of *expanded criticism* provided by Meaghan Morris, Ross Gibson, Eric Michaels, George Alexander, and Paul himself. But on the apocalyptic side, the theory aspect of the magazine has become harder, less open and experimental, more respectfully French; the popular culture angle and feel has been largely lost; and, basically, anything-goes does not seem such a possibility, any longer, for a broad range of tinkerers.

I experienced my own moment of not-so-gentle apocalypse a long time ago, in 1982, right in the middle of the New Wave adventure. I gave a talk during 'POPISM' titled, appropriately, 'Living on the Surface'.[21] It tried to articulate the art/life, media/subjectivity dream, with total optimism and bravado. Not many days later, I do not believe I was hallucinating when I found myself to be the subject of a typical Michael Leunig cartoon in *The Age*: a wan Everyman, entirely oblivious to cold reality, standing on his head (having thrown himself off from atop a road sign pointing alternately to Something and Nothing), mumbling to himself about the fusion of Art and Life...

And so, what to do? Embrace realism? Nihilism, even? Admit the emptiness of all Utopian dreams? After 1983, the particular dream which was New Wave indeed passed away. Sure, anything-goes reappeared, elsewhere – most gloriously in the *Semiotext(e) USA* special of 1987 – but without art, film, TV or pop music.

Is it, then, merely nostalgic to recall the early 1980s as I have done here? Something insists in my brain: not nostalgia, but the desire to refuse this deadly position of 'the dream is over, the era is closed', which usually expresses itself as 'we grew older, we moved on, we got real' – the alibi of all those who have moved up to Yuppieville. (Nanni Moretti's films, in the Italian context, have great fun with these deadly, Yuppie justifications.) I am wary of too strong a demarcation between dream and reality – leading to a won't-get-fooled-again, no-bullshit cynicism beyond any idealism. Such an attitude leaves criticism with only half its work to do: the exposé of romance, myth and platitude whenever and wherever it appears. Yet this stance, it seems to me now, depends on its own, novelistic form of romance: *fatalism*.

Why assume that the dream of any cultural moment – be it Surrealism, punk or New Wave – is merely a fleeting, hallucinatory, youthful interruption in the channel of hard reality, doomed to almost immediate extinction? Of course, situations change and new gestures arise in response to them. Yet, what was symptomatically expressed in the early days of *Art & Text* – the desire for a liberating amateurism, the need to intellectually tinker in a cultural margin, the attempt to feel out the co-ordinates of our contemporary media landscape, the urge to fuse art and life – do not such energies and hunches *underlie* the surface of cultural exchanges, almost constantly?

Perhaps scenes do burn themselves out, and moments do come to an end. But that only means that we will have to look elsewhere, and anew, to find where the dream reasserts its force.

Mass media images recycled in Popism (1982)

Robert Rooney

First published in The Age, *June 23, 1982, Arts, 14.*

The Vietnam War, it has been said, was fought in living rooms of the world via television's instant and saturated coverage of its prolonged history.

The Falkland Islands conflict, as seen on TV, was, by contrast, a curiously distant affair, which was made even more remote by the lack (until now) of important film from official British sources.

This situation forced TV news sources – such as film shot by amateurs and Argentine cameramen, and file film of navy exercises – to match the spoken reports of overseas commentators with suitable visual images.

The TV coverage of the Falkland Islands War made it, for me, into a war of representation. One in which visual images were suppressed, labelled, or appropriated and recycled as stand-ins for its disasters and triumphs.

It is, as we shall see, a useful model for understanding the techniques and ideas behind many of the works in the exhibition
39 'Popism', at the National Gallery of Victoria.

If Popism's 14 artists and groups – selected by Paul Taylor, the editor of 'Art and Text' – have anything in common, it is in the areas of representation, reproduction and the appropriation of images from mass media (TV, newspapers, magazines and books) and popular culture (music and movies).

The use of quotation from existing visual and sound materials gives the works of these artists a cool irony and distance that is at odds with the current epidemic of neo-expressionism, which, as one critic suggests, is now the most acceptable international idiom for contemporary art.

In this way it is often closer to minimalism and conceptual art in its resistance to the self-indulgence and diaristic excesses of much present-day art.

The artists in Popism do not respect the sovereignty of one medium over another. They are likely to use conventional mediums such as painting, drawing and screenprints, as well as music, photography, film and performance (in its more detached forms).

This is true of the work of Richard Dunn, Maria Kozic, Robert Rooney, Imants Tillers and Peter Tyndall, to mention a few.

Most of the exhibitors were born in the 1960s and have grown up with television and have experienced the expansion of the pop music industry. So it is not surprising that elements from these, and other, areas of popular culture are incorporated in their work.

David Chesworth's performance 'Industry and Leisure', Ian Cox and Paul Fletcher's films, and the critical dissection of disco fashion and music by Tsk, Tsk, Tsk under the name Asphyxiation, are specific examples of this.

Also Chesworth, Kozic, Cox, Fletcher, Stevenson and Tyndall are all involved with new music, either in solo projects or as members of groups such as Tsk, Tsk, Tsk, Essendon Airport and Prott.

It should be clear from what I have said, that Popism's artists are not interested in the direct experience of nature. For them, compulsory trips to the You Yangs and other sacred sights of the great Aussie landscape are simply not on.

However, landscape is present in some of their work. In his '52 Displacements', Imants Tillers recognises the fact that Australian artists are made to feel guilty because their knowledge of world art is more likely to come from reproductions than from original works.

Tillers has tackled this problem head-on by purposely using reproductions of paintings and copying techniques. He explores the multiple meanings that occur when 52 seascapes by the American artist, Frederick Waugh (which are themselves American seascapes in the manner of European artists) are copied from a paint-it-yourself book.

Richard Dunn, like Tillers in his other work 'Suppressed Imagery', makes use of a surrealist juxtaposition of unrelated images. Dunn has paired a railway scene with a diagram of the duck/rabbit illusion in one painting, while Tillers makes a fascinating mixture of biological models, pictures from a Latvian children's book and bits of De Chirico in a series of drawings.

Jenny Watson, on the other hand, pairs unrelated images and texts in her 'Conversation Piece' and uses the format of the printed page in her paintings of Twiggy and the front page of the 'Herald'.

Although Peter Tyndall is well represented by selections from his 'A Person Looks at a Work of Art' series, he would have better fitted by the inclusion of a recent work, shown at Art Projects in May, which consisted of images of people pointing at and offering things.

In Robert Rooney's painting 'The Red Card: Australia 1944–45' and other new works, he uses a bland illustrational style to reproduce the loaded imagery of politics, war, propaganda in the 1940s and youth culture from the 1950s.

His screenprint, 'Pilkington Predicts', is, I believe, a reproduction of his 1961 advertisements for armor-plated glass. If you are going to use commercial imagery it might as well be your own!

Juan Davila is represented by two paintings, which, as opposed to the calculated cool of Dunn and Tillers, are hot stuff.

They are sleazy, disjointed narratives that catalogue the images of 1960s Pop artists such as Warhol, Lichtenstein, Lindner and Adami, and Tom of Finland's beefy male stereotypes in crude approximations of their styles.

Maria Kozic has the knack of making something out of even the slightest ideas. This is true of her '500 Fish', which looks good, despite its fragile nature. Her Super-8 film 'Manless' has survived repeated viewings and is a highlight of the film programme.

It is impossible to comment on all the works in Popism – I would have liked to discuss some of the films and performances at length – so I will offer some general comments in conclusion.

As Taylor points out in his catalogue essay, the artists use a variety of amateur art media – ready-made canvas-boards, super-8 film, Instamatics, Polaroids, coloring-in, painting by grids and so on.

For this reason there is less of the smell of the schoolroom than in a lot of current art, although there is an element of didacticism in some of the works.

Unlike some Melbourne critics who are belatedly offering figurative expressionism as the new savoir of Australian art, Taylor is not promoting Popism as a new art movement. He has simply made a personal choice of artists, who, as it turns out, seem to have something in common. "Pop", as he says, "is always with us." (Closes 25 July).

Popism and the Now (1982)

Philip Brophy

Preface: October 2, 2013, where it's now around 4pm.

When I look back at the paper 'Popism and the Now' – which I haven't done since I delivered it some thirty years ago, as it was never published – it reads like a partially cryptic document containing strategic kernels which have sprouted into strange plants throughout my work since. Some people write diaries, autobiographies or (worse) blogs about what they're thinking and feeling at any given moment. I always hated first-person drivel. It's like being subjected to *The Wonder Years*. Whenever I write, it's mostly a response. It's all about the thing; it's not about me.

1982 was the same year I made (as a →↑→ project) the short film *I You We* (made on Super 8, then remade on video in 1983). I got heaps of friends to drop by one night and read out a film title starting with 'I', 'you' or 'we' (the last as duos). The project – like much of what I was doing then – was having fun with linguistic theory and cinema or music. The idea that anything and everything constituted its own unique material language, which then could somehow 'speak' to other things and generate multiple meanings or modes of signification, was a thrill to me when I started encountering such ideas when I was about seventeen. It was the key to unlocking a collapse between all hierarchical discourses on culture, because I could encounter and engage with *anything* and it would have a whole bunch of things to say. Within a few years, I started to realise that the more 'art' something was – and the more valorised it was for being labelled and carried off as 'art' – the less interesting stuff it had to say.

In the early '80s, I was bemused by being caught up in 'art channels' because I was amazed by how limited and limiting so many of its practitioners were. If anything, I got caught in those channels not because I made 'art' (I didn't, and arguably still don't) but because 'popular culture' (what*ever* that meant or means) was deemed to be either relevant, modish, sexy, critical, urgent, politicised, or anything that facilitated discussion on the nexus between art and culture back then. I enjoyed talking and writing: it was never nerve-wracking. To me, being intellectual was always a fun thing. It still is.

I got asked to do a number of panels and the like because I was immersed in the stuff. (Things haven't changed much since.) The 'Popism and the Now' paper was for a 'forum series' run by the Tasmanian School of Art, where Paul Taylor had taught a few years earlier. To tell the truth: until last year, I had actually forgot that I was *in* the 'POPISM' exhibition. I thought I had just spoken on a panel, but it seems →↑→ did the *Asphixiation* performance at the NGV. Anyways, when I wrote up the 'Popism and the Now' paper (very quickly, and likely the night before I presented it) it was mostly a response to being channelled into art under an invented critical rubric by Paul. Some of it I agreed with, but the whole Barthesian shtick I thought I was already dealing with more directly via →↑→'s mutation between linguistic theory and movies and/or records. But Paul's formulation was strategically designed to be comprehensible to art history types of the time (most of whom actually read *Flash Art*). Many people seemed to like French intellectual theorists back then because the key players were gay, and they spoke about sexuality in direct relation to society. I was into glam and treated society like bad theatre, so I always felt like a phantom presence within that realm. In 1981, when →↑→ toured Sydney, I had designed and printed up a T-shirt with a photo of Barthes from the social pages of *Interview*, where he's at a night club with a wet-haired mop-top disco bus-boy. Barthes looks like a Stonewall-era sugar daddy next to this kid. I plastered a big cartoon bubble coming from the kid, saying 'Roland Barthes? Who's he?'

My favourite work by Barthes was *S/Z*: it has none of the socio-political advocacy of his anti-bourgeoisie proclamations, and it's amazingly insular and hermetic. I loved *S/Z* because of its impenetrability and its arcane fabrication of an alternative linguistic universe from the most conservative of sources and protracted of means. Perverse and precise in equal measure, it's the kind of thing I've since aspired to when I write on topics like *Death Race 3: Inferno* or *tokusatsu* special effects. It's all about the thing; it's not about me.

So 'Popism and the Now' is a responsive dismantling of the fabrication of 'POPISM', and speaks from a hands-on experience (via →↑→) of being engaged in making work activated and exacerbated by constructions of the 'self' (i.e., the artist associated with 'POPISM') and 'context' (i.e., the cultural plane where the artist attempts to grapple with those self-constructions). Little did I know that 'the now' would really never go away. And for that, I'm very happy.

Lecture delivered as part of the Art Forum series, Friday July 9, 1982, Tasmanian School of Art, Hobart.

So — we want to know about Popism. We want to talk about Popism. We want to find out about Popism. But let's just freeze things for a moment or two —

'Popism'

— our primary problem is that we have a word and we want to know what the word means. More fundamentally, we are faced with the enigma of *how* the *meaning* got the *word* 'Popism'.

O.K. We pick up the references, extend the lines, position Popism within a list of possibilities: Pop Art, 2nd Degree, Style, New Wave, Fashion, Contemporary Art, Popular Culture, etc., etc. Such are the names from our most superficial references. But what *type* of word (or name) is Popism — is it a style? A form? A movement? An approach? An attitude? A polemic? For example, we could say that Popism is 2nd generation Pop Art, Pop Art of the eighties, etc., but the thrust of such a description would result in radically opposing definitions depending on how we handled and posited the name (i.e., as style, form, movement, approach, attitude or polemic). The description and the definition qualify each other, contextualise each other, as we knead them together in our attempt to extricate substance from the meaning of the word.

So we want to *know* about Popism — but we are confronted with that very word. The word, as Language, points us to what we talk about but then denies us what it is we're talking about. Popism has splattered itself into the public arena of contemporaneity — in other words, it is pleasurably fashionable and painfully hip. Subsequently, we join the queue of consumerism — we want to check it out, find out about it, digest it. But Popism doesn't present itself on a plate for us. To find out what it "means" we have to go past the name, through the word, beyond language. We have to set foot into the wild and random terrain that Language (a name, a word) attempts to put into order. Into that fantastic aggravation that Popism invokes. This is not to say, however, that there is a space, a field, a place "beyond" Language. The most we can ever do is *set foot* into that terrain — without ever standing upright on two feet in it. It is the act or event of penetrating language and getting caught in between it that provides us with a sense (however intangible) of meaning and substance. We have to get ensnared in the word "Popism", entangled in all its meanings, references, locations, and movements in order to get an overview of the world that the word is pathetically trying to govern. We must only use the word Popism as a means to an end. Our object of desire is not the word – we can pick that up anytime, leave it down anywhere. Our real object of desire, our most crucial zone of pleasure, is everything *but* the word.

So we want to *talk* about Popism – but as we speak, we must be precisely aware of the instance and presence of our speaking. We must acknowledge the fact of the 'Now' in which we are situated – temporally, historically, and culturally. If Popism had to be summed up in one word, that word for me would be *NOW* – although to do so I shall have to introduce here a precise list of determined and determinable meanings outside of the mundane connotations that the word 'now' carries. By 'now' I do not mean new, up-to-date, with it, different, unique, original, etc. Rather than a refusal of yesterday's preoccupations, I'm talking about a feverish embrace with everything that has gone before or come before; everything that has occurred in any way in any part of the Past. *Now* means the very instant that the chaotic void of pre-/post-/extra-/non-language is set into Language and compounded into History. Popism is playing in the playground of Now; toying with how it is and is to be consumed by language, appropriated, as it were, *into* writing, criticism, theory, opinion, consensus, hearsay, gossip – into all manners of History.

Through being *now*, existing as a force atemporally within a juncture of the present and its voice, Popism extrapolates all preceding lines of definitional modes (style, polemic, attitude, approach, formal, opportunity, etc.) out of their varying and shifting contextual placings (historical, cultural, social, political, mythical, semiological, etc.) and tangles them all into a throbbing knot. To look at Popism and re-iterate (or regurgitate) that famous call-sign of imperceptions – 'It's all been done before!' – is a failure to distinguish between the meanings of a notion of a 'now'. Popism is not simply an art movement that wears very loud, new clothes, condemning all its predecessors. Popism is involved with the very contradiction that, yes, it *has* all been done before, but that that very fact is what qualifies its newness, its difference to the before – its *nowness*.

The primary dichotomy is between an art that is historicist in its avant-garde existence, and an art that is historical in its avant-garde practice. The word 'avant-garde' is itself an historically fixed/linguistically consumed idea of *now*. 'Avant-garde Art' would then be art waiting to become history, blind to the fact that it already *is* history. Popism is an art awaiting history, forever on the peak of an historicist placing within Art History because it hones in on an eternal dilemma: do we connect the present to the past? What this means is that Popism *has* happened before. And it will happen again. The *now* is forever, and within that infinite range, Popism, as a practice of declaring in and of itself its nature as language, has the scope to be endlessly transformed, depending on the arbitrary (i.e., multiple and non-hierarchical) pushes and flows of its energy. One must never forget that the Present tense lasts as long as you speak it *forever*. Popism exists as you speak it.

So we want to find out about Popism — O.K. It's a critical practice in the most crystalline sense that we have been able to imagine critical practices for some time. The distinction between audience, artist and critic (and all their prolific sub-components) becomes a pedantic issue, a useless tactic. The critical practice that involves and is involved by Popism is an engagement of multiplicities — in particular (and in optional replacement of the audience/artist/critic model) the network of multiplicities of Context and Self — of where the who is placed, how one replicates the other. Let us briefly look at these two major layers within a 'Popimistic' practice one at a time.

SELF: a category that encompasses all the manifestations of the who and the whom — all the voices that speak to us from within, without and on top of the art objects. Who is it that speaks in a painting or whatever? The artist? The painter? The technician? The craftsperson? If we look at the historical tradition of the artist under these conditions, we find that his/her body is of a unified form — s/he speaks to us in a singular voice of artistic intention, painterly skill and conceptual rigour. *Popism* points to the chorus of voices that sing in such an historical tradition. The Popism chorus sings out of tune, with fluctuating tempo, different voices screeching louder than others at odd times. The idea, craft, execution and intention are in a cacophonic state. *Popism* disrupts the harmonic choir, upsetting the unified, singular, unproblematic appearance of the 'artist's voice'.

But we hear more voices — they are the voices of all the paintings, images, objects, gestures, symbols, references, ideas and surfaces that have come *before* the painting. The effect is like a malfunctioning cassette recorder that continually records top layers without ever properly and totally erasing what was previously recorded underneath. The music becomes noise — clarification becomes interference — voice becomes voices. *Popism* speaks in a chorus, because *Popism* exists ironically *without* a speaker. The voice speaks itself: it is spoken. The *Popism* artist plunders, pillages, rapes and buggers art history and popular culture, not even caring to distinguish between the two – or, for that matter, anything. The supreme act of *Popism* is not creation, but appropriation. 'Who did that painting?' Ask that question meaningfully, and you have to be prepared to undertake an endless quest, trapped in an underground catacomb of authorship, voices calling to you from a thousand different tunnels, exits, entrances – all saying the same thing: 'I'. And none of them are lying.

We find *our* 'selfs' caught up in the multiplicity of 'selfs', all mirroring each other and ourselves in the stalemate of language that only *represents* the self. As such, *Popism* refutes the artist – there is no artist; only art. The whole damn history of art. As a critical practice, *Popism* manufactures an object for itself or simply destroys an existing object. We need not be tied down to *Popism* works to perform *Popism*. We can look anywhere.

It is here that we encounter the multiplicities of *CONTEXT*: We find anything and everything everywhere. We find the one thing in all places simply through the act of looking. Inasmuch as *Popism* exists as we speak it, its meanings present themselves as we look for them. The quest is, in fact, quite stupid, but infinitely pleasurable. We can reverse the semantic direction of that old adage 'stupid as a painter' and revel in it, because *Popism* plays in the very surface of stupidity; swimming in the futility of language; O.D.ing on meaning. The notion of *NOW* is tied up with *where* you are *when* you say it.

In realising the multiplicity of contexts, we acknowledge the factionalisation of all modes of practice within a political and cultural history. The range of *Popism* is a squirming mosaic of splinters – strong enough to walk on but impossible to record a map of the walk on. 'Art' is but one of the many squirming trails of splinters, one of the many departments of Culture. To speak only of Art is to adhere to the restricted freedom within a political bureaucracy, to be continually forced to send memos to the other departments (Society, Life, Politics, Theory, etc.) in order to arrange some aimless meeting, behind closed doors, in comfortable chairs.

The play that *Popism* initiates with Context invokes all types of places – institutions, venues, journals, magazines, advertisements, forums – you name it. *Popism* is involved with an act of insertion – inserting *everything* into one place, a place that thrives and survives on its fragmentation, its isolation. We draw up the list of itemisation and play the list against each other, and the items against one another. Medium, Subject, Matter, Presentation, Mediarisation, Audience, Image, Role. A painter makes a film to be shown in a pub that is reviewed in Cleo. Fuck this stale notion of "wrong" place, "wrong" manoeuvre, "wrong" work, "wrong" context. Being 'now' is *being wrong*. The point of assimilation and communication, that instant that Language and History smother something, is the moment of a certain rightness, a certain validation supported by the preceding events, by History.

Just as the Self is all selfs—you, me, them—the Context is all contexts—here, there, everywhere. Just as every sentence you speak is an anagram of grammatical possibilities effecting a desired meaning, every instance of your critical practice is an anagram of contextual references, effecting a desired critique. A kaleidoscope of History and Culture. The act of insertion, of cross-contextualisation is a process of mutation, creating monsters that run loose in any particular faction, be it political, cultural or historical. *Popism* could be making one thing, one work, one object, but distributing it everywhere, investing a germ into the transparent walls that support any system, institution or convention. The walls remain transparent and free-standing, but the decayed cavities are visible. The traces are visible, although their permanence—like that of the walls—is not guaranteed.

Popism is a surface of multiplicity as opposed to a dimension of singularity. It is much more fun, I think, to slip and slide than it is to sink.

Living on the surface (1982)

Adrian Martin

This lecture was delivered on June 23, 1982 within the frame of the 'POPISM' exhibition at the National Gallery of Victoria, Melbourne.

Standing in the midst of this exhibition called 'POPISM', and being obliged to say a few things about it, suggests a few, fairly clear courses of action to me.

First of all, I could imagine myself as the explicator, the spokesperson for a new art movement. Sure enough, there's a minor mythology of Popism (as the name of a movement now, not just an exhibition) already laying in wait to be written, proclaimed and romanticised in some very small book of art-historical scholarship. Such a mythical romance of Australian post-Pop art would be a cross between a tourist guide, a gossip column and a militant theoretical tract, taking in the sites from the Clifton Hill Community Music Centre and Art Projects to The Crystal Ballroom and Inflation disco, from obscene newsletters received privately in the mail to *Art & Text* magazine available at the local newsagent, from forgotten performances given for the benefit of the six people who bothered to show, to albums atop the alternative record charts and video clips on the television show *Rock Around the World*.

Needless to say, this would be a breathless, jazzy, ultra-modern few pages in the grand text of Twentieth Century Art History, written in the style of Andy Warhol's *Interview*, adorned by fashion photos set smartly at oblique angles, and given undeniable intellectual integrity by the size of its bibliography. It would be the story of a subculture growing like a beautiful and deadly weed under the cracked pavements of a so-called dominant culture, the story of cool political subversions and grand-slam theatrical gestures, a rise from humble beginnings between friends to occupation of the National Gallery or The Melbourne Film Festival. Yet, such a fiction, however much fun it is to tell or to live, might prove too fragile or ephemeral once I tried to capture it, document it and evaluate it: best to leave it as a dream.

Then, less romantically, I could take my task as a scholarly, analytical one, and try to position the works of this exhibition inside a fairly short history of a new aesthetic form. In this light,

Andy Warhol beckons to us from the Pop Art of the 1960s as seemingly the instigator of a true historic break in artistic production and cultural contextualisation. Today, we have learnt to love Warhol all over again, and much recent work, such as Maria Kozic's *Two Pages From Warhol's Book* in the exhibition, contains homages that testify to a very real reverence and the recognition of a specific artistic mandate issuing from the Master. Henceforth, after Warhol, nothing will be created and everything will be found; subject-matter will be skimmed off the debris-ridden surface of popular culture; and it will then be transformed, drained of meaning or filled with too much meaning, kicked around, put into play.

The artist as author, as the unique source and controller of his or her work, will more and more seek to deliver himself to death's door (on the good advice of Roland Barthes) to be, like the phoenix, reborn everywhere at once, in the middle of all the fluxes and flows which constitute our society. The Pop artist of today screenprints posters, plays in a New Wave band, designs sets for television commercials, or executes spectacular conceptual gestures to win that requisite fifteen minutes of fame which Warhol promised us all.

An aesthetic history of Popism would be an inventory of the techniques and strategies developed that were and are most appropriate to its aims and philosophy. We would pass by, in turn, the visual devices of repetition and multiplication, quotation and reworking that appear in the work of Kozic and Robert Rooney; we would locate the place of favoured Pop gestures like the grid in Jenny Watson, the mirror reflection in Richard Dunn, the Polaroid photograph in The Society for Other Photography, the pose in the performance of *Asphixiation*, or the studied imitation of children's drawing and painting styles in Howard Arkley. Then we could sort out a characteristic Pop iconography, a store of distinctive images and the way in which they transform themselves from the '60s to the present; an iconography including Marilyn Monroe and David Bowie for Kozic, gay comic strips for Juan Davila, dolls and toys for Paul Fletcher, imagery from commercial film and television for →↑→, and the highly expressive spaces and objects of domestic life for Jane Stevenson.[1]

But such an aesthetic history would be far too neat and accommodating, not to mention reductive. If I use the word Popism (as I shall continue to do), I mean to designate nothing very concrete by it. Neither I nor this exhibition are attempting to foster the illusion of a coherent, organised art movement, a unified, shared style, or even a common origin and inspiration in the Warhol '60s. Popism is just a word – a word taken from somewhere else, from the past. It functions not as a proper name, or an identifying label, but simply as that which serves to bring certain works and certain practices together with the maximum noise and provocation. Perhaps none of the artists represented here would like to identify themselves as Pop artists. That doesn't matter. For there is still something to be gained, something that is at stake, something which can be done by drawing together at this moment.

As for me, I want to follow the works of this 'POPISM' exhibition out along a certain line of flight, to take a walk on the wild side. At its most extreme point of projection into the real world, this current manifestation of Popism seems to suggest to me nothing less than a new way of thinking oneself in relation to things and events, people and places, meanings and histories – what Paul Foss called a 'new politics of life'.[2]

Popism today, as everyone knows, is about style, surface, appearance, about wearing a new image or learning a new dance – but where *new* only ever means *different*, not original or unique. You can pillage the past in any way you like, arrange its treasures in whatever order or combination. The present exists as an open door poised above the bottomless well of history; out of that well is drawn a hundred anachronisms, a thousand hybrid styles, a million dreams. This is not a regressive fixation on the past but a perpetual recreation of it; a transformation of life into art and art into life; a tissue of games, jokes, images and fictions. Popism, in this sense, is not a collection of art objects, but a tone, an attitude, a method, a style which insinuates itself into every aspect of living.

Now, I know what a lousy PR image this Pop lifestyle has. Its surfaces are seen as flat and rigid, its styles are taken as cold and severe, and its practices are described as sterile and unproductive. We will always be encountering in the kitchen at parties spoil-sports like Peter Fuller, ever ready to tell us we are, in truth, hopelessly alienated from ourselves, the sad products of a debased monopoly capitalism, stoned zombies spaced out on a 'megavisual' culture, blinded by the billboards. Let them talk: some people, I guess, have a taste for tragedy. Popism, on the other hand, is an attempt to reclaim the world, to make it bearable and enjoyable, to foster within its multiple surface layers all manner of perversions, ironies and intensities. It is a line of thinking in art and politics that goes back to, for instance, the Surrealists and the Situationists, but today it can marshal an unprecedented number of possible action stations. As life within our culture becomes more splintered and diversified, we stand a good chance of getting lost in its masquerade. And we can enjoy every minute of that.

I talk of living on the surface; I need first to swim up from the depths where I have been too long detained. What a dreary business, what a heavy burden is our fine tradition of significance and richness within works of art. William Routt proposes:

> White intellectual culture is grounded on the search [...] this highly-valued activity in its turn gives rise to a particular sort of aesthetic object, which we may call 'enigmatic'. Works of art [...] are made so as to conceal their 'true meaning', fabricated after the manner of riddles, mazes, and optical illusions.[3]

A world cast through Popism would be all surface, and that does not mean trivial or frivolous. Freed, no longer transfixed in the often cynical search for the deep and the meaningful, we would approach all objects (including art objects) in a more immediate, experimental and utterly disrespectful way. A field of absolute relativity: if it works, if it suggests a possible use, take it; if not, don't waste your time. For, as David Chesworth reminds us in his
38 performance *Industry and Leisure*, 'This is not all you have'.

We need to entirely undo the conceptual apparatus which constrains us in making us consider events, people or artworks in terms of a dichotomy between surface and depth. Traditionally, surfaces are thought as the necessary but troublesome coverings over a centre, a truth, an origin or a self. Hence the cult of the artist as an author with a personality, an insight and a world-view to be deciphered and revealed through her or his work. History, anthropology, sociology—all such disciplines conspire in this operation when they theorise upon the invariant deep structures which supposedly underlay and explain all the vagrant social and personal phenomena of the world. Worst of all, we are constantly reminded of the awesome presence within each of us of something called Human Nature, an inescapable sameness deep within which railroads us into the Brotherhood of Man ... When people like Fuller publish books with titles like *The Naked Artist: Art and Biology*, you know it is time to make a point of acting very silly for a while, just to get back to the surface of the world.

Think for a moment, to take a very Popist example, of the relation between clothing and the human body, costume and skin. According to one traditional argument, clothing is a veil, a disguise, a civilised veneer which covers and represses the natural body. Another, now quite popular argument poses the relation in an only slightly different way, by seeing clothing—along with other privileged sign systems, such as body language and Freudian slips of the tongue – as the surface expressions of one's personal depth, or one's ego, a coded projection, a chart of individualised symptoms. 'You are what you wear.' Now, what is the Pop philosophy on this fashion question? Skin and clothing are, for Popism, utterly reversible, collapsible; one is taken for the other and no mistake is thereby made. Naked flesh is just another costume, and clothing is all skin: more skin, extended skin, folding into layers which touch or remain apart according to wind, movement, contact, pressure ... Skin which expands and contracts across several bodies, a bit of mine, all of yours, the skin of the sheets, the walls of sound that rise up and topple down about us – anyone who has made love, plus those who have only thought about it, know a few things about living on the surface.

None of this need involve some interior self, gripped in the compulsion to communicate its private truth; in fact, quite the opposite is the case. Projected out into the open air, everything becomes games, jokes, laughter, a way of escaping all the tired and congealed doctrines of interpretation and significance. Not only living *on* the surface, but living *as* a surface. If you are what you wear today, you were certainly someone else yesterday.

Obviously, we are not talking here only of bodies and inanimate objects, but also minds, feelings, emotions, attachments. One of the characteristics of Popism is that, while often unwinding on an intense plateau, it never has to make a show of a bleeding expressionist heart, like some other current art styles and practices. Expressionism, old or new, is just another fiction, another play of surface effects and gestures which mistakes itself as an actualisation of inner depths. It is not a style *with* meaning, but only a history *of* meaning, beneficiary of the historical agreement to call certain moves meaningful and others not so – 'conventional acceptances, widely held beliefs, general assumptions, and specious, dogmatic concepts that have accumulated historically into a thick wall of imposing validity', as Philip Brophy has described the process.[4] The sweep of the painter's arm; the touching inclusion in the artwork of autobiographical scraps; the private, unique key of images and symbols – even these most loaded and illusory elements of the expressionist style and philosophy can be brought back to their surfaces and used for the fun of it. This is the hope that Popism offers.

Every surface is part of a black box, in the sense that René Thom has used this term within mathematics and systems theory. (The idea was highly influential upon Jean-Luc Godard's video work of the 1970s.) A black box is opaque, invisible; we will never know it for what it is, if indeed it *is* anything. A black box can only be discerned through experiments to locate the inputs and outputs at the surfaces of its system. A human being is something like a black box, full of holes into which leads are connected, through which things come in, and are then thrown out, projected to create and display other surfaces. David Chesworth's *Industry and Leisure* is about this way of thinking oneself within the world. In it, a voice speaks these words:

> I've lost myself. It was hard to avoid making contact with things. I went all over the place. My bits and pieces were propelled with such force. I offered no more resistance but the pieces were stopped mid-flight by objects. I hit them with such force. I didn't expect it. It all happened so quickly; the mutilation became permanent ... afterwards there is nothing to show except debris. But debris can be interesting.

Debris is indeed interesting. In performances like *Industry and Leisure*, Asphixiation's *What is This Thing Called 'Disco'?*, or the pictorial works of Imants Tillers and Juan Davila, an investigation into a seemingly simple, singular object ends by delighting in a multiplicity of surfaces, extensions and projections every which way. The surfaces encountered are rigid like concrete or flexible like rubber, minute or enormous, calm as the cool world or frenzied as body heat. Disco, or Freud's theory of the unconscious, or perspective lessons from how-to-draw books, are found and imagined everywhere, in religion, in advertising, in art history, in love, transforming them all into mad machines of desire.

This world I have tried to sketch from the perspective of Popism is a pretty nice place to find yourself living in – and, of course, there are completely happy people already there who have never had any need of the works on show in this exhibition. Popism is just one kind of toolbox, or a new pair of glasses to try on, in case things look any better through them. Popism is, as I suggested at the outset, an attempt to reclaim the world. We no longer need to define reality (as many still do) as a dead blank, a bore, a prison – a dark night into which art with its 'aesthetic dimension' will shine a pure, saving light. It is very easy to pose everyday life as lacking, melancholic or dead, to lament the lost world, or to terminate history in an Apocalypse Now. Popism dares you to think differently, to define the world as the sum of its surfaces, its traces, its projections and introjections – a material world which accommodates the immateriality of memory, dream, reverie and speculation. This is a world we can create, complete at every point of its creation.

Going on from these propositions, I would like to say a few things about Popism as an art practice, and the kinds of work it has produced.

First, Popism is an attempt to demystify the traditional relation of separation between art and everyday life, art and reality. It hardly seems to matter at times what language or theory you use – whether you speak of the work of art, or the domain of culture, or of representations and discourses – always implied is an absolute distinction in kind between the base level of reality and the acts of creativity that evolve within it. And there are the familiar institutions, like galleries and art schools, which serve to maintain this distinction – however much their manifestoes of art in the community (or whatnot) might proclaim otherwise.

What happens once this difference in kind has been set into place, as it has been for several centuries? Art, separated from the world, is then asked to entertain a very specific relation to that world, to be a perfect and fabulous mirror, to return our images and feelings to ourselves in a more intense and refined way than we can ever supposedly perceive them in humdrum everyday life. Works of art must speak, embody, create a fullness, materialise the world that we aspire to live in, show the stuff that dreams are made of. Needless to say, all creative work is then under a massive obligation to be representational in some shape or form – if not tied to the world by visible and familiar subject matter (as in realism), then at least analogous to it in its process or intent.

Various styles of abstraction are thereby sorted and redeemed – a Kandinsky or a Rothko deciphered in terms of their bringing to the canvas the colours and forms of an inner, emotional life. The true work of art (so the story goes) is not surface but depth: it possesses a mass, a volume, a weight. Upon this principle, Art History draws up its select list of masterpieces with, lower down the hierarchy, other works acting as filler for the history book, valued for this or that reason as minor or partial successes. Into the category of abject failure shall then fall all those flat, dead, one-dimensional art objects that operate on the plane of mere formalism – those transient, superficial exercises with no claim on history, and no seeming engagement with reality. If you are polite you call them decadent formalist exercises; if you are not so polite, you call them a wank – surely the word of abuse which indicates better than any other the mood and temper of our times.

It is in this sorry category that you will often find listed the works of Popism.

Popism, once again, would want to dismantle this whole way of thinking about art in relation to life. Its work does not want to be seen as apart or separate from the world in the first instance; rather, it seeks to take place as a surface among the multitude of surfaces, colliding with various kinds of social, personal and economic flows and exchanges. Symptomatically, all of Peter Tyndall's works in this exhibition are catalogued as *details*, that is, part of the material contexts like galleries that contain them, subject to particular uses and inflections. They don't aim to reflect the world from some other space; they are *in* the world, they act in the world.

In a similar vein, Popism makes a highly conscious effort to use various creative forms – or languages, if you like – that are part of everyday surface culture, but are for the most part expelled from the canons of expressive art. Hence Jenny Watson's and Howard Arkley's use of children's drawing and painting styles, doodling and scribbling, and small scale canvases; and the anonymous project of the Society for Other Photography to skim a collection of Polaroid snaps off the surface of metropolitan life. The group Asphixiation throw their creative energies into disco music precisely because disco is in the main perceived as 'shallow, cheap and crass',[5] and to perform it with vigour, intensity and a sincere intellectual interest forces a question upon other, more respected forms of art and music, and upon the means by which they bluff their way into a position of respectability.

Although some people claim that these particular efforts and endeavours of Popism constitute just another kind of bourgeois art pining to be 'of the people' – in other words, an illusory type of participation in popular culture still, in fact, locked into an art-culture framework – it is a fact that the crossovers between Popism and actual pop are becoming more frequent, almost to the point of an uncanny reversibility. We not only see the works of Kozic, Brophy or Watson on record covers, postcards, clothes and the front of the *Age Weekender*, we also see their imitators, their doubles, springing up in advertising agencies and glossy magazines everywhere. It is getting harder to tell the difference between first degree and second degree work (using the terms suggested by Paul Taylor), to posit any clear relation between originals and copies. For Popism, it is in fact much better to be lost, beyond the point of caring about origins: everything slides around, objects and gestures belong to everyone and no one, all is available for use.

Popism aims to contribute to the play of surfaces within daily life by folding its layers, drawing connecting lines between objects, events and perceptions (as in Jenny Watson's *Conversation Piece*), and by multiplying the possible angles and viewpoints upon existing phenomena. Look at the Polaroids collected by the Society for Other Photography: they are like windows on the world, but not in the voyeuristic, grasping way in which realist art has always thought itself to be such. There are a hundred windows, a hundred worlds. In Popism, windows are reversible; they open up passageways, inputs and outputs, a projection in and a direction out. A Polaroid on the wall is a perfectly transparent surface, through which we connect ourselves to a disembodied piece of reality — a rose, a statue, a face. In itself it is, of course, a new and extra piece of reality, of the same order and of equal importance as the rose or the face — it is a picture we will carry around, or to which we will lovingly apply the Blu-Tack, in an album or on a wall where it will join other photos to form a fantastic narrative of our own devising. It is an image whose own strangeness of shape, colour and tone will attract our own most intense fetish-making fantasies.

What does a photograph, or any image for that matter, refer to? To a pre-existing object? To itself? To the history of a particular photographic style? To a moment in time? The answer is: all of these, and more. An image works in whatever way you can get it to work; it can be connected to, combined with, anything. This brings me to another important aspect of works of Popism, what I called earlier their absolute relativity. It seizes upon gaps, distances, differences, mismatches; it drives a wedge wherever it can. All the conventional systems of meaningfulness and effectivity are broken apart, pulled into their separate pieces. Objects or symbols no longer mean what they usually mean; the traditional contract of interpretation is cheated. So, too, are all the learnt codes of emotional response that try to pass themselves off as natural or intuitive.

A work of Popism, after one thing, will absolutely go to the opposite extreme in order to achieve it. We can only be gently amused at those people who take in the contrivedly cold, severe and angular works of the 'POPISM' exhibition and then walk away numb, muttering about the chronic depersonalisation, alienation and inhumanity of this latest New Wave; for the joke, truly, is on them. Familiar lines of thought are twisted, confounded and perverted within Popism in order to be reassembled, reconstructed. In Davila's paintings, for instance, the entire elaborate system of Freudian symbolism and psychoanalytic interpretation is at once converted into the purest corn, the slickest list of low puns—and then powerfully volatised, put to work in other directions and other domains, such as homosexual desire and radical politics.

Popism is all about displacements, shifts, crazy associational leaps, and looking through many layers at once. Its images are saturated in history, all kinds of history. In Imants Tillers's *Fifty Two Displacements*, we simultaneously register the sea, plus the labour of the artist's creation of the work itself, painstakingly documented—a cleverly contrived fictionalisation of one of the many myths surrounding the artistic process, once again mounted with a sly humour. Tillers's other piece, *Suppressed Imagery*, is a projection of fantasies and conceits not out of a Gothic, Freudian unconscious, a tortured individual psyche, but rather a social and historical unconscious, bearing all the strange, transformed traces of childhood school lessons, random encounters, and the failures at making sense that litter the fabulous op shops of our minds.

The style of Popism works ceaselessly at hollowing out a space within the ugly constraints of rational thought, ideological socialisation and historical determinism. There comes, finally, a moment of withdrawal from the plots and obligations of convention, a dazzling extrication from the scene of the crime. We have escaped, and we can laugh back at what we have left behind. Popism as a lifestyle, a philosophy and an art practice is about staying on the move, never letting anyone catch you or get a fix on you. Its most subversive and delirious trait is playfulness—games of deceit, bluff, treachery. If, as a Pop artist or Pop theorist, you speak, create or act, you have anticipated definite and immediate reactions to your gesture. But that does not mean you necessarily ever believe what you say. This is what the opponents of Popism find hardest to take, and their inquisitions begin: *just who are you, really? What are you after, finally? What's the real point of all this?* But we do not know the answers ourselves, we don't care—and you can believe that, or not.

Another delight for the artists of Popism is in waste. I am referring to works in this exhibition like Kozic's *Dulux Color Chart* or *The Fish*, and Robert Rooney's series of photographs *AM-PM*. Waste is the opposite of economy, thrift, functionalism. A self-perpetuating, randomly halted process of repetition and multiplication gives, by conventional standards, far too little information, and even less meaning. Again, a contract is cheated and a boundary is blissfully overflowed. Popism finds a pleasure in sterility, uselessness, in the particles that constitute a surface. The *Dulux Color Chart* is a deadly joke upon traditional notions of representation as mimesis, as securing and transferring directly a pre-existing piece of reality. There are forty black and white prints of a color chart — each one possessing a single, real colour sample from the original that has been added to it, right back in its proper place. And that is the joke: to force the prints together in a single mimetic object is to ignore the distribution, the circulation of the original, its multiplication and transformation, and the abundance of sterile differences, sweet nothings, that the work contains.

Popism has been called a theoretical art, and I think it is worth making a few comments about that. Theory is hardly an innocent word these days; it is usually uttered either as a militant rallying cry or a sneering insult. The 1970s gave us a situation that had never quite happened in the same way before in the history of Modernism: the word 'theory' came to designate a particular group of ideas and debates that were threatening to some, and a relief to others. Particularly influenced by radical French thought post-1968 and the film theory contained in the British magazine *Screen*, a solid and imposing materialist theory of culture and politics was developed, drawing from a few modern variations on Marxism and Freudian psychoanalysis, joining forces with the linguistics-inspired study known as semiotics (the study of signs and meanings), and creating — most powerfully on the political level — a new kind of feminist thought within a specific slice of the Women's Movement.

Nowadays, the claims made for this theory, and the results of its advance into practice, seem more than a little dubious to some of us — although there is no doubt that this so-called theory is still hot in the air and thick on the ground, and gets taught, written and spoken about more than ever. Now, there *is* a theoretical art deriving from this work, but it is not Popism. I would identify it by examples of the publication *Photo Discourse* from the Sydney College of the Arts, the American film *Sigmund Freud's Dora* (1979), some of the artists and works represented in the local magazine *Lip* or, to take the supreme example, Mary Kelly's *Post Partum Document* (exhibited in Melbourne at the George Paton Gallery) — which I urge you to compare with the works in 'POPISM'.

There is certainly an important overlap between the interests that feed into Popism and the body of theoretical work I have too briefly designated. Davila is deeply involved in the psychoanalytic ideas of Jacques Lacan, for instance, while the films of Ian Cox or →↑→ rehearse some of the more familiar notions in semiotics about the construction and deconstruction of meanings through image-sound combinations and narrative form. But even these works begin to entertain a sly and subversive relation to the ideas they take on – something which, I have suggested, is characteristic of Popism. A work of Popism can absorb, consume and reproduce any idea or strategy – that is in its method – but this act will always be strictly opportunistic. A theory presents itself as only another fiction, a toolbox, something to be used and exhausted. Unlike that other theoretical art I have cited, it is not engaged in a search for material or political truth, nor is it obsessed with the rather precious and illusion-ridden desire to found a new avant-garde that is so different, so radical and so pleasurable that it will convert the world to Marxist-feminism in a single stroke. Popism could never bring itself to take something that seriously.

'Where in that dead expanse of curtain wall', asks Peter Fuller, 'is there an inch of space for symbols and values beyond the demands of function and necessity?' He goes on to helpfully convey, in his address on 'Aesthetics After Modernism' delivered in Australia, that his hero Ruskin correctly prophesised 'the hell we have made for ourselves'.[6] But when I look around now, out through the doors opened by my engagement with Popism, I see no hell. I see no heaven, either – but that is a reflection for another time. What is wrong with an expanse of curtain wall, if at any moment I can turn it into a surface, a screen for projections, a backdrop for spectacular theatrical tableaux? Does Fuller believe that people are so overwhelmed by the big city that they have stopped living? Popism has given us a glimpse into a lifestyle that continues, a desire that works in whatever way it can.

Popism is the space of fabulous inversions and miraculous recoveries. Any object can be worked over for any effect; a form and a content can go together in any way. In the barest, most minimal situation, excitement can be sparked – and even Alphaville can be transformed into a fun palace. That is Popism's secret delight. For those who can't get in on the joke, Popism will present a face that is proof of all the sad and sorry prognoses that are made of it. When the press started calling the German band Kraftwerk a dehumanised, impersonal quartet ruled over by the tyranny of advanced technology, what did they do? They built life-size dummies of themselves to take on stage with them (sometimes even taking their place) and released an album called *Computer World*. A quintessential Pop gesture – a way of adapting, surviving with a perverse dignity.

Popism, finally, is also a form of delinquency – an immersion of oneself in flippant and inconsistent intellectualism, in suspicious and contradictory moral-ethical codes, in outrageous gestures and insults that bring on lawsuits from damaged egos, in hedonism. That is what living on the surface means. A delinquency which seems validated, if not necessitated, by our (un)fortunate historical placement in a mad, Modernist, Western world. Faced with the many real forms of social collapse, a Popist lifestyle is one way of rebuilding — on a small scale, at least — the world. For the first time, history, imploding in on itself, has freed a generation to do what it can. The surfaces are all ours, while the depths — the sacred traditions of religion, the grand and slow evolutions of culture — have vanished beneath us. We have nothing to live up to. We are the Men and Women Who Fell to Earth, dancing on its surface tension, putting on the Ritz, indulging in play and re-creation, and singing all the while that maddening tune: *I just can't get enough*.

Tall Poppies: a sleight of hand

Judy Annear

In 1983, the Melbourne University Art Gallery held an exhibition
40 guest-curated by Paul Taylor entitled 'Tall Poppies'—'an exhibition of five pictures'. The all-male group of artists consisted of John Dunkley-Smith, Dale Frank, John Nixon, Mike Parr and Imants Tillers. As Taylor wrote in the catalogue essay, 'these five artists have all been selected by non-Australian curators to exhibit abroad. This is their similarity, it is my curatorial acquiescence and also our parochialism.'[1]

The year before, at the age of twenty-four, Taylor had curated 'POPISM' for the National Gallery of Victoria. The first guest curator, and the youngest, in the NGV's history, Taylor organised the first large-scale contemporary art exhibition in that institution since 'The Field' in 1968. 'POPISM', by virtue of taking artists of mainly Taylor's own generation to the museum, was a meteorite in the still pond of the art establishment. Those represented in 'POPISM' could easily be found in the alternative spaces of Sydney and Melbourne. The majority were recent art school graduates, highly literate, curious, and making what American academic Douglas Crimp had called, five years before, 'pictures'.[2] 'Pictures' refers to artworks that call attention to the ambiguities within an image, regardless of the medium used as a platform. Crimp, and his various essays published in *October*, was an important influence on Taylor and this was acknowledged in the 'POPISM' bibliography. 'Tall Poppies' had no bibliography but it did have five 'pictures', which were mostly not the kind of art objects generally referred to as such at that time.

In 1983, and from a pragmatic and political position, Taylor brought together five artists to form the exhibition he called 'Tall Poppies'. He could certainly have chosen a different bunch of five who had been previously selected by foreign curators. Only two of the artists overlapped with 'POPISM'—Imants Tillers and John Nixon (who had appeared as part of 'The Society for Other Photography'). The work in general was different from the studied dilettantism and utilisation of the photographic as outlined by Taylor in his essay for that previous exhibition.[3] Mike Parr was somewhat removed from Crimp's delineation of 'pictures' and Taylor's earlier emphasis on photographic rhetoric. Frank, the youngest (born 1959), was completely removed. 'Tall Poppies' appeared to reorient attention to forms of painting, one of the many sleights of hand in this exhibition.

'Tall Poppies' was utterly dispassionate in selection and presentation. If 'POPISM' had the enthusiasms and effervescence of contemporary pop culture breezing through it (local as much as Warholian), 'Tall Poppies' stripped the artists, their works and the mechanics of the art world bare – they were there because they had been selected by curators from elsewhere. 'How', Taylor asked, 'can we concertina five pictures and gather them together into one bunch to be presented as a gift of five poppies?' What follows in his essay is a succinct analysis of the ways of the art world and its participants. In many respects, this was a more important exhibition than 'POPISM', precisely because the ideas and practices were nakedly presented, and Taylor's writing so focussed and matter-of-fact in regard to context – despite red herrings. For example, a 'bunch of fives' is a fist, so Taylor can be seen to be proposing a punch in the face with the bouquet of poppies.[4] The title was also, surely, a cunning reference to his previous exhibition 'POPISM', and to Andy Warhol.

Another sleight of hand in 'Tall Poppies' is Taylor's manipulation of the term 'tall poppies'. In early 1980s Australia, the term 'tall poppy syndrome' was invented: 'High achievers ... are frequently referred to as "victims of the tall poppy syndrome".'[5] That syndrome meant to be cut down to size, that there existed in society 'a desire to diminish in stature those people who have attained excellence in a particular field'.[6] There is an added twist in that it seems one can be a tall poppy as long as one doesn't act tall, but rather expresses humility and shows no signs of wanting to stand out from the crowd.[7] Further, though tall poppies have been known to exist in other cultures and at other times, the term is particularly linked to modern Australia. The title and therefore the idea of a native anti-intellectualism is, as curator Sue Cramer pointed out in her review of the exhibition, the one aspect of 'Tall Poppies' which could be described as local.[8]

Was Taylor referring to himself as much as the artists? And was excellence here determined by international rather than local kudos? Did it matter who was chosen, by whom and for what context? In the early 1980s it did. Mobility, for most contemporary and experimental artists, was a comparatively recent phenomenon, as it was for Australian curators also. For some, mobility was a thing of the mind but few had the discipline to travel far and wide in their intellects and imaginations only. The desire to be seen in local institutions was rivalled by the desire to be seen with international peers. The strategising toward such visibility was a constant consideration.

The 1970s had seen an expansion in contemporary art activity and support, developments which had the appearance of bearing fruit in the early 1980s. The advent of the Australia Council in 1973 enabled funding for visitors to come and look at art in Australia, and exhibitions of Australian art to be sent elsewhere. Regardless of their content (which was various), these projects forced reflection onto the nature of the culture that was being depicted.[9] Nick Waterlow's 1979 Biennale of Sydney brought younger experimental artists from Europe to both Sydney and Melbourne, enlarging discussions around international contemporary art practice locally; William Wright's 1982 Biennale furthered this. The National Gallery of Australia, with James Mollison at the helm, opened in 1982, dragging state art museums into a new and more professional way of working, one in which contemporary and local practice had to be a part of the program.

The early 1980s was also the tail end of an era in which storming the bastions of social and cultural propriety from the outside was seen to be a viable and necessary activity. As the 1980s wore on, however, most of the smaller interest groups in the artworld and elsewhere remained as smaller interest groups. They were talking to themselves. Women, for example, were not approaching equal representation in contemporary exhibitions, let alone anywhere else in society, and Aboriginal art was seen as having no place at all in the major art museums.[10] Many artists and writers of the era remained wedded to these institutions as they and their progenitors had been for generations, regardless of the nature of their own practice or espoused politics. The inherently opportunistic nature of the art world tended to mitigate against dynamic institutional change. Those thinkers and artists who were seriously interested in transformation often found themselves pigeonholed as alternative, countercultural, or an outsider, by race or gender, or by all of these.

Against such stereotyping, Taylor, through *Art & Text* magazine and his curatorial work, compiled and presented sometimes-conflicting views that bounced off each other and had the potential to enlarge, thereby enabling discussion. Such ideas and practices would no longer exist in parallel or beneath the mainstream, but would co-exist in dynamic interaction. These ideas could then cohere into subcultures that would energise, if not actually subvert, the status quo. Taylor was indeed a tall poppy –

brash and seen as arrogant, determined to bring change and therefore, in the local environment, a threat: someone who needed to be controlled and cut down.

In the exhibition 'Tall Poppies', Taylor presented the works of the artists as signifying 'a crossroad, a meeting place for historical quotation, materialism, opportunism, decoration and the image',[11] rather than as exemplars of the modernist notion of linearity, continuity, and progress. The tall poppies were therefore a gift in the form of a bouquet of contradictions. Cut down, yes, but rearranged to take on new meanings, and not just those associated with a punch in the face.

The contemporaneous responses to 'Tall Poppies' were fewer than those engendered by 'POPISM' the year before. The University Art Gallery was smaller and was seen as a less significant institution; compared with a state gallery, it was not the desired site with the corresponding resources, potential audience, and status. The catalogues for both 'POPISM' and 'Tall Poppies' were, however, similar in scale, despite the 'POPISM' exhibition being nearly three times the size. The tone in the 'Tall Poppies' exhibition and catalogue was subtly elegiac, rather than overtly provocative. Bright colour appeared only in John Nixon's work, and the only movement was John Dunkley-Smith's slide carousel and that of the occasional visitor. At the time, Melbourne University student Juliana Engberg approvingly noted 'the positioning of the exhibition in the hot house of academia', and Taylor wrote in the final paragraph of his 'Tall Poppies' essay that mourning for the conventions of modernism within such confines seemed complete.[12]

Fellow student Naomi Cass reported in the same broadsheet on an evening discussion with Taylor, his opening remarks being, 'I have no message to impart, and write from the position of having nothing to say'.[13] For Taylor, Cass continues, 'the *present* is the only period we can study first hand', however, she notes, 'it is not clear when the present began and how much it is contingent upon and knowable in terms of the past. Notions such as *quotation* and *cover version* ... point to the importance of the past, even though importance must be conferred upon aspects of the past by someone in the present.'

Artist and critic Robert Rooney reviewed 'Tall Poppies' for *Flash Art*. He liked Taylor's 'curatorial selectivity over bland inclusiveness', the latter being common, he thought, to most contemporary exhibitions of Australian art.[14] Rooney also approved of Taylor's 'swift blow to a flourishing fine arts industry, exhuming the gutless corpses of early Australian modernism', and that he seemed 'to thrive on conflict and opposition.'

The most revealing contemporaneous account of 'Tall Poppies' and Taylor's modus operandi, however, came from the man himself, in an interview with writer Christina Davidson. Taylor's seriousness, as much as his provocations, are evident in statements such as these:

> the function of an art critic is to be someone who brings particular roles and ideas, bodies of work and audiences together on certain points and then allows them to disperse again. It's a way of opening up a debate and an argument and that's a very healthy thing, a way of artists seeing their work in an entirely different way...[15]

Or: 'artists are critics first and foremost. Behind every artwork is another artwork that the piece we are looking at is in some way a response to and a challenge to and a variation of.'

When asked to explain his contradictory statements and writings, given he said he had nothing to say, Taylor replied: 'When I have been most clear ... is when I have made connections between things that weren't there before ... I'm very fond of contradicting myself. I think that inconsistency and error are becoming more important.'

On 'POPISM': 'I got a big shock seeing the show up and I realised that there was a much greater kinship between pictorial signification and the process of cultural reification than I had expected. In fact the show was almost describing rather than deconstructing the order of meaning.'

On 'Tall Poppies':

> If Australians are going to be reflexive about their regional situation, it's going to be to understand the position of combative anti-modernist thought which is really the tradition of Australian art ... A lot of the backdrop to Australian art was quite antagonistic to an intellectual culture ... The Tall Poppies are the artists who have this situation as their backdrop: they don't really have a lineage within Australian art, they are just isolated instances.

Key, then, is what Taylor learnt from 'POPISM' and channelled into 'Tall Poppies' — that art could not be positioned in such a way so that it appeared, even if only to the curator, to describe anything, just as Taylor's own words had to momentarily crystallise a set of ideas which would then dissolve in order to re-form elsewhere and in another way. This made Taylor quite different as a thinker and curator from those who were visiting Australia at the time he was active. Germano Celant, Achille Bonita Oliva and others tended to gather a coterie of like-minded artists around them and form a 'school', which, for someone like Celant, had meant Arte Povera and, for Bonita Oliva, transavantgarde art. Taylor refers to Bonita Oliva in a 1982 essay for *Flash Art*, noting that the visitor 'suggested our TransAvantGarde art might resemble a pop art because popular culture and imagery have constituted our major historical tradition'.[16] Bonita Oliva was thinking of painting and where Australian artists might fit within his ideas. His interests were more in line with the kind of emotionally loaded expressions of Dale Frank and Mike Parr than the cooler intellectual work of the artists who had appeared in 'POPISM'.[17]

Cultural theorist Adrian Martin, paraphrasing Philip Brophy, has described the 'wilful dilettantism' of Taylor and many of the artists associated with 'POPISM' who thereby embodied personal, professional and intellectual risks.[18] Such dilettantism was often commonplace amongst the eclectic collection of artists, writers, theorists, filmmakers, curators and musicians at that time and nowhere more so than for Taylor himself. This approach was also reflected through and between the covers of *Art & Text*.

'Tall Poppies' was no exception in terms of Taylor's thinking. The majority of the five artists, however, are now no longer part of the margins and may never have aspired to reside there, or as part of subculture(s), in the first place. The artists' backgrounds in diverse media and ideas coalesced momentarily into five different 'pictures' in one context. For little more than a month in 1983, the pictures came together at the behest of Taylor who was curious to see what might happen in consideration of the attention the artists had garnered from curators from elsewhere. This was his 'curatorial acquiescence', just as Australia's parochialism was refracted through the title, 'Tall Poppies'.

Paul Taylor's '70s

Rex Butler & Susan Rothnie

Take a typical Tom Nicholson work like *2pm Sunday 25 February 1862* (2005) or *Action for 2pm Sunday 6 July 1835* (2005). The two works refer to historic meetings between Europeans and Aborigines in colonial Australia, although the exact circumstances of these meetings are lost to history and there is some dispute as to not only the dates of these meetings but whether they took place at all. It is not, however, that Nicholson actually intends to restage the original event. Rather, like one of those time travel stories in which a small change in the past leads to a widening series of divergences in the future, we might say that we could not have had this reconciliation between white and black in the past in order to produce the present in which Nicholson produces his work. That is, it is not so much a matter of Nicholson meaning to change history as thinking through the impossibility of changing it, with the present we inhabit arising only as the condition of a certain repression or forgetting in the past (and with Nicholson commemorating these non-events in the past in the only appropriate way as a certain non-event in the present). In a subtle distinction from any historical revisionism, Nicholson is attempting to think the very absence or non-event that makes his thinking of history possible. It is undoubtedly for this reason that commentators are able to describe his work as an 'evanescence in the present', because what we see there stands in for its own impossibility, and appears only to remind us that the events it speaks of could never have taken place.[1]

Nicholson's work is, of course, insistently contemporary, but it is also insistently 1970s with its posters, banners, utopian politics and marching crowds. (And Nicholson has made a whole series of other works, such as *Seven Days (Action)* (2003) and *Marches for May Day* (2005), in which crowds march with more general blank or generic banners and placards.) And, we want to suggest that, among the many absences the work wants to think—think as the very impossibility of doing so—is that of the 1970s. It would be the '70s not as any rendezvous with the future or subsequently revealed truth of the work, but as an always missed rendezvous and the lack of any final truth to the work. It would be the '70s as a period—and here the parallel with those historical events the work seeks to commemorate – that is always excluded or left out to produce the art-historical present we now inhabit: the contemporary. The '70s would be left out to produce the contemporary, which at once represses the '70s and is indebted to it. The missed meeting between an event and its public in Nicholson's works refers not only to a past (and contemporary) event that did not eventuate, but also to an art-historical '70s, with all of its utopian and soon-to-be-disillusioned hopes for an art that would change the world.

The Marxist cultural critic Fredric Jameson once wrote an essay entitled 'Periodizing the '60s' (1984), which took up some of these issues. In his essay, Jameson looks at the '60s decade of society and culture, which he characterises in terms of its 'poly-valence', 'heterogeneity' and lack of any 'unified field theory', and which we might equate here in Australia with our '70s. Jameson's point – despite the title of his essay – is that the '60s is in fact very difficult to periodise. Or that, for all of the attempts to do so – the essay lists, amongst others, 'Third World Beginnings', 'The Politics of Otherness', 'Digression on Maoism' and 'The Withering Away of Philosophy' – they all properly fail to do so. There is always something about the '60s, for all of its decisive transitional character, that obdurately refuses to fit the existing (or any possible) historical schema. It is a period that is not only culturally and politically, but historically and even historiographically, excessive. The radicality of the '60s, we might say, lies not just in its content (any particular one of its qualities) but in something like its form (the fact that it embodies so many contradictory qualities). As Jameson admits with regard to the limitations of his own Marxist method:

> Yet the forces [that the State] must now confront, contain and control are new ones, on which the older methods do not necessarily work [...] Such newly released forces do not only not seem to compute in the dichotomous class model of traditional Marxism; they also seem to offer a realm of freedom and voluntarist possibility beyond the classical constraints of the economic infrastructure.[2]

And all of this is carried on in Jameson's 1973 essay 'The Vanishing Mediator: Narrative Structure in Max Weber'. There he addresses German sociologist Max Weber's well-known thesis that Protestantism is the missing link between the medieval world and capitalism. That is, in order to have capitalism, there must first be something like the ethics of 'saving' or 'thrift' of Protestantism, but once capitalism is established Protestantism is unnecessary and is written out of history (capitalism as the liquefaction of all prior values and beliefs). As Marx makes clear, capitalism is an idea that needs to conceive of itself as existing forever. It understands itself as subject to no evolution or 'pre-history', but rather as a 'universal history' that has existed unchanged from the beginning. However, in order to have this 'universal history', which is not simply wrong, we need the missing link of Protestantism. It is precisely Protestantism that allows capitalism to be self-explanatory. Protestantism thus acts like the 'vanishing mediator' of capitalism.[3] Protestantism is what allows us to get from medievalism to capitalism, but after capitalism it disappears, even though it is its secret explanation. It is swallowed up by its own success, as is the case for every truly revolutionary force in history.

Paul Taylor, more than anything else, was a critic who was interested in, indeed obsessed by, the 1970s. He realised that it was an obstacle to the particular form of Australian art he wanted to bring about and would have to be written out. And Taylor was right: increasingly since his death, the '70s have emerged not as something that disappears in the passage between modernism and postmodernism, but as what we might speak of as the 'vanishing mediator' between the modern and the contemporary. Indeed, if anything, it is the 1980s—Taylor's postmodernism—that is now disappearing in accounts of Australian art, that has become increasingly harder to give shape and meaning to (and already the recovery efforts have begun, with a recent show at the University of Queensland Art Museum, 'Return to Sender', which takes up that generation of Queensland artists who moved interstate or overseas while Bjelke-Petersen was in power, and the more recent 'Mix Tape 1980s' at the National Gallery of Victoria, which actually runs together the '70s and '80s). But we would say that all of these efforts are ultimately doomed. The 'vanishing mediator' having recently been discovered, the history of Australian art is increasingly being written from the perspective of the '70s. And we have a sense of all of this with the 'Impresario' conference attempting to remember or commemorate Taylor, who was once surely the most ubiquitous and often-quoted Australian art critic since Bernard Smith, as though his legacy is in danger of slipping away. But, to explain...

From the very beginning, Taylor was keen to distinguish what he was doing from what came before, which he characterised broadly as the distinction between the 1970s and the 1980s. Taylor was famous for his whole attitude, which soon became a style, imitated by others, of dismissing high culture, feminism, humanism, political correctness, the original work of art and art history. Against this, there was his assertion of homosexuality, disco, the fake, popular culture and the 'second degree'. There was his provocative riposte to the feminist journal *Lip* (or was that Adrian Martin?),[4] his curt dismissal of Greenberg in an interview,[5] his levelling of cultural distinctions, his flaunting of self-contradiction. It was all done undeniably with a certain flair and desire to provoke. (Part of its charm, or let us say its tolerability, was its deliberateness, the fact that it appeared not so much a real emotional or intellectual response as a conscious strategy.) It is an approach that won him as many enemies as friends, from the lame rip-off *Art & a Texta* to Marxist academic Stan Anson,[6] art school teacher Gordon Bull,[7] feminist critic and curator Julie Ewington, and University Professor Virginia Spate (and a number of these critiques Taylor even published in *Art & Text*).

But Taylor's critics (and advocates) invariably missed what was original about Taylor's argumentative style. The distinctions he drew were not so much between one period and another, both equally full of artistic qualities, as between one period, the '80s, and nothing. It is this that constitutes the absolute novelty of what Taylor was doing, which he was the first to introduce into Australian art writing and which has become its default mode ever since. (We are using it here, for instance.) Taylor does not so much argue against what comes before him as double it, revise it, give it an explanation that it does not itself possess. We begin to get some insight into this when we look at his 'Editorial: On Criticism' for the first issue of *Art & Text*. In his editorial, Taylor does not characterise the '70s as a particular style or even series of styles (which would allow him to periodise it). Rather, he speaks of it as a plurality of styles, which prevents any attempt to summarise or comprehend the period or make it work artistically or critically. This plurality of styles lacks *a* style or meaning (and hence *any* style or meaning). As Taylor writes:

> The counter-cultures of the early and mid-seventies which espoused pluralism as an alternative have become themselves an institution; their critical apparatus has become a block to analysis [...] As such, pluralism and its related alternative institutions of power compels the experimenter to transgress further boundaries.[8]

And Taylor's aim – in a gesture or 'transgression' he repeated throughout his work – is not so much directly to refute, oppose or dismiss the '70s as to give it a meaning. Now there is no longer a pluralism, but this pluralism is a sign of, stands in for, something. And this something is the *sign*. The sign of postmodernism is not a content – something real that is opposed to the '70s – but a form. Postmodernism repeats or has the same content as the '70s (it can encompass anything), but it has a different form. As Taylor writes in his catalogue for a touring show of Australian art, 'Eureka!', in 1982, drawing a contrast between the postmodernism he advocates and the art of the '70s:

> This [postmodernism] is an art involved in plotting the play of meaning rather than the search for meaning. It takes as its primary materials the body as signifier, pre-existing technology, images and modes of representation, and thereby attempts to short-circuit the mimetic attachment to 'natural' materials.[9]

And, indeed, there was a very acute awareness by several of Taylor's better critics that what Taylor was introducing was an opposition, distinction or hierarchy (one thing explaining another) where there was none before. As Ewington wrote in her 'Fragmentation and Feminism' of 1982: 'Do not suppose that what is at issue here is an actual opposition of a simple kind, between the darlings of Postmodernist criticism, between the New Image/Bad Painting and the chic semiotic delinquency of sophistication and Political art which sets about purposeful analysis and didactic image-making'.[10] And, as Spate argued in her 'Whatever Happened to the Art of the Seventies?', Taylor's '80s was only a repetition of what had come before, but in a different mode or model. That is, many of the strategies that claimed to be postmodern – like quotation, self-parody, juxtaposition and disjunction – had already been employed by socially critical modernist forms that 'call on the spectator's necessary participation in the processes of creating relationships'.[11]

However, we must be more precise here. Spate is obviously correct in suggesting that Taylor's postmodernism is a continuation of what we already know as modernism. Its tactics of montage, quotation and the incorporation of items from popular culture are already to be found in Dada and Surrealism, amongst other art movements. But Taylor is not *opposed* to modernism (as we shall see, his Popism is more properly considered a continuation of modernism). Rather, he is opposed to the '70s. He is opposed to the non- or anti-modernism of the '70s. That is, again, he is not opposed to the '70s insofar as it is something. He is opposed to the '70s insofar as it is nothing, insofar as it cannot be summarised, insofar as it is plural, ahistorical, non-critical and non-teleological. And in a brilliant conceptual doubling, this meaningless pluralism is rewritten by Taylor as the sign of something. It is, indeed, understood as allowed, made possible, by the sign: 'The [photographic] caption embodies the involvement of the verbal in an emptied pictorial sign – it is the supplement that directs and anchors meaning and whose use increases as the image's specific meaning decreases'.[12] And this sign, in turn, is always the sign of a certain distance or provincialism. Again, as Taylor writes: 'This art [of the 1980s], born in mediation, has gestated within the camera where things are naturally upside down and is expressed in a carnivalesque array of copies, inversions and negatives'.[13] After Taylor (this is Taylor's hope), we can never look at the '70s as such, but only as a symptom, as standing in for or having to be explained by something other: the '70s would be both something standing in for the sign and something peculiarly Australian.

This is the meaning behind Taylor's 1984 anthology on the '70s, *Anything Goes: Art in Australia 1970–1980*. Paradoxically, the argument of *Anything Goes* is that, for Taylor at least, not anything goes or not anything went. The whole book is structured so that Taylor's own 'Australian "New Wave" and the "Second Degree"', originally published in *Art & Text* in 1981, comes at the end, serving as its summing up and retrospective truth (and the oddness of the selection is indicated by the fact that Taylor's is the only essay in the book that deals with the '80s, which of course is after when the book is meant to end). Thus we have Ann Stephen on women's art, Janine Burke on community murals, Julie Ewington on political postering, Christine Godden on amateur photography, Memory Holloway on Minimalism, and Patrick McCaughey on Colour Field painting, but with all of these '70s tendencies taken into account by Taylor at the end of the book when he writes:

> To such inhabitants of the 'second degree', nothing except the manner and power of a quotation is new. The only quality in a fiction seems to be in its retelling [...] Consequently, the artists discussed above can successfully display the variety of means by which the conventional signification and preconception about natural modes are subverted.[14]

Taylor is opposed to feminism, performance, political art, the counterculture and consciousness-raising – and he says as much – but the deeper, more profound aspect of his criticism is that all of these seemingly divergent tendencies are in fact the same. All must be understood in the 'second degree', as not only mediated but actually brought about by the sign, as arising out of the effects of mechanical reproduction. All of them are made equivalent insofar as they are seen as signs of the '70s: the plural no longer as plural but as signifying plurality, no longer resistant in its excess to art history, but merely another moment within this history.

It is all of this that is to be seen in Taylor's famous 1982 show 'POPISM'. The underlying argument of the show, ultimately derived from Paul Foss's 1981 essay 'Theatrum Nondum Cognitorum', is that Australia is a creation of the map.[15] It exists in reproduction before being discovered in reality. (Foss's is an essay that is duly noted, along with many others, in the footnotes to Taylor's catalogue essay, giving it the look of one of Juan Davila's paintings of the '80s, in which all of its various artistic sources or appropriations are listed on the canvas.) In the show, we have Maria Kozic's reproductions of images from Warhol, Imants Tillers's quotations from Aboriginal art, Jenny Watson's deliberately naïve paintings of photos by Richard Avedon, Super-8 films by Paul Fletcher and Jane Stevenson, semi-random snapshots from the Society for Other Photography, and Davila's *Hysterical Tears* (1980) and *Miss Sigmund* (1981). And this art of the second degree is seen to correspond to something deeply 'unoriginal' in Australian culture, the fact that we never see reality directly in our art but only as mediated by the sign:

> When in Australia last year, Achille Bonita Oliva suggested that our Transavantgarde art might resemble a Pop Art because popular culture and imagery have constituted our major visual tradition. Popism, however, focused itself upon the rhetoric of photography, rather than painting, as the bearer of a specifically Australian utterance.[16]

But, again, in a strategy typical of Taylor – it is the way a new master-signifier works to requilt the field in which it is inserted – in remarking this provincial pluralism, the works in 'POPISM' also seek to overcome it. The enunciation that is able to speak of Australian cultural dependency is necessarily outside of it (the peculiar and self-contradictory privileging of the critic in Taylor, for all of his assertions of unoriginality). That is, in a famous paradox – perhaps brought to Taylor's attention by Tillers in his essay 'Locality Fails', but also to be seen in a certain reversal in Foss's 'Theatrum Nondum Cognitorum', in which 'it is no longer we who act as balance or sponge for the artefacts of a European civilisation'[17] – in speaking of provincialism, the artist or critic triumphs over it. In making a sign of it, there is also produced a certain place or exception not subject to it. As Taylor writes in a later explanation of the show, setting out the distinction very clearly: 'Our art and criticism have recently sought to reverse the shame of earlier generations concerning cultural alienation and instead exploit that alienation as part of a multi-national strategy'.[18]

Taylor hence inaugurates the long period of postmodernity or even post-coloniality, which in many ways we are still living through. The classic accounts of Australian art history move straight from 1968 to 1982, from 'The Field' to 'POPISM', the modern to the postmodern, without stopping in between.[19] We have either postmodernism as the critique of modernism (as Taylor would have it) or modernism as already postmodern (as Spate would have it). It makes no difference. We can see 'POPISM' either as a break with 'The Field' – contesting its imported American avant-gardism – or 'The Field' as already Popist – Ian Burn's and Nigel Lendon's interpretation of the show as evidencing a type of 'cultural distancing'.[20] This revisionism is the method Taylor applied to the 1970s, and it henceforth becomes the prevailing logic of Australian art history. We do not so much contest the canon or introduce new figures into it as re-read the canon in order to reveal how the past is an effect of the present. This method, which leads to a kind of historical relativism that nevertheless exempts its own position, can be seen for example in the most recent instalment of the Adelaide Biennale, 'Parallel Collisions' (2012), which describes itself as showing 'how ideas emerge, converge and re-form over time'.[21] And it is to be seen even in one of Nicholson's works for the show, *Evening Shadows* (2010–11), in which he removes the original H.J. Johnstone *Evening Shadows* (1880), a painting of an isolated Aboriginal family camped at the end of a billabong as the sun goes down, from the wall of the art gallery, and replaces it with many amateur copies of the work, exactly as an emblem of the many readings the work has received over the years, many of which make the point that, as opposed to Johnstone's prediction, Aborigines are not a 'dying race' and have not been assimilated within white society.

Historical revisionism in Australia is always accompanied by something like Taylor's ironic restatement of Australian identity as empty, the mimetic reproduction of other cultures. We have the rewriting of the landscapes of Nolan and Williams, in the light of such Tillers works as *The Nine Shots* (1985) and *The Antipodean Manifesto* (1986), as the attempt to represent not so much a place as the space between places. That is, we are meant to see in Nolan and Williams's landscapes, with their high horizons that bring the back of the canvas to the front, an attempt to figure the distance or emptiness that defines Australia. But, of course, after Nolan and Williams, we discover the same spatial organisation everywhere in Australian landscape, from the empty middle grounds of Eugene von Guérard's cattle stations to the abysses of Augustus Earle's Blue Mountains, all the way back to the melancholy and tentative dabs of the distant shores in the First Fleet artists. And, moving forward, we see the same fundamental insight into the 'emptiness' of the landscape and the attempt to record a kind of pure distance in the desert waterholes of John Olsen, the Sydney Harbours of Brett Whiteley, the *Mirror Pieces* and *Blue Reflexes* of Ian Burn, in Tim Maguire's corrugated iron watertanks, which can be seen as a response to Burn, and even in the Baroque 'up from under' of the rainforests of William Robinson. The entire Australian landscape tradition can now seem not the expression of any *genius loci* or the attempt to represent a specific light, land or people, but rather the paradoxical attempt to paint nothing, a non-place, a (in Foss's terms) nondum. And, similarly, after Taylor's 'POPISM', every Australian artist seems a proto-appropriator, stitching together elements from other cultures in an ironic playing out of our provincialism: from Thomas Watling's 'mongrel' vernacular (Ross Gibson),[22] through Margaret Preston's 'bracketting' of the Indigenous elements in her still lives (Nicholas Thomas),[23] Nolan's 'mocking the idea of dependence' (Ian Burn)[24] and on to Albert Namatjira's 'mimicry' of his teacher Rex Battarbee's artistic language (Burn and Ann Stephen).[25] Again, all of these artists appear as virtual Tillers before their time, seeking to 'reverse the shame of earlier generations concerning cultural alienation' and instead exploring that alienation 'as part of a multi-national strategy'.

But wait. In order for these readings or re-readings to work—in Tillers, obviously, but also in Nolan and Williams and all of those others—we need to conceive of the country as empty. That is, for all of its rhetorical invocation of Aboriginality, its comparing of European Australian artists to nomadic 'white Aborigines', Popism is finally a rhetoric of 'terra nullius'. And against this reading of Williams—itself disappointingly absent in the recent

National Gallery of Australia retrospective of his work[26] – we might think of those speckled black dots and smudges in his canvas as symptomal indications of an Indigenous presence, or, as has often been noted, of Nolan's black-helmeted Ned as a stand-in for displaced Aborigines. And all this might be thought in another sense. Popism is a brilliant response to the well-known 'provincialism problem'. Tillers is quite right when he insists that he does not follow the logic of Terry Smith's essay on the topic but argues against it, ironically mimics it in order to overturn it. But, of course, in another way, Smith is right: provincialism is proved in its exceptions. As he writes in his 'The Provincialism Problem' of 1974: 'The system is structured so that several artists every few years have to "break the bind".'[27] Perhaps, indeed, in all of this the more profound point is that Popism revives the provincialism problem (in the form of its supposed refutation) exactly at a time when it no longer applied. Even Bernard Smith in the second edition of his *Australian Painting* argued that by 1970 'there were indications that Australia was beginning to create nascent metropolitan situations in its main capital cities'.[28] That is, Popism is a retrieval of a national or nationalist art, no matter how ironically, at a time when it was dying out. Taylor's 'multi-national' strategy – and he is explicit on this – is still a form of nationalism, just as Tillers's fantasy of the provinces sending back their copies to the centre is ultimately a replay of Bernard Smith's *European Vision* and its contention that it was the fauna and flora of the South Pacific that led to the Romanticism that overturned Neo-Classicism back in Europe.

We speak of Taylor's Popism as the revival of nationalism at a time when it was dead. When could it be said to have died out, no longer to compel artists as a way of making art? Bernard Smith suggests that it was by the beginning of the '70s. And we would agree. It was the '70s, with its Conceptual and mail art, its collaborations and reproductions, its non-critical, non-historical and non-progessivist notion of art, that was already global, already an overcoming or, better, a forgetting of the provincial. The '70s was already an era of a non-national UnAustralian art, of what we might call a certain 'globalism before globalism'. (And, indeed, if we go back to that great 'Australian' exhibition, 'The Field' of 1968, one peculiar aspect of it, virtually never noted in all of the commentary, is just how many of the artists in it were either not Australians or Australians living overseas at the time of the show: Mel Ramsden, James Doolin, John White, Ian Burn, Michael Kitching, Ron Robertson-Swann. This is the truly innovative thing about the show, the actual way it ushers in the '70s, as opposed to that tired old question of whether it is modern or postmodern.) Taylor's Popism, that is, proposes a national art at a time when the national was no longer the ruling assumption in either Australian art or art historiography.

In fact, it is in this connection that we might see the true logic of Popism and the deepest cultural affiliation of Taylor. When we look at Taylor's 'POPISM' exhibition, three things are particularly notable. It is an argument about national identity, the fourteen chosen artists are all figurative in some way, and twelve of the fourteen come from Melbourne. What is it, then, that 'POPISM' reminds us of? Not 'The Field', the exhibition it is always paired with, also held at the National Gallery of Victoria, some fourteen years before, but Bernard Smith's 'The Antipodeans', held at the Victorian Artists' Society rooms in Melbourne, some twenty-three years before. Smith's show too was a protest against internationalism and the perceived loss of Australian identity. It too featured figurative art as opposed to abstraction. And it was a show of Melbourne artists, as opposed in those days — but what really has changed? — to artists from Sydney, who were seen as internationalist in their abstraction. Here is Taylor on 'POPISM': 'The imagery speaks of two things — a domestic, close-at-hand and suburban image pool, one that is particularly child-like (with an attendant "innocence"), and one which operates in a close relation to current cultural reproduction'.[29] And here is Smith on The Antipodeans: 'Destroy the living power of the image and you have humbled and humiliated the artist, have made him a blind and powerless Samson fit only to grind the corn of the Philistines. As Antipodeans we accept the image as representing some form of acceptance of an involvement in life.'[30]

But, of course, to begin with, 'Australian' art is not confined to that made in Melbourne — or Sydney. It is also made in Adelaide, Perth, Hobart, Brisbane, Yuendumu, Papunya — and London, Paris, Belle-Île, Seattle, New York, Hawai'i, and so on. It is the '70s and not the '80s that explains how we got from modernism not to postmodernism, but to what we might call the contemporary. It is the '70s that is already global, plural, post-critical, relational, Aboriginal, an art about 'others'. It is, in fact, its very plurality, its inability to be spoken of critically or summed up historically, its lack of one defining medium, the fact that it does not stand in for anything, that makes the '70s a forerunner to today. It is the '70s, in its very unrecuperability, its unnarratabilty, our inability to give it any art-historical consequence or say it leads to anything, that makes the period our art-historical vanishing mediator. Indeed, in that double anachronism we see in Nicholson's work, it is in saying that the '70s never happened that we might also say that the '70s have never ended. To paraphrase a Pop song from the period, we're still living in the '70s.

And is this not, finally, what certain feminist critics of the time recognised? They may not have recognised Taylor's strategy, but they responded to it and in many ways even repeated it themselves. For, if we read again Spate's 'Whatever Happened to the Seventies?', we can see her speaking of certain 'obdurate' artistic practices of the '70s that live on despite their historical 'denial'.[31] If we read again Ewington's 'Fragmentation and Feminism', we can see her at once complaining about the 'loss of diversity' of Taylor's '80s and speaking of the way that, against this, the '80s should themselves be characterised as a 'pluralist ideology', with Taylor's semiotic-based art only one of many different alternatives.[32] In other words, if Spate and Ewington do not exactly grasp Taylor's own strategy of rewriting the '70s, they nevertheless attempt themselves to rewrite his '80s. It is not the '80s that seeks to foreclose on '70s pluralism, but the '80s that must themselves be seen as a continuation of this pluralism. It is not the '80s that is the retrospective truth and destiny of the '70s, but the '70s that make possible the '80s. And, perhaps as much as anything, Australian art history is today suspended between these alternatives — with the very choice between them, if not the actual choice we will make, owing everything to Taylor.

Part III

Sources: Interviews

Deliberately provocative
Patrick McCaughey interviewed by Janine Burke

April 16, 2012

JB: Patrick, in the early 1970s, you were invited to start the Visual Arts Department at Monash University. Can you tell me about your vision for it?

PM: Well, I suppose the thing which was utmost in my mind when I went out to Monash was that I really didn't want to bore the students by talking about what was remote from them in time and culture. I mean, University of Melbourne had a perfectly good Fine Arts department, but they start with the pyramids and then took ages to work through Classical Antiquity – which is so remote from students coming to Monash. There's so much in Western art history which is really good and interesting and exciting; why not start with that? So we started with what I call the beginning of the modern period; we began with Giotto. And they were just the most marvellous students. They came in on the Red Plan and the Yellow Plan and all those wonderful schemes that Whitlam introduced, so that people of character could come to university. One of my students used to say, 'we used to spell Giotto J-o-t-t-o', and I thought, well, these are the right people that I'm talking to. And the one thing I wanted to make sure of, from the beginning, was that they had a real sense of engagement with art of their time and in their space. So the first term was about the Italian Renaissance, the Italian Revolution; the next term we did nineteenth and early twentieth century, and in the third term we did the rise of modern architecture from about 1870. We took everyone on a bus all around Melbourne, showing them the rise of modern architecture via Melbourne examples. And that was very exciting for both me and the students.

JB: Paul Taylor was one of your students, at BA level. What are your memories of him?

PM: I think Paul was in the first intake. From the beginning, he was fantastically independently minded. 'Pleasantly obstreperous' is how I would describe him. Always questioning, never taking the stuff for pap, sometimes reading the article which you hadn't read which you should have read, and so on – and very much dining out on it. We got on very well personally. I admired him as a student as his papers were lively. I was recently shown again his final year honours thesis, on sculpture in the 1960s; it was a very careful, well thought out work. As a Monash student, he could also take courses at the University of Melbourne. He decided in his final year to take a course with Margaret Plant on Marcel Duchamp and his influence. And I would have to say that I think that particular course, taught brilliantly by Margaret Plant, was probably as influential as anything in Paul's undergraduate career. I mean, he was faintly patronising in his attitude to me ever afterwards – but I didn't take offence.

JB: Can you tell me about some of Paul's contemporaries who were your students at that time?

PM: Paul came with a very gifted first intake, and I can remember them all quite vividly. Many of them went on to have very successful careers in art. Jan Minchin was, at one stage, a very gifted curator at the National Gallery of Victoria; she did a wonderful exhibition which we called 'The Fox and the Bunnies' ['The art of Rupert Bunny and E. Phillips Fox: paintings from the collection of the National Gallery of Victoria', 1984], which was on Emmanuel-Philips Fox and his wife, and Rupert Bunny, out at that awful outpost of the National Gallery, the dark side of wherever it was [Banyule Gallery] ... And there was Jenepher Duncan, who later became a curator at Monash and now of contemporary art at the Art Gallery of Western Australia. So it was a very rich matrix of students from which Paul came. And Paul was clearly the kind of intellectual leader of the group – there I would have no hesitation at all. They didn't bow down to him, they weren't obsequious; but you could see that there was a level of respect even when he was an undergraduate.

JB: And who were some of the other staff?

PM: Memory Holloway. John Gregory. One of the things which we did early on at Monash was to introduce film, and we had quite a successful early film series. David Hannan became a very successful lecturer in that. This was the kind of mix that Paul really wanted, I think. He already had a feeling that visual arts were extending themselves way beyond simply easel paintings and formalist sculptures.

JB: Paul's thesis was 'Sculpture and the Spectator 1962–1967'. Do you know why he would have chosen that? Would that have been in consultation with you, or would this be his own interest?

PM: The choice of his final year thesis essay on sculpture in the '60s probably came out of conversations with Memory Holloway, who I think supervised it. I think he was looking to refute Michael Fried, who had a view that Minimalism was all bad because it was only the spectator in response to it — a terribly theatrical circumstance, according to him. Whereas Paul had the sense that Minimal sculpture absolutely belonged to the great history of modernism; he wanted to dispute the Fried line that it was all spectator sport. I think Paul was right and Fried was wrong in this instance.

JB: Eventually, Paul left the academy and began *Art & Text*. Did he have any discussions with you about *Art & Text*? What were your impressions of the journal?

PM: I think Paul told me about it, and more or less said I was welcome to write for it — not over-enthusiastically. I have to say that, in those days, *Art & Australia* was a pretty institutionalised magazine, and there was really nothing else around. *Art & Text* was deliberately provocative, seeking out the new author, the new artist, the new writer, and so on. And it really did come with a kind of breath of fresh air and a kind of edge to it. In the late '70s, Melbourne was deadly. Paul gave the scene a real impetus with the journal. He took it very, very seriously.

JB: Then you left Monash and took the helm at the National Gallery of Victoria, as its director. Can you discuss the evolution of 'POPISM'?

PM: Well, if you're talking about the origins of 'POPISM', the one word you could not use is 'evolution' — because that's not how Paul worked. Paul came and told me that he wanted to do this exhibition, adding 'so what would the date be?', before there was any opportunity to discuss it with the curators or the Trustees or my Deputy Director or whomever. But I liked from the beginning that it had a real idea to it. He said, very early, that Pop turns out not to be simply a time-bound style, as Abstract Expressionism was. Pop turns out to be a great, mutating style, with a continuing shape and influence over artistic practice today — long after the Lichtensteins and the Warhols of this world had gone into the Pantheon, into the canon. That idea attracted me enormously. And he also talked about artists who might do the work, some of whom I knew very little about, others I knew quite well. It seemed to me that the most important thing in contemporary art was this: in this great sea of images and possibilities and forms and objects and non-objects and installations and videos and god knows what, here's somebody who had a real view about what was coherent and central at this moment of contemporary art. And anyway, it'd take a braver man than me to have turned Paul Taylor down. My deputy director Ken Hood hated the exhibition from birth and I think he refused to go to the opening. But I remember the whole thing just had this sense of clarity and purpose, which I really admired in Paul.

JB: When you saw the works up on the walls — you know, Jenny Watson, Juan Davila, a whole range of breakthrough artists at that time — what were your visceral responses to the show? Were you shocked, excited, numbed? What were some of the responses you had?

PM: I was really delighted and astonished by 'POPISM' when I finally saw it. It was livelier, it was less ideological than I thought it might have been. I mean, Paul, for all of his avant-garde attitudes, was a great lover of art — an art lover. That's a wonderfully old-fashioned phrase, but he actually liked objects. 'POPISM' was a tremendously object-based show. It ranged fantastically. The pieces I can remember so vividly were Howard Arkley and his fantastic arrangement of chairs, and the Maria Kozic pieces — those flying fish all over the space. 'POPISM' mixed installation, object and simply very good, strong works of art like Juan Davila's. It was based in objects — not in any ideology.

JB: I think this was one of the first exhibitions where Paul insisted that the artists be paid to participate. Do you remember that discussion?

PM: There was a great flap about that; it was kind of terrible. It was the first time it was ever done, and everybody was shocked: the National Gallery of Victoria paying artists! But, in the end, Paul made his point. I do think we were going to get benefits from it, and the crowds were going to pay to see it: it was a popular show, so there was a certain logic to it. But there was a bit of a flap at the Gallery at the time.

JB: Do you remember a good response from the general public to the exhibition? Was it a breakthrough exhibition – or a little bit difficult for people?

PM: I recall a tremendous *artistic* success. I mean, for all of about five minutes, the National Gallery of Victoria's stocks rose with contemporary artists from Melbourne: as a result, everybody is popular for fifteen minutes (to adapt Andy Warhol) – even at the National Gallery of Victoria. I don't think it brought the crowds. My memory was that I was a bit disappointed that it didn't draw a wider public. The reviews were strangely tepid, for some reason or other. They were not of the kind that were inclined to bring an audience in. And the kind of people that went along were partly intimidated by Paul Taylor, they didn't want to get into a row with him! So it wasn't an overwhelming public success.

JB: After Paul left for New York, did you continue to have contact with him?

PM: I did see him from time to time. I remember once, when he was putting together the *Anything Goes* anthology, he very generously said to me: 'Well, I'd like to include two of your pieces in this'. I thought it was a good housekeeping seal of approval from the succeeding generation to be approached by Paul in that way. I saw him a couple of times in New York; he was steaming around, certainly getting to know the scene – he told Robert Hughes that he wanted his job, which didn't go down wildly well with Hughes, but he was still the old Paul Taylor. He was pushing the envelope, pushing the edges, and so on. Now, New York is a big scene and there's more than one Paul Taylor floating around at any given moment. But I have no doubt that, had Paul lived, he would've been a real force, and a remarkable force, on the critical art scene in New York. And I rather would have hoped for him that he might have found a kind of position in art criticism somewhere. It's a shame: nowadays, he's the sort of critic that the *New York Times* would've absolutely taken to its bosom, whereas in those days its art criticism was very conservative indeed; the Paul Taylors of this world wouldn't have got a look in the door.

JB: Looking back, finally, at the 'POPISM' catalogue, it has quite a few resemblances to *Art & Text* itself—and a very extensive bibliography at the back. Do you think this bibliography, and Paul's scholarship in general, relates to his years at Monash?

PM: I'd like to claim credit for the extensive bibliography that Paul put into this—not without a tad of pretension, believe you me—but this is really all Paul's own work. I'm sure he came along, and—just as he muscled me into having the show—I'm sure he went down to the in-house designer, a very nice woman in those days, and muscled her into designing the rather (I have to say) flimsy catalogue of 'POPISM', along the lines of *Art & Text*. But Paul could muscle people with the greatest degree of charm, and they would come out in the end being grateful to him. That was part of his finesse as a human being.

John Nixon interviewed by David Homewood

February 8, 2013

DH: When were you first introduced to Paul?

JN: To be honest, I can't exactly remember how I was introduced to Paul. I probably would have first met him at Art Projects. In terms of his coming into the scene, Art Projects and *The Virgin Press* would have both been in existence. And in that sense, Paul, Ashley Crawford, and myself belonged to the same moment. And so I think Paul thought, 'If John can do this, and if Ashley can do this ... I can do a magazine'. The vision was there that an individual can do something, that an individual can do something to change the situation. Together, the three projects (Art Projects, *Virgin Press*, and *Art & Text*) created an atmosphere of discussion and involvement that allowed people from different scenes to come together. There was also an attempt to involve writers and artists from the Sydney scene within the local context. It was a matter of gathering around yourself other like-minded people who were pro this kind of activity, who were actually encouraging, who would say, 'Paul, that's a great idea', rather than, 'why would you want to do that?' or, 'why would you care?' The idea to work with one another was good, as a way of defining ourselves against the older generation, against the existing system. Paul had the initiative and the strength of character to actually make things happen. He wasn't going to be beaten at anything. If he really wanted to do it, he found a way. He basically made the first issues of *Art & Text* single-handedly. And the work in those days wasn't done on a computer, it was typewritten and typeset.

DH: So there was a strong affinity, then, between the DIY ethos governing your own practice, and that of the artists with whom you were associating, and Paul's will to start his magazine?

JN: Yes. You see, Paul was very socially able, very friendly, socially curious, he really liked to be informed. He wanted to ask you what was going on. While he learnt a lot from theory and reading books, he also learnt a lot from the people he was in association with.

I don't even really know who else he studied with, he seemed to be flying solo in that respect. He wanted to be with the artists, hook, line, and sinker. A certain image of Warhol, or Warhol's persona, was important to Paul. Warhol was much more than just an artist; he was also an advocate for lots of different activities. Paul liked this aspect of Warhol's work: having a place like the factory enabled everyone to come together and have fun. In some ways Paul's parties were like this. He had a lot of parties in his lovely apartment in South Yarra, in an apartment building called 'Beverley Hills.' Everything about this building was perfect for Paul's socialising. It was a very nice old Art Deco building with a swimming pool, like what you would have found in California. It was wonderful!

DH: Who were Paul's closest associates?

JN: He was very friendly with Philip Brophy, Maria Kozic, Vivienne Shark LeWitt, and Denise Robinson (who at that stage was director of the George Paton Gallery). Also with Judy Annear, Janine Burke, and Jenny Watson, and some other people who I didn't really know, like Adrian Martin and Christopher van der Craats. There was a group of young women from Melbourne University who were on the scene at Paul's parties: Robyn McKenzie, Christina Davidson, Sue Cramer and Louise Neri, and the Biltmoderne architects. Of the artists associated with Art Projects, John Dunkley-Smith, Peter Tyndall, Tony Clark and Lyndal Jones were good friends with Paul.

DH: Were you close to Philip and Maria at that time?

JN: Well, they were younger; I had my Art Projects group, so that was my cadre. Philip and Maria represented the Northcote side of Paul's friendship group, while Jenny Watson and I represented the Prahran–St Kilda division of the friendship group. Adrian was also very good friends with Philip and Maria.

DH: But you would have come into contact with Paul's Northcote clique at the Clifton Hill Community Music Centre (CHCMC)?

JN: Yes, but Clifton Hill wasn't really the central meeting point. It was more a subgroup within the art-music scene involving David Chesworth, and some of the older men associated with La Trobe music school, like Warren Burt. We would definitely go there but it was much less social. Paul's personal interest in music was disco; I think he found Philip and David and the musical scene in which they were involved very interesting, but he loved disco and dance music.

DH: To what extent did your Anti-Music ensemble converge with music performed or discussed at Clifton Hill?

JN: The two were quite distinct. It seems that it was something that happened concurrently rather than being influenced by it or anything like that. Anti-Music ran sort of counter to Clifton Hill. The artists involved in Anti-Music were the same as those involved with Art Projects.

DH: Who were the other visual artists involved in the Clifton Hill Community Music Centre?

JN: I don't know.

DH: Maybe there weren't many visual artists involved with Clifton Hill?

JN: I don't think so. Peter Tyndall might have gone a few times. I went a few times. I don't know whether Tony Clark ever went.

DH: You were by no means, then, a regular attendee.

JN: No, no, no. It was also this thing between living in St Kilda or living in Northcote. They seemed a long distance from one another. For the people in Clifton Hill, the CHCMC was the primary outlet for their creative work. They set up a place there to promote what they had done, similar to what I had done with Art Projects, where the artists constituted the principal audience for the work.

DH: To what extent did Paul's socialising feed into his curatorial practice?

JN: That he was able to do a show like 'POPISM' at the National Gallery of Victoria as a young man not long out of university shows something about his wide network of friends, as well as his gall, his intellect, and his ability to convince someone else about his project. 'POPISM' might have even been the first exhibition curated by a non-staff member at the National Gallery of Victoria. You don't normally get that gig: in-house curators are normally employed to do it. Paul would have gone to Patrick McCaughey, the Director at the time (who had also previously taught Paul in the Fine Arts department at Monash University), and said: 'I want to do this show, etc.'.

DH: Maybe we can talk about the curatorial agenda driving an exhibition like 'POPISM'. It seems to me, from a distance, that Paul's interest in your work might have been linked to his preoccupation with the artistic strategy of appropriation.

JN: Postmodernism was a particular attitude in our culture at the time Paul was studying, and this helped to shape his ideas for *Art & Text*, the sorts of essays he would publish in the magazine and also the type of thesis he would follow in making an exhibition. Through his interest in Warhol, Paul had a primary interest in Pop art ('Popism' is the title of a Warhol book) and he looked to gather artists with a pop sensibility for his exhibition. When he came to me to choose work for the exhibition, he selected the Polaroid project I devised under the banner of The Society for Other Photography – rather than my work as John Nixon – because The Society seemed to better conform to his curatorial concept. I was happy to be included, but there were artists like Robert Rooney, Maria Kozic, Howard Arkley, and Jenny Watson who were the full-forwards of the pop team. I was somewhere in the back pocket. I wasn't leading the argument. The other artists were definitely more involved in this pop sensibility, working with found imagery, scavenged material, and so forth.

DH: Your contribution to 'POPISM' as The Society for Other Photography was quite different from that of the artists you just mentioned, in the sense that it was more closely linked to the legacy of, say, Conceptual art, than Pop art. You're not recycling imagery...

JN: Yes, I pointed the camera at things I found interesting. The imagery came from daily life – it wasn't coming from the landscape, or from photos of the moon or something. In a sense, this everyday quality might have been how the works fitted in with the broader thesis of the show.

DH: In these photographs, were there any further criteria you used to determine where you would point the camera? Or was it more intuitive?

JN: Pretty much purely intuitive. Whereas the photography of Ed Ruscha or Robert Rooney was based on serial repetition, my photographs were composed more in line with constructivist principles; I often composed using diagonals. Sometimes, for example, I would go to an amusement park, where I would find strange imagery, like of the Ferris wheel, for example, in which the depicted subject matter would not immediately be apparent. So there was a level of abstraction inherent to this series that is still evident in the photography I practice today.

DH: And what camera were you using?

JN: A Polaroid SX70.

DH: In order to draw out the difference between your own understanding of your practice and Paul's understanding of your practice, I want to read a passage from Paul's 1981 article 'Australian "New Wave" and the "Second Degree"'.

JN: Which I'm not mentioned in.

DH: Well, not explicitly, but Paul does discuss Arkley's reconstruction of de Stijl furniture.

JN: Ah yes. I helped Howard with that.

DH: Here is the quote: '...the history of Modernist art itself is being interpreted by many New Wave artists as a series of signs and as a style which can be quoted. Adopting a pose at once cynical and naïve, many young artists are juggling with Modernist conventions – retrieving and synthesising them while collectively "forgetting" the conditions which spawned them. In this context, these artists are directing our attention to the question of Modernism's decline.'[1] Did you see your own work at the time as engaging in a practice of 'quotation' that was at once 'cynical and naïve'?

JN: It's a matter of how you see it. Say you're looking at an artwork made in 1910: Looking with your left eye, it's about the end or death of modernism, whereas with your right eye, it's about influence and continuity. These two attitudes co-existed in the early 1980s. It wasn't always a cynical attitude [the left eye] that took over at this moment, there was also a different approach, one of genuine appreciation of past art, its just that this attitude lay outside the postmodernist theorist's focus and thus tended to be overlooked... Now that the cloud of postmodernism has passed, we can move back to the idea of influence in art. I'm not saying that Paul was wrong, it was the way that he saw it and it was true of many of the artists he associated with.

But in my case, because I was older, I was interested in Constructivism before postmodernism hit. I learned about it through my interest in Minimal art, especially reading texts by the Minimal artists, who in the 1960s were themselves inspired by Constructivist art, not as 'quotation', but as a form of continuation. So I was the one saying, 'No, hang on a minute, there are certain works that might be influenced by van Gogh, or Duchamp, or other aspects of modernism without being cynical. I was always a believer, and as a believer I had faith. In my mind, postmodernists had no faith and said, 'let's just quote or appropriate this or that for our own end'. But Paul had his own approach and sometimes you just have to let people have their own say: they see it their way.

DH: But your painting practice from 1977 onwards seems to be explicitly engaging with the history of art in a way that the work of Malevich and the Suprematist circle wasn't: their work is often understood as a break with what had come before. If we are prepared to admit your post-1977 work as 'modernist', then it is a different kind of 'modernist': one that is prepared to go back and selectively borrow from certain past conventions.

JN: Constructivism radically changed the focus of art. You could argue that it was the first type of art to throw away realism. These artists developed a new language. At the same time, they still brought some things from the past like the icon, and the corner piece. The invention of abstraction was one of those breakthroughs that actually affected the whole world. We can reflect on this now with the 2013 exhibition 'Inventing Abstraction 1910–1925', at the Museum of Modern Art in New York. And there is no cloud of cynicism surrounding this exhibition, it's all blown away. Without the baggage of postmodernism, we can now better appreciate that the relationship of my work to the history of abstraction is one of influence rather than appropriation. Many other artists are continuing this tradition in their own way, like Ellsworth Kelly for example. For me, it is very interesting how an artist like this, through learning from the pioneers, has built a whole program and been able to sustain it throughout a lifetime of work. What the pioneers of abstraction did was to open up this possibility. It's the same with Robert Ryman. You could say of his work, 'Well its just an endless quotation of a *White Painting* by Malevich', but it's not helpful, nor accurate to say that. It's like telling an architect that their steel and glass building is 'just like a Mies van der Rohe, so why bother building it?' It's accepted in a discipline in which, from time to time, rules are fractured and new groundwork laid, allowing fresh questions and answers to be formulated.

DH: Did your dialogue with Paul stop after he left Australia?

JN: I visited him twice in America towards the end of his life. I remember staying with him in New York. He had a very lovely big apartment; I could sleep on the couch. So the friendship endured after he left Australia. And I'm sure he maintained contact with many other Melbourne friends. At the same time his allegiances did shift when he moved to America. He was ambitious, so a part of him leaving Australia was his desire to participate in a larger, international context. He wanted to be part of the bigger picture, and had the talent and ability to make this happen. It's just very unfortunate he died young.

Clifton Hill Community Music Centre and early music (including Essendon Airport)

David Chesworth interviewed by Jon Dale

This interview was initially conducted for an article which first appeared in The Wire, *issue 272 (October 2006), www.thewire.co.uk. Reproduced by permission.*

JD: How did you become involved with the Clifton Hill Community Music Centre (CHCMC)?

DC: I was enrolled in the music course at La Trobe University, which had been set up a year earlier by Keith Humble. The course approached the idea of music from a very broad and experimental perspective. We didn't need to have prior instrumental skills. Contemporary music was positioned alongside art history, so we had a larger perspective on the art scene. I started the course with the intention of studying sound engineering, not imagining that I would get into creating music.

28 Around this time, guitarist Robert Goodge and I were already familiar with the rock scene and were now checking out many contemporary classical music performances happening around town which were mainly associated with university departments, such as the Victorian College of the Arts under Richard David Hames and the Melbourne Conservatorium under Barry Conyngham, plus non-traditional jazz venues around Melbourne like The Commune in Fitzroy, where you could hear free jazz by established performers like Brian Brown, Bob Sedergreen and Dura Dara. The National Gallery of Victoria (NGV) even had occasional contemporary music presentations. We also went to the fledgling Clifton Hill Community Music Centre. We just soaked it all up wherever we could find it.

After being at La Trobe for about a year, Warren Burt, who was my main lecturer, rang one day out of the blue in the 1977 summer break and asked me to take over from him organising the CHCMC performances. I think he had received a big Australia Council grant (many artists of his generation were receiving grants from the newly formed Australia Council) and needed time to travel and work on his own music, film and videos. Through Warren, I met up with Philip Brophy, who had briefly been a student of music and film at La Trobe University. Through Philip,

I connected with the post-punk scene in inner Melbourne, which was a small, emerging scene but very active and in direct opposition to everything else that was happening in the tiresome mainstream music scene.

The CHCMC was a very small concern when I became involved. Initially, CHCMC was conceived by Ron Nagorka and Warren Burt as a community music-making space. It mainly attracted friends and associates of particular performers. It was not originally intended as a space solely for experimental music, rather experimental music was just one of the kinds of music that could be heard there. Some nights had barely an audience, sometimes nobody or just two or three people.

The idea of the CHCMC was always about giving anyone the opportunity to make music and perform rather than providing entertainment for an audience. It was up to those who attended to get what they could from a performance. After all, they hadn't paid to attend.

When I took over, I was able to build on Ron Nagorka and Warren Burt's initial concept for the space, which gave artists more control and less dependence on organisations like universities and state orchestras, etc. The structure also gave more power to the audience, who became equal participants in a creative exchange.

The often stated idea of CHCMC – that being that anyone could present there – was sometimes tested, as I dissuaded certain posturing (without irony) New Wave bands. There was no operational budget at all. Our regular upstairs space was a small, run-down, warehouse-like space that had a few mismatched old school chairs and a couple of tables. You could get up to about thirty people in there. The second space was fitted out as a small theatre with a stage that sat about a hundred (it was the venue for the New Theatre group, which has an interesting history of its own). The theatre space wasn't used initially until audiences began to build. There was a third space downstairs where we would sometimes have installations. I remember installation works by Les Gilbert, Ros Bandt and Bill Fontana being staged there. It was my job to arrange equipment for performances, which usually meant borrowing from a University department or bringing my own gear in. The performers brought their own gear too. Then I'd help people set up if needed – the usual stuff. Philip Brophy and Ernie Althoff designed the posters. Ron Nagorka would photocopy the posters at Melbourne State College where he worked. Ron and Warren Burt both held senior tertiary music teaching positions at this time, which was radical and significant in itself.

We had about four performance seasons a year, and sometimes two performance nights per week, Mondays and Wednesdays. A concert might be one person or a band doing a whole performance. At other times, it might consist of works by several unrelated performers who often presented works with vastly different conceptual approaches, often from opposite sides of the Cagean fence.

Importantly, no one was charged an entry fee. Audiences never applauded at the end of performances. It was not what you did at CHCMC. Actually, this felt quite natural at that time because the audience considered themselves to be on equal footing with the performers. There was no perceived creative or intellectual hierarchy or superiority between performers and audience. This was a good outcome, as it helped demystify the otherwise 'special' or privileged process of making art. It was a pretty relaxed atmosphere. People would hang around and chat between each performance.

Experimental music – or 'New Music', as it was then known – soon became the centre's main activity, as that was the scene I was now most familiar with. Performers who played more conventional styles of music weren't really interested in performing there *because* of its structure (as audiences weren't charged money, performers weren't being paid), and so the few people who had an interest in non-conventional music started to gravitate to the space.

There were several key people always ready to present new work, but often I had to do some talking and convincing to get others to commit as they were new to public performance.

By 1980–81, audience numbers had increased considerably and we were attracting a range of visual artists as well as musicians and composers. Artists such as John Dunkley-Smith, John Nixon, Peter Tyndall and writer Paul Taylor were coming along as audience members and to present their own work. CHCMC developed as a space for cross-disciplinary art practice, with many music-based performers getting into filmmaking, video art, and performance making, and visual artists made films and music works.

JD: You studied at La Trobe for a few years with Warren Burt?

DC: I did first year composition with Warren as main lecturer and later with Graham Hair and Jeff Pressing, who taught jazz theory. Both Warren and Jeff were from the States. In Warren's course, we studied experimental music and art music forms starting from the very present and then moving backwards through the twentieth century. The emphasis was on American and English experimental music rather than the European contemporary composers. It probably reflected Warren's influences. Experimental music was more focused at the non-specialist music maker and conceptual ideas that the non-specialist could readily grasp. It was great to not have European modernism thrust in our faces as was happening at most other institutions.

In relation to the broader contemporary musical scene, experimental music seemed to represent the one viable political rebellious approach to music making that a composer could become involved with. You did not need to have privileged access to orchestras or invitations from the mainstream arts communities or universities in order to create music. It could be done with few resources and without traditional musical skills. Anyone could do it. Personal computers were yet to make an appearance, and so we used the only instruments at our disposal, which, for a band, were drums, guitars, synths, cassette recorders, and small cheap instruments including toys. We tended to explore ways of playing these instruments that were not so correct.

At the same time, the brief burst of Melbourne punk had given way to a growing post-punk scene that was making waves in new inner-city music circles. It was happening outside of the universities, which, up to that time, had been considered the hub for new ideas in music.

There was something of a shared philosophy between punk and experimental music (anyone can do it, just do it, you don't need skills, finding your own new spaces and audiences, etc.). However, the difference, I think, is that experimental music up to this point in time had represented modernism's alternative radical edge and was therefore primarily preoccupied by continually evolving the structures of musical form, particularly its inner structures, while the post-punk (and perhaps the postmodern) aesthetic was expressed through re-contextualising existing musical form and changing the 'act' of its performance.

What experimental music and post-punk had in common, however, was that you no longer needed to be a musical expert or skilled in playing traditional instruments. *Anyone* could contribute to and make music. You just needed ideas and any means to produce a sound or make a gesture.

JD: You held the longest tenure as coordinator of CHCMC—five years, 1978 to 1982. What do you feel were the most important developments over the time you coordinated?

DC: It was great to be part of that energy at the time. The paradigm was shifting away from modernism into uncharted waters. This period was just prior to the emergence of sound art as a discrete, non-musical practice. Some of us at CHCMC were starting to challenge the dominance and authority of both the Western musical canon and to pick apart popular culture. We preferred to look at music and sound from conceptual and textual perspectives that lay outside of purely musical considerations. We were less concerned about the score, and more concerned about performance (something we were also quite new at). Many of our performances were about the act of performing itself. Our works tended to be self-analytical, exploring performance narratives and musical structures and exposing hidden exchanges embedded within music.

During this time, Philip Brophy and I formed Innocent Records to release our music. John Campbell and I engineered and produced most of this material. John did the first →↑→ EPs and Essendon Airport's *Sonic Investigation of the Trivial*, and fixed up *50 Synthesizer Greats* by adding spring reverb and removing hums. I recorded and engineered the rest. I remember I mixed the whole of *Palimpsest* in a night. I had keys to the La Trobe Uni music department recording studios and I could get in at night and on the weekends, mostly without the knowledge of the department.

I also worked on mastering the first two Laughing Hands albums and engineering or co-producing the rest of the Innocent releases. Philip Brophy had the major say in the production of the →↑→ recordings. In general, Philip did most of the album artwork and I did most of the recording. I would often assist Philip and Maria Kozic in screen-printing the covers.

Philip and I produced a magazine called *New Music*. It was based on the notion that someone saw and reviewed a performance at CHCMC and then gave the review to the artist/performers to read. An interview then took place between the two parties, which was recorded and transcribed. The process was actually drawn-out and labour intensive to transcribe and edit, and it was always hard to find reviewers. However, it lasted for five issues and was an extension of the CHCMC notion that anybody could be a performer. Here, anyone could be a reviewer and it allowed the performer a right of reply after the review was written. Rainer Linz, who also performed at CHCMC and went on to edit *NMA* (*New Music Articles*), infamously subverted the whole process by faking the interview part by interviewing himself, which caused a great stir when the subversion was exposed. There was great moral outrage from some. This foreshadowed another later publication also involving Rainer, called *Art & a Texta*, that parodied Paul Taylor's *Art & Text*. More outrage ensued.

CHCMC presented a convergence of experimental music-making. There were a lot of process pieces by Warren Burt, Ron
27 Nagorka, Graham Davis, Ernie Althoff and others – these were still based on scores, but radically different scores that might just be a series of performance instructions rather than notation. These works utilised cheap, lo-fi technologies like cassette players, small radios, walkie-talkies or 'found' instruments. There were also acoustic music-making machines and installations by Les Gilbert, Ros Bandt, Graeme Davis and Ernie, as well as complex synth pieces made on cutting-edge electronic instruments, such as the Serge Tcherepnin Synthesizer and DAISY created by Warren Burt (who also explored his interest in different scales and modes), Chris Wyatt, and myself. Warren had arranged to get a couple of these modular synths into the country. I was the part-owner of one and composed many pieces for it.

Most of the music was live, often with a distinct performance element attached. Musique concrète and tape-based pieces were not so common. I played my new album *Layer on Layer* in a CHCMC concert, where three versions of the record were played simultaneously on three record players. There were also video works, films (Super 8), performance works, and even the occasional non-original work, such as a section of Beckett's *Play*: a performance devised by Paul Taylor. There are no posters or fliers to my knowledge about this performance, and it was deliberately left off the posters, as Paul did not want to advertise it. It did take place, though, as I was one of the performers. It involved several performers reading excerpts of Beckett's texts from behind a screen on which other text was projected.

We all explored new creative areas. Peter Tyndall pursued an interest in music; Warren Burt, Philip Brophy, Adrian Martin, Paul Fletcher, Jayne Stevenson and I turned to filmmaking. Andrew Preston made some performance works. It was open slather at CHCMC, you could do anything.

In the greater Melbourne post-punk scene, several other smaller creative enclaves had emerged, perhaps conjured up by the alternative music press. There was the Fitzroy Beat, which I never really pinpointed (Whirlywirld and Primitive Calculators, perhaps?). There was the Little Bands scene, which was a group of performance artists/bands/sound poets who performed at the Champion in Fitzroy and later at the Seaview Ballroom, partly under the guidance of Alan Bamford. There were a string of bands with hero figureheads generally made up of private-school kids, such as the Boys Next Door. We were the 'puritanical theorists' at CHCMC, who apparently took ourselves far too seriously. I can recall several confrontations with people bearing serious CHCMC or Essendon Airport grudges, accusing us of being pretentious wankers (in fact, we knew where the pretensions really lay, and it wasn't with us). There was always the accusation that there was no booze, sex or drugs at CHCMC and little chance of getting laid.

29 Groups like →↑→ and Essendon Airport were now performing at the many new alternative pub venues, such as the Crystal Ballroom and art gallery spaces like the Ewing and George Paton Gallery and Roslyn Oxley Gallery in Sydney. Judy Annear curated CHCMC groups into events at the George Paton Gallery. Both Essendon Airport and →↑→ were becoming more popular. Essendon Airport played at the 1982 Sydney Biennale supported by Adrian Martin's group, The Connotations. By this stage, Paul Taylor became a regular attendee at CHCMC, and many of us went to his Beverley Hills parties and swimming pool events. Philip and Adrian were invited to write for *Art & Text*, including a review by Adrian of my LP record *Layer on Layer*.

JD: I've a good idea of the broader 'ways of going on' of the CHCMC, but I'm particularly interested in the moment when the CHCMC met with post-punk, pop, disco, etc....

DC: Around 1977–78, the whole punk and New Wave scene was in full swing and, from a musical perspective, it felt to me as though modernism was in its death throes, although it was still very dominant in the universities. The modernist music appeared heavily codified and set in its ways. There was a sense that works undertaken outside these 'academic' styles were not taken seriously within the academic world, and were considered an embracing of commercial culture. The academy was generally unaware of the emergence of the new inner city subcultures taking place. It was becoming clear that we were beginning to experience a creative shift from the academic institutions to the outside world.

There were new accessible channels of distribution opening up too. Our records, which we had found ways to make and release ourselves, would get played on newly emerging public radio stations like 3CR and 3RRR, 2SER and 2MBS. They were self-distributed to new independent record shops that were springing up around the country, like Missing Link in Melbourne. There were also several cassette publications that carried some of this music. Philip and I would sometimes take the train from Melbourne to Sydney to personally distribute our Innocent Records to shops. The group Laughing Hands also released several records on their own label.

Engaging directly with punk or disco was really the territory explored by →↑→. Essendon Airport's *Talking to Cleopatra* was as close as we got to disco. However, Essendon Airport had started to write music that people could dance to. This music was intended for a different audience than CHCMC.

JD: And furthermore – were there any ideological showdowns between factions? I wondered about Ernie Althoff's comments regarding 'French-based arts theory and criticism' infiltrating the CHCMC, in his *New Music Articles* (*NMA*, an independent magazine edited by Rainer Linz and Richard Vella), documented the CHCMC's history...

DC: I think Ernie is referring to the arrival of the postmodern, which was played out on the floor of CHCMC, in my opinion. There were ideological showdowns between emerging factions and generations. It got a bit tense there for while. It was quite exciting. There were special meetings called to thrash out the political and creative approaches of CHCMC. Ernie was right: French theory had become influential. Several of us attended the film course at La Trobe University, which was heavily influenced by European theory. *Screen* magazine was a big influence, and of course, Godard and other French New Wave filmmakers. Adrian Martin was also (at a very young age) teaching film at Melbourne State College, while also creating works at CHCMC. French New Wave filmmaking was self aware, interrogating both itself and society, and this no doubt influenced many of us. The late '70s and early '80s was a time for interrogating discourses. In the case of music, this resulted in a structural unpicking of the form and content of pre-existing musical styles. There was lots of smart use of quotation, juxtapositions of musical forms and gestures, plus irony, which worked perfectly well then, but is perhaps a little harder to appreciate retrospectively. There was so much material that could be used as subject matter for us to appropriate and present alternative viewpoints.

The continual modernist push to 'make it new' started to give way to works that challenged existing, accepted structures hidden behind the creator/audience transaction.

Although there was no acknowledgment of this at the time, some of us were certainly aware that the regular performers at CHCMC could be separated into two generational groupings: the slightly older generation of artists and performers (in their thirties) would tend towards indeterminacy and non-hierarchical musical structures and processes that had their roots in John Cage or perhaps Alvin Lucier, and us younger folk (early twenties) wanted to pursue (rather than negate) the idea of desire and explore aspects of the signifier/signified relationship as it was played out within mainstream culture. Suitable subject matter might include Minimalism, Pop, jazz, set theory, pop culture and, in the case of →↑→, even the Bible and the law.

JD: How did Essendon Airport form, and what were the goals/ intentions of the initial duo format with Robert Goodge?

DC: We were pretty bored with much of the music that immediately surrounded us—pop, modern classical, jazz or experimental '70s rock. All these existing forms seemed, for us, to exist within performance and presentation contexts that were tired and exhausted. Our aim was simply to try to figure out music that could work in a new way. We just started playing together, layering and repeating little phrases and rhythms against each other until something felt good to us. And then we repeated it. The music's ironic minimalism was pedantic, but also created a new fresh extended sound field, which had a new direction and feel. It was as if, by adding a few simple phrases together, we got something that was greater than the sum of its parts. Robert Goodge's guitar playing has a great feel and these simple phrases transitioned into something special. It really started to work at places like the Crystal Ballroom where our feel rubbed up against the tastes of the New Wave.

Essendon Airport released *Sonic Investigations of the Trivial*, adding a drum machine borrowed from →↑→ (it was built from a kit and bought via the *Trading Post*). As I can hardly play the piano, I used to play as few notes as possible and as close together as possible. In the end we just combined what we knew and what we enjoyed. It was CHCMC that enabled us to perform in public and eventually lead us to performing at the emerging post-punk venues. Our music connected with a certain subset of that audience. Later, Essendon Airport became a four-piece when we were joined by Ian Cox on sax, who, like Robert, had a great feel and Paul Fletcher, whose wild drumming always added an unpredictable element. We eventually grew to five with the addition of Barbara Hogarth on funky bass.

JD: I've always thought those earliest recordings and associated documentation were humorous, in quite a dry manner—the *Sonic Investigations of the Trivial*, etc. In the self-conducted interview with Ian Cox in *NMA* 1, he discusses Essendon Airport as structuralist. Was Essendon Airport about exposing the processes of pop/rock, its formal qualities, and the shadowplay that goes on within rock discourse (i.e., ideas of 'authenticity' etc.)?

DC: At the outset we were not political, but we became so. Robert Goodge and I both studied film at La Trobe and through that became familiar with Marxist and structuralist theory. →↑→ were incorporating structuralism into their works at CHCMC. Ian Cox, our sax player, became very interested in politics too. We were now aware that choices of performance style and musical content had political and cultural ramifications, and we increasingly played with these ideas in our music. This was often achieved intuitively and hilariously by recontextualising musical languages and styles and endlessly repeating the result. This used to antagonise some audiences. Back then, some got what we were doing and many didn't.

Our flyer for *Sonic Investigations of the Trivial* reads:

> songs which combine many of the most facile and insipid kinds of music in a redeemingly dignified manner ... creating new trivia out of old. All this takes place along with a kind of pedantic fetishism for small-repetition games—the music travels in circles, spirals and solid blocks of sameness and difference.

JD: What was your relationship with pop music at that point? Essendon Airport recordings work, I think, because they display strong engagement with pop—French pop, bossa, post-punk electronics, etc. What did you source from pop?

DC: Everything and nothing. Pop was all-pervasive and had a constant presence in our daily lives. It was constantly marketed at us, as it was making so much money for the record companies. Pop is both a vacuous vessel of effects and also a text containing lots of cultural information relating to who played it, where it came from, who sang it, what instruments were used, what the lyrics were about, what else the pop tune might be referencing. It was always evolving and providing a mirror to other aspects of popular culture. We all avidly followed it week by week, if only to groan and laugh. Pop music was so malleable. It was something we inevitably incorporated into our music, both ironically and for the pleasure of it.

As many of us at CHCMC saw it, something quoted and played incorrectly had as much or more to say to an audience than a virtuosic guitar solo. Competence and context became compositional tools in themselves. One of Adrian Martin's groups at this time was aptly called 'Competence/Performance'.

JD: How do you look back on the *Palimpsest* era, and what led to the fracturing and demise of the group? (Several members regrouped as I'm Talking, didn't they?)

DC: Our album *Palimpsest* re-uses various musical texts with deadpan irony and humour. Many of the lyrics in *Palimpsest* are derived from popular songs from the 1920s through to the 1950s. We kept the original lyrics or just the title but changed the music. Essendon Airport tended to work intuitively in our music-making. By contrast, →↑→ and Adrian Martin's group The Connotations tended to write theoretical notes that accompanied their performances or wrote songs with lyrics that directly addressed the subject matter of the song. I think Ralph Traviato was the main lyric writer for →↑→ and Philip wrote most of the music.

Paul Taylor gravitated to these activities at CHCMC and then proceeded, through *Art & Text*, to provide an analytical voice to what was going on. *Art & Text* was able to feed from what we and other art spaces were already offering and which many other publications were either ignoring or deliberately marginalising. I think it was crucial for *Art & Text* that spaces like CHCMC were already established and happening. Paul was stimulated by them. They provided a reservoir for the more interesting art, artists and writers who were operating on the edges and margins of art at that time.

As some members of Essendon Airport were becoming quite political, there was a desire for some in the group to move into mainstream pop culture and to work from 'within the system', like what the group Scritti Politti were doing at that time. At the end of 1983, various performers from CHCMC were invited to the Paris Autumn Festival. I left for Paris and stayed overseas for a few months. Essendon Airport decided to call it quits at this time as, frankly, we needed a break. I don't see it as unusual that the group should break up. It had been five or six years, which was a long time for a band back then. By this stage we were headlining at places like the Crystal Ballroom in St Kilda. It had been great fun but we were becoming tired and a bit over it. After we split, Robert, Ian and Barbara Hogarth from Essendon Airport formed I'm Talking with Kate Ceberano. They appeared on *Countdown*, which brought them into a mainstream context. Although I haven't personally analysed this music, I have reason to believe it is full of political theory and clever ironic word games, while masquerading as disco pop music.

'He was the devil incarnate': Paul Taylor, *Lip* and *Art & Text*

Janine Burke interviewed by Helen Hughes

January 15, 2013

HH: How did you meet Paul Taylor?

JB: I first met Paul in 1979 in Hobart, where he was a tutor at the art school. Next, he arrived at Victorian College of the Arts to have lunch with Elizabeth Gower and me, and he brought each of us a red rose. He had such presence and style. Carrying a red rose—for anybody else it would have looked totally ridiculous. It did look slightly ridiculous, but Paul could carry it off. He liked parody. Paul was ebullient. He wanted to engage with everybody he possibly could. There was no sense that he was pushing a particular line at that stage. He wasn't discussing particular theorists or artists. Mainly he was talking about his work at Hobart, and the people he knew there. For example, he was a good friend of Carol Jerrems. He knew Vivienne Shark LeWitt when she was a student there. But he had plans to relocate to Melbourne.

Paul kept in touch with everything that was going on. But then we all did. It was a very small scene, so you could get to know everybody very quickly. The art world wasn't atomised like it is now. Though everybody had quite different points of view, nonetheless at any one opening—at Realities Gallery or Powell Street Gallery—Jenny Watson and John Nixon would be there. Patrick McCaughey. Kiffy Rubbo. Fred Williams. You could see everyone in one environment, which you can't do anymore. When I started writing art criticism in 1973, when I was twenty-one, I found it was easy to engage with pretty much all the networks.

HH: How did it come about that Paul asked you to write for the first issue of *Art & Text*?

JB: I think he identified me as a key feminist critic and curator. I'd been a co-founder of the Women's Art Movement in 1975 and *Lip* the following year. In 1980, my book *Australian Women Artists: 1840–1940* was published. Women's art was hot property at that time: it was shaping the culture and had been doing so for several years. Some senior curators and critics like Daniel Thomas were encouraging about women's art, so that upper level of disregard or criticism for feminist activities wasn't so apparent.

It was welcomed in a way. Though probably not by a lot of the male artists! And there were several women academics and curators who were totally opposed. So Paul would have seen me in that context: that I was a historian and I was also a contemporary art writer, a curator, and a teacher, like him, in an art school.

Paul launched himself into the Melbourne art world. This ebullience was reflected in *Art & Text*—he cast the net very wide. He wasn't interested in a narrow perspective on art and culture. He was simultaneously trying to draw in people like Patrick McCaughey and Bernard Smith and Terry Smith. Regarding my essay 'Collaborations: Artists Working Collectively', Paul certainly didn't say, 'I want you to write about such and such', or 'I want you to write about feminist art criticism'. When I suggested writing that article, he was enthusiastic. He enjoyed the idea of it. He loved the article and made no cuts or changes. I wanted to do something fresh for *Art & Text* because there was a lot, I could see, riding on what he wanted to do.

Maybe Paul wanted to take a leaf from my book. I'm not sure if I was the first guest curator at the National Gallery of Victoria. But in 1980, Robert Lindsay invited me to curate the Bea Maddock
31 Survey Show and, in 1981, I curated the Joy Hester retrospective. The following year, Paul did 'POPISM'.

HH: Could you sense the gap that *Art & Text* eventually filled, in relation to the landscape of contemporary art writing, editing and publishing at that time?

JB: Not immediately. It was only around the early 1980s that theory began to emerge as a major force with the 'Futur*Fall' conference and with the writings of Meaghan Morris. There were a lot of competing forces. Peter Fuller, the English critic who started the journal *Modern Painters*, was in Australia in 1982. He was telling art students, 'Oh, they don't teach you anything. Why aren't you learning life drawing?' You know, 'Why aren't you learning how to be a real artist?' And many of my students at the VCA were like, 'Yeah, we want to learn life drawing, we want to be real artists'. Fuller was a conservative character and his attitudes towards art education and art itself were widely discussed.

Also ROAR Studios opened in Fitzroy in 1982. A group of disaffected art students (several from the VCA) organised a collective whose unofficial leader was the talented painter David

Larwill. They were reacting against what they saw as the minimalist and conceptual aesthetic of the Melbourne art world. I imagine they would have loathed *Art & Text*. Their painting style was figurative and expressionist. In fact, ROAR Studios looked like just another upmarket art gallery – but it shows the energy and diversity of the Melbourne scene at that time.

There was also the impact of large-scale, neo-Expressionist painting coming out of New York as well as Italy and Germany. Achille Bonito-Oliva was impresario of the so-called Transavantgardia. Mary Boone Gallery in New York represented highly publicised painters like Julian Schnabel and Jean-Michel Basquiat. All of a sudden, a generation of young male artists were international celebrities, some making fantastic sums of money. The 1982 Sydney Biennale introduced many of these works to an Australian audience. The contemporary art world went berserk and revelled in its status as a booming, global market. It was all pretty venal and disgusting.

HH: Did you sense a shift in what theory was being read, from the 1970s to the 1980s?

JB: There was a huge shift. Suddenly, we were immersed in Foucault, Lacan, Kristeva, Barthes, Derrida. For me as a critic, involved in radical critiques of cultural history, Foucault knocked me out. I read *Madness and Civilisation*, which is a dazzling polemic about the dark side of the Enlightenment, underpinned by this brilliant original research. There was also the new approach to language – it was as though language was being reinvented. I'd started reading Freud and that took me on a journey to Lacan, then back to Freud. I found Freud more juicy than Lacan. *The Interpretation of Dreams* was a key text for me, especially as I was in psychoanalysis at that time. I was also on the editorial board of *Meanjin* and Judith Brett, the editor, was interested in psychoanalytic theory. We were lucky in Melbourne because two Lacanian analysts, Maria-Ines Rotmeiler de Zentner and Oscar Zentner, who had fled the regime in Argentina, had settled here. Maria-Ines founded the Freudian School of Melbourne and published *The Papers of the Freudian School*. Juan Davila was a friend of the Zentners.

But it was a curious fact that, although Foucault, Derrida, etc., were as left as left could be, the manifestation of their theories, popularised as they were in the early '80s, often seemed to be in the hands of conservative forces. It seemed like a denial of radicalism. Because one of the biggest shifts was in terms of politics. The

’70s were left-wing. We were all part of collectives. My ‘Collaborations’ essay reflects that.

HH: It includes the photograph of the 1975 sit-in at the NGV.

JB: Exactly. I wasn’t at that sit-in, but I was on the committee (that also included Terry Smith and John Davis) that formed afterwards to demand a curator of contemporary Australian art. We met for about a year, until finally Robert Lindsay was appointed in 1977. The sit-in reflected the dissatisfaction that artists and the art community felt about the way contemporary Australian art was represented at the NGV. Well, the way it *wasn’t* represented.

HH: So, a change in politics?

JB: A shift in politics to the right with the decade of Margaret Thatcher. It was massive and it filtered down. Prior to that, the art world had prided itself on its raffish, down-at-heel style, like, ‘Who cares about how you look?’ Then everybody was wearing black and younger folk were in Comme des Garçons and boasting about how much it cost. Paul was very fashion- and style-conscious. He was zipping around in his red MG sports car. He loved looking good and wearing expensive clothes. He did it with a great sense of camp style. I mean, the bow-tie is obviously mimicking Patrick McCaughey, who made the bow-tie famous. Paul was quoting Patrick, whom he no doubt admired a great deal. He might have wanted to contest Patrick, but at the same time Patrick must have been a role model.

So, for the feminists, from beating our breasts and being in May Day marches, suddenly this was just seen as ‘Oh, so terribly old fashioned’. The word ‘feminist’ literally became a term of derision overnight.

HH: Why do you think ‘feminist’ became a term of derision at this time?

JB: Feminism, or the women’s art movement, grew out of a social movement, and that movement and those politics were suddenly seen as irrelevant. Plus there was that great wave of neo-Expressionism, coming from Europe and New York, and there were virtually no women in that scene. All the Italian artists in the Transavantgardia were male, plus there was Markus Lupertz and

Anselm Kiefer from Germany and then the Americans Schnabel and Basquiat. It was daunting. Women were gone. Off the map in any kind of a major, visible, influential way.

HH: How was Paul's emergence onto the art criticism scene received by your *Lip* and feminist colleagues at that time?

JB: Oh, they [the *Lip* collective] were horrified. They hated *Art & Text*, they hated Paul. Well, some of them, at least. Because he got a big grant and we never got any grants. So, he was the devil. Annette Blonski and Jeannette Fenelon wrote a critical essay about 'POPISM' in *Lip*. It was really a reply to an article Paul wrote in 1981, lambasting *Lip* in *Meanjin*. I'd left in 1980, and I was glad to be away from it. Like most small cultural groups where everybody's doing everything for nothing, it's exhausting and the forces that bring you together are not going to maintain you, usually. So it fractured from within.

And I wondered about its relevance. What did *Lip* have to say and to whom was it speaking in 1980? That phase of Australian cultural history was—necessarily—focused on the prefix 're': rediscovery, restore, remember, recall. We had to excavate the past to find the present. When I did 'Australian Women Artists: 1840–1940'—this was the 1975 exhibition before the 1980 book—many women artists said to me, 'Now my work has a context. Now I can see where I belong in Australian art history.' That was a strong element of *Lip*'s enterprise—researching the women artists or filmmakers or playwrights who'd been neglected or ignored.

But, connected to that, was a problem I found with *Lip* and that was you weren't supposed to criticise other women. For the first issue in 1976, I reviewed 'Experiments in Vitreous Enamels: Portraits of Women'—a collective show at the Ewing and George Paton Galleries, which included Vivienne Binns, Frances Budden, Marie McMahon and Toni Robertson. I was critical of the younger artists, writing that while Vivienne emerged as sophisticated and inventive, the younger ones seemed less able to present convincing imagery and deal with the techniques involved. I described the imagery as 'neutral'. Ann Stephen wrote a rebuttal of my review in the same issue of *Lip*, called 'A Process of Deneutralising', which Paul reproduced in *Anything Goes*.

Despite the fact that some members of the *Lip* collective considered Paul to be the devil incarnate, many of his women friends were staunch feminists: like Judy [Annear], Denise [Robinson], Lyndal Jones and me.

I think that for some of the women associated with *Lip*, their approach to art and theory was instrumental. They weren't interested in reading new theory because they felt they'd read theory – Simone de Beauvoir or Mary Daly or Shulamith Firestone. Plus, there were the new feminist histories like Anne Summers's *Damned Whores and God's Police*. Some weren't prepared to sit down and bang their heads against Derrida's *Of Grammatology*. They saw these texts as the new authority figures and isn't that exactly what feminism was trying to subvert!?! You know, the patriarchy? It was about language and who had the power over it. Feminists had felt they did. But then the ground was swept from under their feet.

I mean, if members of the *Lip* collective had said to Paul, 'We're interested in whether or not Julia Kristeva is a feminist and we want to write that for *Art & Text*', I'm sure he would have been delighted. But parading one's politics, for instance, would put Paul off. His interest would be sparked by somebody who was up-to-date with the latest theory, who might be able to speak persuasively and articulately about that. Then he'd try and get that person writing for *Art & Text*. And he would nag you. He never stopped nagging me for another essay. That's how he got things out of you.

I admired what Paul was doing with *Art & Text* and, by 1982, I thought it was streets ahead of *Lip*. But I think Paul looked closely and carefully at *Lip* because *Lip* was a stylish statement. We put so much effort into making the magazine look beautiful. That was something we cared about a great deal. There were political and art publications around that were roneoed sheets, stapled together. *Lip* had an elaborate, decorative, feminist sensibility. Paul's taste was minimalist, which was also part of the '80s shift.

But Paul worked in a curiously feminist way because everything for him was about the personal relationship. He valued close, intimate friendship. He wanted to know everything about you, what you were doing, where you were going and (usually) could he come along, too!

Paul developed an agenda. He probably looked at us [the *Lip* collective] and thought we'd had an agenda, too. Perhaps we portrayed ourselves as maybe a little more innocent or naïve than we actually were. We had made changes in the art world by focusing exclusively on women. For a short time, maybe only for a year or two, maybe 1977 to 1979, I wrote only about women. I announced that. You know, 'Sorry, not writing about you guys'. It pissed off some of the male artists. My early articles in *Art & Australia* focused on men: John Firth-Smith, Donald Laycock, Clive Murray-White, Syd Ball.

Apparently, the *Lip* gang could be quite threatening. Women who didn't want to be involved with us – you know, some younger women artists – have told me subsequently, 'You were really terrifying, all of you feminists'. At the time, we thought we were being so open and welcoming, but we seemed quite severe to those who didn't want to engage politically in the art world.

What was important about Paul was his openness, his willingness to engage. With *Lip*, because we were feminists, we were excluding a lot of people from publishing with us. Whereas for Paul it was the opposite: it was open slather.

HH: So there was already some antagonism on the part of *Lip* towards Paul because of the funding awarded to *Art & Text*, then he went on to fan the flames by publishing 'Lip-Reading', his negative assessment of *Lip* in *Meanjin*, where he claims that *Lip*'s art criticism suffers because it is a) subjugated to the service of the feminist cause and b) is therefore able to 'evade theorising'. It sounds as if, by the time you left in 1980, you and Paul may have connected on this point?

JB: It was a reason for being attracted to one another's views. But there remained a political divide which was part of the early '80s shift. You could be talking about art and cultural change and a whole range of other issues and not even mention the shade of someone's politics. And this kind of unwillingness to engage, for whatever reason – there were probably lots of complex reasons – made some of those associated with *Art & Text* look right-wing.

Nor did Paul make it easy. Once *Art & Text* was up and running, he didn't go around trying to explain it to people. It got to the point with him, quite soon, I mean, you were either on board or you weren't.

The dynamic that surrounded *Art & Text* was, firstly, there was no collective; the editorial decisions were all Paul's. Perhaps he'd heard his feminist friends complaining about the endless *Lip* meetings and how we had to do all the design and layout ourselves! Plus, *Art & Text* was Paul's full-time job. *Lip* was only ever part-time. The collective not only had full-time jobs – there was also our critical writing, curating shows and one's own practice.

Paul wanted a very high profile in the Australian art world, to have the broadest of broad connections. Court controversy. You know? In, in a flamboyant, old-fashioned way – like Diaghilev. 'Impresario' was a not term that we used at the time about him, but it was certainly how he would have seen himself.

HH: You didn't write again for *Art & Text*, did you?

JB: I was finishing my MA on Joy Hester, which I rewrote as a book. Plus, I was curating the Hester retrospective for the NGV. Also, I was moving into writing fiction, which precipitated a break with Melbourne and with the art world for several years. It was a time of intense change and dislocation for me. It was exciting, but also disturbing and schismatic. Around the beginning of each decade I think this happens culturally—many different currents start to converge.

That's how theory entered my work—through fiction. I found it didn't suit my art historical practice. I remember one review of *Joy Hester* and it said, 'My god, she didn't mention Lacan!' *Speaking* (1984) is built from post-structuralism which taught me that structure can *itself* be political and I wanted to write a big, political, feminist novel. *Speaking* is littered with references to Foucault, Freud and Hélène Cixous. Theory gave me a lot of confidence to really tear into the text, to tear it apart, to subject it to interrogation. It was exhilarating. I'd escaped from the straightjacket of art history! *Second Sight* (1986) is, in part, a homage to Barthes's *Camera Lucida*, and I named the central character Lucida after his book. Photography is a central theme in that novel, though it is also strongly autobiographical.

HH: What was the social scene of *Art & Text* like?

JB: Few people had children. People were in couples or they were single or whatever, but, apart from one or two exceptions, there were no kids in that scene. So we were still leading a youthful 'Let's go out, let's take drugs, let's party' sort of existence. Paul liked to be the ringleader. 'Come on, we're going to Inflation!' Paul didn't have a partner. I mean, he had lovers. He certainly had his heart broken, but he refused to be comforted, refused to be sentimental. He'd be dismissive: 'Oh, who cares about that?' I was never quite convinced by these protestations. He was proud. He didn't want to show hurt. Paul was single in a (largely) singles scene. It was kind another advantage for him and another way he viewed the culture as working fluidly, as not being constrained by the demands of home and family, by certain kinds of responsibilities. That said, Paul adored his mother Pat and was close to his brothers—Greg and Philip. Greg and his wife Janice also lived at Beverley Hills and I'd see them at Paul's parties. Once you entered Paul's life, you entered all of it.

I spent time with Paul in his gay world. He would take me to parties and I'd be the only woman there, in a room of, like, forty men. It was weirdly liberating, because if I were in a room with forty straight men as the only dame, I would probably feel nervous. So this world was a different world to the art world. There were no art people in it. These were guys who might run a clothing store, or they might be a drug dealer, or they might be a young guy who'd just left school. It was quite amorphous, that world, and it wasn't necessarily made up of middle class people, either. I remember thinking – of course, this was before AIDS hit – that it was an optimistic scene. You didn't need credentials apart from your own smarts or good looks. A person could make all sorts of valuable connections. Class and money had nothing to do with it.

It was another area of Paul's life. Sometimes it was sort of secret because it was sexual. Sometimes it was flamboyant. He wanted to shock. I remember him taking me to The Seahorse, which was a transvestite club. It was the first time I'd seen guys wearing ball gowns, with hairy chests and beards and wigs and make-up. Paul was keen to hear your reaction: he didn't judge, which made him an ideal companion. You could let your hair down. But there were boundaries. He'd say, 'When you go out with me, you're *my* girlfriend.' I mean, when a gay man has a friendship with a straight woman, it doesn't exclude erotic elements like jealousy and flirting.

HH: You and Paul seem to share an obsession with photography. There's your work on Albert Tucker's photographs, but also your own book of photographs, *Personal View: Photographs 1978–1986*, which was recently published by Monash University Press. While Paul's interest in photography was shaped by his idea of 'photo rhetoric', the idea that a photograph is always framed, cropped, then crystalised into a surface, your recourse to photography seems to be shaped by your interest in and work as a social and art historian (for instance your work on Hester and Tucker, but also the Reeds and the wider Heide circle, which looks at the art produced by that circle as inextricably entwined with its social context). Can you tell me a little about your recourse to photography as an art historical tool? And did you ever discuss photography with Paul?

JB: That's interesting. I recall the 1982 spring issue of *Art & Text* with (then prime minister) Malcom Fraser's photo on the cover. Of course, Fraser was a much hated figure. Paul gave me a copy, hot off the press. We were at Pellegrini's in Bourke Street. I said, 'Why would you have Fraser on the cover?' Paul replied, 'It problematises the image.' I didn't think that was an adequate answer. But perhaps it reveals our differing positions. During the '70s, a quite brilliant group of women photographers had emerged in Melbourne, including Carol Jerrems, Sue Ford, Micky Allan and Ponch Hawkes. The work of Ford, Allan and Hawkes appeared in *Lip*. Plus I selected them for 'Self Portrait/Self Image', an exhibition I curated in 1980. So there was a local feminist photographic practice informing my theoretical and curatorial practice. I developed an optics that meshed a social context – of an intimate kind – with high aesthetic standards. It shaped the photographic aspect of my Heide research.

I guess it's because, for me, the visual is a fundamental explanation for the word, the thought, the idea. It's a concentration, a coalescing of the culture at any one point. I feel that photography captures that better than any other medium. It makes time palpable. You look time in the eye. I admire the 'photo journalists' like Robert Capa, Henri Cartier-Bresson and Jacques Henri Lartigue. They record the drama in the moment. It's stark but also rich and layered. Tucker's photographs – and my own – were 'accidental'. There was no agenda – but, unconsciously, it's clear we were fascinated by our contemporaries and we had a sense that this was a special time and demanded to be recorded.

32 That photograph I took of Paul at Heide in 1982 – he looks as innocent as a flower, and as brightly coloured. It's interesting, of course, because that's where Bert took many of his photographs, of Joy, Nolan and the Reeds. It's a palimpsest. We're in Sunday's kitchen garden, the one she made near Heide II. It's what I did and what Bert did – cart our cameras around and take pictures of our friends.

I'm not even sure which is the greater reality for me – word or image. Much of my writing has concerned itself with visual culture – as a way of attacking and subverting norms and omissions. Even in my novels, like *Speaking*, *Second Sight* and *Company of Images* (1989), there are artists making work. In fact, *Company of Images* is a satire of the art world, which has a character based (very loosely) on Paul.

HH: I only labour the point because this methodology, which underpins a lot of the books you've written and the projects you've done, seems to have spilled over into the symposium, and subsequently into this publication, which focuses on Paul as a person in a particular place, at a particular time, and as one member of a distinct group of artists, musicians, critics, etc. So I'm wondering, what specifically do you hope to get out of this approach to looking at Paul's legacy as an art critic in his own right? And do you think Paul would have approved of this approach, as someone who is more interested in 'photo rhetoric' rather than photo content?

JB: It's important to have one's work addressed seriously and critically, and treated as an oeuvre. That's what *Impresario* sets out to do, though we've focused only on the Melbourne years. *Impresario* places Paul in his time. I don't think he'd have a problem with that. It gives him the opportunity to speak from his own time, amid a constellation of other voices. It begins to defines him and that becomes the legacy. Unless a creative person – and this particularly applies to women – is contextualised, they're dead to history. Much of my work as a feminist historian has been digging up the dead. And you have to sort of dig up the whole graveyard, you know? You have to discover the cultural connections to make sense of the individual within it. That lone hero stereotype has been destructive and not only for women but for the culture as a whole. It thins and reduces it and ends up by falsifying and misrepresenting it. In *The Gods of Freud: Sigmund Freud's Art Collection* (2006), I wrote about Freud the collector from within the context of his life and experiences, his frustrations and desires.

My approach to culture in general and art history in particular favours the biographical. I've been criticised for that. You know, 'Janine Burke writes about sex!' Perhaps it's a feminist perspective? I see art and sexuality, culture and gender as indissolubly linked. It's dialectical. It amazes me how prudish the art world is about sex and about the personal life – things which are the pulse of creativity. I've come to love the shocking and inspiring truthfulness of facts. Facts are more astonishing than anything you can imagine. It's why I returned to art history after writing fiction for a decade. Heide – how could you invent that?

Paul Taylor: Impressions

Lyndal Jones interviewed by Janine Burke

July 23, 2012

JB: I wonder if you could recall your first impressions of Paul Taylor?

LJ: I have a very clear first impression of Paul. I'd lived in London for a number of years and returned to Australia and had a job at Monash, running the theatre office. As my first act, I had curated an exhibition of four artists – with videos by Bill Viola, then a dance workshop led by Nan Hassell, films by John Dunkley-Smith and sound works by Bill Fontana. There were these strange little bunker rooms at the bottom of the Menzies Building, and the works were shown there. Once, thinking that no one would be there, I snuck in when Bill Fontana's beautiful sound work was up in the space just to listen to it again, and there was this kid dancing. I discovered later that it was actually Paul. I don't think he saw me there, he was just by himself in the space dancing. He must've been a first-year student at the time. Afterwards, it was a wonderful image to hold on to, especially around the time of his death.

I remember, much later, staying with Paul in Hobart in this kind of stable at the back of someone's very glamorous house. We sat up all night talking about art, gossiping about people. Paul could always find fabulous places to live. He lived for a long time in a small place in the famous Beverley Hills apartment building in South Yarra, with its grotto swimming pool that he loved to show off. He had wonderful parties, but he had a way of having in-depth conversations with individuals at the same time.

JB: You said you'd just come back from London. Perhaps you could talk a little bit about your own practice at that time?

LJ: I had gone to London in time to escape the new nationalism in Australia. I came back and there was now a distinctive 'Australian' voice. It was wonderful to find it everywhere moving from being an explicit to an assumed part of artists' works in art, in theatre, in writing, in song. I couldn't quite understand the gravitas that a lot of the more 'essentialist' works were given, however.

JB: Can you just explain 'essentialist'?

LJ: At the Pram Factory, for instance, it seemed that a lot of the work was about looking at what was different about us as Australians, and so I would include that as a kind of essentialist idea of this culture. I was also intrigued at that time by something I had missed the beginning of ... the women's art movement, as it took hold in Sydney and in Melbourne. I'd missed Lucy Lippard's visit and the beginning of *Lip* magazine, but I was fascinated by what had happened so quickly. I was also curious about the kind of 'homemade-ness' of a lot of the work. I remember writing quite critically about that. I think that's where Paul and I actually had something in common; we were both interested in problematising rather than simplifying ideas. For me as a woman the importance of feminism was to increase choice, and to increase and to enable us to have an equal platform to speak from, and to speak through. Paul and I had spent a lot of time talking about some of those kinds of ideas. My own solo performances of the time had a number of voices – ones that told contradictory stories, others that stood outside and 'explained' what might have been happening. This approach came from an ongoing concern about being able to be contradictory rather than having to try and find a singular voice.

JB: Going back to your point about the kind of intellectual dialogue that took place with Paul, did you feel that was also represented in *Art & Text*? Did this act as a forum for you, both professionally and personally, as a cultural form, a way of observing what was going on, or a selection of what was going on in the culture?

LJ: Before *Art & Text*, there was Art Projects, and it seemed to me that *Art & Text* very much came out of a wonderful dialogue that was enabled by this space created by John Nixon and a group of other Melbourne artists. A whole range of people were starting to engage with this very new idea of a gallery and Paul was, at first, a young voice amongst many. Then I remember the time he announced 'I've decided on the name for the magazine', without understanding myself the possibilities of what he was setting out to do. I think that the name itself actually started to bring together something that was pertinent to the discussions at that time, as it became an introduction to philosophical ideas that might be made manifest in artworks, might start to place them as part of a cultural debate.

JB: It was one of Paul's strengths, to bring contemporary intellectual ideas and theories smack bang into the art world. Probably one of his most startling achievements in the early 1980s. Some women saw *Art & Text* as anti-feminist, as not being engaged sufficiently with feminist discourse.

LJ: It was unfortunate that, at that time, Elizabeth Grosz, Luce Irigaray, Judith Butler and a whole range of women's voices—apart from Mary Kelly, who epitomised it beautifully and whose work was shown in Australia at that time—were not seen to be part of that discussion. If those voices had been included, I think it might've enabled a richer contribution within *Lip* magazine, for instance. But, faced with a barrage of French male theory, I think there was probably the thought, 'well, hang on a second, we're struggling to find our voices here and the discussion is being framed through male voices again'. Paul was impatient with our hesitation, completely impatient with it, and he and I had lots of fights about these feminist issues.

JB: What are your recollections of 'POPISM'?

LJ: Before 'POPISM', there was a night at the George Paton Gallery that speaks well of Patrick McCaughey's invitation to Paul to curate that exhibition. And it speaks interestingly of Paul, too. It was a seminar and four of us—Patrick, Paul, Peter Tyndall and myself—were invited to speak. The subject of the discussion was the role of the artist, as I remember it, and the George Paton Gallery was packed with people sitting and standing everywhere—many of them women who had clearly come only to hear Patrick speak. Patrick, when I last saw him, still remembered it as the worst night of his life! The three of us had been mentored by Patrick. He was Paul's teacher at Monash. He had been a mentor to Peter Tyndall through his reviews of Peter's work in *The Age* at a time when nobody else seemed to understand it ... and I had been in his first-year English tutorial at Monash before the Visual Art department had started. We all respected him deeply. However, it seemed to us that the role of the Australian artist, and especially the role of women artists, was being severely neglected by the National Gallery of Victoria. And so we went for it. We all did it in poetic ways, but the audience was furious with us, of course, for challenging Patrick. There was pandemonium. Why I speak of that before I speak of 'POPISM' is because it was a distressing night for Patrick. I don't think he had been challenged about his role at the gallery to that extent. Later, he was able to turn around and provide a central space for Paul to make this huge exhibition. As is the way with artists, whether or not our work was relevant to it, those of us who were not in it were really pissed off! I'd never had anything to do with the central ideas of 'POPISM', but it was so much a show about contemporary Melbourne art I remember saying to Paul, 'well why aren't I in it?!' He just laughed and I laughed too. It was a wonderful show. I can remember Maria Kozic's works were being given a powerful voice. →↑→ performed. There was this sense of an extraordinary energy.

But a later memory of 'POPISM' was of sitting with Paul at a bar in New York and becoming aware of his bitterness about the responses to the exhibition. He actually said that the public critique had been so unfair and so negative that he had left Australia because of it and he felt he couldn't go back. And the negative public response was huge at the time. Interestingly, from his friends at least, it was probably more a silence than any critique. He couldn't hear anyone defending the show.

Later he did return, but as an acknowledged international writer. Once he stayed (at the magazine's expense) at the Como Hotel, which had just opened and was very chic. Paul was delighted with his suite with its mezzanine bedroom, a large spa bath at the top of the stairs, a reception room downstairs and the fact that it was costing him nothing. He threw a big party of course! People were partying – even in the bath on top of the stairs. I remember that there was this sudden scream from above as the bathtaps took on their own life. Water was pouring down the double glass windows into the room where we stood. Paul, I remember, was white with horror as he clearly realised the consequences of having his friends at the Como Hotel! But he loved the social-ness, the sense of bringing people together to discuss ideas. I'm sure other people who are interviewed will talk in much more detail about the rigour of his relationship with art and philosophy and the way in which it was able to articulate and frame our works as we struggled to come to terms with a complex political time. Here, I would simply like to point to the atmosphere of friendship within which he was able to frame these ideas in ways that proved enormously enriching and helped us all to think and continue in more conscious ways.

Imants Tillers interviewed by Helen Hughes

September – October 2013

HH: Your essay 'Locality Fails' (1982) is undoubtedly one of the most important texts in postmodern Australian art history in the way it dismantles the former stranglehold of the centre-periphery dynamic. How did you come to write it?

IT: I sketched out the essay largely in Paris in early 1982 when I was on my way to participate in the exhibition 'Eureka!: Artists from Australia', curated by Sandy Nairne and Sue Grayson at the Serpentine Gallery and the Institute of Contemporary Arts in London. The catalyst for writing it was that Paul Taylor had just started the magazine *Art & Text* and wanted artists, in particular, to write 'pieces' for it. I had met Paul through John Nixon and Jenny Watson, when I began to exhibit with Art Projects in Melbourne. The key inspiration for this essay was a fascinating book by Gary Zukav, *The Dancing Wu-Li Masters*, which attempts to relate the latest thinking in quantum physics to certain aspects of eastern philosophy. This is where I came across 'Bell's Theorem' and the strange counterintuitive phenomenon of the 'failure of locality', which can occur at the quantum level of reality. Scientific ideas did not daunt me, since as a high school student I had excelled at maths and science and had won a place in 1967 at the International Summer Science School at the Nuclear Physics Foundation of Sydney University, an initiative to groom talented science students to pursue a career in science. By 1982 I had chosen a career in art rather than science (or architecture, for that matter, which I had studied at Sydney University). Thus Bell's Theorem provided me with a scientific metaphor for playfully solving the so-called 'provincialism problem' in Australian art.

HH: You are currently in London for the 'Australia' exhibition at the Royal Academy. To what extent do theories of Australian identity impact on your most recent work? Say, for instance, in your collaborations with Michael Nelson Jagamara?

IT: My work has never been driven by theory. Undoubtedly, I've been interested in ideas, but I find that one's work needs to develop intuitively, almost in parallel to the ideas. There is nothing worse in my mind than art which is simply an illustration of theory. For me, the 'Australia' exhibition at the Royal Academy in London confirms that the big story in Australian art is the co-evolution and cross-fertilisation of contemporary Aboriginal art with the non-indigenous stream of contemporary art. It is a phenomenon which I believe is unique to Australia, and I like to call this exciting new phase which we have entered as 'post-aboriginal'. Indeed, my collaborations with Michael Nelson Jagamara over the last decade are part of this 'post-aboriginal' phenomenon. A month after 'Australia' opened in London at the Royal Academy, another significant exhibition opened at the Museum of Aquitaine in Bourdeaux, France—'Vivid Memories: an Aboriginal Art History'—and one of our 'post-aboriginal' collaborations, *Fatherland* (2008), was given a prominent position in the unfolding story.

HH: How has your attitude towards the artistic strategy of appropriation changed since the early 1980s and your involvement in exhibitions like 'POPISM'?

IT: The power of 'appropriation' as not only a way of connecting diverse imagery and narratives but also as a technique for understanding—as something crucial for an epistemological investigation—has not lessened in my practice as an artist. To be frank, I have never identified with the 'Pop Art' of Andy Warhol, Roy Lichtenstein or Claes Oldenburg, nor that of many of the Australian artists in Paul's 'POPISM' exhibition at the NGV in Melbourne, in its exploration of popular culture, consumer culture and the mass media. Warhol's appropriation of Brillo boxes or Campbell soup can labels left me cold!

Recently, however, I've been excited by a recognition that Western ideas of originality have little traction in Aboriginal culture. To the contrary, all Aboriginal art could be said to be based on a form of quotation or 'appropriation' in the sense that the repetition of forms, stories and symbols (Dreamings) through the passing generations has been essential to maintaining the very existence of their world. Here, too, there is a strange resonance with some of the writings of Martin Heidegger, in which 'appropriation' occurs as a key concept in the emergence of 'being' itself.

HH: It has been said that Paul was incredibly committed to your work, perhaps more so to yours than to that of any other Australian artist, and that he took it upon himself to make your work known to international audiences—particularly in New York.[1] Why do you think Paul felt this international framing was such an imperative?

IT: The German painter Markus Lupertz once said: 'Every ten years, the doors of art history open and then we start running'. Such a moment occurred internationally at the beginning of the 1980s with the exhibitions 'A New Spirit in Painting' at the Royal Academy in London in 1981 and 'Zeitgeist' at the Martin-Gropius Bau in Berlin in 1982. Even though I did not see either exhibition, the experience of participating in Documenta 7 in Kassel in 1982 quickly brought me up to speed with what was unfolding on the international stage. And further exhibition opportunities coincided with the possibilities and portentousness of the moment, galvanising my art practice and taking it to another level. Paul was a new enthusiastic ally and friend who also took notice of what was happening.

By the time Paul moved to New York in late 1984, I had already exhibited at Documenta 7 (1982), staged my first international solo exhibition at Matt's Gallery in London (1983), exhibited in New York for the first time as one of three artists in John Kaldor's 'An Australian Accent' at PS1 (now part of the Museum of Modern Art) (1984), been taken into the stable of the young New York gallerist Bess Cutler, and indeed was presenting my first solo exhibition there to coincide with the Guggenheim Museum's group exhibition 'Australian Visions' (1984). Between 1984 and 1989, I had four solo exhibitions with Bess Cutler and a fifth solo exhibition at a University Gallery in Portland, Oregon, and was included in many significant group exhibitions across the United States and Canada. A highlight was being included in Howard Fox's summation of the decade in his exhibition 'Avant-garde in the Eighties' at the Los Angeles County Museum of Art in 1987. Paul's ongoing presence in New York gave me some added encouragement and I met some interesting people through him, though he didn't write about me or curate my work into any exhibitions. It certainly wasn't a matter of deliberate 'international framing', rather events and opportunities would present themselves and both Paul and I were 'running', joining in and contributing in our different ways to the unfolding spectacle and narrative of the decade.

HH: You once mentioned that you gave Paul the first canvasboards from your Book of Power series. What was painted on the boards? And what made you decide to give them to Paul?

IT: The first canvasboard series was called *Suppressed Imagery* (1981) and it consisted of forty-nine pencil drawings on canvasboard panels arranged in a seven-by-seven grid formation. This work looked back to the preceding series (*One Painting*, 1980–1983) relating to the Basilica of Saint Francis at Assisi but also incorporated some new elements including some imagery from Giorgio di Chirico, whose later work (post-1919) I'd just discovered. *Suppressed Imagery* was one of my pieces in Paul's 'POPISM' exhibition, photocopies of these panels were part of my installation at the Serpentine Gallery in the 'Eureka!' exhibition in London in 1982, and the source for many of these drawings (a series of polaroid photographs) were part of my exhibit at Documenta 7. Although I completed this work in 1981, it was not until 1986 after my exhibition at the Venice Biennale that I decided to give this work to Paul. It was to thank him personally for acting as the Australian Commissioner for my participation there. My exhibit had received significant critical acclaim and led to further opportunities for me, including the solo exhibition at the Institute of Contemporary Arts in London in 1988, curated by Iwona Blazwick. At that moment, I felt that Paul really believed in me both as a person and as an artist, and as *Suppressed Imagery* dates back to the period when I first met him, I felt it was an appropriate act of recognition and acknowledgement of our friendship.

Reacting with enthusiasm

Juan Davila interviewed by Janine Burke

July 23, 2012

JB: I wonder if you can recall your first meetings and first impressions of Paul Taylor.

JD: My memory is that we met at the Clifton Hill Community Music Centre, which was a place where all the artists went; Maria Kozic, Tony Clark, John Nixon and others. It was based around music, so I saw him in the crowd and we said hello but he seemed too smart for me!

JD: We met properly in 1981 at Tolarno Galleries, where I had a show which had a lot of psychoanalytic quotation in the works. So Paul enquired about me, and we met then.

JB: Did getting to know Paul introduce you to *Art & Text* as well?

JD: Yes, that's how it happened. Because at that point, my [quotational] artwork was not considered by the scene. Paul was the only person who reacted to it with enthusiasm. So he connected me to others—because I worked alone until then—and then he introduced me to the *Art & Text* scene. So I became a part of that group in a way, which was wonderful—a bit of life!

JB: Was *Art & Text* an exciting publication to you? Did you compare it with international publications you were aware of, or did it seem an especially Australian manifestation?

JD: I wasn't in the 'international scene'. I was from Santiago in Chile and I went from that scene to this one. That scene was all photocopying, self-publishing and so on. I had little interest in the international scene. What I found here was a stale, conservative, middle class sort of taste. Galleries, and the National Gallery of Victoria, had this suffocating English-ness. Not all of them were like that, because there were other issues being addressed like art and social commitment, discussions about sexuality, what exists between black and white. But reading *Art & Text*, I thought: this is astonishing. It was theoretical discussion where there was none, at least from what I could tell.

JB: Did Paul invite you to publish in *Art & Text*?

JD: Yes. The first thing was in regard to my connection to the Freudian School of Melbourne with Oscar Zentner and Maria-Ines Rotmiler de Zentner. I had shown work there, presented as a conference paper. I did a small piece called 'Spider Woman in Australia', and that began a relationship that was somewhere between friendship and cultural work, if you like.

That was a crucial moment at least for me, because in Australia we had the International Freudian Association, which was very conservative. So, to find Lacanian theory here caused a lot of ripples and debate. *Art & Text* also caused the same ripples, because the whole scene was invested in a 'Toorak set' and social climbing. Only some artists were seen as truly Australian, such as Fred Williams, Sidney Nolan and Arthur Boyd. There was nothing else, from what I could tell. So *Art & Text* was like a door opening to intellectual life.

JB: You also started a collaboration with Howard Arkley during those years. Did that grow out of you both showing at Tolarno? Was that also part of Paul and *Art & Text*, or did that have a separate kind of energy?

JD: It came separately. I went round all the galleries with photographs of my work and I was rejected in a polite way. They said 'oh, you're not from Victoria', when in fact I was living here. Others I won't name said 'there is nothing I can do for you'. This is except for Georges Mora, who saw the work and said, 'I'll give you a show'. It was very simple. Howard had come into the gallery at that very same time, so we became friends, and found a sort of ambience between friendship and creating art.

JB: I wondered too if your connection with Paul may have been due to his own interest in Latin America. Was that already there, or did you feel you helped engender it?

JD: I hope I helped him engender that; there was a strong debate between art and politics and psychoanalysis. As a result, Paul had developed a certain curiosity, and the result of that interaction was in 1996, number 31 of *Art & Text* was devoted to Nelly Richard, who was a theoretician in Chile. I worked with her because I kept coming and going between Australia and Chile. In typical Paul Taylor fashion, we were in a sports car at high speed with Nelly. He decided that he'd give the whole issue to an essay by Nelly Richard on an 'avant-garde movement at the end of the world' in Chile and the military regime. Paul wasn't just an entrepreneur or game player, he had true serious intent in matters like that. Migrants didn't exist, and he made a very strong gesture. We spoke of the avant-garde utopia, and the fight against the system—in our case, the dictator in Chile. It wasn't a challenge, it was a life and death situation, and you worked not with slogans but with manipulating language to say more than what's allowed, to go in the cracks and fissures of things. In Australia, the reaction towards art in Latin America was minimal. Some academics said, 'oh, it's an overrated place for mediocre artworks', and because it didn't fit the academia of Latin America and the States, there was no career in getting interested in that. Paul had mixed feelings about it all, as he did with everything.

JB: Can you say what some of that mixture of feelings was?

JD: Well it was totally out of fashion—who cares about a small group in Chile when then it was all geared toward mainstream Europe and America? That was the world. Australians only repeated that, to think of 'The Field' exhibition and copycats, so this was something out of the blue. And I mean for the migrants, it was quite astonishing to see themselves in English with a work, so that was one of Paul Taylor's great moments.

JB: What are your recollections of 'POPISM'?

JD: My recollection is of what happened before and after 'POPISM'. Before, [the National Gallery of Victoria] didn't do Australian art, and, if they did, it was put in an awful little corridor that looks into the courtyard. I can't remember the dates, but Ivan Durrant killed a cow to protest this treatment of the local artists. So it was a place not unlike today. 'POPISM ' was totally against what they were like. The National Gallery of Victoria collected what was sort of conservative, like an accountant's view of Australian art; it had to be landscape. The Depression was just accepted. Any image of Aboriginality was rejected. So with 'POPISM' you have, as if another world, debates about the construction of French theory, brought to the local scene, to our issues; issues of provincialism, identity, the systems of power within the arts, so it was something and you see that in the projection that it provoked, and later in the splitting of opinions from academics and cultural studies who absolutely loathed these abstracts.

JB: So 'POPISM' did a good job, then?

JD: It did a good job. Paul had a talent for connecting, communicating and stirring.

JB: Yes, he was definitely a provocateur.

JD: He loved that role, so life wasn't dull near him. I remember visiting him in New York. He was testing how it would be there. I gifted him a painting, one of the quotation paintings, which his wonderful family has now, I'm very pleased with that. The first thing he said was, 'is that the best you can give?' That was Paul.

JB: What did you say?

JD: Silence, of course it was the very best! His ego was really something.

Personality portraits

Jenny Watson interviewed by Kelly Fliedner

March 24, 2013

KF: When did you first meet Paul?

JW: I met Paul at a party in 1977. I was teaching at Caulfield Institute of Technology, now Monash University, which had some very interesting students including Nick Seymour of Crowded House. Nick Cave had just dropped out. There were people like Wendy Bannister who was a model and sister of Jenny Bannister, the fashion designer. There was a really interesting bunch of people and, apart from teaching, it was a fun social life in Melbourne. I went to a party where a very young Paul Taylor was a guest. He was finishing his honours thesis off at Monash on some American minimalists like Robert Morris. He knew who I was and he knew that I was teaching and he asked if he could visit my studio.

KF: Where was your studio at the time?

JW: I had a little old stable building in a backyard in St Kilda that had been the stables of a grand house a long time ago. That house had been divided up into flats and I was using what had been the stables as a studio. Paul visited me there for the first time.

KF: So he had seen your previous work at exhibitions in Melbourne and was interested in meeting you?

JW: I had my first show in 1973 of works on paper at Powell Street and then my first painting exhibition in 1974. It was a gallery full of large horses. I had shown my series of suburban houses in 1977, but had painted them between '75 and '77. I was an up-and-coming Melbourne artist, and he knew my work before he knew me.

KF: Why do you think Paul was interested in your work in particular?

JW: Well, because he had been looking at this quite academic

American work, I think he was interested in local artists who were making work about local issues. He loved the suburban houses, he loved my personality portraits. When he came to my studio, I was in the process of painting my Twiggy painting, which is in the National Gallery of Victoria. I was doing a whole lot of paintings on board with very think oil paint. They were still very traditional paintings, but the subject and the placement were pretty radical. He loved that painting and asked me to name it after him, which I did.

I did that at his request and actually a dealer said to me later, 'I wish you hadn't have done that, it's not so good to be identified with anyone in particular'. We were very unprofessional in those days and didn't think about the ramifications of things like that.

After the Twiggy exchange, Paul then said, 'look, there's a bunch of you who are making images from your experience of having grown up with television, which makes you very different to generations before, and I'm going to do something about that'. And that became 'POPISM'.

KF: Do you have any other memories from the 'POPISM' exhibition and how that came together? Was it after long conversations with Paul?

JW: Well, because Paul was a very social guy he wanted to know everyone who was making anything. He wanted to bring everyone from different groups together. He was a party animal. We all started to go to the same clubs and restaurants and quite often met at Paul's flat in South Yarra. He connected me with people like Juan Davila, Philip Brophy, Maria Kozic, and Judy Annear. Those people were not any particular kind of set before Paul made the introductions, and the rest is history.

KF: The group of artists and writers involved with the *Art & Text* and 'POPISM' projects had such gravitas, in retrospect. When I think of that time in Melbourne, it has a commanding presence within Australian art history. How was your practice affected by the 'POPISM' exhibition?

JW: Yes, 'POPISM' helped me define who I was and what kind of artist I was going to be. I had made this very radical shift from traditional paintings. I had exploded the paintings out by using small canvasboards. The first work in Australia in that format was my work *Conversation Piece* (1981). Everyone knows that Imants

Tillers found the use of the canvasboard very inspiring. It went from there. I then not only exploded the grid, I thought I could use language and I could use fabric. Exploding the painting out from that normal traditional format opened up the work I have been doing for the last thirty years.

We were interested in music and fashion and culture in general. However, broader Australia was a very conservative place at the time. I wanted to use language. I wanted to use my thoughts and ideas, my autobiography and personal stories. I felt that if I stuck to a traditional painting format it would be too slow. I had to deconstruct the imagery and work out a format that was faster and so I started using my big personal script. I had a lot of ideas and I needed formats that could integrate those ideas quickly instead of taking me years and years to do photorealism.

KF: Getting back to 'POPISM', what kind of a curator was Paul? What was he like to work with? Did he dictate, or pick and choose your work in the exhibition, or was it developed over time through conversations between the two of you?

JW: No, he was quite tough. He had very clear ideas about what suited his philosophy and what didn't. He was a tough curator. He had his own agenda. I think he realised early on that Australia was not going to be big enough for him. I think *Art & Text* and the book *Anything Goes* were very clever vehicles. They were calling cards to New York in a way, where he became very successful very quickly.

KF: There was a certain amount of animosity for him from conservative aspects of the arts industry, because he so heavily pushed international theory, such as French poststructuralism. Exhibitions like 'POPISM' were challenging and difficult for the broader public and general audience. Do you want to comment on this opposition?

JW: Yes, there was opposition. My '77 exhibition of suburban houses was very much the comment that Australia is not a big open burnt landscape. Most people live in suburban houses in Australia. That was my comment. The Australian landscape was something that we had looked at enough. Paul was on the same wavelength. He didn't want to absorb the myths or the boogies of the time. The Antipodeans, the symbols at the time, the work that they had made. Yes, it's good work but it *still* dominates the auction houses to this day, which is ridiculous. There is a real resistance in Australia to get hip and to get modern. People really want to hang onto an idea of Australian art as that before the '50s. Australia does not really accept anything after that. Australia has a modernist culture and does not accept a postmodernist culture, let alone a post-feminist culture, and that was frustrating for Paul. We had all catapulted into the twentieth century and no one wanted to acknowledge it.

KF: Do you remember the *Art & a Texta* incident? I'm intrigued, obviously Paul was upset about the parody, but do you have any more thoughts into what he may have been thinking at the time?

JW: I thought at the time that that sort of criticism of what was a very interesting journal was very Australian, the Tall Poppy syndrome, someone putting in a whole lot of energy into something so negative. It was very Australian and I'm glad that he fought it. His brother was a lawyer so you know it was a family thing, to not let this guy get away with that. Australia is a very small culture, it's getting better all the time and people travel more and we have international guests. But the city of Melbourne is a small city at the bottom of a huge continent that is a long way from anywhere and it is very prone to that sort of thing; more so than, say, New York, where no matter what you say your project is going to be, people say 'Good for you!' It's a recurring problem.

KF: Paul was an advocate for your work in Melbourne and New York. It's not always that curators go out of their way to advocate for artists. It's always great to be part of a community and to support those around you, but there is no guarantee that someone is going to advocate that strongly for you in the same way as Paul did for yourself and others of your generation.

JW: Absolutely not, that is true. He really went out on a limb, but I think that's because we were friends first. Back in those old days, artists didn't really lobby curators, there wasn't the networking and connecting that seems to be necessary now. We were just friends and we stayed friends all through the business side of things of 'POPISM' and emerging into New York. I alerted him to places like the Crystal Ballroom and the bands there and other Melbourne painters who were a little more retiring than others that were part of that scene. He wouldn't have known about that, he was into disco, a sort of upmarket scene, expensive, fancy drinks, dressing up. It was very different to the St Kilda underground that I was part of. I alerted him to that and I think he was grateful. I think he was able to make an amalgam of what was happening at the time in Melbourne culturally, and we know the rest is history.

KF: He was obviously really good at seeing the potential in particular artists and particular groups of people, as well as having a strong curatorial oversight to bring everyone together...

JW: In some ways, after working with some pretty great dealers, Paul had the qualities of an art dealer, he could pick someone and talk to them and develop them. And the sad thing about that was that he wasn't in a position to make a lot of money out of it. But he could have been an agent type person, he almost was, unofficially.

KF: A question directed at the music scene, the Crystal Ballroom, The Go Betweens, Nick Cave. Obviously, like the art world, there were many various and separate tribes of musicians. Did you ever head over to the Clifton Hill Community Music Centre?

JW: Yeah, we did. And that was Paul's legacy, he introduced all of these factions. You could go to the Crystal Ballroom one night and you could go to Clifton Hill another night and see a very early version of Essendon Airport. Philip Brophy started there. You could pick and choose. There were jokes ... we used to say, Janine Burke needed a passport to get out of Carlton. Because all her activity was Carlton-based. For some people, all their activity was Clifton Hill-based. I used to do the rounds, but my spiritual home was the Ballroom. It created a cabaret-type set up for a whole lot of suburban people who didn't want to live like their parents.

KF: Do you remember any particular events or nights where Paul was present?

JW: I remember introducing Paul to Nick Cave. Nick back then was really scrawny, bad hair, bad teeth, a real St Kilda punk. And Paul was a polished South Yarra boy with fancy glasses and nice hair and I kind of remember them checking each other out and thinking, 'well, Jenny has all sorts of friends.'

KF: Could you talk a little about *Art & Text*? You were written about in *Art & Text* by writers such as Richard Dunn, Frances Lindsay, Sue Cramer and Paul himself. Paul clearly used the journal as another forum to endorse a group of artists that you were part of. How did you feel at the time, about having these quite heavy theories overlaid onto your work?

JW: I talked to him about this at the time and I said to him, 'artists do the work they do and then what happens is in a particular time in history a curator will see a certain amount of links and then say, "These are the postmodernist artists we should look at. These are the post-feminists we should look at."' But it actually comes from the work. A problem with young artists these days, that I have noticed with my students, is that a lot of them read theory and try to make some art that fits in with it. It's one way to go, but in my day it was the artists who made the work and then theory circulated around it.

KF: You didn't feel like you were part of that conversation? Did you feel detached from it?

JW: It's the way I make my work, the way I have always done. There will always be critics or writers or curators saying, 'I'm going to put you in a show about this'. I make my work in a very old fashioned, solitary way. I see a reason to pair some text with an image on a particular piece of fabric. Although my work doesn't look old-fashioned, my way of working is. It's absolute studio practice.

KF: But whether artists liked it or not, Paul did create divisive tribal lines within the art world and you were either part of it or you weren't. I guess particularly with a lot of the members of the *Lip* collective, the feminist crew, had issues with *Art & Text* and the 'POPISM' crew. Feminist themes resonate through your work and you once wrote for *Lip*, did you ever feel at times like you were stuck in the middle?

JW: I think, yes, I would have been aware that there were different points of view and it was divisive to pick a bunch of artists and say, 'these are the interesting people', like Paul did. But the Australian art world at that time needed a shake up. I was aware there were all these divisive elements, and to get out of all that division I bought a horse and, in 1982, moved to the country and natural life, and that was the beginning of the end for me. Paul came out to my house outside Melbourne, probably in 1984, when he was just about to go to New York, and I remember he couldn't get away fast enough. 'Yep, okay, I can see what you're into, but it's not for me.' He wanted to get back to Toorak Road in his MG and the life he knew and loved.

We got on very well. He was a Virgo and I was a Libra. We got on very well, it was almost a familial type of relationship.

Paul Taylor and the Brisbane sound

David Pestorius interviewed by Helen Hughes

March 5 – June 30, 2013

HH: Your text 'The Brisbane Sound: An Illustrated Chronology' notes that Paul Taylor visited Brisbane in 1981.[1] What were the circumstances of his visit?

DP: He delivered a lecture at the Institute of Modern Art on Thursday July 16, 1981. The second issue of *Art & Text* had just been published and the title of the lecture was '*Art & Text* in the Australian Art Context',[2] which suggests it was probably an echo of his 'On Criticism' editorial from the first issue. However, Taylor was not only in Brisbane to promote his new art magazine. He was also here to see Howard Arkley's exhibition, 'Wall Painting: Muzak Mural', which had opened at the IMA the previous week and for which he had written the catalogue essay.[3]

HH: At the time, John Nixon was not only the IMA director and curator of the Arkley exhibition, but also an artist with an active exhibition and studio practice, which included the collaborative Anti-Music project. The Arkley show conflated painting and muzak at the same time as Taylor and Philip Brophy were raising the formula of disco as a way to think through the prevalence of appropriation art in Australia. How do you see these different modes of music (Anti-Music, muzak, disco) functioning as theoretical tools for Taylor here?

DP: I don't think this rhetoric around disco came into it at all. Basically, Taylor was positioning Arkley's installation within a history of wall painting, from Renaissance frescos to Constructivist environments (Lissitzky, Buchholz, Mondrian, etc.), to the chapels of Matisse and Rothko, to 'the vagaries of interior decoration'. In other words, he saw the work within a kind of Minimalist lineage, which was about activating the viewer and rendering them reflexive. What's especially interesting is how he inserted the Cagean notion of 'all sound is music' into the equation. Taylor makes the point that 'both walls and muzak are greater than the spectator, they surround and manipulate yet so often go unnoticed'.[4] Arkley's IMA wall painting was therefore not only concerned with the spatially receptive viewer, but also one who is acoustically receptive. At the time, Cagean thinking was hugely influential on artists internationally. Back in the day, Dan Graham spoke of the important links between the New York No Wave groups and Cage, while one only needs to read the hyperbolic pronouncements of Anti-Music, especially those of Peter Tyndall's Invisible Music and Gary Warner's Forced Audience, to get a sense of how important Cage was in the local context. Incidentally, Taylor also mentions Cage in the 'On Criticism' piece, which was more or less contemporaneous with these Anti-Music texts.

HH: Do you think Anti-Music coloured Taylor's reading of Cage?

DP: He would have been familiar with the manifestos of Anti-Music, but, as I say, Cage was very much in the air at the time. Dan Graham's observations were published in April 1982 in the catalogue for the first major international survey of the new crossover culture.[5] That pioneering exhibition did not take place in New York, London, or Berlin, but under the umbrella of that year's Biennale of Sydney. Curated by Bill Furlong, the British artist whose *Audio Arts* cassette magazine had only months earlier released an Anti-Music sampler, the survey featured over forty projects, with many coming from cities around Australia. There were also many contributions from New York, including by Laurie Anderson, Glenn Branca, Rhys Chatham, Brian Eno, Dan Graham, Kim Gordon, Thurston Moore, and Lee Ranaldo. Furlong's curatorial rationale was that Cage was the glue that held it all together. Many of the artists close to Taylor participated, including Philip Brophy, Maria Kozic, David Chesworth, John Nixon and Peter Tyndall. It's curious that the catalogue for the Sydney show was omitted from the bibliography published in the catalogue for Taylor's famous 'POPISM' show, because all of these artists resurfaced in that context a few months later. Of course, by then, this new crossover culture had been fermenting in diverse contexts, here and overseas, for some time. For instance, only weeks after Arkley began to channel muzak in Brisbane, Judy Annear curated 'Noise & Muzak' at the George Paton Gallery and Taylor wrote a catalogue essay for that show too.[6] Incidentally, Bill Furlong participated in 'Noise & Muzak', which overlapped in many respects with his sound survey at the Biennale of Sydney the following year. And, just to continue on the theme of muzak, earlier the previous month, Invisible Music published a manifesto

in *Pneumatic Drill*, the newsletter of Anti-Music.[7] Obviously, the group name Invisible Music was strongly evocative of Cage, while the manifesto brilliantly summarised how his philosophy was being thought about locally at the time. With respect to muzak, the manifesto had this to say: 'Invisible Music encourages the development of muzak and other musics intended for specific uses. However, it recommends that, to develop further, muzak needs to be first stripped of any vestiges of tune.'[8] Gary Warner's Forced Audience manifesto, a few issues later, in a kind of 'call and response' approach, involved a witty reiteration of the Invisible Music polemic. Paul Taylor was very close to all of this and it was fitting, I think, that he would make the photomontage that graced
37 the final issue of *Pneumatic Drill*. The photomontage depicts a family of desert Aborigines sitting down with a portable audiocassette tape recorder/player and appears under the title 'The Art of White Aborigines'. The cassette tape recorder was the quintessential instrument of Anti-Music and represented the new democratic possibilities of the new art/music. The title and the composite image must be understood as a kind of graphic analog to Taylor's Popist theory, while also perhaps pointing to the emerging phenomena of contemporary Aboriginal art.

HH: What exactly do you mean by 'new crossover culture'? What were the main channels for this crossover, beyond exhibitions?

DP: It was the latest break with 'official' art—its forms, contexts and systems of value—that began with Conceptual art in the late 1960s. I think what sparked it was punk, which had a lot in common with Conceptual art, the actions of the Situationists and, of course, Dada. During the post-punk years, the rock context was seen as offering new outlets, audiences, and opportunities for a kind of anti-rock with roots in a fine arts tradition. In other words, there were discernable links to performance art, Cage, experimental music and advanced theatre. Melbourne had quite an elaborate infrastructure for this activity, with multiple overlapping scenes, including the Clifton Hill Community Music Centre, The Crystal Ballroom in St Kilda, the Little Bands in Fitzroy, Art Projects, and the George Paton Gallery. In Brisbane, the scene was much smaller and most of the activity was self-organised in small inner-city halls and seedy little clubs. Nixon's collaborative Anti-Music project, aspects of his program at the IMA, his Q Space project, and Jeanelle Hurst's One Flat Exhibit, were also important crossover contexts here in the early 1980s. The Brisbane scene also had a political edge that was largely absent in other cities around the country. Obviously, the performative work was the main game, but the new crossover culture also manifested itself in unconventional forms of exhibition, vinyl records, audio cassette recordings, Super-8 films, Polaroid photography, photocopied zines and other publications, including Bruce Milne's audiocassette magazine *Fast Forward* and Ashley Crawford's *The Virgin Press*. In 2010, I tried to capture this diverse mix in the exhibition 'Melbourne><Brisbane: Punk, Art & After' (Ian Potter Museum of Art, Melbourne), which included over 20,000 words all over the walls in an attempt to critically build the context, but unfortunately there was no stand-alone catalogue.

HH: What other ways did Taylor collaborate with Nixon? I think you suggested that Taylor was involved directly with Nixon's Society for Other Photography?

DP: I think the photomontage for the final issue of *Pneumatic Drill* in 1983 was his only direct contribution to Anti-Music. Having said that, it's clear Taylor was closely associated with Nixon in the early
34 1980s. He appears wearing headphones, presumably listening to an Anti-Music recording, in one of the large Polaroid pieces by The Society for Other Photography, one of Nixon's many projects at that time. One of these pieces was included in 'POPISM', although it's rarely, if ever, mentioned in dispatches because it doesn't sit so well with the brash appropriation art that so dominated the
39 discourse. The same goes for the 'POPISM' catalogue, which has the slightly dry look of 'classic' conceptual art. Its design is also strongly evocative of El Lissitzky, which, in my eyes, points again to Nixon, whose work in the early 1980s involved a multifaceted re-working of Russian Constructivism. Of course, there were other artists in 'POPISM' who were toying with the tropes of Constructivism, with Robert Rooney and Richard Dunn coming to mind.

HH: Were there other direct channels of influence between the cities? For instance, do you think Paul Taylor and *Art & Text* had an impact on the Brisbane scene?

DP: It's hard to measure the impact *Art & Text* and Paul Taylor had on Brisbane. I know in certain quarters there was antipathy because of all these Melbourne directors of the IMA — John Buckley, Nixon, and then Peter Cripps — who were seen as 'blow-ins', people not really interested in the local scene. Taylor and

Art & Text would have been seen as part of that. I actually think Peter Cripps's engagement with local artists but also Brisbane's recent past, especially the new crossover culture, was quite remarkable and I tried to point this up in the 'Melbourne><Brisbane' exhibition. People are also quick to forget that Nixon, with his art dealer's hat on, represented a number of Brisbane artists at Art Projects, not the least being Robert MacPherson. There's a tendency today to present Art Projects as a kind of proto-ARI space, but this is quite misleading. The truth is it was a dealer gallery that held monthly changing exhibitions and represented, promoted and sold the work of a small group of artists.[9] One need only look at the Art Projects ads in *Art & Text* to get a sense of this. It's almost inconceivable in today's highly institutionalised world of art that John could wear so many hats, but back then it was more possible. He had extraordinary drive and ambition ... and he still does! Perhaps he could have done more for Gary Warner, who was represented as part of the Anti-Music collective and whose diverse material production would have been a good fit in 'POP-ISM', which did not include a single Brisbane artist. Again, I think it's hard to be too critical here because Gary was also a member of perhaps the most promising of the Brisbane Sound groups, Peter Milton Walsh's Out of Nowhere. In mid 1981, they collaborated with Anti-Music on a split-cassette, but I think there was soon a perception that Gary had forsaken art for a life in rock'n'roll.

HH: Most commentaries on *Art & Text* note the impact of capital-T 'Theory' on the production and interpretation of art in Melbourne from the early 1980s onwards. Was there a similar shift towards Theory in Brisbane at this time? What were the main channels (i.e., was there a Brisbane journal undertaking similar/related projects to *Art & Text*)?

DP: Certainly artists here read the theory-laden pages of *Art & Text* religiously in the early years. But there was a healthy skepticism too. For example, in April 1983, *Art Walk* – which was one of the offset-printed magazines produced in connection with Jeanelle Hurst's One Flat Exhibit project – published one of the most insightful critical rejoinders to the invocation of French theory in the name of art by Taylor and others in the early 1980s, although today this remarkable text languishes in obscurity.[10]

Part IV

Sources: Reflections

As I was saying,
Vivienne Shark LeWitt

'There was never any need to worry about Paul ... and wherever he is now, he's probably having a better time than you or me.'

When these closing words to my address at Paul Taylor's memorial in 1992 were published a few months later in *Art & Text*,[1] I was dismayed to see the final 'me' had been changed to an 'I'. This small act of correction seemed to ring the last, irrevocable change of the times. Paul was gone and wouldn't be coming back.

An excellent writer himself, as an editor Paul was surprisingly laissez-faire – if it was good enough to publish, it was good enough to stand on its own feet and fight for itself. Yet so much was Paul identified with the magazine he founded that everything published under its aegis became, as it were, a part of himself. His attitude towards contributing writers was as such rather 'parental' – with all the expectations, demands and keen disappointments that characterise parenthood. It was always a case of the querulously assumptive: '*When* are you going to write something for *Art & Text?*' and not, '*Would* you write something?'

I wrote two essays for *Art & Text* in the early '80s – both quite ridiculous in different ways, but both published intact, precisely as I originally presented them. The first one marked the beginning of the brief captivation with French philosophy I shared with Paul.[2] The second marks my disenchantment and escape from it.[3] Like many of his friends could say, fragments of our conversation often wound up in print. In my case, woven through the essays he and I both wrote over those years is the thread of a forever-unresolved argument about cultural sincerity, meaning and faith. Predictably enough for people just over twenty-one, it all started in the contested field of pop music and everything it stood for.

Before I officially met Paul at the School of Art in Hobart, I'd already spotted him once or twice in the record shop at Sandy Bay (no doubt looking through the Disco section). He, in turn, had stolen a march on me. 'I've heard of you', he said, citing an article I'd written on Punk and New Wave for *The Tasmanian Review*.[4] Not long after, across the table at a dinner party, I was to hear him mischievously quoting it – 'Some people say "The history of art is a history of quibbling" but I don't agree' – with a slight smirk in my direction. And sparring partners we became.

I moved to Sydney about six months later, keeping up a correspondence with Paul. He recruited me as his emissary a few times – insisting I go to things and meet people I would normally be too intimidated to go near – his exasperated nagging being the more dreaded of outcomes. His letters were always spiked with exhortations: 'Are you entering the sculpture triennial? Are you writing? Why not write for *Art Network*? What are you reading? Don't let your brains turn to mush.' He was never too impressed with my preference for fiction, but it was actually a John Fowles novel that made me look up Roland Barthes.

Leafing through a copy of *Roland Barthes by Roland Barthes* in a Paddington bookshop, I came across the entry called 'The second degree and the others'.[5] It sounded familiar, a bit like the habit of always seeing reminders of things in other things, connections that weren't necessarily there literally but could be made on some other, subjective level. Barthes may not have meant what I thought he meant, but it seemed to encapsulate the intellectual trap of self-consciousness that is part of any creative action. It would be the lynchpin for the essay on the Mod revival I was planning for the as-yet unnamed magazine Paul was setting up. I sent off a postcard letting him know. He wrote straight back in his usual heat-seeking missile way, 'When you come down, would you please bring Roland Barthes's thing on 2nd degree which you mentioned? – I'd like to read it all. Don't forget!'[6]

The Guerrilla Girls have a line about women artists getting to 'see their ideas live on in the work of others' – but as an art *critic* Paul saw a far wider potential for the second degree idea. He gave it a true home in his flagship essay 'Australian "New Wave" and the "Second Degree"',[7] which, combined with his salutary editorial on art criticism, launched the first volume of *Art & Text* and established Paul Taylor as an intellectual force to be reckoned with. Meanwhile, he judiciously held my effort back for a later volume.

It was a trick of Paul's to niggle away at the edge of one's consciousness, at what to others would be barely perceptible differences in opinion and belief, but which to those involved meant everything. My essay on Mod, for all its 'epistemological and ontological' nonsense, was genuinely concerned with the loss and recovery of credible social and political meaning. By comparison, Paul's article stressed the very 'pleasure of dislocation' – the forgetting of the past as a strategy for recasting meaning more towards its construction than its particular content – more the how than the what. What I interpreted in Barthes as a moral warning about 'language losing its good conscience', Paul interpreted as the liberation of ideas and method. The intellectualism of his writing often confounded the shallow and the deep at the same time – aligning him always with the paradoxical 'profound superficiality' of Andy Warhol. But, needless to say, better this by far than the horrors of the 'superficially profound' – which Paul could detect at a hundred paces.

He was not, however, unaffected by the somewhat romantic vision of the aftermath of postmodernism I proposed in my second essay for *Art & Text*, 'The End of Civilization Part II: Love Among the Ruins'. As I've written elsewhere,[8] 'Love Among the Ruins' was in many ways a response to Paul's exhibition 'POPISM'.[9] But there was also a parallel between my attempt to retrieve some old values of religiosity and symbolism, and what Paul called the 'return of the repressed' – crushed so poetically beneath the chariot wheels of his next curatorial venture, 'Tall Poppies'.

The 'Tall Poppies' catalogue essay provides an elegant account of 'the collapse of the Modernist paradigm', seeing historical order where my battle of 'iconoclasts and philistines' saw only chaos. Paul's essay makes a connection between the postmodern condition and the resort to classicism after World War I, and folds both into the cold reality of modernist culture never being welcome (in Australia anyway). 'Love Among the Ruins' intuitively but unwittingly bore this out, and had I understood Paul's conclusion to 'Tall Poppies' – 'attempting to recuperate for art its greatness and uniqueness, and for the artist his vision, we mourn by self-immolation the loved one who has past away'[10] – I might have wondered if he was sending me up.

Paul would always catch the drift of your thinking and then outsmart you. He ran rings around us all, but repeatedly said he wanted to see his friends do as well in life as himself. And towards that end he took a real and practical interest. It was he who thought to reproduce my paintings alongside the mod article. It was he who insisted I was the only candidate to assist Denise Robinson at the George Paton Gallery. And it was he who sat up half a night working out my nom de plume.

At the airport next morning, he made me try it out. I dutifully gave the name Vivienne Shark LeWitt at the stand-by desk and sat down to wait with Paul. When a halting voice struggled to pronounce it over the loudspeaker, he burst out laughing.

Nineteen-eighty-two
Ralph Traviati

This must have happened on a Saturday in 1982 after March 29th. That was the day that Sparks – the American pop group so subtly smart that most people thought they were English – released a new album with one of their funnier titles.

On that Saturday, Paul Taylor came to our place for lunch. I was living with Jane Stevenson – also a member of art collective/group/buddies/band →↑→ – and Paul was interested in the group and us as members of it. Jane was a good cook and we cared a lot about what we ate. I can't remember what we prepared that day, but I'm sure it was wholesome, vegetarian and probably involved heavily iced carrot cake.

We were living in a narrow terrace house in Brunswick, on a very narrow street way up Sydney Road. This was not Paul's usual stamping ground. He lived in South Yarra in that beautiful, old (for Melbourne) apartment complex called Beverley Hills. And that was one of the things that struck you about Paul at the time: his unapologetic embrace of material pleasure, good living, the lovely things that wealth can bring. We assumed he was from a rich family but never really enquired. What was interesting about it at that time was that it felt as though he was using those trappings to kick things around, create dissonance, maybe even discomfort, chip away the punky crustiness still in the air.

I remember two details from that lunch. First, Paul arrived with a white paper bag containing some of those Polish potato cakes which appear to be woven out of thin strips of the vegetable. I was pretty sure he had bought them on Acland Street because of the white bag and the obviously professional skill with which they had been made. But when he handed them to me, he gave me a twinkly look – I don't think I ever saw him untwinkly – and said he had made them himself. I don't think he said it because he saw that we had gone to some effort, but probably because a white lie was more fun than a boring truth, a little frisson instead of bland and forgettable earnestness. And which would you have preferred? The idea of challenging the truthfulness of his claim didn't cross your mind. Instead, you tacitly agreed to go along with the twinkly-eyed act (sidebar: the potato cakes connected back to something in the real world – a shop on Acland Street – so their provenance was verifiable; art and art theory, for instance, a little less so).

The second thing was to do with the Sparks album. Central to its sound was a swooshy kind of live drum feel, where the sounds of each of the different components of the drum kit spilled and splashed over each other. This was particularly noticeable because at the time, with disco going strong, the neat separation of snares from cymbals from kick was the thing. Anyhow, when he walked in we were playing it really loud. It was new to Paul and, given the 'we really dig this' volume, he asked what it was. *Angst in my pants* by Sparks. I don't think he knew who Sparks were and I don't think his connection to music was as strong as his connection to art. But he loved the title and the photo on the cover, which was of the two Mael brothers getting married, one of them in a glittery silver tuxedo and the other one, the one with the moustache, in a beautiful wedding dress and veil. We didn't discuss it beyond my providing a little info on the band, its origins, past hits and so on, and I couldn't tell you what reverberations the album title might have had inside Paul, but he did use it as the title of a subsequent issue of *Art & Text*. It could have been to do with that pluralist notion of putting things together from disparate sources (pop music and contemporary art theory). Or maybe he liked the sense of the phrase itself and the way it made fun of angst and Freud. Or maybe it was the silly play on the phrase that begins with 'ants'. Whatever the reason, plunked on the cover of a serious art magazine, with its flippancy, it had the ring of steely provocation.

The last time I saw Paul was in New York. He had just moved there permanently, after many visits, and I was there for the first time, full of awe and dread. We had tea in his apartment, which I'm pretty sure was below 14th Street, and when I left I remember thinking that he was really on his way and, in fact, soon he was being named in the same breath as the earlier Australian art critic who had made NYC both his home and court. Was he the new Bobby H? We never found out, alas, but I'm pretty sure he would have been, but with less angst and more twinkle.

Everyone gets lighter*

Denise Robinson

In Montaigne's famous chapter on the art of conversation, he was insistent that 'The most fruitful and natural exercise of our mind, in my opinion, is discussion. I find it sweeter than any other action of our life ... It is not vigorous and generous enough ... if it is civilised and, artful, if it fears knocks and moves with constraint.'[1] This remarkable sixteenth-century inventor of the essay form then elevates conversation over writing. And here is Gertrude Stein, speaking of the loss of conversation in the twentieth century: 'And that is because talking and writing have got more separated. Talking is not thinking or feeling anymore. It used to be but it is not now, writing is, and naturally writing needs more refusing.'[2]

26 It's possible that Paul Taylor intended to make his way partly to reinvigorate that place where 'talking and writing have got more separated', along with Montaigne's desire for it as 'sweeter than any other action', and, I would add, crucially, its afterlife, its affect. In Reva Wolf's introduction to *I'll be Your Mirror* (2004), an all but definitive collection of interviews with Andy Warhol, she comments on Paul's interview with Warhol – 'The Last Interview'. 'This tongue-in-cheek flirtation developed out of a previous interaction between Taylor and Warhol', she writes, 'and because, in this instance the interviewer played along with, rather than resisted, Warhol's game rules ... sometimes this "personal" approach to the interview went much further – and was much funnier'.[3] Paul's rhetorical nous almost always had the effect of generating a kind of ongoing event – out of the liminal space between conversation and interview. It's worth considering the
45 photograph of Paul taken by Robert Rooney in the early '80s and featured in the media material for the conference held at Monash University in 2012, 'Impresario: Paul Taylor / *Art & Text* / POPISM'. It is perfectly poised, suggesting something more open and contingent than you would expect of an impresario. Here, Paul is posed in front of a mirror, but turning away, just enough to ensure his reflection is in profile, and nearby, just inside the frame, is his ventriloquist's dummy – surely an opening to consider where speech might come from.

In the spirit of the impresario, the work Paul undertook was in excess of any singular nomination of a role – as editor, writer, publisher or curator. Perhaps his impresario-like manner was contingent on what it was like to be his kind of 'smart'. Paul's work was initially shaped in Melbourne alongside his collaborations with artists, writers and musicians amidst New Wave and post-punk's diffidence in relation to any consensus on culture, all of which underscored his engagement with post-structuralism in *Art & Text*. Then, with his move in the mid '80s to New York, his engagement with art, primarily through journalism, struck another register. In an interview in *The Bulletin* during the late '80s, Paul indicates something of his commitment to style:

> Nowadays journalism is really important [...] you can see from my pieces that there is a philosophy and a mood in all of them, I am not being catty about Mary Boone or Illena Sonnabend [...] I would apply that tone to anything. It's satire really [...] Swift was my hero [...] It's a hard thing.[4]

To indicate how incendiary his writing could be, Anthony Haden-Guest in his book *True Colors* cites Paul quoting Mary Boone. On being questioned about dealing with 'slow moving artists', she says 'Get them into debt ... get the artists to have expensive tastes ... get them to have expensive habits ... that's what I love, that's what drives them to produce.'[5]

This preoccupation with the limitations of style in relation to language is in the service of enabling him to say precisely what should not be said, pace his article critiquing Mary Boone's role in relation to the manipulations of the art market with potentially costly — albeit avoided — consequences for him.[6] A price worth paying to overcome the writer's plague, self-censorship. He was consistent in this regard, infuriating the then-Director of the National Gallery of Australia, James Mollison, on his New York visit, by berating him for his regressive position in relation to contemporary art in Australia. These were strategic jolts to power.

There's no doubt that there is now a reconsideration of the 1980s in Australia, with some emphasis on Melbourne, and with considerable focus on Paul's work during this period. While in 2009, Rob McKenzie's publication *The &-Files: Art & Text 1981–2002* focussed on Paul Foss's editorship of *Art & Text*, recent events like the 'Impresario' conference at Monash University and the exhibition 'Mix Tape 1980s: Appropriation, Subculture, Critical Style' at the National Gallery of Victoria in 2013 refocused attention on the impact of Paul's work in this period; in the instance of 'Mix Tape', in encountering the effect of Paul's critique of curatorial practices in relation to the Museum,[7] which the NGV recirculates in the present under the 'the popular' as marketing rubric.

Paul's presence in 'Mix Tape' was as curator of the exhibition 'POPISM' at the NGV in 1982, an exhibition that both literally and figuratively permeates many aspects of the latter exhibition. At the time, 'POPISM' sought to develop and sustain a critique, embedded in and through the work of the artists – artists working with the implications of postmodernism and post-colonialism in a privileging of the significance of pastiche, bricolage and quotation. In fact, these artists required strategies, amongst other things, precisely in order to avoid being reduced to the 'popular' – or that other side to the 'popular', the game of shock. This was hard won, not popular. What may have been at stake for those artists and intellectuals who were taking 'popular culture' seriously, held no relation to the NGV's tendentious idea of the 'popular'.

'POPISM' did not propose an alternative to the museum – a strategy formed through the 1960s and 1970s – rather it proposed to take it over, to cut it adrift, temporarily maybe, but in anticipation of what could be done with the fallout. There was a politics of the provisional at play, in line with the practices of appropriation and postmodernism. However unacknowledged, it also owed something to earlier shifts in the strategies of feminism. For example, as the director of the George Paton Gallery at the time, it was clear that there was a shift away from the idea of an 'alternative' – an idea that risked simply leaving the power that nominated it intact. Meaghan Morris in *The Pirate's Fiancée* argues that 'when feminine specificity is taken as a point of departure, or as defining the contours of a problem, then we are on the verge of a "something else"; a re-organisation, major or miniscule, in the articulation of power and knowledge'.[8]

Writing from London thirty years later, there is a strange indication of some of the historical fallout in the current representations of the history of 'Australian culture' in England. In the recent BBC series titled *The Art of Australia, Strangers in a Strange Land*, fronted by Edmund Capon, the director of the Art Gallery of New South Wales throughout the 1980s, the parameters of this representation are made clear: its remedial subtitle reading 'how art helped Australian settlers come to terms with such an unfamiliar land'. The reference to the early Europeans as 'settlers' is not innocent, it's troubling, and it's indexical of a failed attempt at veiling the presence of colonial hegemonic thought.

'Australia' is reprised in an eponymously titled exhibition at the Royal Academy, London, organised with the National Gallery of Australia. 'Landscape' is its theme, along with the attendant mythologising of the foundations of culture in Australia. Its media release reads, 'the story of Australia [is] inextricably linked to its landscape and for Australian artists this deep connection has provided a rich seam of inspiration for centuries', while profiling Anthony Gormley's comment, 'The Red Continent comes to the heart of London'.[9] At the entry to the Royal Academy courtyard are cruel and extraordinary indicators: merino sheep corralled around a statue of the founder of the Royal Academy, Joshua Reynolds, leaving droppings on the eighteenth-century statue's pedestal (it is the sponsors' promotion of merino wool), while inspiration's 'rich seam', in a kind of slip, invokes that other dark source, mining. As it was with the BBC series, the ubiquitous presence of Shaun Gladwell's work appears in the entrance to the exhibition, as if the interpreter of 'Australian identity' in an overwhelmingly large-scale projection, *Approach to Mundi Mundi* — a baffling purification of the iconography of *Mad Max*. And where is cinema in this two hundred years of history, or some sense of the brilliant and necessary work done that has been vital in countering such forays into colonial hegemony over the past decades in Australia — including those writers, artists and intellectuals in the early 1980s?[10] For example, Meaghan Morris, writing on the photographs of Lynn Silverman in an issue of *Art & Text* in 1982, writes '"The desert" is always a pre-existing pile of text and documents, fantasies, legends, jokes and other people's memories, a vast imaginary hinterland ... But the enduring seductiveness of the myth resides in the reversibility of its meanings.'[11] And in the same issue, Paul Foss writes in 'Meridian of Apathy' that: 'The centre is really quite a new place, and sings with a different logic — whether we can hear its tune or not.'[12]

There was a particularly charged work commissioned by the George Paton Gallery in 1983 that arose from Paul's suggestion to commission artists to combine their work in a reprise of the Surrealist chance encounter, 'Exquisite Corpse'. The artists invited were Howard Arkley, Maria Kozic and Juan Davila, each having in some way collaborated with the other previously. There's a kind of gravitational pull here towards the game of Exquisite Corpse, with both the critique of authorship and originality in postmodernism and an embrace of the Surrealists' privileging of the unconscious — a form of automatic writing. Four drawings on four large panels were installed in the window of the Rowden White Library as a display;[13] here, there's a certain harmony with the Surrealists' encounter with the commodity as fetish. And lets not forget just how underfunded most projects were, the fees for these artists were nominal, a few hundred dollars. I understand the work is now with the Roslyn Oxley Gallery in Sydney, one section having been lost, then 'turning up at auction' in 2012. In my addressing this work's fate, I was told in a whispered aside that it now has a high market value, making it strangely talismanic – what kind of power is being attributed here?

This issue of an historical view through a 'window of time' can be finessed, for there is always something in excess, a remainder. Consider the international context during this period, as the publication of a special issue of *Art & Text*, 'Margins and Institutions: Art in Chile Since 1973', goes some way in addressing. Not only did Juan Davila initiate this project, he ensured its full realisation. The publication, written by the Chilean theorist and critic Nelly Richard, was commissioned by Paul Taylor and edited and translated by Paul Foss and Juan Davila. It may have been published in 1986, however the impetus for, and the work to realise it, accrued over a period of several years in both Australia and Chile – notwithstanding the artists and producers in Chile working under the effects of a dictatorship. Acts of translation extend further and are made more complex through both the attendant exhibition touring Australia, and the loaded ambivalence of its reception.[14]

In comparison to the current art scene in Australia, the 'scene' in the early 1980s was small and this retrospective allocation of the term 'impresario' to Paul goes some way in understanding his role in the continuing amplification of this scene. Rex Butler has spoken of how *Art & Text* managed to articulate postmodernism and post-structuralism with such rhetorical force, as a measure of its difference from other art theoretical journals and magazines. It was Paul's achievement to sustain this force across the territories of journalism, publishing, writing and editing, as well as his highly charged interventions into the institutional presumptions of exhibition making – he was everywhere, talking to everyone.

In my conversations with Paul, there were prompts, prompts veiled as questions at times, convincing me that something vital might be at stake. He cajoled me, 'why don't you get a student loan and join me in the US?' I did, it was 1981, and in the midst of our tours of post-war collections and the incendiary fun we were having, we saw the first broadcast of Robert Hughes's *The Shock of the New*. Paul did as he always did, 'why don't you interview him?' I did, in 1983, in Melbourne, and Paul charmed his way to join us in the interview, on the promise that he would not say anything – unimaginable. Paul's gestures seemed incidental at times and had the generative capacity of fragments, and his continuing influence, upon me, cannot be underestimated.

> The word *museum*, which I use to designate this house, is a survival of the time when I was working on plans for my invention, without knowing how it would eventually turn out. At that time I thought I would build large albums or museums, both public and private, filled with these images. Now the time has come to make my announcement: This island and its buildings, is our private paradise. I have taken some precautions – physical and Moral – for its defense: I believe they will protect it adequately. Even if we left tomorrow, we would be here eternally, repeating consecutively the moments of this week, powerless to escape from the consciousness we had in each one of them – the thoughts and feelings that the machine captured. We will be able to live a life that is always new, because in each moment of the projection we shall have no memories other than those we had in the corresponding moment of the eternal record, and because the future, left behind many times, will maintain its attributes forever.[15]

To quote these words from Bioy Casares's novel *The Invention of Morel* – with its conflation of the museum, history, and his cinematic 'invention', producing a simulacrum of a specific period of time – indicates something of my wary approach. Without sufficient archives, I am at times cast into an aporia of remembering. I can't spoil the plot of the Bioy Casares novel, other than to say that to sustain our endeavours in relation to history uncritically has consequences.

Recollections of Paul

Sue Cramer

I was fortunate to start out in the visual arts during the Paul Taylor/Art Projects era; both galvanised the scene and were defining for me. Paul's brilliance and wit gave it a formidable focus, both socially and intellectually, something to pit oneself against, though in a modest kind of way. A recent Melbourne University graduate and fledgling curator, I had set myself the task of learning about contemporary art since, in those days, a degree in 'Fine Arts' (as art history was then called) scarcely touched on the subject. I met Paul and Ashley Crawford, editor of *Virgin Press*, around 1983 at John Nixon's gallery Art Projects, which together with Paul's Beverley Hills apartment in South Yarra, was a chief meeting place for a core community of artists, but also writers, curators and other supporters. Everyone was active, often fulfilling more than one role; the idea of artists working as curators and writers was important to the unspoken DIY ethic of the group. Gatherings at Beverley Hills were more eclectic, extending to include architects, designers and other select high-flyers. I briefly met Don Dunstan at one of Paul's soirees, the urbane former Premier of South Australia who, among other important reforms, decriminalised homosexuality in that State.

Dauntingly clever and stylish, Paul could be great fun to be with—the first sports car I rode in was his. By encouraging me to write, he was throwing me a challenge, to see what I could come up with. Through his contacts, I started with lengthy reviews for Sydney's *Art Network* magazine of shows, like Denise Robinson's 'Comic Stripping' at the George Paton Gallery. An articulation of second-degree-ism, it included work by artists who re-purposed the graphic style and content of comic magazines, like Howard Arkley, Juan Davila, →↑→, Linda Marrinon, Peter Tyndall and Christopher Van Der Craats. I also wrote on Paul's 'Tall Poppies' exhibition at Melbourne University Gallery. With large and impressive works by John Dunkley-Smith, Dale Frank, Mike Parr, Imants Tillers and Nixon, 'Tall Poppies' aspired to a certain gravitas and was largely unconcerned with sub-cultural style or appropriation. This showed a side to his curatorship that was different in tenor and almost contradictory to 'POPISM'. As a Warholian and post-modernist, Paul was unfazed by contradiction.

He invited me to write for *Art & Text* on the exhibition 'Vox Pop Into The Eighties', held at the National Gallery of Victoria in 1983. Organised by NGV curator Robert Lindsay, this survey of local art from the early eighties was arguably a reply to 'POPISM', which the gallery had staged the previous year, but was a more conservative exhibition. It uneasily brought together two opposed streams, the popists and figurative expressionists. In May 1984, I became weekly art critic for *The Age*, an unexpected opportunity directed my way by the position's former incumbent Memory Holloway. Paul had been Memory's student at Monash University, so perhaps he put a good word in for me.

I saw 'POPISM' in 1982 on the cusp of my initiation into the art world. Paul's legendary audacity in gaining a spot for the exhibition in the state gallery's program allowed him to work at the centre of the local art scene, inserting an oppositional view right where it was most visible. I remember him in a conversation dismissing the seventies idea of critiquing the mainstream by being alternative or fringe. He was headed for the main stage, eventually New York. John and I stayed with him in his apartment there and among other excursions he took us to New York's spectacular and politically charged Halloween Mardi Gras Parade — an all-nighter for him, an early-ish night for us. Paul never gave his approval away easily and he always kept you on high alert with the sharpness of his commentary, wicked humour and considerable charm. He set the bar very high. I am grateful for his generosity towards me as a mentor and friend, it counted for a lot.

About Paul

Maria Kozic

How did I get into this situation? There was some sort of scuffling, grunting sound wafting through the streets. It's 4am and nobody's around, except for Paul and myself, like two bad secret agents, walking sideways with our backs against an incredibly narrow laneway between two buildings. After hearing the somewhat mysterious sounds in the distance, Paul had decided that we needed to investigate. I finally succumbed to his will and agreed to accompany him on this latest quest. Glimpses of moving shadows appear around corners as we move closer to the sounds. Paul could hardly contain his snickering and glee about the situation. I could hear my heart beating louder than the sounds we were creeping towards. There was excitement in the warm Venice air and our footsteps, even as we were careful, could be heard on the uneven cobbled pathways. We were hoping not to be noticed. At the edge of the narrow lane we saw light. And there, underneath a single streetlamp, we saw what we were looking for. Two US naval men in a heated argument, slow moving with an occasional glint from the knives they were wielding. They were itching to slice pieces off of each other. It was ominous. Shadows were cast across the courtyard and everything looked like it was in black and white. Like we had just entered a film noir movie. Dangerous and beautiful at the same time. We left before seeing the outcome.

That was Venice 1986, where no one could pull off wearing a canary yellow suit the way Paul did. He looked fabulous!

Just as always, Paul is never forgotten in conversations; so many stories, he is impossible to forget. When he left Melbourne to relocate to New York City, he was very much missed, but we all relished his new endeavors and adventures. His letters were priceless and always made me smile. Although there was a gap in town without him, it was great he was in NY and doing his thing, raising hell and creating amazing new projects. When he came back for visits, he'd always get people together for dinner and it was great to see him. He remained the supportive friend he was before he left. And very much loved.

First time I met Paul was when he came to my apartment in 1981. Just out of the blue arranged to come over. He'd been working in Tasmania and was back in Melbourne where he'd been checking out shows and what people were doing. He was so charming, funny and incredibly knowledgeable, and he talked about a magazine he was about to start up. Notably, *Art & Text*. After he left, I just thought, 'wow, who is this guy? Where has he been?' It was friends at first sight. And he instantly became such an important contributor to the art world. His writing was brilliant and his thinking innovative.

The thing with Paul was that he was someone who readily shared his knowledge with everyone. He was very generous in that way. He would be introducing people to each other in order to help people make connections. He always had opinions on everything that was going on in the art world. He always knew what was going on and wouldn't be shy of letting you know what he thought sucked. He could be very blunt. But he had a genuine hunger to see people do well in their field. He rejoiced in it. To him, the more people doing interesting stuff, the better. It was a time where there was such an abundance of creative activity. From this, he developed the show 'POPISM'. It was exciting.

And something else that particularly stood out about Paul was that, with all his brilliance and intellectualism, he had at the same time a sense of fun and a mischievousness that would ultimately cause trouble at times. The parties he'd throw and the dinners of heated conversation, skinny-dipping pool parties and overflowing hotel spas where it got out of control (making him very annoyed). So much fun was had.

His laugh is forever etched in my memories. That snigger. It always sounded like he had just performed a magic trick on you and caught you out. As a kid, he had a magic set where he'd perform tricks for family and friends. It seemed a part of that childhood carried on to his adulthood, which was what made him so much fun to be with, although at times his mischievousness could be infuriating. But that was part of the fun; we'd always end up laughing in the aftermath. Like that time I was with him in his little red sports car with the top down tearing through the streets nearly getting squashed by a tram as he hurled us in front of it, just squeezing through by an inch, with him laughing that devilish laugh the whole time. I nearly threw up and was furious, which made him laugh even more. Urrrrgh. Never a dull moment with Paul. And hardly a time he is not in my thoughts.

Whenever I watch Hitchcock's *Strangers on a Train*, the character Bruno played by Robert Walker always reminds me a bit of Paul, with that mix of mischievous charm and brilliance.

Paul Taylor: 1957–1992 (1992)

Peter Tyndall

Written in 1992 and published in Agenda, *Nos 26 & 27 (November 1992 – February 1993), 45.*

> He quickly looked back down at the paper, hoping perhaps that by the time he looked up again the improbable vision would have vanished. But when he did, there was that man still staring at him.
>
> The orator at the graveside.
>
> — Milan Kundera, *The Book of Laughter and Forgetting*

On Thursday September 8, 1982, Paul Taylor and I (and a gallerist who never came) were to address the seminar topic 'Art in the '80s' in the Art Department of the Prahran Campus of Victoria College. Shortly before the seminar began, Paul asked me if I'd prepared anything for the occasion. I said that I had. He said that he hadn't.

I spoke first, reading my prepared paper based on Rembrandt's *The Anatomy Lesson of Doctor Tulp*, projected onto a screen behind us: 'Rembrandt's painting, perhaps is a predictive scenario that has awaited this moment to be a mirror image. Is this body on the slab the waiting body of our History...'

When I had finished, Paul stood up and asked that the image remain. 'I'll speak to the same image', he said, his problem solved.

Irony upon irony, we gather again like Dr Tulp and his company.

I recently saw on TV an Argentinian remembrance ceremony in which, as the names of the dead were read out, those who had known them in life answered, 'presente'.

Those who knew Paul personally will, at this time, be similarly holding him 'presente' in a great number of colourful recollections.

I first met Paul in 1975 when he was at the start of his Arts degree at Monash University. Patrick McCaughey was head of the newly created Visual Arts Department and I was artist-in-residence.

One day, Paul made an appointment to interview me for *Lot's Wife*, the student newspaper. I remember that he arrived with a gift, a drum of Cool Mints, and that he quickly set about establishing credibility and relationship: me to him, I to others, he to the stars. He told me that this was his third interview for that week, the other two being with Glenda Jackson and Elton John.

The next-to-last time I saw Paul was in an encounter similar to the first. It was in Venice, in the busy week leading up to the official opening of the Biennale. I was there as a participant in the Aperto section and Paul was there doing something for the BBC, I think he said.

33 I chanced upon him looking at my installation. We stood nearby for a while and as we talked Paul provided a running commentary on those who paused to look at my work. 'She's head of ... department at ... museum. She's good on ... but is generally second rate. That's... He's...' and so on. I knew next to no one. It amazed me that in just four years since he'd left Australia, Paul seemed to know everyone who was a shaker or mover in the Art World.

Leo Castelli came up to say 'Hello, Paul.' 'Leo, this is Peter Tyndall. That's his work over there...' (*Thanks, Paul. Leo looks decidedly less than interested.*)

'What did you think of my article on Julian (Schnabel), Leo?'

'It was very good, Paul. Very...'

'I've spoken to Jasper (Johns, representing the USA at that Biennale) and we've decided to leave the interview until we get back...'

And so it went.

I've been told that in Melbourne, only weeks before he died, Paul was still enthusiastically seeking out information about certain young artists who had emerged since he left. His capacity for broad, critical engagement was extraordinary. In retrospect, it was inevitable that he would need to leave Australia, to relocate himself where the greatest number of practitioners were concentrated, at the heart of the Art World machine, where flux and energy were seen to be greatest.

From start to finish, from Monash to New York, Paul seemed to be compulsively attracted to all points of new cultural energy, be they individuals or 'scenes'. First, personally engage with the energy; then, through writing, exhibitions and publishing, feed that engagement into the critical consciousness of a larger audience. Then, move on, keep things moving.

In Melbourne, in the early '80s, Paul placed himself at the centre of a very energetic vortex that had been brewing and developing since the late '60s. By the late '70s and early '80s, there was a great spread of informed, critical, artistic activity. My experience of this was centred on the Clifton Hill Music Centre, the inner-city pub music scene, the George Paton Gallery and Art Projects.

A flagship was needed. Six months or so before the appearance of *Art & Text*, I attended a small meeting at Art Projects, called by John Nixon in the hope of starting a magazine that would reflect this local energy. On this occasion, none of those present were prepared to attempt it. It needed someone especially committed to make it happen.

Winning assistance in advance from the Visual Arts Board, Paul edited and published the first issue of *Art & Text* in Autumn 1981. He brought to it a critical sharpness, a cool passion, subversive playfulness and a new professionalism. Unhampered by editorial boards or fossilised ideological adherence, he concentrated his sights on 'The recent role of art criticism in Australia...' (the first words of *Art & Text*, 1. 'Editorial: On Criticism') asserting that 'our entire enterprise of art-writing is being underrated and neglected'.

Art & Text was projected as a 'forum for critical and artistic re-examination [*Art & Text* 8, the 'Australian Summer Pool-side Issue', was titled 'WHAT IS THE USE OF INTELLECTUALS?'] and experimentation' set against 'the incomprehension of a large section of our art world to newer art and the tightening of opportunities for artists and writers (that) threatens the potential of art in the coming years'.

Metathesis

Paul Foss

I first met Paul Taylor, in Sydney, around 1981 or 1982. In 1983, he ran a French translation of mine in *Art & Text*, based in Melbourne, around the same time that it appeared in the Semiotext(e) publication, *Simulacra and Simulation*. But for this quirk of fate, perhaps Paul might never have brought me to the magazine when he moved to New York the following year. On reflection, the coincidence is significant. Apart from various astrological and other portentous signs surrounding this moment, some textbooks now claim that *The Matrix* film, written and directed by the Wachowski Brothers, may have been influenced by this translation, 'The Precession of Simulacra', as well other writings by Jean Baudrillard from the early 1980s.

This is not the place to discuss my long association with *Art & Text* and its later avatar, *artUS*, which I published in Los Angeles between 2003 and 2012. All that is more or less covered in an interview, with the Melbourne-born artist Rob McKenzie, published in *The &-Files: Art & Text 1981–2002* (2009). With this publication and the almost eighty issues of *Art & Text*, as well as the 1995 anthology of Paul's New York journalism, *After Andy: SoHo in the Eighties*, which I sealed and delivered after his early demise in 1992, there's a lot for future historians and other interested parties to consider.

In the interview and other documents contained in *The &-Files*, I tried to describe the history of both magazines and my views on analogue publishing in general. I further developed these thoughts in 'A German Requiem for Print and Social Media', a special introduction to the *Collector's Edition* of the last three issues of *artUS*, published earlier this year by Intellect Books in the UK. On this occasion, I propose to do something rather different, and possibly more controversial. By returning to the 'primal scene' of my association with *Art & Text* and Paul Taylor all those years ago, I hope to draw out some of the unforeseen consequences of that encounter in the larger scheme of things. If that helps to situate Paul outside of the parameters of his already established renown, then so much the better.

Paul Taylor was a genuine character. He also happened to possess extraordinary powers of observation, especially concerning what is comically called the human condition. His natural wit and charm, along with an uncanny ability to remember whatever you'd said at a party about so-and-so and so forth, catching you unawares, helped to fill the sails of his odyssey and win valuable friends and allies, both back home in Australia and among the bohemian set then encamped in SoHo and the East Village, where he quickly earned a reputation as the new Wizard of Oz, though his spell didn't work on everybody.

Paul had the distinction to arrive in New York at a time when the art scene was going through a meltdown, when so much of the revolutionary fervour of the 1970s had evaporated like mist, and what emerged, in theory at least, was a kind of new romantic 'anything goes'. It was a time of scavenging, appropriation, the Garage and the Saint – and the Emperor's New Clothes.

As a young man, he had made a splash in Melbourne with his embrace of what used to be called postmodernism. In fact, it now seems incredible how this guy from *On the Beach* territory could ride the new wave into Metropolis and hit the ground running. He schmoozed up to Warhol, 'discovered' Jeff Koons, hung out with the likes of Barbara Kruger and Julian Schnabel, got slapped in public by art historian Barbara Rose, and generally made a nuisance of himself. Art in the 1980s was a dominant cultural force, driven by skyrocketing prices and, in the pages of fashion and art magazines, a misplaced sense of manifest destiny.

By the close of the decade, however, after the Berlin Wall and the Soviet Union came down, Wall Street and the country and soon much of the planet woke up with a hangover. Beginning with a series of lightning recessions, and culminating in an even louder crash a decade or so later, the scene and the scenario were no longer the same. The personal computer and the Internet and the telecommunication fix and Terrorism had begun to take hold, lapping at the shores of what is ironically called social networking today.

Paul was a hunter and gatherer, of people, things, contacts. Yet he was also a collector in the technical sense – specifically, a lightning rod, conductor, or Leyden jar. He accumulated current from the air or in the grid, and stored it, like static electricity, between the electrodes of his mind. This ability seemed to come naturally to him, although the suspicion that he deliberately chased thunderstorms and stood out in the open can't be dismissed. A 1986
36 photograph of Paul adorning the back cover of *After Andy*, taken by Robert Mapplethorpe, manages to catch that incandescent storage capacity perfectly.

This glowing image also provides a link to the 1988 opening of the 'Impresario: Malcolm McLaren and the British New Wave' show at the old New Museum on Broadway. It must have been the 'in' event of the season, since a long line of people had gathered outside. The ground floor was turned into a gigantic dance club-cum-bathhouse, festooned with period clothes, vintage posters, documents, jungle gyms, and musical paraphernalia, arranged to look like a re-creation of the 1970s Too Fast To Live Too Young To Die store on Kings Road, London, first called Let It Rock and later renamed SEX. His research was impressive. I recall going with Paul to a room at the Chelsea, where he proceeded to rummage through some moth-eaten clothes rack. He seemed familiar with every stitch and thread of punk and new wave fashions, from Vivienne Westwood (McLaren's former girlfriend) to the leather fetish wear of the New York Dolls.

Somehow, I managed to cadge a ride over to the museum in a black stretch limo, seated in the back with Paul, the 'original' impresario, whom he idolised, and actress/model girlfriend Lauren Hutton. All in all, this was a Paul Taylor production, so there must have been a lot of backstage drama. Yet even if the show didn't get the plug it deserved, it is undoubtedly his most accomplished exhibition, thanks in no small part to the organisational skills of director Marcia Tucker. Paul mentioned afterwards that he had fought her tooth and nail to have his memorabilia mounted in the way he saw fit, damn the expense.

In this screenplay, apart from the 'collector' or capacitor trope raised earlier, the other 'striking' thing about Paul is best conveyed by that much overused, yet semantically rich word, *character*. The Greek noun *kharakter* (from *kharax*, or 'pointed stake') originally meant an 'engraved mark', or 'instrument for marking'. By the mid fifteenth century, its meaning had branched out in a number of Romanic languages to include, as in the Old French *carecter*, 'the practice of sorcery through symbols or tracings' and something like 'psychic impressions', from which are derived the current, more theatrical and eccentric, usages of the term. Far from emphasising Paul's dynamic and sometimes outrageous personality, his display of showmanship, and great acting skills, here the word character is precisely used to denote his ability to store up and plug into his surroundings, to 'catch' them, through and by his voltage. This act of scoring is indistinguishable from Derrida's notion of erasure, or else the baseball expression, striking out.

All told, Paul spent eight years in New York. His final days also happened to coincide with the *Götterdämmerung* of the art scene, as well as the brave new world of cell phones, emerging mobile networks and markets, the dawn of internalised state security, micronised military advance warning systems, and much more besides. Rather like today's android-based microconsoles, the metacognitive and meta-levels mix and compound.

In those days, in the air and on the ground, the present-future tense seemed preoccupied with – and haunted by – footage taken from movies like *Tron*, *The Terminator* and *Videodrome*. Consider, as further examples of this transitional era, such biotechnological time machines as *1984*, both Orwell's postwar dystopia and the revamped version of it; Terry Gilliam's *Brazil*, released in 1985; Kubrick's *2001* from 1968, the same year that Philip K. Dick published *Do Androids Dream of Electric Sheep?*, the precursor of *Blade Runner* (1982); and the much underrated creature feature *Lifeforce*, also from 1985. Over the horizon lay the new reality of 'posthuman society', as witnessed by the advent of drone strikes, smart bombs, handheld gadgetry, and electronic mass media. As historians and diplomatic hackers now like to point out, entire populations were on the verge of getting an extreme makeover, of being prosthetically linked or 'wired up', held in check by intelligence gathering and the spectre of Global Warming and the New World Order vampire.

Meanwhile, in the early 1990s, the logistical and medical breakthrough that was about to reverse the course of the global pandemic, if only in fits and starts, had yet to kick in. These were busy yet amazingly scary times.

That cultural references like the above seemed to anticipate many of the military-industrial and administrative novelties of the new millennial era is not a unique phenomenon in the history of science and technology. Consider the NASA space program of the 1960s and '70s, which in the beginning took many ideas from Jules Verne's 1865 novel *From the Earth to the Moon*, including 'the correct velocity required to escape gravity, the use of rocketry for steering and braking, even the places for blastoff and splashdown'. In his 1978 translation and annotated edition of this famous work of fiction, Walter James Miller claims that NASA even considered using Verne's space gun when new, less explosive propellants became available. But one of the most enduring (and enigmatic) popular fictional time warps remains the American-Australian movie, *The Matrix* (1999).

This cyberpunk film is no doubt familiar enough to require no detailed analysis, but let me at any rate recall its general drift. Its scene is set anywhere today. A computer programmer moonlights as a hacker, known as 'Neo'. Vague references to 'the Matrix' start appearing on his computer, piquing his curiosity. Trinity, another hacker, calls him out of the blue and suggests that he contact someone called Morpheus. After meeting him and taking a red pill, Neo discovers that the so-called real world is in fact an elaborate simulation set some 200 years in the future, where intelligent Machines are keeping countless humans in a state of suspended animation, harvesting their body heat and bioelectricity via a system of tubes and cables. Back on the Matrix, everyone is kept docile and contained in a holodeck-like trance, unaware that, in the movies as in real life, the Machines have taken over.

After a lot of toing and froing, Neo eventually learns that he has been chosen as 'The One' to lead the charge against the Machines by 'unplugging' enslaved humanity. A mysterious Oracle is not so sure about this prophecy, so she casts a love spell over Trinity as a backup plan. A final battle between the rebel ship and the sentinels ensues. The mercurial Agent Smith tries to foil the renegades by dueling with Neo to the death, aided by a 'precession of simulacra'. After a magic kiss from Trinity in the real world revives the slain Neo in the virtual one, he seems to defy the odds by gaining superpowers over the Matrix. The film ends on a note of bionic and cosmic reconciliation, with Neo flying into the skies of a make-believe worldwide web after promising to work it out with the Machines. (Later episodes in the franchise seem to equivocate over this neo-Kantian ending.)

This is the point, as with those framing devices (or *Rahmenhandlungen*) employed by film noirs, when the storyline starts to unravel and dissolve in a series of flashbacks. I refer to the *Urszene* mentioned earlier, the one concerning the Baudrillard translation that initiated my involvement with *Art & Text* and Paul Taylor three decades ago. Even if the *Matrix* connection is a stretch, at least it gives me something to go on here, rather than yield to sentiment and what Freud calls, in full Darwinian mode, *Erinnerungsspuren* ('mnemic traces').

In other words, my reboot of *The Matrix* is a roundabout way of drawing attention to the enigma of nomination, of *nomos* (from *nemein*, 'appointing or naming by Law'). Uncovering the truth about 'The One', either Platonically or through the agency of self-replicating machines charged with beaming back and forth between the different zones at the back of the Cave of computer or holographic reality, is, as that Greek word (as well as Neo's appointment with destiny) would suggest, something you do at your own risk when attempting to connect, or link up. But new technology is both a control panel and a pretext for breaking into and damaging central command. The collective mind meld is a contest with normal programming, prescriptive usage, the genitive case – namely, those regulations controlling access to the world-wide registry or server.

World history abounds with various kinds of resistance-training, as first responses to the rise of other forms of sentience or interference, which all machines and media in general, even brute animals (and blocked users), have always represented for *Homo rationale*: disconnection, doubling, alienation, metamorphosis, transposition, and, more recently, detachment via a sort of cerebral implant or supplement, along with widespread cultural immersion in texting and networking. Everything gets stored in a Dantesque limbo of total recall, where signals of private and social meaning circulate aimlessly in the stratosphere (thus making them even more prone to wiretapping).

To explore another connection with *The Matrix* by way of Roman times, the act of nominating someone, of solving the riddle of access, of cracking the code for every program, application, node and hyperlink in the universe (like the 'Keymaker' character in *The Matrix Reloaded*), is the classic double bind, or blind study. It falls somewhere in the moment between logging on and signing off: between entering the database of the *nomen nudum* ('naked name') – that is to say, between finding out that the username, the 'Prime Program', is a misnomer or contradiction as it currently stands – and pulling the plug on the metathesis *Nomen [est] omen*, according to which, both technically and as a species, we are all programming errors in the long run.

Character study is a work in progress, as are the work of mourning and the challenges presented by the enigma of the name (the Greek verb *ainissethai* literally means 'to speak in riddles'). No doubt that is why impressions of Paul Taylor continue to fly around the matrix. By allowing us access to protocols and domain names now mostly blocked on the Google search engine, the asynchronicity of his online identity will better enable us to tag and use them.

Ecce Homo

Edward Colless

It's one thing to deliver a eulogy or an elegy; it's another privilege – one that requires being silent and stoic – to be pallbearer, and escort the deceased. When I was approached by Janine Burke and Adrian Martin to present a talk at the symposium celebrating Paul Taylor as the impresario of the 1980s Australian art world, timed to a significant anniversary of his untimely death, I impulsively seized on the morbid if also vain pun 'Pallbearer' as a title. This was a flippant gesture for conducting that legacy (for me manifest in the journal he founded with visionary and polemical largess, *Art & Text*) toward the destiny of its critical memorial. I quickly realised, however, that I was assuming an undeserved honour as much as I was anticipating an unappealing fate: a bit like a caryatid standing at the edge of a temple sanctuary, and bearing on its head the loaded entablature of Taylor's bequest to Australian art and art criticism. I have neither the resolve nor nobility for that. Nor would any monument to *Art & Text* demand that kind of rhetorical ostentation or sanctity. If anything, the *Art & Text* I identify as catalyst of and commentary on postmodern Australian art (despite its enduring off-shore avatars since) was actually buried alive in the late 1980s; not quite in the ambience of a Gothic premature burial, but instead more like the Chernobyl nuclear reactor encased in its concrete sarcophagus. *Art & Text*'s legacy is a half-life of hidden radiant decay, as a type of poisonous revenant importunity lodged inside a bunker. I suspect that an archaeological dig into the journal's eclectic aesthetic tastes might well exhume the 1980s equivalent of a secretly diseased portrait of Dorian Gray: a cauldron of campy nihilism and fetishistic teen nostalgia that lusciously swilled the art criticism hatching out from the laboratories of subcultural studies and poststructuralist philosophy.

From our historical perspective, we can treat this critical legacy as if it were a contaminant in a time capsule; like the stories (not all of which are urban legends) of dormant and forgotten viral contagions nested in the stuffing of antique furniture that mysteriously infect the upholsterers restoring them. But that mode of critical restoration of the treasured object is patient, demure, delicate and tasteful, even if accidentally unleashing a surprise toxin. I propose another method for the critical, historical assessment of *Art & Text*, one that spoils its history by crypto-archaeological invention. In part this conjures up the audacity and cunning of a legendary tomb raider – attractively disrespectful of heritage – and in part also elicits the misfortune of a grave robber stumbling into a plague pit. And it is with this gesture of defiling the dead (rather than defaming them) that the stolid, critically virtuous obligations that go with the role of being 'Pallbearer' to *Art & Text* can be dismissed. Digging up that oddly sepulchral pirates' treasure of the early years of *Art & Text* is like breaking the seal on a grave that has been cursed, for Australian postmodernism of the 1980s is both a grave and a curse. Disinterring the sinister portrait of that era would involve the flourishing command of prophecy – of the veil being torn away – rather than patiently forensic, academic propriety: it's too horrible, too obscene a thing, to be neatly and gradually uncovered with tweezers and a brush. I'll officiate at its excavation instead with a sweeping gesture of proclamation that is outrageous, impious and extravagantly exemplary: '*Ecce Homo*'.

For anyone unfamiliar with the episode from the Christian Passion that this Latin phrase derives from, it's recorded in the Gospel of John (chapter 19 verse 5) and is uttered when the Roman procurator or 'prefect' Pontius Pilate, presiding – seemingly ineffectually – over Jesus's trial and under some pressure from a seething mob outside the praetorium in which Jesus is at first interrogated and then whipped, brings the accused out from this secret space of confinement and torture. 'Behold the man!' he announces (in the English of the King James Version), steering a blood-drenched Jesus sporting the crown of thorns – and who, having insult added to his injury, is loosely draped in regal purple – into public view. Immensely popular as a devotional image in Christian Europe through the fifteenth and sixteenth centuries in particular (although it originates in less well-known iconography of ninth-century Syrian orthodoxy and later medieval illuminated Books of Hours), this scene cut such an iconic cast that its ecclesiastical Latin (from St Jerome's fourth-century Vulgate translation of the Christian Testament) stuck with it – even till now – as a sort of soubriquet.[1] The trial of Jesus is described in all four of the canonical gospels (Matthew, Mark, Luke and John), as well as in the Acts (attributed to the author of Luke), although surprisingly this piquant phrase is only recorded in John.[2] Incidentally, in the original Greek of John, the term *ὁ ἄνθρωπος* has been contextually interpreted to connote a tone of almost colloquial pathos, and a lapse in the formal etiquette of Roman legal conduct that insinuates a benevolent characterisation of Pilate into the narrative, as if he were to say, 'Here is the poor fellow'.[3] Simultaneously, the epithet *anthropos*, in the Hellenistic Judaic usage familiar to this gospel's author (and its Christian readership in the cosmopolitan city of Ephesus), may have been also an eschatological title, which nuances Pilate's speech with a prophetic allusion. Hence the double edge of the more ceremonial Latin version; and the almost philosophical as well as legal precision and concision of Pilate's interrogation of Jesus in *John*. Of course, I'm hardly citing '*Ecce Homo*' in a spirit of Christian piety. I have in mind instead how, having just completed *The Antichrist* in 1888, Friedrich Nietzsche used the phrase *Ecce Homo* with delicious sacrilege – followed up with doses of egoism and vulgar pomposity in the accompanying text – as the title for his autobiography. Now that's exemplary!

Strictly speaking, however, Nietzsche's turn of the phrase is a bad example. There are two reasons for this. The first is to do with rhetoric. The invocation of *Ecce Homo* really only succeeds for biography rather than autobiography, because it's a rhetorical gesture that puts someone other than oneself on show, paraded as if on a catwalk as an object in front of an audience. It's a scenario that has something of the stereotypical formula of objectification, particularly for the objectified body allegedly captured in the voyeur's gaze. And indeed, for many European Christians in the later medieval and early modern eras, the suffering body of Christ as man of sorrows was both beautiful and adorable: a passionate object for the worshipper not only to emulate but also to desire. Even though the words are so eloquently and tersely uttered by Pontius Pilate, what assumes equal consequence is the clamorous relation between the accused, Jesus, and the mob that accuses and (depending on differing theological apologetics as well as historical conjectures) judges and sentences him. In the schema of the devotional imagery – particularly in its more rhetorical formats of address – the pious viewer before the painting or the sculptural tableau is placed in the position of the mob calling for blood, and is coaxed into acknowledging his or her personal complicity with the mob's murderous intent – which, in the reflective penitent soul would not be pictured as a single particular crime but a generalised sinfulness of humanity, and hence as an inescapable guilt, constitutive of the self. The devout would hear Pilate's words delivering Jesus into a show trial as an accusation not of Jesus, but of them: 'you asked for the accused, well I give him to you'. *Ecce Homo*. And there is the second reason why Nietzsche sets a bad example: from an ethical perspective. There is no sense of self-accusation – not even self-pity – in Nietzsche's confessions. 'Why I write such brilliant books', 'Why I am so wise' … these chapter titles set the overall tone of his confessional magniloquence. All the more exquisitely irreverent and profane. It's this turn on *Ecce Homo* that we also hear, now, in the Passion of Julian Assange, when he stands on the first floor balcony of London's Ecuadorian Embassy.

So, don't get me wrong. It's bad examples such as these that provide the method for profaning, which means not just violating but also desublimating or earthing, the sanctity and sanctuary and even secrecy of an inviolate or doctrinal legacy. In this spirit, I'd like to propose a bad example from *Art & Text* in the fashion of the rhetorical profanation of *Ecce Homo*, which comes from a piece of critical writing of Paul Taylor's, unrecognisable as it may be in the chain of associations that leads me to hijack *Art & Text* in celebration of Pontius Pilate. Admittedly, this is not the most spectacular, commendable or stylish citation of Taylor's work; in fact, it's from an essay that seems so stylistically compromised and awkward within Taylor's usual confident editorialising that it seems far more symptomatic (and thus vulnerable to profanation) than expressively commanding. This article is called 'Self and Theatricality: Samuel Beckett and Vito Acconci', published in *Art & Text* 5 in 1982 but – apart from a short prefatory page – was actually written in 1979. This is a clumsy piece of writing: a conjunction of slender and enervated references to Vito Acconci's performance works and an unsurprising, even pedestrian, exposition of Samuel Beckett's radically pared down theatre and radio work from the 1960s and '70s – such as the famously disembodied mouth floating in the dark void of the play *Not I*, ranting with shreds of memories it clutches or disowns. Intended perhaps as an editorial statement, as most of the issue content deals with performance art, it's however so unmarked by Taylor's characteristic editorial polemic that (apart from the disjoined preface) it reads like a recycled undergraduate assignment or dutiful undergraduate lecture – the topic of which has been edited out, and with it the argumentative purpose of the essay. Moreover, it is written in a style routinely modelled on Rosalind Krauss, in fact resembling the explication of a critical doctrine, and spinning off a remark of hers about Acconci performing 'the drama of the shifter'.

To make matters worse, my interest in this essay is only with a fragment of it: a sentence near the start when, after introducing various ways in which the 'self as subject matter' appears in recent art (notably in feminist narratives), Taylor suggests:

> These self-representations are above all artistic self-emanations, 'ripples' circling outward from a pebble of creativity, like the social conventions, outward appearances and other exteriorities which we romantically believe surround and shroud a true self.[4]

It's a tangled sentence, and by no means unique as a critical or sociological insight, but it could be situated like the pebble it imagines occupying the position of a false creative self, at the centre of a radiating and radiant world of appearances. Art, indeed, is a pattern of discharges from a focal fallacy, an aesthetic nucleus with the inscrutable density of a fundamental particle: the self. A rather predictable exegesis of this proposal would be: dispel the romanticism of the self, as if it were some archaic superstition, and this implies we see that everything we otherwise took as emanations of a nature or essence to be instead conventions of performance. Art (in its essence, and not just its effective artistry) is such a performance, which means that it is nothing but presentation. It will present well or present badly, but not truthfully or falsely because, since it does not present 'itself', these latter words don't mean anything; and whether it presents well or not will depend on the knack of the presenter. This knack—at its apogee of superlative control, manifested through an unfurling exteriority, facility with appearance, and exploitation of social conventions—is the domain of the impresario. Successful art is an art that deals in these appearances without any superstitious romance with creativity: or rather, creativity is the cynical guise of pure enterprise with an economy of scale that is disproportionately profitable enough to be fancifully ingenious. (Today, we applaud this fantastically profitable ingenuity of artifacts—from communication devices to diets, from cars to virtual financial products—as 'smart'.) Disenchanted, art's magical success formula is a magic act, or a trick or vanity of the eye. Supposedly, one can hardly blame impresarios like Warhol or McLaren, or for that matter Jeff Koons or Damian Hirst, for the downstream development of the miserable managerialism of a globalised creative industry employing a creative class administered by self-basting cultural agencies networked through international exchange exhibitions, art fairs and global party nomads appropriating residency circuits, nor the cynical doctrine of contemporary arts 'practice' which accrues its success stories in the mode of ABC TV Arts or *Weekend Age* 'lifestyle' profiles of artists undertaking home renovation and enjoying media celebrities dropping by their studios. We can't blame the extravagant ingenuity of our Popist impresarios for the neo-liberalism of the market that fabricated contemporary art as a creative industry. They are all just players on its stage, seizing the opportunities of canny self-interest that the market provides without really believing the self is anything but the moves of appropriation within that market.

But let's go back for a moment to that gospel story. Having commanded Jesus's entrance, Pontius Pilate quickly tries to slip out of the picture: and he goes down in history or legend, or at least in one trajectory of the history of this story, as the emblematic instance of someone avoiding moral and political responsibility for their actions, or at least disposing of their liability. But what actually is the charge that Pilate doesn't want to touch? Don't get caught up in the backstory quarrel about whether the plaintiff was claiming to be the messiah; that's not what Pontius Pilate's announcement refers to. Remember, he washes his hands like Lady Macbeth quite theatrically of that whole affair: he abstains from judgment.[5] Indeed, what is rather clever about his *Ecce Homo* manoeuvre is its absolutely performative force: 'Behold the man' is the gesture of a director rather than a judge. This is a demonstrative gesture, and it's the type of expression that in linguistics would be called deictic: expressions that can include Krauss's 'drama of the shifter' such as 'I', 'you', 'here', 'now'; and the meaning of which depends on their context and timing (their eventfulness). Or, put another way, this is the type of expression the sense of which is determined utterly by presentation. Presentation here is the scope and possibility of mobile but empty or unoccupied positions from which an utterance can be delivered, and delivery means display. Presentation is thus the tactics of appearance: by which things become manifest, they make an appearance. Think back to the proclamation of *Ecce Homo* and it's hard not to picture the sweep of a hand in a magical – as well as ceremonial – flourish of conjuring; and so, if *Ecce Homo* is a phrase uttered by a director rather than a judge, then it is a creative action; that's to say its art is in its artistry and, in particular, the sort of artistry that traditionally has a devious magic to it. Unedifying and entertaining. Theatre. Nietzsche's *Ecce Homo* cannot set an edifying standard not because it is iconoclastic but because it theatrically upstages the *Gospel of John*. Can we also see Pontius Pilate as a character whose performance, far from being sidelined, upstages Jesus; perhaps even as a character whose motivation, rather than being ineffectually neutral, is beyond good and evil? Perhaps Pontius Pilate might not be the miserable fence sitter of the gospels (predetermined in this role by a God who needs a weak puppet to occasion the death of Jesus) but, in that one flickering magical gesture that damns Jesus, Pilate could be a flamboyant, unruly and undisciplined agent of creative enterprise. Should we call Pontius Pilate an impresario?

Is not this impresario figure a magically diseased portrait of Dorian Gray for the 1980s, preserving the performative artifice of charismatic, affluent and fluent lifestyle in a zombified spell by interring its putrescent essence, its putrescence? A noxious radioactive core entombed in a concrete coffin – which, like that inscrutable pebble, emanates self-representation in a decaying half-life. And, yet, doesn't the gospel story we have raided to unlock this abominable curse also describe an unnerving twist on the scenario of a cynical performativity of the art life, and of the theatre of the art life, a ghastly secret worthy of Poe or Lovecraft – indeed an exhumation of the putrescent life of art that is not just crypto-archaeological in method but crypto-ontological in consequence: that, when its sanctuary, its tomb, is opened, there is no body there? *Ecce Nihil.*

Notes

Foreword – Janine Burke

1 Janine Burke, *Field of Vision, A Decade of Change: Women's Art in the Seventies* (Melbourne: Viking, 1990), 13–14.
2 Paul Taylor, ed., *Anything Goes: Art in Australia 1970–1980* (South Yarra, Melbourne: Art & Text, 1984), 7.
3 In his editorial, Taylor wrote that Holloway's review of 'POPISM' was 'a series of deliberate mistakes ... [Holloway's] review was intended to smear not only her readers' knowledge of the show but also the character and career of its curator.' Paul Taylor, 'Pool Talk', *Art & Text*, No. 8 (1982/83), 6–7.
4 Paul Taylor, 'Lip Reading', *Meanjin*, Vol. 40, No. 4 (December 1981), 529–533.
5 Annette Blonski and Jeannette Fenelon, 'Born Again Pop: A discussion of the exhibition POPISM', *Lip, a feminist arts journal*, No. 7 (1982/83), 47–49.
6 Taylor, 'Pool Talk', 6–7. In the same editorial, Taylor accused the editorial board of *Art Network* as being 'Luddite'.
7 I had left the *Lip* collective in 1980 (together with the Women's Art Movement) due to what I perceived as a lack of direction and relevance. It marked the beginning of a longer process of disengagement where I quit art writing and research to write fiction for the next decade. Like Taylor I left Australia in 1984, relocating to Europe.
8 Hopkins had printed the first issue of *Art & Text*. *Art & a Texta – a New Australian Art Magazine* was intended as a one-off publication. Hopkins, under the pseudonym Les Hopwood, also contributed to *Art & a Texta*. Anson contributed under the pseudonym Donatello Bourke.
9 Devised by the poets James McAuley and Harold Stewart, the fictitious poems by Ern Malley took as their target *Angry Penguins*, edited by Max Harris, Sunday Reed, John Reed and Sidney Nolan. Duped, the editors published the poems in *Angry Penguins* and shortly afterwards, the hoax was revealed.
10 Stan Anson, 'On Being Difficult, The Conservatism of *Art and Text*' [sic], *Meanjin*, Vol. 42, No. 2 (June 1983), 203. I would like to thank Ted Hopkins for providing me with 'John and Betty Go to Court' (1983), a collection of documents relating to the court case, and for information about the case. Ted Hopkins, e-mail correspondence with the author, June 18, 2013.

Introduction: Paul Taylor, presente – Nicholas Croggon & Helen Hughes

1 Peter Tyndall, 'Paul Taylor: 1957–1992', *Agenda*, Nos 26 & 27 (November 1992 – February 1993), 45. Reproduced on pages 278–280 of this book.
2 Paul Taylor, 'Sculpture and the Spectator 1962–1967', Honours thesis, Faculty of Arts, Department of Visual Arts, Monash University, Melbourne, 1978.
3 See Rex Butler, *An Uncertain Smile: Australian Art in the '90s* (Sydney: Artspace, 1996); Rex Butler, *What is Appropriation? An Anthology of Writings on Australian Art in the 1980s and 1990s* (Brisbane: Institute of Modern Art, 1996); Charles Green, *Peripheral Vision: Contemporary Australian Art 1970–1994* (Sydney: Craftsman House, 1995).
4 Paul Taylor, *After Andy: SoHo in the Eighties* (Melbourne: Schwartz City, 1995).
5 Adrian Martin, Vivienne Shark LeWitt, Gregory Taylor, Thomas W. Sokolowski, Leo Castelli, Richard Prince, Carol Squires, and Allan Schwartzmann, 'Paul Taylor 1957–1992', *Art & Text*, No. 44 (January 1993), 12–17.
6 Heather Barker, 'A Critical History of Writing on Australian Contemporary Art,

1960–1988', PhD diss., School of Art History, Cinema, Classics and Archaeology, University of Melbourne, Melbourne, 2005.

7 Paul Foss, Rob McKenzie, Ross Chambers, Rex Butler, and Simon Rees, *The &-Files: Art & Text 1981–2002* (Brisbane: Institute of Modern Art, and Florida: Whale & Star, 2009).

8 Rooney wrote of his own screenprint, '"Pilkington Predicts", is, I believe, a reproduction of his 1961 advertisements for armor-plated glass. If you are going to use commercial imagery it might as well be your own!' Robert Rooney, 'Mass media images recycled in Popism', *The Age*, June 23, 1982, Arts, 14.

9 Paul Foss, 'Theatrum Nondum Cognitorium', *The Foreign Bodies Papers*, ed. Peter Botsman, Chris Burns and Peter Hutchings (Sydney: Local Consumption Publications, 1981), 15–38.

10 Imants Tillers, 'Locality Fails', *Art & Text*, No. 6 (Winter 1982), 51–60.

11 Paul Taylor, 'Popism: The Art of White Aborigines' (1983), reprinted in *What is Appropriation?*, ed. Butler, 87.

12 Rex Butler, *Radical Revisionism: An Anthology of Writings on Australian Art* (Brisbane: Institute of Modern Art, 2005).

13 Butler, introduction to *What is Appropriation?*, 13.

14 Peter Osborne, *Anywhere or Not At All: Philosophy of Contemporary Art* (London and New York: Verso, 2013), 17.

15 Hal Foster, Yve-Alain Bois, Rosalind Krauss and Benjamin Buchloh, *Art Since 1900: Modernism, Antimodernism, Postmodernism* (London: Thames & Hudson, 2004).

The return waltz – Adrian Martin

1 Michel Foucault, 'The Life of Infamous Men', in *Michel Foucault: Power, Truth, Strategy*, ed. Meaghan Morris and Paul Patton (Sydney: Feral Press, 1979), 76–91.

2 See page 176 of this book.

3 Michel Foucault, 'Dream, Imagination and Existence', introduction to *Dream and Existence*, by Ludwig Binswanger, ed. Keith Hoeller (Atlantic Highlands, New Jersey: Humanities Press, 1993), 31.

4 Foucault, 'Dream, Imagination and Existence', 31.

5 I have discussed the contents of early *Art & Text* issues from a more general perspective in my 'Before and After *Art & Text*', see pages 140–156 in this book. I also wrote an obituary tribute for Paul, relating personal anecdotes not included here: 'Paul Taylor 1957–1992', *Art & Text*, No. 44 (January 1993), 12–14.

6 'Producing the Line: Paul Foss interviewed by Rob McKenzie', in *The &-Files: Art & Text 1981–2002*, ed. Paul Foss, Rob McKenzie, Ross Chambers, Rex Butler and Simon Rees (Brisbane: Institute of Modern Art and Miami, Florida: Whale & Star Press, 2009), 31.

7 Ibid.

8 Graham Willet discusses several of these texts in his essay 'Paul Taylor's gay Melbournes' in this book, see pages 76–85. Russell Walsh also includes them in his bibliography on pages 321–328 of this book.

9 Paul Taylor, 'Editorial: On Criticism', *Art & Text*, No. 1 (1981), 5–11.

10 Stan Anson, 'On Being Difficult: The Conservatism of *Art & Text*', *Meanjin*, Vol. 42, No. 2 (June 1983), 212.

11 Antoine de Baecque, *Camera Historica: The Century in Cinema* (New York: Columbia University Press, 2012), 112.

12 de Baecque, *Camera Historica*, 110.

13 Paul Taylor, 'Lip Reading', *Meanjin*, Vol. 40, No. 4 (December 1981), 529–533.

14 Annette Blonski and Jeannette Fenelon, 'Born Again Pop: A Discussion of the Exhibition POPISM', *Lip, a feminist arts journal*, No. 7 (1982/3), 47–49; Gordon Bull, '*Art & Text* and the Second Degree', in *Sex, Politics and Representation*, ed. Peter Botsman and Ross Harley (Sydney: Local Consumption, 1984), 107–116.

15 Paul Taylor, *Art & Text*, No. 8 (1982/3), 7.

16 Juan Davila, 'POPISM Transgresses', *Art Network*, No. 8 (Summer 1983), 48.
17 Paul Taylor, untitled postcard, *Art Network*, No. 8 (Summer 1983), 48.
18 Mary Eagle, 'New journal draws the debating lines', *The Age*, May 8, 1981, 10.
19 Paul Taylor, *Art Network*, No. 10 (Winter 1983), 46–47.
20 Either Tom Thompson, John McDonald, or both, *The National Times*, c. 1985 [undated clipping in author's collection].
21 See Guy Debord, *Cette mauvaise reputation* (Paris: Gallimard, 1993).
22 Frieda Grafe, 'Theatre, Cinema, Audience: *Libelei* and *Lola Montès*', in *Ophuls*, ed. Paul Willemen (London: British Film Institute, 1978), 53–54 [translation amended and emphases mine].

Why a record review in an art magazine? – Chris McAuliffe

1 See Mark Sladen, Ariella Yedgar and Barbican Art Gallery, *Panic attack! Art in the punk years* (London: Merrell, 2007); Kunsthalle, Wien, *Punk. No one is innocent. Art-style-revolt* (Nürnberg: Verlag für moderner Kunst, 2008); Dominic Molon et al., *Sympathy for the devil: art and rock and roll since 1967* (New Haven: Yale University Press, 2007); CCAC Wattis Institute for Contemporary Arts, 'Rock my world: recent art and the memory of rock'n'roll', California College of Art and Craft, San Francisco, 2002. Significant Australian exhibitions include 'Noise & Muzak', curated by Judy Annear, George Paton Gallery, Melbourne, 1981; 'Know your product', curated by Ross Harley, Institute of Modern Art, Brisbane, 1986; and 'Melbourne><Brisbane: Punk, art and after', curated by David Pestorius, Ian Potter Museum of Art, Melbourne, 2010.
2 Bernard Gendron, *Between Montmartre and the Mudd Club: Popular Music and the Avant-Garde* (Chicago: University of Chicago Press, 2002), 7.
3 Peter Wollen, 'Ways of thinking about music video', *Critical Quarterly*, Vol. 28, No. 1–2 (1986), 167.
4 Ibid., 169.
5 Ibid., 170.
6 Ibid., 168–169.
7 Jody Berland, Terry Blake, Philip Brophy, Rolando Caputo, Ted Colless, Mary Eagle, Adrian Martin, John Nixon, Andrew Preston, William Routt, Vivienne Shark LeWitt and John Young all wrote on, and around, popular music in the early issues.
8 Adrian Martin, 'Review: David Chesworth, *Layer on layer*', *Art & Text*, No. 3 (Spring 1981), 87. This issue of *Art & Text* featured eight articles referring to popular music and/or written by musicians, including a special section dedicated to music-related practices.
9 Paul Taylor, 'Editorial: On Criticism', *Art & Text*, No. 1 (Autumn 1981), 8. Taylor cited Xavier Rubert de Ventos, *Heresies of modern art* (New York: Columbia University Press, 1980).
10 Michel Foucault, 'Fantasia of the library', cited in Taylor, 'Editorial: On Criticism', 9.
11 Lillian Roxon, 'Creedence Clearwater Revival – the band that means business', *Sydney Morning Herald*, January 23, 1971, reprinted in Robert Milliken, *Lillian Roxon: mother of rock* (New York: Thunder's Mouth Press, 2005), 351.
12 Mick Farren, 'The Titanic sails at dawn', *New Musical Express*, June 19, 1976, 5. Reprinted in *Uncut*, Vol. 1, No. 2 (2002), 8.
13 Mike Drayson and Anthony O'Grady, 'David Bowie interview', *RAM*, No. 11 (July 26, 1975), 19.
14 For all the post-facto hair-splitting, New Wave was essentially a label coined to distinguish forms of punk-inspired minimalism from the perceived violence of the original punk bands. In January 1978, the American trade newspaper *Billboard* published a special supplement on New Wave, reassuring readers that all major labels now featured New Wave acts and responding to the likes of Farren with the declaration that New Wave offered 'a fresh, honest approach and a sense of cultural involvement between artists and audience'; Greg Shaw, 'New trends of the new

wave', *Billboard*, January 14, 1978, 62. (Shaw was the director of the LA-based independent label, Bomp.)

15 Renato Poggioli, *Theory of the avant-garde*, trans. Gerald Fitzgerald (Cambridge, Massachusetts: Belknap Press of Harvard University Press, 1968), 32.

16 Simon Frith and Howard Horne, *Art Into Pop* (London: Methuen, 1987).

17 Flaming George, 'Nothing better to do on a Sunday night', *Honi Soit* [Sydney], No. 13 (June 30, 1980), 10–11.

18 Dave Laing, *One chord wonders: power and meaning in punk rock* (Milton Keynes: Open University Press, 1985), 128.

19 Tim Johnson in Peter Cripps, *Interviews* (Brisbane: Institute of Modern Art, 1986), 21.

20 Chris McAuliffe, *Jon Cattapan: possible histories* (Carlton: University of Melbourne Press, 2008), 31.

21 Craig Wilcox, 'Slugfuckers, SCA concert review', *Z/X* [Sydney], No. 4 (June 1979), 8.

22 A parenthetic comment on the 'dull and limited selection of music' at the Last Laugh disco in an early student newspaper article is the exception that proves the rule; Paul Taylor, 'Waiter, there's a circus in my soup', *Lot's Wife* [Melbourne], June 27, 1977, 14.

23 Taylor, 'Editorial: On Criticism', 6.

24 These prescient remarks made in a Sydney trade journal; John Clare, 'Music in the subconscious', *Music Maker* [Sydney], Vol. 38, No. 20 (January 1971), 17.

25 See, for example, Colin MacInnes, 'Sharp schmutter', *The Twentieth Century*, August 1959. Reprinted in his *England half-English* (New York: Random House, 1961), 146–157. 'Schmutter' is a polari (London gay slang) term for clothing. The parallels between MacInnes and Taylor are intriguing: entrepreneurial, expatriate, gay, writing on art and youth subcultures, at home in both art criticism and journalism, determined to register the cultural impact of popular music.

26 Drayson and O'Grady, 'David Bowie interview', 19.

27 Gendron, *Between Montmartre and the Mudd Club*, 272.

28 Anon., 'Letters', *RAM*, No. 24 (January 30, 1976), 30.

29 Anon., 'Laurie Richards', *TAGG* [The Alternative Gig Guide], November 29 – December 12, 1979, 4. Richards ran the Crystal Ballroom at St Kilda's Seaview Hotel.

30 H. Wayman, 'St Kilda rocks', *TAGG*, March 19 – April 2, 1981, 63.

31 Mark Ferrie quoted in Neil Bradbury, 'Models', *Vox Muzepaper*, No. 9 (December 1981), 16. Ferrie played bass guitar with the Models and is now more familiar as a member of the house band for television's *RocKwiz*.

32 Paul Taylor, 'Australian "New Wave' and the "Second Degree"', *Art & Text*, No. 1 (Autumn 1981), 23.

33 Paul Taylor, introduction to *Noise & Muzak* [exh. cat.], curated by Judy Annear (Melbourne: George Paton Gallery, Melbourne, 1981), 4.

34 Ibid.

35 Ibid.

36 Dick Hebdige, *Subculture: the meaning of style* (London: Methuen, 1979), 94–95.

37 Ibid., 101.

38 Ibid., 117–118. Hebdige's primary interest lay in the ways in which popular music revealed a succession of responses to black culture in the United Kingdom.

39 Hebdige, *Subculture: the meaning of style*, 129.

40 Taylor, 'Australian "New Wave' and the "Second Degree"', 24.

41 Ibid., 27.

42 Paul Taylor, 'Jenny Watson's "Mod"ernism', *Art International*, Vol. 24, Nos 1–2 (September–October 1980), 214.

43 Ibid., 218.

44 Ibid.

45 Philip Brophy, 'Subculture: the meaning of style', *Art & Text*, No. 1 (Autumn 1981), 69.

46 This and subsequent quotations are from Philip Brophy, 'Visions of reality', *Stuff*, No. 4 (December 1984), n.p.

47 In this iteration The Connotations were: Chris Astley, Kim Beissel, Gerard Hayes and Adrian Martin. Off stage: Philip Stromei. On tape: Linda Baron and Michelle

Wild. On film: Maria Kozic (who also contributed a drawing to the flier).

48 This and subsequent quotations on 'Rock journalism' are from an A4 photocopied flier for April 29, 1981 performance. Collection of the author.

49 A later performance, 'Let's go native!', re-presented a set of 'jungle', 'voodoo' and 'primitive' songs, mainly from Hollywood movies but including Suzi Quatro's 'Primitive love' in order to 'understand what "going native" means to us today, how it is similar to and different from its previous cultural manifestations'. Undated A3 photocopy fliers. Collection of the author.

50 Anon., 'New genital discovered', *Honi Soit*, February 23, 1981, 10.

51 See Terry Blake, 'The dis-corpse of Althusser: a paranoic fantasy', *Cogito*, No. 3 (1979), n.p. Blake (singer for the Slugfuckers) opened a lengthy assault on Althusserian critics of Feyerabend with lyrics from the Sex Pistols' 'Anarchy in the UK' and concluded with lyrics from X Ray Spex's 'Oh bondage, up yours'. *Cogito*, the journal of the University of New South Wales Socratic society, was edited by another Slugfucker, Graham Forsyth. The cover featured a scabrous portrait of Descartes by John Young. In the same issue, Slugfuckers personnel also offered a translation of Guattari's 'Towards a micro-politics of desire', a review of *Anti-Oedipus*, and a punk-inspired appreciation of Philip K. Dick. Slugfuckers' publications were kindly provided to me by Graham Forsyth and John Laidler.

52 Paul Taylor, 'Poofta bashing bashed', *Lot's wife*, July 25, 1977, 2.

53 Taylor, 'Jenny Watson's "Mod"ernism', 214, 216, 218.

54 Meaghan Morris, 'Politics now (anxieties of a petty-bourgeois intellectual)', in her *The pirate's fianceé* (London: Verso, 1988), 177.

55 Ibid., 176.

56 Anon., 'Honi Soit presents some perspectives on New Wave punk', *Honi Soit*, October 1977, 8–9; Mick Makhno, 'Ace Punk Prophet Into Mincer', *Honi Soit*, March 14, 1978, 6–7; David Connolly, 'Punk: dole queue music', *Lot's Wife*, June 19, 1978, 18–19.

57 The comments appear in an artist's book, presented as an LP, and including notes, clippings and correspondence relating to an unrealised proposal for exhibitions and performances: Vivienne Shark LeWitt, *Never mind the exhibition, here's the problems*, [1978], National Gallery of Art, Canberra, NGA Acc. no. 1980.3818.2 and 1980.3818.1.

58 Shark LeWitt, *Never mind the exhibition, here's the problems.*

59 Vivienne Shark LeWitt, 'Why Egyptian mods didn't bother to bleach their hair, or, More notes about parkas and combs', *Art & Text*, No. 3 (Spring 1981), 81.

60 George Melly, *Revolt into style* (Garden City, NY: Anchor Books, 1971), 10. First published in the UK, 1970.

61 Lawrence Grossberg, 'Reflections of a disappointed popular music scholar', in *Rock over the edge: transformations in popular music culture*, ed. Roger Beebe, Denise Fullbrook and Ben Saunders (Durham: Duke University Press, 2002), 27.

Strategic Aboriginalism: Paul Taylor, postmodernism, neo-Expressionism and Aboriginal art — Ian McLean

1 Charles Baudelaire, *The Painter of Modern Life and Other Essays*, trans. Jonathan Mayne (London: Phaidon, 1995), 9.

2 Bell's Theorem (not to be confused with Richard Bell's 'Bell's Theorem'), which refers to the entanglement of quantum particles, was used as a metaphor by Tillers in his argument against regionalism: Imants Tillers, 'Locality Fails', *Art & Text*, No. 6 (Winter 1982), 51–60.

3 Gilles Deleuze and Félix Guattari, 'Nomad Art', *Art & Text*, No. 19 (October–December 1985), 16–23; Stephen Muecke, 'The Good Oil Company and the Bad Oil Company', *Art & Text*, No. 9 (Autumn 1983), 3–13; Stephern Muecke, 'The Discourse of Nomadology: Phylums in Fulx', *Art & Text*, No. 14 (Winter 1984), 24–40.

4 The catalogue listed them as: Clifford Possum Tjapaltjarri, in part assisted by his brother Tim Leura Tjapaltjarri, *Warlugulong*, 1976; Tim Leura Tjapaltjarri assisted

by his brother Clifford Possum Tjapaltjarri, *Anmatjera Aranda Territorial Possum Spirit Dreaming,* 1980; and Charlie Tjapangati, *Tingari Dreaming,* 1981. See Bernice Murphy, *Australian Perspecta 1981* [exh. cat.] (Sydney: Art Gallery of New South Wales, 1981), 136.

5 Paul Taylor, 'Popism: the Art of White Aborigines', *Flash Art*, No. 112 (May 1983), 48–50.

6 See Terry Smith, 'A New Spirit in Painting? The Royal Academy Meets Modern Art', *Art Network*, Nos 3/4 (1981), 14–15 at 14.

7 Indeed, in 1981 Terry Smith criticised new-expressionism in a similar tone to his later criticism of Taylor (cited above), as being empty rhetoric and 'arch, self-conscious flippancy'. Ibid., 15.

8 Roland Barthes, *Mythologies*, trans. Annette Lavers (New York: Hill and Wang, 1982), 129.

9 Paul Taylor, 'Australian "New Wave" and the "Second Degree"', in *Anything Goes: Art in Australia, 1970–1980*, ed. Paul Taylor (South Yarra: Art & Text, 1984), 158–167 at 159.

10 George Alexander, 'Conference Postscript', in *The Foreign Bodies Papers*, ed. Peter Botsman, Chris Burns and Peter Hutchings (Sydney: Local Consumption Publications, 1981), 159–160 at 159.

11 Paul Taylor, 'Australian "New Wave" and the "Second Degree"', *Art & Text*, No. 1 (Autumn 1981), 23–32.

12 Suzi Gablik, 'Modernism and Morality', *Art & Text*, No. 1 (Autumn 1981), 4348 at 43.

13 Barthes, *Mythologies*, 133. Nevertheless, Barthes believed that poetry was as much if not more prey to myth than any other cultural expression.

14 Tillers, 'Locality Fails', 54.

15 Suzi Gablik, 'Report from Australia', *Art in America*, January 1981, 29–37 at 32.

16 Ibid., 35.

17 Ibid., 31.

18 Ibid., 29.

19 Murphy, *Australian Perspecta 1981*, 11.

20 Ibid., 13.

21 Robert Lindsay, 'Relics & Rituals', in *Anything Goes : Art in Australia, 1970–1980*, ed. Paul Taylor (South Yarra: Art & Text, 1984), 108–115 at 110.

22 Murphy, *Australian Perspecta 1981*, 14.

23 Typical is Richard Shone, '"London" a New Spirit in Painting at the Royal Academy', *The Burlington Magazine*, 123/936 (March 1981), 182–183, 185.

24 Christos M. Joachimides, 'A New Spirit in Painting', in *A New Spirit in Painting*, ed. Christos M. Joachimides, Norman Rosenthal and Nicholas Serota (London: Royal Academy of Arts, 1981), 14–16.

25 Peter Schjeldahl, 'The New Painting: Return to the Sublime', *New York Times*, April 18, 1971, Arts and Leisure, D23.

26 Daniel Thomas, 'Art & Life: The Actuality of Sculpture', in *Anything Goes : Art in Australia, 1970–1980*, 98–107 at 98.

27 Susan Heller Anderson, '"Spirit" show highlights contemporary paintings', *New York Times*, February 5, 1981, http://www.nytimes.com/1981/02/05/arts/spirit-show-highlights-contemporary-painting.html. Accessed October 9, 2013.

28 Imants Tillers, 'Fear of Texture', *Art & Text*, No. 10 (Winter 1983), 8–18 at 12.

29 Murphy, *Australian Perspecta 1981*, 13.

30 Tillers, 'Fear of Texture', 11. In the mid-twentieth century the Angry Penguins had turned Australian modernism away from existing European models and towards the vernacular of the outback and Aboriginal Australia.

31 Janina Green, 'Roar or Whimper?', *Art & Text*, No. 14 (Winter 1984), 86–91.

32 Imants Tillers, 'Locality Fails', 53.

33 Alternatively he may have seen it performed on its Australian tour.

34 Giorgio Colombo, 'The Mirror without a Memory', *Art & Text*, No. 1 (Autumn 1981), 16–22 at 22.

35 Karoline Kirst, 'Walter Benjamin's *Denkbild*: Emblematic Historiography of the Recent Past', *Monatshefte*, 86/4 (1994), 514–524 at 515.

36 Interestingly, the image is adjacent to Taylor's seminal article, 'Australian "New

Wave" and the "Second Degree"', and was preceded on the previous page by an emblematic image of a photograph of the heads of a peasant and murderer, which are morphologically nearly similar as if each is a mirror image of the other.

37 Juan Davila, 'Spider Woman in Australia', *Art & Text*, No. 4 (Summer 1981), 15–19.

38 Jennifer Phipps, 'Marina Abramović/Ulay: Ulay/Marina Abramović', *Art & Text*, No. 3 (Autumn 1981), 43–50 at 50.

39 Ibid., 46.

40 Ibid., 47.

41 For example, Julie Ewington, 'Fragmentation and Feminism: The Critical Discourse of Postmodernism', *Art & Text*, No. 7 (Spring 1982), 61–73.

42 Baudelaire, *The Painter of Modern Life and Other Essays*, 28.

43 See for example the very next page after the Abramović and Ulay interview: 'recent art ... seems to interpret culture as a set of "givens" and creatively intervene by means of *bricolage*: the strategies of juxtaposition, framing, fragmentation, recontextualization, collage, quotation and staging.' Paul Taylor, 'Speical Section: Introduction', *Art & Text*, No. 3 (Spring 1981), 51–56 at 51.

44 Philip Brophy, 'What Is This Thing Called "Disco"?', *Art & Text*, No. 3 (Spring 1981), 59–66 at 64.

45 John Nixon, 'Pneumatic Drill', *Art & Text*, No. 3 (Spring 1981), 58.

46 Ted Colless and David Kelly, 'The Lost World', *Art & Text*, No. 3 (Spring 1981), 67–75.

47 Paul Taylor, 'From Deserts the Profits Come', *Art Press*, No. 74 (October 1983), 32–33 at 32.

48 Adrian Martin, 'Paul Taylor 1957–1992', *Art & Text*, No. 44 (January 1993), 12–14 at 12.

49 Paul Taylor, Untitled, in *Eureka! Artists from Australia* [exh. cat..], ed. Sue Grayson and Sandy Nairne (London: Institute of Contemporary Art and the Arts Council of Great Britain, 1982), 61–67 at 61, 62.

50 Paul Taylor, *POPISM* [exh. cat.], curated by Paul Taylor (Melbourne: National Gallery of Victoria, 1982), 3.

51 Taylor, 'Popism: the Art of White Aborigines', 48.

52 Paul Taylor, 'Angst in My Pants', *Art & Text*, No. 7 (Spring 1982), 48–60 at 50.

53 Ibid., 60.

54 For example, see: Christiana Davidson, 'Interview: Paul Taylor', *Art Network*, No. 10 (Winter 1983), 46–47 at 47. The source of this argument can be found in his 1982 interview with Rosalind Krauss, who pointed out that if Foucault is right, then new-expressionism must be a form of postmodernism. (Rosalind Krauss and Paul Taylor, 'Rosalind Krauss Paul Taylor', *Art & Text*, No. 8 (Summer 1982/83), 31–37 at 31–32.

55 Taylor, 'From Deserts the Profits Come', 32. Translation by Paris Lettau.

56 Imants Tillers, phone call with the author, September 17, 2013.

57 Imants Tillers, 'One Painting Cleaving (Triangle of Doubt)', in *Eureka! Artists from Australia*, 36.

58 Tillers, 'Locality Fails', 57.

59 Imants Tillers, phone call with the author, September 17, 2013.

60 Martin, 'Paul Taylor 1957–1992', 12–14.

61 Sue Cramer, '"Masterpeice" out of the Seventies and "Tall Poppies"', *Art Network*, No. 10 (Winter 1983), 42–45 at 44–45.

62 Paul Taylor, *Imants Tillers: White Aborigines* (London: Matt's Gallery, 1983).

63 Cramer, '"Masterpeice" out of the Seventies and "Tall Poppies"', 44.

64 Douglas Crimp, 'Pictures', in *Pictures* [exh. cat.] (New York: Committee for the Visual Arts. Inc, 1977), 3–29.

65 Paul Taylor, 'Tall Poppies', *Art & Text*, Nos 12/13 (Summer/Autumn 1983/84), 49–53 at 52.

66 Ibid., 51.

67 Davidson, 'Interview: Paul Taylor', 47.

68 Ibid.

69 Taylor, 'Tall Poppies', 51.

70 Cramer, '"Masterpeice" out of the Seventies and "Tall Poppies"', 45.

71 The article was first published in the first issue of *On the Beach*, which came out in

Autumn 1983, and shortly afterwards in *Flash Art*.

72 Taylor, 'Popism: the Art of White Aborigines', 48–50.

73 Ibid., 50.

74 Tillers, 'Fear of Texture', 8.

75 Ibid., 15.

76 Ibid., 16–17.

77 Ibid., 15.

78 Ibid., 8.

79 Ibid., 15.

80 Ibid., 18.

81 Tillers, 'Locality Fails', 60.

82 Tillers, 'Fear of Texture', 18.

83 Bernice Murphy, 'General Introduction', in *XVI Bienal De São Paulo: Australia*, ed. Bernice Murphy (Sydney: Aboriginal Arts Board of the Australia Council, 1983), 3–4 at 4.

84 See Terry Smith's obituary in *Art Network*, No. 5 (Summer/Autumn 1982), 70.

85 Kenneth Coutts-Smith, 'Australian Aboriginal Art', *Art Network*, No. 7 (Spring 1982), 52–55 at 54.

86 Robert Lindsay, *Vox Pop: Into the Eighties* [exh. cat.] (Melbourne: National Gallery of Victoria, 1983), 10.

87 Patrick McCaughey, 'Preface', in *Vox Pop: Into the Eighties* [exh. cat.] (Melbourne: National Gallery of Victoria, 1983), 5.

88 Ibid., 28, 32.

89 Ibid., 32.

90 Suzanne Pagé, *D'un Autre Continent: L'australie Le Rêve Et Le Réel* [exh. cat.] (Paris: ARC/Musée d'Art Moderne de la Ville de Paris, 1983).

91 Jill Montgomery, 'Australia: The French Discovery of 1983', *Art & Text*, Nos 12/13 (Summer 1983 – August 1984), 2–15.

92 Philip Brophy, 'Not the Black and White Artist Show', *Art Network*, No. 13 (Spring 1985), 53.

93 Imants Tillers, phone call with the author, September 17, 2013.

94 Imants Tillers, 'In Perpetual Mourning ', in *Imants Tillers: Venice Biennale 1986 Australia* [exh. cat.], ed. Kerry Crowley (Sydney and Adelaide: The Visual Arts Board of the Australia Council and Art Gallery Board of South Australia, 1986), 16–19 at 18.

95 Raphael Rubinstein, 'Neo-Expressionism Not Remembered', *Art in America*, February 2013. Accessed October 1, 2013, http://www.artinamericamagazine.com/news-features/magazine/neo-expressionism-not-remembered/.

96 Taylor, 'Popism: the Art of White Aborigines', 48.

97 Tillers, 'In Perpetual Mourning ', 18.

98 See Imants Tillers, 'A Conversation with Ian North', *Artlink*, Vol. 21, No. 4 (2001), 36–41.

99 Rex Butler, introduction to *What Is Appropriation?*, ed. Rex Butler (Brisbane and Sydney: Institute of Modern Art and Power Publications, 1996), 13–46 at 30–37.

100 Tillers, 'In Perpetual Mourning', 18.

101 Ibid., 19.

102 It first appeared in a joint issue of *Art & Text* and the New York journal *ZG*, and was reproduced in the catalogue of Tillers's work when he represented Australia at the 1986 Venice Biennale. Tillers then had a growing international presence.

103 Adrian Martin, 'Before and after *Art & Text*', *Agenda*, Vol. 1, No. 2 (August 1988), Special Supplement: 'Art: The Present and Recent Past of Australian Art and Criticism', 15–19 at 18.

104 Heather Baker and Charles Green offer a different assessment – see Heather Barker and Charles Green, 'No More Provincialism: Art & Text', *emaj*, No. 5 (2010). Accessed June 26, 2013. http://www.melbourneartjournal.unimelb.edu.au/E-MAJ/pdf/issue5/GREEN%20AND%20BARKER_emaj%202010.pdf at 19–20. However their claims are not evident in Taylor's many articles written in New York. These show that Taylor quickly became a successful paparazzi-type critic of the New York

scene — see Paul Taylor, *After Andy: Soho in the Eighties* (Melbourne: Schwartz City, 1995). Imants Tillers, who frequently showed in New York in the second half of the 1980s and stayed with Taylor several times, remembered that 'Paul was good to have in New York because he was always eager to pass on the latest art moves in the east village, but once there he lost interest in my work' (conversation with the author, August 2013).

105 For a description of *Art & Text* after Taylor moved to New York, see Martin, 'Before and after *Art & Text*', 18–19.

106 Juan Davila, 'Aboriginality: A Lugubrious Game?', *Art & Text*, Nos 23/24 (March–May 1987), 53–56.

107 Paul Taylor, 'Primitive Dreams Are Hitting the Big Time', *New York Times*, May 21, 1989, H 31, 35. All subsequent quotes by Taylor are from this article.

108 Hal Foster, 'The "Primitive" Unconscious of Modern Art', *October*, No. 34 (Autumn 1985), 45–70 at 55.

109 Barker and Green, 'No More Provincialism: Art & Text', 20.

110 Jane Rankin-Reid quoted in ibid., 19.

111 Imants Tillers, phone call with the author, September 17, 2013.

112 Rex Butler's review of Emily Kame Kngwarreye that appeared in *Art & Text* in 1998 suggestively raises these issues but does not develop them. See Rex Butler, 'Emily Kngwarreye: Queensland Art Gallery, Brisbane February 20 – April 13, 1998', *Art & Text*, No. 62 (May–July 1998), 94–95.

Art & sex: Paul Taylor — Ashley Crawford

1 The original group all contributed story ideas. They were Robin Barden, G.J. Burchall, Andrew George, Suzzi Salamanca and myself.

2 Ashley Crawford, 'The Art of New Wave', *The Virgin Press*, No. 6 (August 1981), 12–13.

3 Martin Armiger, 'Pushing the art of pop', *The National Times*, July 11–17, 1982, 24–25.

4 Paul Taylor, written correspondence with the New Art A Magazine collective, January 20, 1983.

5 'John and Betty', written correspondence with Paul Taylor, January 26, 1983.

6 Biltmoderne were Dale Evans, Roger Wood and Randall Marsh.

7 Pearce's co-founders of the Fashion Design Council were Robert Buckingham and Kate Durham.

8 Paul Taylor, Denise Robinson, Ashley Crawford and John Nixon, written correspondence with Paul Clarkson, Director of the Victorian Ministry for the Arts, c. 1984.

9 Paul Taylor, 'Angst in My Pants', *Art & Text*, No. 7 (September 1982), 48–60.

10 Arminger, 'Pushing the art of pop', 24–25.

11 Paul Taylor, written correspondence with the author, c. 1987.

12 A reference to the publication *Visual Tension*, which accompanied the exhibition of the same name curated by John Buckley and myself at the Australian Centre for Contemporary Art, Melbourne and, with Peter Cripps, at the Institute of Modern Art, Brisbane in 1985.

13 Jenny Watson was notorious for lashing out when feeling under-appreciated. The argument referred to occurred between this author and Watson on a crowded Melbourne tram.

14 Paul Taylor, written correspondence with the author, March 4, 1985.

15 *On The Beach* was launched in Sydney in 1983 by editors Mark Titmarsh, Lindy Lee, Ross Gibon, Sam Mele and Mark Thirkell.

16 Paul Foss and Juan Davila went on the attack in the pages of *On The Beach* over the exhibition 'Visual Tension' curated in 1985 by John Buckley and this author.

17 Paul Taylor, written correspondence with the author, June 3, 1985.

18 Paul Taylor, 'Robert Mapplethorpe's Climax', *Tension*, No. 13 (June 1988), 28–33.

19 Paul Taylor, written correspondence with the author, November 12, 1990.

20 Paul Taylor, written correspondence with the author, June 23, 1990.

Three entrepreneurs du chic — Merryn Gates

1 Presented by entrepreneurs Julie Purvis and Jillian Burt, AKA Party Architecture. These parades were more than just catwalk fashion. Many of the designers were artists and saw the parade as an extension of their art practice. The nights included comedy and live bands around the building. Original music was composed for each designer by Dean Richards.

2 Rob McKenzie, 'Explicit Content, The Early Issues', introduction to *The &-Files: Art & Text 1981–2002*, ed. Paul Foss et al. (Brisbane: Institute of Modern Art, and Miami, Florida: Whale & Star Press, 2009), 17.

3 Lee Tulloch, 'Remember POP?', *Vogue Australia*, July 1982, 40.

4 Sylvère Lotringer, 'My '80s: Better Than Life', *Artforum,* Vol. 41, No. 8 (April 2003). Accessed September 9, 2013, http://artforum.com/inprint/issue=200304&id=4509.

5 Paul Taylor, 'Australian "New Wave" and the "Second Degree"', *Art & Text*, No. 1 (Autumn, 1981), 23–32.

6 Philip Brophy, 'Book review: Subculture: the meaning of style by Dick Hebdige', *Art & Text,* No. 1 (Autumn 1981), 73.

7 Party Architecture, *Fashion 82* and *Fashion 83*, Seaview Ballroom, St Kilda.

8 'Noise & Muzak', curated by Judy Annear, Ewing and George Paton Gallery, University of Melbourne, Melbourne, 1981.

9 Andrew Bolton, 'Punk: chaos to couture', Metropolitan Museum of Art, New York, 2013, and Geoffrey Marsh and Victoria Broackes, 'David Bowie is', Victoria & Albert Museum, London, 2013.

10 Claire Wilcox, 'Radical fashion', Victoria & Albert Museum, London, 1996 included commissions for original music for each of the featured designers.

11 Marcia Tucker, preface to *Impresario: Malcolm McLaren and the British New Wave* [exh. cat.], curated and edited by Paul Taylor (New York: New Museum and Cambridge, Massachusetts: MIT Press, 1988), 7.

12 Paul Taylor, *POPISM* [exh. cat.], curated by Paul Taylor (Melbourne: National Gallery of Victoria, 1982).

13 Maria Kozic, interview with the author, New York, June 2013.

14 Maria Kozic, 'I Was a Teenage Pyjama', Oz Print Gallery, Brunswick Street, Fitzroy, 1979. The works have stood the test of time, as many have ended up in public collections.

15 Maria Kozic, interview with the author, New York, June 2013.

16 'It started with t-shirts, because I loved silk screening. I was huge at silk screening. I did t-shirts and started trying to sell them in stores by myself. You know, I didn't try to do it in a big way. I did that series of "horror heads". I did those as paintings too, but then made them into t-shirts. And I did that series for the MCA show — like they were four different shows. I was trying to merchandise. My little mini merchandising.' Maria Kozic, interview with the author, New York, June 2013.

17 Maria Kozic, interview with the author, New York, June 2013.

18 'Rip it up and start again', Orange Juice lyric, 1983.

Paul Taylor's gay Melbournes — Graham Willett

1 Raymond Williams, *Marxism and Literature* (Oxford: Oxford University Press, 1977), 121–127.

2 Wayne Murdoch is conducting important research on this period. For indications of his findings to date, see his '"Phone Me Up Sometime": Melbourne's Homosexual Subcultures in the Interwar Years', in *Queen City of the South: Gay and Lesbian Melbourne, La Trobe Journal*, ed. Graham Willett and John Arnold, No. 87 (May 2011), 19–31 and his many chapters in *Secret Histories of Queer Melbourne*, ed. Graham Willett, Wayne Murdoch and Daniel Marshall, Australian Lesbian and Gay Archives (ALGA), Melbourne, 2011.

3 Murdoch, '"Phone Me Up Sometime"', 25–26.

4 Graham Willett, 'Val Eastwood', in *Secret Histories of Queer Melbourne*, 79–80.
5 For the Hotel Australia see Richard Petersen, 'The Australia, the Woolshed and the Sexual Gaze', in *Queen City of the South*, ed. Graham Willett and John Arnold, 32–41.
6 Peter C. Langford, 'A Fleeting Impression', *Campaign*, October 1975, 11. This and the following discussion draws heavily upon my 'The New Camp Scene of the 1970s', in *Secret Histories of Queer Melbourne*, 102–105.
7 'Guide to Gayer Melbourne', *Campaign*, May 1978, 21–39.
8 Langford, 'A Fleeting Impression', 11.
9 Jamie Gardiner, 'Mixed Sauna has a Long History', *Melbourne Star Observer*, December 18, 1987 - January 1, 1988, 5.
10 Graham Willett, 'Society Five' in *Secret Histories of Queer Melbourne*, 109–111, and, for the broader national context, see: Graham Willett, *Living Out Loud: A History of Gay and Lesbian Activism in Australia* (St Leonards: Allen and Unwin, 2000), 33–52.
11 Graham Willett, 'Into the Streets: Gay Lib in Melbourne', in *Secret Histories of Queer Melbourne*, 116–119; Willett, *Living Out Loud*, 53–71.
12 Ibid., 108–131.
13 The Homosexual in Society, leaflet, 1974, ALGA Ephemera Collection.
14 Homosexuality on Campus, n.d. [1977], ALGA Ephemera Collection.
15 Andrew, 'Thinking a Bit About Things...', *Lot's Wife*, September 8, 1975, 6–7.
16 *Lot's Wife,* May 31, 1976, 8.
17 'Hi Mum I'm a Poofta', *Lot's Wife,* July 25, 1977, 13.
18 Paul Taylor, 'The Elocution of Benjamin Franklin', interview and review, *Lot's Wife,* July 18, 1977, 22.
19 Gordon Balfour, 'Taylor's Aim', letter, *Lot's Wife,* July 25, 1977, 2.
20 Stephen McLardie, 'Poofta Bashing Bashed', letter, *Lot's Wife,* July 25, 1977, 2.
21 Paul Taylor, untitled, *Lot's Wife,* July 25, 1977, 2.
22 Bebe Loft and Virginia Johnson, 'Perversions', letter, *Lot's Wife*, July 25, 1977, 26.
23 Willett, *Living Out Loud,* 122.
24 Ibid.
25 [Women's Liberation Group], letter, *Lot's Wife*, April 28, 1975, 20.
26 Ross Moor, letter, *Lot's Wife*, April 28, 1975, 20.
27 'Tom and his Pigs', *Lot's Wife*, June 2, 1975, 13; John R. Gaden, letter, *Lot's Wife*, June 2, 1975, 17.
28 Willett, *Living Out Loud*, 124.
29 Phil, 'Report from the National Homosexual Conference', *Lot's Wife*, September 1, 1975.
30 Willett, *Living Out Loud*, 196ff.
31 For this section see Graham Willett, 'Australian Gay Activists: From Movement to Community', and Willett, *Living Out Loud*, 196–218.
32 Phil Carswell, 'Life Behind Bars', *Gay Community News*, May 1980, 31. The 'best traditions' is used ironically here.
33 On Carrigan and Lee see Graham Willett, 'The Adelaide Homosexual Alliance and the Origins of the Gay Community', in *Intimacy, Violence and Activism: Gay and Lesbian Perspectives on Australian Politics and Society*, ed. Graham Willett and Yorick Smaal (Melbourne: Monash University Press, forthcoming). For Craig Johnston's ideas and interventions, see *A Sydney Gaze: The Making of Gay Liberation* (Sydney: Shiltron Press, 1999). For *GCN*, see Phil Carswell, 'Clones', *GCN*, November 1980, 24–25 and letters debate, December 1980 - January 1981, 4, 40.

A pink Moke, fur coat and the flying duck collection — Jonathan Holmes

I am very grateful to the following individuals and institutions for permission to include original documents and photographs for this essay: Paul McGillick, Noel Frankham, Janine Miller, the Australia Council, the University of Tasmania's Tasmanian College of the Arts. Thanks also to Gerrard Dixon for scanning archival photographs.

1 Here I need to state at the outset that I was on the Visual Arts Board at the time that *Art & Text* was being considered for funding: in the first instance in 1980, and during the second round of funding of the magazine in 1981. I do recall noting in the relevant Board Meetings that there was a potential conflict of interest insofar as I was working with Paul Taylor at the Art School, although there was never any question that as Board Members we could not offer advice to applicants about their applications and, as will be noted later, re-reading the draft of Taylor's initial application, I have no hesitation in stating that it was written entirely in his own voice!

2 Cited in a two page curriculum vitae submitted to the Visual Arts Board to accompany Taylor's application for funding to attend the Eleventh International Sculpture Conference in Washington, D.C. in June 1980.

3 Of particular note was the visit of Hamish Fulton who created his work/walk *Tasmania: A Slow Journey* (1979, gelatin silver photographic prints with lettering; four works, each 105.5 × 87.0 × 2.5 cm). Mario Merz's lecture was one of the most memorable performances of the period: speaking entirely in Italian for well over the expected hour scheduled, he mesmerised the audience with a bravura display of drawing using only a roll of transparency sheet and an overhead projector. Other notable visitors during that year included the American photographer Robert Cumming, as well as Tom McCullough, Michael Leunig, Jillian Orr, Ron Radford, John Lethbridge, John Davis and Frank Watters.

4 See Clement Greenberg, *Arts 54*, No. 6 (February 1980); also Paul Taylor, 'Clement Greenberg and Post Modernism, an Interview', *Art & Australia*, Vol. 18, No. 2 (Summer 1980), 141–144. Another noteworthy interview by Taylor in 1980 was with Graeme Murphy: Paul Taylor, 'Graeme Murphy (Interview)', *Tasmanian Review*, No. 3 (Autumn 1980), 10–11.

5 Paul Taylor, *Tasmanian Sculpture and Three-dimensional Art* [exh. cat.], curated by Paul Taylor (Hobart: Tasmanian School of Art Gallery, Tasmanian College of Advanced Education and University Fine Arts Gallery, University of Tasmania, 1980), 1.

6 *Tasmanian Sculpture and Three-dimensional Art*, 3.

7 Discussing Pachucka's use of materials such as crocheted hemp and jute in her 'environmental tableaux', Taylor writes: 'Their essential softness, not simply desirable for visual effect, aptly conveys a sense of being inside the body, a condition to which the complimentary attitudes of stiffness and repose and relaxation and attention are crucial. By these means a remarkable sense of fatigue, even languor is suggested, describing a fine line between vacuity and nothingness' (2).

8 Although a few of Marek's remarkable surrealist paintings are on public display in Australia, his career remains relatively obscure. The author Bernice Murphy's *Dusan Marek Art* (Sydney: Macquarie Galleries, 1979) is the most comprehensive survey of his oeuvre. His paintings received belated attention in the National Gallery of Australia's 1993 exhibition, 'Surrealism: Revolution by Night', shortly after Marek's death in the same year. See also: Danni Zuvela '"A Haze of Visions": Dream Work in Early Australian Avant-Garde Cinema', *emaj*, No. 6 (2012). Accessed September 16, 2013. http://emajartjournal.com/2012/11/14/danni-zuvela-unorthodox-dreams-modernist-aesthetics-in-early-australian-artists-film/

9 The letter to Katrina Rumley is referred to in footnote 2.

10 Paul Taylor, *Submission for Assistance for a journal of new Australian art and criticism*, unpublished and handwritten ms, [n.p.] 1980, 8 pp. Collection of the author.

11 Australia Council, *News from the Visual Arts Board* (North Sydney: Australia Council, October 1980).

12 Minuted copy of unpublished letter to Nick Waterlow from Paul McGillick, November 28, 1980 [registered in Australia Council Visual Arts Board Sub Registry, December 3, 1980].

13 This wasn't strictly true of *Art & Australia* with recent issues carrying articles on the Sydney Biennale, performance art, and new work by Imants Tillers.

14 Taylor, *Submission for Assistance for a journal of new Australian art and criticism*, n.p.

15 Paul Taylor, 'Editorial: On Criticism', *Art & Text*, No. 1 (Autumn 1981), 5–11.

16 Paul Taylor, written correspondence to Geoff Parr requesting leave of absence, October, 1980. File held by the Tasmanian School of Art, Tasmanian College of the Arts, University of Tasmania.

Provincialism no more: *Art & Text* – Heather Barker and Charles Green

1 This essay is a new, revised and expanded version of our paper, 'No More Provincialism: *Art & Text*'; since that essay's publication, we have reconsidered and altered our assessment of the longevity of the *Art & Text* circle's arguments about the geo-politics of inauthenticity; we now see those "theories" as far more circumscribed by their Cold War origins and less the culminating, most coherent solution to a geo-cultural situation than they seemed until recently; the distinction might at first sight seem small but is significant in the more panoramic perspective of a history of Australian art writing's attempts to formulate a new understanding of Australian art as contemporary art (we are tracing that history in a forthcoming book); to that end we have here introduced an expanded explanation of *Art & Text* 1's reception; for the earlier essay, see Heather Barker and Charles Green, 'No More Provincialism: *Art & Text*', *emaj*, No. 5 (2010). Accessed June 26, 2013. http://www.melbourneartjournal.unimelb.edu.au/E-MAJ/pdf/issue5/GREEN%20AND%20BARKER_emaj%202010.pdf.

2 Michael Denholm, 'Art Magazines in Australia 1963–1990: A Study of Values, Influence and Patronage' (MA diss., Australian National University, 1994), 94.

3 Terry Smith, 'The Provincialism Problem', *Artforum*, Vol. 13, No. 1 (September 1974), 58.

4 Les Levine wrote, 'the institution's great strength is its openness to new ideas and its aim to move with educational needs as they arise. It is, then, an empirical, self-defining institution in a continual process of adjustment, a process helped by the school's informal posture.' See Les Levine, 'Letter from Australia', *Art and America*, Vol. 59, No. 10 (July/August 1973), 15.

5 Jonathan Holmes, Taylor's senior colleague at the Tasmanian School of Art, was also a member of the Visual Arts Board (VAB) between 1977 and 1981. Of the application, he later recalled 'talking about it a lot' with Taylor.

6 Jonathan Holmes, e-mail correspondence with the author, November 19, 2003.

7 Ashley Crawford, conversation with the author, Melbourne, May 6, 2004.

8 Ibid.

9 Nick Waterlow, 'Paul Taylor', *Art & Australia*, Vol. 30, No. 3 (Autumn 1993), 336.

10 Ibid.

11 'Visual Arts Board Publication Grants', in Australia Council for the Arts, *Australia Council for the Arts Annual Report 1980–81* (Sydney: Australia Council for the Arts, 1981), 149.

12 Charles Green, 'Empire', in *Meridian: Focus on Contemporary Australian Art*, ed. Rachel Kent and Russell Storer (Sydney: Museum of Contemporary Art, 2002), 10–15.

13 Jean Baudrillard, 'La precession des simulacres', trans. Paul Foss, *Traverses*, No. 10 (February 1978), 3–37. Paul Foss referred to his own translation.

14 Jean Baudrillard, *Simulations*, trans. Paul Foss, Paul Patton and Philip Beichtman (New York: Semiotext(e), 1983). Also see Jean Baudrillard, *Simulacres et Simulation* (Paris: Galilée, 1981). For a commentary on Baudrillard, see John Storey, *Cultural Theory and Popular Culture, An Introduction* (Harlow, UK: Prentice Hall, 2001).

15 See Paul Foss, 'Theatrum Nondum Cognitorum', in *The Foreign Bodies Papers*, ed. Peter Botsman, Chris Burns and Peter Hutchings (Sydney: Local Consumption Publications, 1981), 15–38; and Meaghan Morris and Anne Freadman, 'Import Rhetoric: Semiotics in/and Australia', in *The Foreign Bodies Papers*, ed. Peter Botsman, Chris Burns and Peter Hutchings (Sydney: Local Consumption Publications, 1981), 122–153.

16 Donald Brook had argued since the 1960s that theories had not kept up with art; see Donald Brook, 'Theory and Criticism', *Art & Australia*, Vol. 5, No. 1 (June 1967),

390–392. The editors of the first issue of *Other Voices* (June/July 1970), Terry Smith and Paul McGillick, had suggested in 1970 that Australian art writers must import ideas from overseas.

17 See Ian Burn, 'Gary Catalano, *The Years of Hope: Australian Art and Criticism 1959–1968*', *Art Network*, 3 & 4 (Winter/Spring 1981), 49.

18 Meaghan Morris and Anne Freadman, 'Import Rhetoric: Semiotics in/and Australia' in *The Foreign Bodies Papers*, ed. Peter Botsman, Chris Burns and Peter Hutchings (Sydney: Local Consumption Publications, 1981), 125.

19 Morris, 'Import Rhetoric: Semiotics in/and Australia', 127.

20 See Green, 'Empire', 10–15; also see Charles Green, 'Australian contemporary art, 1995–2010', *Grove Art Online. Oxford Art Online*. Accessed January 24, 2010. http://www.oxfordartonline.com.

21 Morris, 'Import Rhetoric: Semiotics in/and Australia', 127.

22 Ibid.

23 Margaret Preston (1875–1963), arguably Australia's most famous woman artist, was a modernist painter who produced an extraordinary quantity of still-life paintings, prints, decorative work, ceramics and domestic art including quilts, cushion and rugs. Preston was deeply inspired by indigenous art and used Aboriginal motifs in her work from the 1920s onward. She took the view that a national Australian art must incorporate indigenous images. Mainstream art history cast her as a passionate champion of a national Australian art but Preston can also be seen as a white artist who took images from an already exploited culture without any understanding of the meaning of the images or their traditional owners.

24 Morris, 'Import Rhetoric: Semiotics in/and Australia', 127.

25 Ibid., 128.

26 Peter Timms, *What's wrong with contemporary art?* (Sydney: University of New South Wales Press, 2004).

27 See Morris, 'Import Rhetoric: Semiotics in/and Australia', 129; Morris explains an 'apologetic' as 'an argumentative defence which serves as a means of enabling speech; an apologetic poses an Other (who shifts between "the reader" and someone else s/he knows) as a someone who is about to be offended.'

28 Ibid.

29 Ibid.

30 Paul Foss, 'Ozimeandering, or the Theatre of Here-Nor-There' (paper presented at ARCO Madrid, Madrid, c. late 1990s); in a lecture delivered in the late 1990s at ARCO, the Madrid contemporary art fair, Paul Foss recalled, 'Back then, I was attempting to position debates about centre and periphery in the strict terms of postcolonial discourse, contrasting these debates with narratives about the legendary hollowness or never-never-land thinking that dominates Australia's historical and cultural relationships to itself and to the rest of the world.'

31 Paul Foss, e-mail correspondence with the author, August 14, 2003.

32 Ashley Crawford, conversation with the author, Melbourne, May 6, 2004, noted, 'A great editor? No, but choosey. He recognised talent and placed it. Paul was a bower bird.' Martin Armiger wrote that Taylor 'moved with the confidence of a man with an idea whose time has come.' See Martin Armiger, 'Pushing the Art of Pop', *National Times*, July 11–17, 1982, 25.

33 Paul Taylor, 'Editorial: On Criticism', *Art & Text*, No. 1 (Autumn 1981), 5–11.

34 Ibid., 5.

35 Ibid., 6.

36 Margaret Plant, 'Quattrocento Melbourne: Aspects of Finish, 1973–1977', *Studies in Australian Art* (Melbourne: Department of Fine Arts, University of Melbourne, 1978); Taylor took three quotes from Plant's essay, referring to it as a 'most intelligent and straightforward assessment of the mid-seventies Australian art scene'. See Taylor, 'Editorial: On Criticism', 7; Taylor knew Plant well, as one of her younger students; she was McCaughey's successor at Monash University's Department of Visual Arts, a transitional figure in writing on Australian art, a perceptive, precise commentator on late 1960s and 1970s art who commented little

on contemporary art after that.

37 Taylor, 'Editorial: On Criticism', 8.

38 Ibid., 6.

39 Ibid., 8.

40 Ibid., 9.

41 Ibid., 10, cites Roland Barthes, 'Musica Practica' (1970), reprinted in *Image, Music, Text*, ed. and trans. Stephen Heath (London: Hill and Wang, 1977).

42 See the citation of Robert Venturi, *Complexity and Contradiction in Architecture* (New York: Museum of Modern Art, 1966), in Taylor, 'Editorial: On Criticism', 10–11.

43 Taylor, 'Editorial: On Criticism', 11.

44 Ibid.

45 On the strength of his work at the magazine, Gibson was able to move to New York as managing editor of *Artforum*'s literary sister-journal, *Bookforum*, and then to become the managing editor of *Artforum* itself.

46 Crawford, 2004. In the first eight issues of *Art & Text* there were essays by artists John Nixon, Peter Tyndall, Imants Tillers and Richard Dunn, all associated with John Nixon's Art Projects; Philip Brophy and Adrian Martin from the Clifton Hill Community Music Centre; artists Juan Davila and Vivienne Shark LeWitt; and curator Judy Annear. But there were also articles by well-known, mainstream writers and curators such as Bernard Smith, Patrick McCaughey, Donald Brook, Julie Ewington, Ian Burn and Terry Smith, with all of whom Taylor was on at least reasonable working and speaking terms. The magazine consistently drew on a wide range of subjects including the pedagogical perennial ('What Can We Do With the Art Class' by Donald Brook in *Art & Text*, No. 4 [Summer 1981], 39–43); the art historical ('The Sixties: Crisis and Aftermath' by Ian Burn in *Art & Text*, No. 1 [Autumn 1981], 49–65); and the feminist ('Feminism and Fragmentation' by Julie Ewington in *Art & Text*, No. 7 [Spring 1982], 61–73) as well as an increasing component of French Theory.

47 Paul Taylor, 'Australian "New Wave" and the "Second Degree"', *Art & Text*, No. 1 (Autumn 1981), 23–32.

48 Ibid.

49 Ibid., 23; see Dick Hebdige, *Subculture: The Meaning of Style* (London: Methuen, 1979). Hebdige's book immediately became the definitive text on subculture; it was Paul Taylor's major reference; Taylor commissioned a review of the book by Philip Brophy for *Art & Text*'s first issue. Hebdige's book analyses youth subcultures in post-World War II Britain. He looked at teddy boys, mods and rockers, skinheads and punks; he applied semiotic theory, especially Roland Barthes, along with Gramsci's theory of hegemony, to argue that subcultures adopted styles—'those emphatic combinations of dress, dance, argot, music, etc' (101)—that deliberately subverted conventional codes and set out to provoke.

50 Emphasis in the original. Hebdige, *Subculture: The Meaning of Style*. Adrian Martin, 'Before and After *Art & Text*', *Agenda*, Vol. 1, No. 2 (August 1988), Special Supplement: 'Art: The Present and Recent Past of Australian Art and Criticism' (papers delivered during a programme of six discussions held on consecutive evenings May 2–7, 1988, at Theatreworks, Acland Street, St Kilda), 16; Martin's paper is a retrospective and nostalgic account of the very distinctive Melbourne subculture that embraced *Art & Text*. It successfully evokes the social context of *Art & Text*—but it tells only one part of the story of Australian art writing in the early 1980s.

51 Terry Smith and Adrian Martin were both speaking in 'The Present and Recent Past of Australian Art and Criticism'. According to endnote 2 (19) of Martin's paper, Smith's comment was made in his paper 'Art Criticism in Australia: The Mid-1970s', but it does not appear in the edited paper published in the *Agenda* supplement. See Martin, 'Before and After *Art & Text*', 17.

52 Taylor, 'Australian "New Wave" and the "Second Degree"', 23.

53 Ibid.

54 Ibid., 24.

55 The terms 'bricoleur' and 'bricolage' were adopted from Hebdige, *Subculture: The Meaning of Style*; he used 'bricolage' to describe a technique that re-assembles signs to create a new discourse; see 1–19 and 103.

56 Martin, 'Before and After *Art & Text*', 16.

57 Ibid., 15.

58 Carol Squires, 'Paul Taylor 1957–1992', *Art & Text*, No. 44 (January 1993), 16.

59 Martin, 'Before and After *Art & Text*', 17.

60 Philip Brophy, email correspondence with the author, June 17, 2004. The core members of →↑→ were Philip Brophy, Maria Kozic, Ralph Traviato, Jane Stevenson and Leigh Parkhill, however, there was an 'organically changing personnel' and more than sixty people were involved in →↑→; for further information, see John Jenkins, 'Philip Brophy', in *22 contemporary Australian composers* (Melbourne: NMA Publications, 1988). Accessed December 7, 2010, http://www.rainerlinz.net/NMA/22CAC/brophy.html.

61 Ashley Crawford, 'Tch-Tch-Tch', *The Virgin Press*, July 5, 1981, 12. The name of the band was actually →↑→, a name that Brophy invented in 1977 to indicate three descriptions of volume: length, width and height. →↑→ appears in different spellings, sometimes hyphenated and sometimes not. Brophy was the spokesman for the group in the interview and gave the following explanation in the *Virgin Press* interview, 'The basic approach of the band's work is to pick an area of interest to us, which is usually part of an area of popular culture such as television, disco music, rock, muzak, Hollywood movies and we dissect these things looking from the point of view of them being constructed objects and we de-construct them and try to present everything back to an audience showing them these parts and how they operate ... Semiotics comes into our work not as dogma or something we follow really rigorously, more than anything it's a very practical analytical process we can use.'

62 Paul Taylor, 'Popism: the Art of White Aborigines', reprinted in *What is Appropriation? An Anthology of Critical Writings on Australian Art in the '80s and 90s*, ed. Rex Butler, (Brisbane: IMA Publications, 1996, 85–87). The essay 'Popism: the Art of White Aborigines' was commissioned for the international magazine, *Flash Art* and first printed in *On the Beach*, No. 1 (1982).

63 Chris McAuliffe, 'Let's Talk About Art: Art and Punk in Melbourne', *Art & Australia*, Vol. 34, No. 4 (Summer 1997), 502–512. Chris McAuliffe's remarkable evocation of this moment examines the relationship between art and pop music, proposing that art schools were places where high and mass culture met: 'punk rock was the ultimate art school music movement'. McAuliffe was a student in Melbourne during the early 1980s and a young contemporary of the group Adrian Martin wrote about in 'Before and After *Art & Text*'; see Simon Frith and Howard Horne, *Art into Pop* (London: Routledge, 1987), 2–3, 125.

64 McAuliffe, 'Let's Talk About Art: Art and Punk in Melbourne', 505.

65 Adrian Martin, 'Paul Taylor, 1957–1992', *Art & Text*, No. 44 (January 1993), 14. Sadly, apart from 'Before and After *Art & Text*', many of the recollections of Paul Taylor appeared in obituaries after he died in 1992, aged just thirty-five. Such recollections are hardly objective but they convey a sense of the impact of his personality on *Art & Text* and beyond.

66 Vivienne Shark LeWitt, 'Paul Taylor', *Art & Text*, No. 44 (January 1993), 14.

67 Martin, 'Before and After *Art & Text*', 17.

68 Stan Anson, 'On Being Difficult; The Conservatism of *Art & Text*', *Meanjin*, Vol. 42, No. 2 (June 1983), 203–214

69 Christina Davidson, 'Interview: Paul Taylor', *Art Network*, No. 9 (Autumn 1983), 46.

70 Julie Ewington, 'Fragmentation and Feminism: the critical discourses of postmodernism', *Art & Text*, No.7 (Spring 1982), 61–73.

71 Martin, 'Before and After *Art & Text*', 17.

72 Ibid.

73 Ibid.

74 Ibid., 15.

75 Taylor, 'Australian "New Wave" and the "Second Degree"', 23. Taylor broke Barthes's sentence to omit the word 'also'.
76 Ibid., 24.
77 Ibid., 30.
78 Vivienne Shark LeWitt, 'Paul Taylor 1957–1992', *Art & Text,* No. 44 (January 1993), 14.
79 Squires, 'Paul Taylor 1957–1992', 16.
80 Ashley Crawford, conversation with the author, May 6, 2004.
81 Jane Rankin-Reid, email correspondence with the author, September 14, 2005.
82 'Editorial', *Art Network,* 3 & 4 (Winter/Spring 1981), 5.
83 For instance see Judy Annear, '*Art & Text*: Autumn 1981', *Art Network,* 3 & 4 (Winter/Spring 1981), 49; Richard McMillan, 'Writing about Criticism', *Art Network*, 3 & 4 (Winter/Spring 1981), 49; Ian Burn, '*The Years of Hope: Australian Art and Criticism 1959–1968* by Gary Catalano', *Art Network,* 3 & 4 (Winter/Spring 1981), 49–51.
84 Annear, '*Art & Text*: Autumn 1981', 49.
85 Annear was an associate of the Lip collective in 1981. Suzanne Davies recalled in 2004 that Annear was emphatically opposed to publishing writing by men in *Lip*, even including a tribute to Kiffy Rubbo by Gary Catalano; Suzanne Davies, conversation with the author, Melbourne, August 3, 2004.
86 Annear, '*Art & Text*: Autumn 1981', 49.
87 McMillan, 'Writing about Criticism', 49; Burn, '*The Years of Hope*', 49.
88 Paul McGillick, 'The Decline of the Australian Art Critic', *Quadrant,* Vol. 22, No. 12 (December 1978), 48–51.
89 McGillick, 'The Decline of the Australian Art Critic', 48.
90 Ibid., 49–50.
91 Burn, '*The Years of Hope: Australian Art and Criticism 1959–1968* by Gary Catalano', 49.
92 The first quote is from McMillan, 'Writing about Criticism', 49; the second quote is from Burn, '*The Years of Hope*', 49.
93 Bernard Smith, 'Critical Reformation', *The Age Monthly Review*, March 1, 1982, 9.
94 Ibid.
95 Ibid.
96 The essays were David Bromfield, 'Adrian Hall. An Artist in Australia', *Art & Text,* No. 3 (Spring 1981), 3–12; Janine Burke, 'Collaboration: Artists Working Collectively', *Art & Text*, No. 1 (Autumn 1981), 33–44; Patrick McCaughey, 'David Wilson's New Sculpture', *Art & Text*, No. 2 (Winter 1981), 27–32; Memory Holloway, 'Reel Women: Narrative as a Feminist Alternative', *Art & Text*, No. 3 (Spring 1981), 3–12; Mick Carter, 'The Re-education of Desire', *Art & Text*, No. 4 (Summer 1981), 20–38; Peter Tyndall, 'Culture Corner', *Art & Text*, No. 2 (Winter 1981), 39–48; Peter Tyndall, 'Slave Guitars', *Art & Text*, No. 4 (Summer 1981), 44–46; Edward Colless and David Kelly, 'Lost World 1', *Art & Text*, No. 3 (Spring 1981), 67–75.
97 Smith, 'Critical Reformation', 9.
98 Imants Tillers, 'Locality Fails', *Art & Text*, No. 6 (Winter 1982), 51–60; Meaghan Morris, 'Texts', *Art & Text*, No. 6 (Winter 1982), 61–73; Paul Foss, 'Meridian of Apathy', *Art & Text*, No. 6 (June 1982), 74–88.
99 Patrick McCaughey, 'Director's Introduction', *POPISM* [exh. cat.], curated by Paul Taylor (Melbourne: National Gallery of Victoria, 1982), front cover.
100 Paul Taylor, *POPISM* [exh. cat.], curated by Paul Taylor (Melbourne: National Gallery of Victoria, 1982), 1.
101 Ibid.
102 Ibid.
103 Ibid., 2. The article was illustrated by one of the first Imants Tillers canvasboard paintings, *Suppressed Imagery*, 1981, his famous painting that reproduces a blurred postcard of the Church of St Francis at Assisi; reprinted in Butler, *What is Appropriation?*, 85–87; 'Popism: the Art of White Aborigines' had been commissioned for the international art magazine, *Flash Art*, in 1983 but was published first in *On the Beach*; Taylor wrote the catalogue essay for the exhibition 'Eureka! Artists from Australia', in London, in 1982.
104 See also Butler, *What is Appropriation?*; Rex Butler's 'Introduction' to *What is*

Appropriation? remains the only detailed periodisation of Australian postmodernism.

105 Paul Taylor, 'Popism: the Art of White Aborigines', reprinted in Butler, *What is Appropriation?*, 86.

106 Ibid.

107 Ibid., 87.

108 Butler, *What is Appropriation?*, 16–17.

109 Ibid., 20.

110 Paul Taylor, 'Clement Greenberg and Post Modernism, an Interview', *Art & Australia*, Vol. 18, No. 2 (Winter 1980), 141–144. The fourth essay in 'Antipodality' is Paul Foss, 'Meridian of Apathy', 74–88; as Taylor explains in the Introduction, this is Part 2 of Foss's previously published 'Theatrum Nondum Cognitorum'.

111 Imants Tillers, 'Locality Fails', *Art & Text*, No. 6 (Winter 1982), 51–60.

112 Gary Catalano, 'A trespasser confronts an unlikely hero,' *The Age*, May 31, 1989, 2.

113 See the simplified explanation of Bell's theorem in Gary Felder, 'Spooky Action at a Distance: An Explanation of Bell's Theorem', 1999, http://www.felderbooks.com/papers/bell.html. Accessed September 13, 2013. Felder defines locality as 'the principle that an event which happens at one place can't instantaneously affect an event someplace else.' In 1935, Einstein, Podolsky and Rosen had published a paper that predicted the breakdown of locality, showing that putting a particle in a device at one location could instantly and arbitrarily influence another, far distant particle. They refused to believe that this could happen and it was Einstein who called the result 'spooky action at a distance'. In 1964, J.S. Bell published a paper that showed that no theory that preserved locality could explain results predicted by quantum mechanics. Bell's Theorem states that 'no physical theory which is realistic and also local in a specified sense can agree with all of the statistical implications of Quantum Mechanics.' Tillers took the idea of the failure of locality out of its scientific context and used it to support an entirely different and unrelated argument about cultural identity.

114 Tillers, 'Locality Fails', 55–56.

115 See De Andrade, *Manifesto da Antropofagia*, 1928, http://www.uol.com.br/bienal/24bienal/nuh/i_manifesto.htm, accessed 2010; Marcelo Guimarães Lima, 'São Paolo Bienal: Cannibalism and Identity', *New Art Examiner*, June 1999, 37–8. He writes, 'Against the fear of the enemy or other, the "Manifesto da Antropofagia" proposes to cannibalise it: devouring the enemy, absorbing the other as nourishment, destroy (or deconstruct) it and use the energies thus liberated to invigorate the self.' The 1998 Sao Paolo Biennale revisited the *antropofagia* movement and curator Paulo Herkenhoff adopted 'Only anthropophagy unites us', the opening declaration of the Anthropophagite Manifesto, as its theme.

116 Meaghan Morris, 'Texts', *Art & Text*, No. 6 (Winter 1982), 61–73, and Lynn Silverman, 'Photographs', *Art & Text*, No. 6 (Winter 1982), 61–73.

117 Silverman said of her work in 1980, 'I like the notion of anchoring the reading of an image by using other images in sequential, collective, or paired relationships. Each photograph derives its meaning from the others around it within the series. The photographs all comment on one each other.' See Judy Annear, *Frame of Reference: Australian Tour 1981–82* (Parkville, Victoria: George Paton Gallery, Melbourne University Union, 1981), 24.

118 Morris, 'Texts', 64.

119 Ibid., 65.

120 Ibid., 72.

121 Jane Rankin-Reid, e-mail correspondence with the author, September 20, 2005.

122 Ibid., 2005.

123 Donald Kuspit, 'Imants Tillers at Bess Cutler', *Art and America*, 73/3 (March 1985), 158.

124 Graham Coulter-Smith, *The Postmodern Art of Imants Tillers: Appropriation en Abyme, 1971–2001* (Southampton: Fine Arts Research Centre, Southampton Institute, 2002), 80.

125 Donald Kuspit, 'Australian Drawings at CDS', *Art and America*, 73/3 (March 1985), 154.

126 Ian North, 'StarAboriginality' in *Postcolonial + art: where now?*, ed. Charles Green

(Sydney: Artspace, 2001, n.p.); reprinted by Hawke Research Institute, University of South Australia (*Working Paper no. 20*), 2002; anthologised in Klaus Stierstorfer, ed., *Return to postmodernism: Festschrift, in honour of Ihab Hassan* (Heidelberg: Universitätsverlag, 2005), 151–66.

127 Ian Burn, Nigel Lendon, Charles Merewether and Ann Stephen, *The Necessity of Australian Art: An Essay About Interpretation* (Sydney: Power Publications, 1988).

128 Burn et al., *The Necessity of Australian Art*, 8, 9.

129 Ibid., 145.

130 Ibid., 4–9.

131 Rankin-Reid, 2005, commented, 'He was quite ambitious on behalf of this goal and was quite successful I believe.'

132 Crawford, 2004.

133 Rankin-Reid, 2005.

134 See Paul Taylor, 'US Art Theorist Suzi Gablik', *Art Network*, No. 2 (Spring 1980), 13–15; Paul Taylor, 'Introduction. Special Section: Antipodality', *Art & Text*, No. 6 (Winter 1982), 141–144; Paul Taylor, 'Rosalind Krauss' *Art & Text*, No. 8 (Summer 1982–83), 31–37.

135 See Australia Council, *Art & Text* file, document 10, Paul Foss to Project Officers—Publications, Visual Arts Board. This letter on an *Art & Text* letterhead is headed 'Application for Publications (Periodicals) *Art & Text* magazine 1985–1986'.

136 See Australia Council, *Art & Text* file, document 10, Paul Foss to Project Officers—Publications, Visual Arts Board.

137 See Australia Council, *Art & Text* file, document 29, Paul Taylor to Ross Wolfe, April 1, 1985, n.p.

138 Australia Council, *Art & Text* file, document 40 (a postcard), Paul Taylor to Ross Wolfe, January 9, 1986, n.p.

139 Charles Green, *Peripheral Vision: Contemporary Australian Art 1970–1994* (Roseville East: Craftsman House, 1995), 6. 'In early 1990, passing through New York, I met Paul Taylor, the founder of *Art & Text*, for the first time. By the end of the evening I had been convinced that the project I outlined to Paul—this book—could be realised, and I am indebted to him for his example of a generous participant in the world of contemporary art.'

140 Imants Tillers, 'In Perpetual Mourning', *Art & Text*, No. 15 (Spring 1984), joint-issue with *ZG* [London], No. 11 (Summer 1984), 22–24; Philip Brophy, 'A Face Without a Place: Identity in Australian Contemporary Art Since 1980', *Art & Text*, No. 16 (Summer 1984–85), 68–80; see Rex Butler, ed., *Radical Revisionism: an anthology of writings on Australian art* (Brisbane: Institute of Modern Art Press, 2005).

Before and after *Art & Text*—Adrian Martin

1 Originally published in *Agenda*, Vol. 1, No. 2 (August 1988), Special Supplement: 'Art: The Present and Recent Past of Australian Art and Criticism', 16; then in Rex Butler, ed., *What is Appropriation? An Anthology of Critical Writings on Australian Art in the '80s and '90s* (Brisbane: Institute of Modern Art, 1996), 107–118.

2 Roland Barthes, 'Lecture', trans. R. Howard, *October*, No. 8 (Spring 1979), 14.

3 Terry Smith, in the course of his talk on 1970s art criticism at Theatre Works, May 3, 1988; from my notes.

4 Paul Taylor, 'Australian "New Wave" and the "Second Degree"', *Art & Text*, No. 1 (Autumn 1981), 23–32.

5 For the essential text of the period, see Dick Hebdige, *Subculture: The Meaning of Style* (London: Methuen, 1979); and Philip Brophy's review of the book in *Art & Text*, No. 1 (Autumn 1981), 69–74.

6 Taylor, 'Australian "New Wave" and the "Second Degree"', 23.

7 John Nixon, 'Manifesto For A Renewed Art Practice 1980', *Art & Text*, No. 2 (Winter 1981), insert; punctuation and layout as in the original.

8 For a helpful documentation, see John Nixon, 'Art Projects 1979–84', *Art & Text*,

No. 28 (March–May 1988), 20–37.

9 See for an example Stan Anson's 'On Being Difficult: The Conservatism of *Art & Text*', *Meanjin*, Vol. 42, No. 2 (1983), 203–214.

10 For a theorisation of this from the period, see Richard Dunn, 'The Pursuit of Meaning: A Strategy of Parts', *Art & Text*, No. 6 (Winter 1982), 16–30. Dunn subsequently sharply separated himself from tendencies associated with 'POPISM' or *Art & Text*; see, for instance, his 'Argument With Design (Annotated)', *On the Beach*, No. 10 (Winter 1986).

11 John Young and Terry [Terence] Blake, 'On Some Alternatives to the Code in the Age of Hyperreality: The Hermit and the City-Dweller', *Art & Text*, No. 2 (Winter 1981), 4–17; John Young, 'Three Facts by Imants Tillers', *Art & Text*, No. 4 (Summer 1981), 62–63; Imants Tillers, 'Locality Fails', *Art & Text*, No. 6 (Winter 1982), 51–60; Imants Tillers, 'Fear of Texture', *Art & Text*, No. 10 (Winter 1983), 8–18; John Young, 'Anything Still', *Art & Text*, No. 11 (Spring 1983), 62–66. For further Blake, see 'Image is the Measure', *On the Beach*, No. 6 (Spring 1984), and 'Nothing to Declare', *Tension*, No. 9 (1986); his current (2013) webpage is: http://terenceblake.wordpress.com/.

12 See for instance Philip Brophy and Adrian Martin, 'The Archaeology of Culture, or How To Say Everything at Once', *Cantrills Filmnotes*, No. 37/38 (April 1982). See also Adrian Martin's forthcoming e-book *Golden Eighties: Early Writings 1978–1987* (Melbourne: Screening the Past, 2014).

13 Ted [Edward] Colless and David Kelly, 'The Lost World', *Art & Text*, No. 3 (Spring 1981), 67–75; 'The Lost World 2: The Way We Were', *Art & Text*, No. 7 (Spring/September 1982), 4–11; 'The Lost World 3: Signs of Life', *Art & Text*, Nos 12/13 (Summer 1983), 84–89—all reprinted (without images) in Edward Colless, *The Error of My Ways* (Brisbane: Institute of Modern Art, 1995); Jody Berland, 'Popular Music and the Post-Pop Avant-Garde', *Art & Text*, No. 6 (Winter 1982), 3–15.

14 Jean Baudrillard, 'Is Pop An Art Of Consumption?', *Tension*, No. 2 (September–October 1983), 33–35.

15 Paul Taylor, 'Tall Poppies (catalogue entry)', *Art & Text*, Nos. 12/13 (Autumn 1984), 51.

16 Dick Hebdige, 'Digging for "Britain": Postmodernism, Popular Culture, and National I.D.' (paper presented at University of Sydney, Sydney, July 7, 1987).

17 Jenny Watson, 'Urgent Images', *Art & Text*, No. 14 (Winter 1984), 73.

18 The two soundest are Julie Ewington, 'Fragmentation and Feminism', *Art & Text*, No. 7 (Spring/September 1982), 61–73; and Gordon Bull, '*Art & Text* and the Second Degree', *Local Consumption*, No. 5 (subtitled: 'Sex, Politics, Representation', April 1984).

19 William D. Routt, 'Disco Hoodoo', *Art & Text*, No. 3 (Spring 1981), 79.

20 This phrase is taken from Germano Celant, 'From Alpha Trainer to Subway', *Art & Text*, No. 9 (Autumn 1983), 69.

21 See pages 167–179 of this book.

Living on the surface—Adrian Martin

1 Jane later altered her name to Jayne Stevenson. For an account of her film work to 1983, see my 'Letter to Jane', *Cantrills Filmnotes*, No. 41/42 (June 1983), 13–18.

2 Paul Foss, 'Meridian of Apathy', *Art & Text*, No. 6 (Winter 1982), 84.

3 William D. Routt, 'Disco Hoodoo', *Art & Text*, No. 3 (Spring 1981), 79.

4 Philip Brophy, 'What is This Thing Called "Disco"?', *Art & Text*, No. 3 (Spring 1981), 65.

5 Brophy, 'What is This Thing Called "Disco"?', 63.

6 These quotes were transcribed by me at Fuller's lecture, 'Aesthetics After Modernism' (paper presented at the Power Institute, Sydney, April 5, 1982). The material was recast by Fuller into his book *Aesthetics After Modernism* (London: Littlehampton Book Services, 1983).

Tall Poppies: a sleight of hand — Judy Annear

Research for this essay was assisted by Jacqueline Au and the Art Gallery of New South Wales Research Library. Useful comments were provided by Vivienne Shark LeWitt.

1 Paul Taylor, *Tall Poppies* [exh. cat.], curated by Paul Taylor (Melbourne: University Art Gallery, University of Melbourne, 1983), n.p. For example, Dale Frank had been selected by Achille Bonita Oliva to show in Italy, Mike Parr had substantial international contacts particularly in Europe and had exhibited there since the 1970s, John Nixon and Imants Tillers had been selected for 'documenta 7' by Germano Celant. In 1982 John Dunkley-Smith had been selected by PSI, New York for a residency there in 1982.

2 'Pictures was the title of an exhibition ... which I organized for Artists Space in the fall of 1977. In choosing the word pictures for this show, I hoped to convey not only the work's most salient characteristic — recognizable images — but also and importantly the ambiguities it sustains. As is typical of what has come to be called postmodernism, this new work is not confined to any particular medium; instead, it makes use of photography, film, performance, as well as traditional modes of painting, drawing, and sculpture. Picture, used colloquially, is also nonspecific ... Equally important for my purposes, picture, in its verb form, can refer to a mental process as well as the production of an aesthetic object ... I think it is safe to say that what I am outlining is a predominant sensibility among the current generation of younger artists, or at least of that group of artists who remain committed to radical innovation.' Douglas Crimp, 'Pictures', *October*, Vol. 8, No. 102 (Spring 1979), 75.

3 Paul Taylor, *POPISM* [exh. cat.], curated by Paul Taylor (Melbourne: National Gallery of Victoria, 1982), 1–12.

4 *Bunch of fives* was also the name of a 1970s English children's television show about two fifth formers who start a school newspaper.

5 Bert Peeters, 'Tall poppies and egalitarianism in Australian discourse', *English world-wide*, Vol. 25, No. 1 (2004), 12.

6 Susan Butler, ed., *Macquarie dictionary of new words* (Sydney: The Macquarie Library, 1990), 357; as quoted in Peeters, 'Tall poppies and egalitarianism in Australian discourse', 13.

7 Peter Weir quoted in Peeters, 'Tall poppies and egalitarianism in Australian discourse', 18. Hugh Mackay quoted in Peeters, 'Tall poppies and egalitarianism in Australian discourse', 21.

8 Sue Cramer, 'Masterpieces and Tall poppies', *Art Network*, No. 10 (1983), 45.

9 See for example, Paul Taylor, *Eureka!: artists from Australia* [exh. cat.] (London: Institute of Contemporary Arts and Arts Council of Great Britain, 1982), 61–67.

10 See Imants Tillers, 'Locality fails', *Art & Text*, No. 6 (Winter 1982), 51–60 for a discussion on the complexity of responses to the question of Aboriginal art, for instance, at that time.

11 Taylor, *Eureka: artists from Australia*, 61–67.

12 See Juliana Engberg, 'Maxi crop — a review of *Tall poppies*', *Melbourne University Fine Arts Students Society Broadsheet*, Vol. 2, No. 2 (1983), 15 and Taylor, *Tall Poppies*, n.p.

13 Naomi Cass, 'Discussion evening report — Paul Taylor critic, ed. *Art & Text*', *Melbourne University Fine Arts Students Society Broadsheet*, Vol. 2, No. 2 (1983), 1–2. Emphases in the original.

14 Robert Rooney, 'Tall poppies', *Flash Art*, No. 114 (November 1983), 74.

15 All five quotes from Taylor can be found in Christina Davidson, 'Interview: Paul Taylor', *Art Network*, No. 10 (1983), 46–47.

16 Paul Taylor, 'Popism: the Art of White Aborigines', *On the beach*, No. 1 (Autumn 1983), 30.

17 See Achille Bonito Oliva, 'Contributions to a symposium', *Art & Text*, No. 8 (Summer 1982/83), 72–75.

18 Adrian Martin, 'Popism/art in the age of mechanical reproduction', *The Virgin Press*, August 1982, 9. The descriptors used for those quoted in this essay describe them as

they were in the early 1980s. With a few exceptions these people were in their twenties.

Paul Taylor's '70s – Rex Butler & Susan Rothnie

1 Anthony Gardner, 'Which Histories Matter?', *Third Text*, Vol. 23, No.5 (2009), 613.
2 Fredric Jameson, 'Periodizing the '60s', in *The Ideologies of Theory: Essays 1971–1986*, Vol. 2 (London: Routledge, 1988), 208.
3 Fredric Jameson, 'The Vanishing Mediator: Narrative Structure in Max Weber', *New German Critique*, Vol. 1 (1973), esp. 75–77.
4 Actually, it was both of them. See Paul Taylor, 'Lip Reading', *Meanjin*, Vol. 40, No. 4 (1981), 529–533; and Adrian Martin, 'Don't Give Me No Lip', *Virgin Press*, January 21, 1983, 9–11.
5 'Greenberg and Post-Modernism, An Interview with Paul Taylor', *Art & Australia*, Vol. 18, No. 2 (Summer 1980), 141–144.
6 Stan Anson, 'On Being Difficult: The Conservatism of *Art & Text*', *Meanjin*, Vol. 42, No. 2 (June 1983), 203–214.
7 Gordon Bull, '*Art & Text* and the Second Degree', Local Consumption Series 5, 1984.
8 Paul Taylor, 'Editorial: On Criticism', *Art & Text*, No. 1 (1981), 11.
9 Paul Taylor, *Eureka! Artists from Australia* [exh. cat.] (London: Institute of Contemporary Arts, 1982), 65.
10 Julie Ewington, 'Fragmentation and Feminism: The Critical Discourses of Post-Modernism', *Art & Text*, No. 7 (1982), 63.
11 Virginia Spate, 'Whatever Happened to the Art of the 'Seventies?', *Art & Text*, No. 14 (1984), 76.
12 Paul Taylor, *POPISM* [exh. cat.], curated by Paul Taylor (Melbourne: National Gallery of Victoria, Melbourne, 1982), n.p.
13 Paul Taylor, 'Popism: the Art of White Aborigines', *On the Beach*, No. 1 (1982), 30.
14 Paul Taylor, 'Australian "New Wave" and the "Second Degree"', *Art & Text*, No. 1 (1981), 32.
15 Paul Foss, 'Theatrum Nondum Cognitorum', in *Foreign Bodies Papers*, ed. Peter Botsman, Chris Burns and Peter Hutchings (Sydney: Local Consumption Publications, 1981).
16 Taylor, 'Popism: the Art of White Aborigines', 30.
17 Foss, 'Theatrum Nondum Cognitorum', 24.
18 Taylor, 'Popism: the Art of White Aborigines', 30. And along with the sign and provincialism, there is perhaps a third 'suspension' in Taylor's work: the homosexual. We might illustrate this here with an anecdote. One of us was once invited to visit Juan Davila's studio in Melbourne. After a pleasant lunch, the artist invited us down to his studio. Contrary to our expectations of a Hannibal Lecterish bloodbath, it was in fact immaculately tidy. As we walked in the door, we saw *Nothing if Not Abnormal* (1991), which features the then-Prime Minister Bob Hawke pulling up a singlet to reveal breasts and his deposed Deputy Paul Keating parting his buttocks and blowing a fart at the spectator. Davila beckoned us closer. 'Look into Keating's arsehole', he softly commanded. We did – and to our surprise saw what appeared to be a miniature Fred Williams landscape there. Here exactly is what we might call the framing or bracketing of the 'Australian' by the homosexual. And it immediately occurred to us that this was like looking out the window through the surrounding darkness in Tom Roberts's *Shearing the Rams* (1890). In other words, in an extraordinary way, Davila turns Roberts's male shearing shed into an arsehole. To complicate what we have previously suggested, we might say the sign, the provincial and the homosexual each explain one another in Taylor: the sign arises because of the provincial, Australia's provincialism can be understood as a kind of homosexuality and homosexuality is a particular relationship to the sign.
19 See, for example, Christopher Allen, *Art in Australia: From Colonization to Postmodernism* (Melbourne: Thames & Hudson, 1997), 180–186. For a more general account of

this absence, see Heather Barker, 'A Critical History of Writing on Australian Contemporary Art 1960–1988' (PhD diss., University of Melbourne, 2006).

20 Ian Burn and Nigel Lendon, 'Purity, Style, Amnesia', in Ian Burn, *Dialogue: Writings in Art History* (North Sydney: Allen & Unwin, 1991), 97.

21 Alexie Glass and Natasha Bullock, introduction to *Parallel Collisions, 12th Adelaide Biennale of Art* [exh. cat.], curated and edited by Alexie Glass and Natasha Bullock (Adelaide: Art Gallery of South Australia, 2012), n.p.

22 Ross Gibson, '"This Prison This Language": Thomas Watling's *Letters from an Exile at Botany Bay* (1794)', in *Islands in the Stream: Myths of Place in Australian Culture*, ed. Paul Foss (Sydney: Pluto Press, 1988), 23.

23 Nicholas Thomas, *Possessions: Indigenous Art and Colonial Culture* (Melbourne: Thames & Hudson, 1999), 140.

24 Ian Burn, 'Sidney Nolan: Landscape and Modern Life', in *Dialogue: Writings in Art History* (North Sydney: Allen & Unwin, 1991), 69.

25 Ian Burn and Ann Stephen, 'The Transfiguration of Alert Namatjira', in *Dialogue*, 58–59.

26 Anne Gray, *Fred Williams: Infinite Horizons* [exh. cat.] (Canberra: National Gallery of Australia, 2011).

27 Terry Smith, 'The Provincialism Problem' (1974), in *Transformations in Australian Art*, Vol. 2 (St Leonards: Craftsman House, 2002), 119.

28 Bernard Smith and Terry Smith, *Australian Painting 1788-2000* (Melbourne: Oxford University Press, 2001), 334.

29 Taylor, *POPISM*, n.p.

30 Bernard Smith, 'The Antipodean Manifesto', in *The Antipodean Manifesto: Essays in Art and History* (Melbourne: Oxford University Press, 1976), 166.

31 Spate, 'Whatever Happened to the Art of the 'Seventies?', 77.

32 Ewington, 'Fragmentation and Feminism', 72. And another feminist critic offers a similar insight, thinking the '70s as something that runs up to and characterises the present: 'The historical era referred to as "the 1970s" was also encountered during the 1980s (as it still is now) ... The 1970s effect was not universal, and was not — as much art-historical and museological convention, and much of the current curatorial nostalgia, would have it — somehow magically contained within this decade', Denise Robinson, 'You Got to Burn to Shine', in *When You Think about Art: The Ewing and George Paton Gallery, 1971-2008*, ed. Helen Vivian (Melbourne: Macmillan, 2008), 84.

John Nixon interviewed by David Homewood

1 Paul Taylor, 'Australian "New Wave" and the "Second Degree"', *Art & Text*, No. 1 (Autumn 1981), 23–32.

Imants Tillers interviewed by Helen Hughes

1 Secondary market art dealer and critic Jane Rankin-Reid has said of this relationship: 'I would say that Paul's most significant contribution around in his first year in Manhattan was in inserting Imants Tillers's work and theories into the Manhattan Appropriation mix. ... He went in to bat for Imants in a way that he rarely did for other artists.' See note 122 in Charles Green and Heather Barker, 'Provincialism No More', on page 56 of this book.

Paul Taylor and the Brisbane sound — David Pestorius interviewed by Helen Hughes

1 This text was published as part of an artwork by Leni Hoffmann, which was first

presented in 'Melbourne><Brisbane: Punk, Art & After', curated by David Pestorius, Ian Potter Museum of Art, Melbourne, February 24 – May 15, 2010.

2 The IMA's printed announcement for the Taylor lecture includes the date, time and title of the lecture, but nothing more. In 2013, John Nixon, the IMA director who invited Taylor to give this lecture, had no independent recollection of the occasion, but agreed with this hypothesis (John Nixon, e-mail correspondence with David Pestorius, July 23, 2013).

3 Paul Taylor, *Howard Arkley: Wall Painting (Muzak Mural 1981)* [exh. cat.] (Brisbane: Institute of Modern Art, Brisbane, 1981), n.p.

4 Ibid.

5 Dan Graham, 'The Static', interview with William Furlong, in *Vision in Disbelief: The 4th Biennale of Sydney* [exh. cat.], curated by William Wright (Sydney: Biennale Committee, 1982), 191.

6 Paul Taylor, introduction to *Noise & Muzak* [exh. cat.], curated by Judy Annear (Melbourne: George Paton Gallery, Melbourne, 1981), 4.

7 All sixty issues of *Pneumatic Drill*, the one-page Anti-Music newsletter, which were issued on an occasional basis between April 1981 – October 1983, were produced as a bound volume for 'The Brisbane Sound', David Pestorius Projects/Institute of Modern Art, Brisbane, February 9 – March 8, 2008.

8 *Pneumatic Drill* [Melbourne], No. 4 (special issue: Invisible Music) (June 1981), n.p.; republished in book form as John Nixon, ed., *Pneumatic Drill* (Brisbane: David Pestorius Projects, 2008).

9 For a discussion of how Art Projects was structured as a commercial gallery, see David Pestorius, 'An interview with John Nixon in early 1999', in *John Nixon* (Berlin: David Pestorius Gallery, 1999), 8. The 'alternative' view was first given currency in the exhibition 'Pitch Your Own Tent: Art Projects | Store 5 | 1st Floor', Monash University Museum of Art, Melbourne, June 23 – August 27, 2005.

10 Heather Killen, '2nd degree art; 3rd degree theory, the new art /criticism', *Art Walk*, No. 3 (1983), 4–5.

As I was saying, — Vivienne Shark LeWitt

1 Vivienne Shark LeWitt, 'Paul Taylor 1957–1992', *Art & Text*, No. 44 (1993), 14.

2 Vivienne Shark LeWitt, 'Why Egyptian Mods Didn't Bother to Bleach Their Hair or more notes about parkas and combs', *Art & Text*, No. 3 (Spring 1981), 80–86.

3 Vivienne Shark LeWitt, 'The End of Civilization Part II: Love Among the Ruins', *Art & Text*, No. 10 (Spring 1983), 1–6.

4 Vivienne Thwaites, 'So This is Real Life? The Continuing Dissensions of New Wave Music', *The Tasmanian Review*, No. 1 (1979), 11–13.

5 Roland Barthes, *Roland Barthes by Roland Barthes* (New York: Hill & Wang, 1977), 66.

6 Paul Taylor, written correspondence with the author, May 8, 1980.

7 Paul Taylor, 'Australian "New Wave" and the "Second Degree"', *Art & Text*, No. 1 (Autumn 1981), 23–32.

8 Vivienne Shark LeWitt,'The end of civilization part II: Love among the ruins, George Paton Gallery 28 July – 26 August 1983', in *When you think about art, The Ewing & George Paton Galleries 1971–2008*, ed. Helen Vivian (Melbourne: Macmillan, 2008), 142–145.

9 'POPISM', curated by Paul Taylor, National Gallery of Victoria, Melbourne, June 16 – July 25, 1982.

10 Paul Taylor, *Tall Poppies* [exh. cat.], curated by Paul Taylor (Melbourne: University Gallery, University of Melbourne, 1983), n.p.

Everyone gets lighter — Denise Robinson

* The title of an exhibition of John Giorno poem paintings, 2013.

1 Michel De Montaigne, *The Complete Works*, trans. Donald M. Frame (UK and USA: Everyman's Library, 2003), 855–856.

2 Gertrude Stein, *How to Write* (New York: Dover Publications, Inc., 1975), xiii.

3 Reva Wolf, introduction to *I'll be Your Mirror, The Selected Andy Warhol Interviews, 1962–1987*, ed. Kenneth Goldsmith (New York: Carroll & Graf Publishers, 2004), xvi.

4 Paul Taylor quoted in Andrew Olds, 'Man on the Make', *The Bulletin*, October 25, 1988, 139.

5 Anthony Haden-Guest, *The Real Life of the Art World* (New York: Atlantic Monthly Press, 1996), 197.

6 Paul Taylor, 'Mary Boone and Michael Werner', *Manhattan, Inc.*, June 1986, reproduced in *After Andy: SoHo in the Eighties* (Melbourne: Schwartz City, 1995), 29–36.

7 'Mix Tape 1980s' was a survey of works from the 1980s in Australia, interestingly based on the NGV's extensive collection from this period, and which included many of those artists originally shown in the 'POPISM' exhibition that Paul curated at the National Gallery of Victoria in 1982.

8 Meaghan Morris, *The Pirate's Fiancée* (UK and USA: Verso, 1998), 66.

9 'Australia', *Royal Academy Exhibitions*, http://www.royalacademy.org.uk/exhibitions/australia/about-the-exhibition/; Accessed October 31, 2013.

10 It is important to note that the works of Aboriginal artists are included in this exhibition, yet they are 'contained' by this context. There is also the work of contemporary artists, a small selection, a token. There is not the room here for me to comment further.

11 Meaghan Morris, 'Two types of photography criticism located in relation to Lynn Silverman's series', *Art & Text*, No. 6 (Winter 1982), 64.

12 Paul Foss, 'Meridian of Apathy', *Art & Text*, No. 6 (Winter 1982), 74–88.

13 Produced to be installed to scale in a large display window at Rowden White Library, adjacent to the George Paton Gallery, Union Building, University of Melbourne.

14 See the contribution by Juan Davila elsewhere in this publication for a discussion of this project.

15 Adolfo Bioy Casares, *The Invention of Morel*, trans. Ruth L.C. Simms (New York: The New York Review of Books, 1964), 76. Actually I am quoting notes written by the character 'Morel' and found by the first-person narrator in the novel. The notes were to be read to his intended 'subjects'—but were never read. The 'reality' of the first person narrator is also in doubt.

Ecce Homo—Edward Colless

1 Colum Hourihane, *Pontius Pilate, Anti-Semitism, and the Passion in Medieval Art*, (Princeton and Oxford: Princeton University Press, 2009), 220–226; 328–356.

2 *John* is the latest of these canonical texts, dated by scholarly consensus at 85–95 CE, and written in Ephesus during the imperial reign of Domitian. The composition of *Mark* is attributed to a Roman author for a gentile (formerly pagan) Christian readership, between 60 and 70 CE. *Luke-Acts* was likely written sometime between the early 60s and early 80s CE for a community of Jewish converts in Antioch and draws strongly on the narrative in *Mark*. *Matthew* probably dates to between 80 and 90 CE, for a Greek-speaking community in Antioch. *Luke-Acts* and *Matthew* also have common sources in an older extra-textual tradition identified as Q. These different circumstances of composition—geographic, political, theological, rhetorical and social—provide varying proportions and vantages on the role and character of Roman law and governance of the province of Judaea, demonstrated by Pilate. Other episodes and interpretations—mainly negative—on Pontius Pilate's administration turn up in the Jewish writers Philo of Alexandria (*Legatio ad Gaius* and *In Flaccum)* and Josephus (*Jewish War* and *Antiquities of the Jews*). Philo, for instance, remorselessly refers to Pilate as cruel, violent, stubborn, spiteful, but also

weak. The recipe of vacillation mixed with callousness gives us the prominent Western tradition of Pilate as corrupt, decadent and diffident. But there is also a considerable apocrypha corpus on Pilate (most famously the *Gospel of Nicodemus* or *Acta Pilati* that may have been composed in the fourth century CE), which depicts Pilate, particularly for the Eastern and Coptic traditions, with quite divergent destinies: as a convert to Christianity, even as a martyr. In the Ethiopian church, he is a saint!

3 M.W.G. Stibbe, *John as Storyteller: Narrative Criticism and the Fourth Gospel* (Cambridge, UK: Cambridge University Press, 1992), 108.

4 Paul Taylor, 'Self and Theatricality', *Art & Text*, No. 5 (Autumn 1982), 2.

5 More accurately, his abstention is a complex of disposing judgment onto other players in the drama, and is dispersed across numerous permutations of the trial proceedings, involving not only the variously described constituencies of the 'mob' outside the *praetorium*, but also the council of the Sanhedrin and the provincial Roman legal hierarchy and its Jewish agents, such as Herod in Caesarea. For a detailed account of Pilate's characterisations in both Jewish and Christian accounts of the first century CE see Helen K. Bond, *Pontius Pilate in history and interpretation* (Cambridge, UK: Cambridge University Press, 1998).

Paul Taylor: Publications 1977–1984

Compiled by Russell Walsh

Shortly before he died, Paul Taylor compiled, typed and circulated a 'Curriculum Vitae' that included publications by and about him. It contained several errors and omitted much, perhaps intentionally, but it has also provided an invaluable foundation for what follows: a more comprehensive list of publications by and about Paul Taylor for the period of his activity in Australia prior to his move to New York (late 1984). To this end, the list also includes his Juan Davila volume, *Hysterical Tears* (1985), which was conceived and at least partly developed before his departure. (He returned to Australia briefly to launch it in 1985.) Critical responses to that publication, some emerging as late as 1986, have also been listed.

In preparing this bibliography, I benefited from the editorial support of Helen Hughes, especially, and Nick Croggon. I also remain grateful to Adrian Martin for generously sharing resources from his personal archive. At a late stage in our work, Chris McAuliffe drew Helen's attention to Paul Taylor's prescient undergraduate publications, for which we both owe him thanks. As always, Michael Graf has offered me professional and personal support throughout the project; I cannot thank him enough.

The State Library of Victoria holds most, but not all, of the listed items.

A: Publications edited by Paul Taylor

Unless otherwise stated, all issues of *Art & Text* are published in Melbourne.

1981

— *Art & Text*, No. 1 (Autumn 1981)
— *Art & Text*, No. 2 (Winter 1981)
— *Art & Text*, No. 3 (Spring 1981)
— *Art & Text*, No. 4 (Summer 1981)

1982

— *Art & Text*, No. 5 (Autumn 1982)
— *Art & Text*, No. 6 (Winter 1982)
— *Art & Text*, No. 7 (Spring/September 1982)
— *Art & Text*, No. 8, subtitled: 'What is the use of intellectuals? Pool-side issue' (Summer 1982–1983)

1983

— *Art & Text*, No. 9, subtitled: 'Image scavengers' (Autumn 1983)
— *Art & Text*, No. 10, subtitled: 'The art of appearance and the appearance of art'

(Winter 1983)
— *Art & Text*, No. 11 (Spring 1983)
— *Art & Text*, Nos 12/13 (Summer 1983 – Autumn 1984)

1984
— *Art & Text*, No. 14 (Winter 1984)
— *Art & Text*, No. 15, subtitled: 'Double trouble' (Spring 1984), joint issue with *ZG* [London], No. 11 (Summer 1984)
— *Anything Goes: Art in Australia 1970–1980* (Melbourne: Art & Text, 1984)

1985
— *Hysterical Tears* (Melbourne: Greenhouse Publications, 1985)

B: Published writings and transcripts (excluding exhibition catalogues)
Unless otherwise stated, all publications are Australian and in English.

1976
— 'Reviews: Three modern musicals...', *Lot's Wife*, Vol. 16, No. 2 (March 8, 1976), 18.

1977
— 'Cinema at Monash: Interview with James MacBean', *Lot's Wife*, Vol. 17, No. 5 (April 4, 1977), 14.
— 'Letters: Book Co-op rip off??', *Lot's Wife*, Vol. 17, No. 7 (April 25, 1977), 2.
— 'Theatre: *Tarantara! Tarantara!* & *The Club*', *Lot's* Wife, Vol. 17, No. 10 (June 6, 1977), 21.
— 'Theatre: *Waiter, There's a Circus in My Soup*', *Lot's Wife*, Vol. 17, No. 13 (June 27, 1977), 14.
— 'Theatre: *The Elocution of Benjamin Franklin* (interview & review)', *Lot's Wife*, Vol. 17, No. 15 (July 18, 1977), 22–23.
— 'Letters: Poofta bashing bashed (response)', *Lot's Wife*, Vol. 17, No. 16 (July 25, 1977), 2.
— 'Theatre: *The Cherry Orchard*', *Lot's Wife*, Vol. 17, No. 16 (July 25, 1977), 24.
— 'Films: *"Tis Pity She's a Whore"*', *Lot's Wife*, Vol. 17, No. 17 (September 19, 1977), 17 [signed: John Russell Taylor].

1979
— 'A dance of raw passion', *The Examiner* [Launceston], June 20, 1979, 31.
— Letter to the editors, *Art Network*, No. 1 (November 1979), 10.

1980
— 'Interview with Graham Murphy', *The Tasmanian Review*, No. 3 (Autumn 1980), 10–11.
— 'Is there progress in art? Suzi Gablik interviewed by Paul Taylor', *Art Network*, No. 2 (Spring 1980), 13, 76.
— 'Clement Greenberg and post modernism, an interview', *Art & Australia*, Vol. 18, No. 2 (Summer 1980), 141–144.

1981
— 'Jenny Watson's "mod'ernism"', *Art International* [Lugano, Switzerland], Vol. 24, Nos 5/6 (January–February 1981), 209–218.
— 'Editorial: On criticism', *Art & Text*, No. 1 (Autumn 1981), 5–11.
— 'Australian "new wave" and the "second degree"', *Art & Text*, No. 1 (Autumn 1981), 23–32.
— Editorial, *Art & Text*, No. 2 (Winter 1981), inside cover.
— 'The strategy of presence in two works at the Triennial', *Art Network*, No. 3/4 (Winter–Spring 1981), 30–31.
— 'A Melbourne gallery guide', *The Age*, Weekender, August 7, 1981, 10–11.
— 'Special section: Introduction', *Art & Text*, No. 3 (Spring 1981), 51–56.
— 'A portrait of an artist', *The Age*, Weekender, October 31, 1981, 24.
— 'Contemporary art and the role of the museum', in *Contemporary Art and the Role of*

the Gallery, ed. Judy Annear (Melbourne: George Paton Gallery, Melbourne University Union, 1981), 2–11 & passim [transcript of panel presentation at seminar, George Paton Gallery, Melbourne, September 17, 1981].
— 'Lip-reading', *Meanjin*, Vol. 40, No. 4 (December 1981), 529–533.

1982
— 'Learning the art', *The Age*, Weekender, January 29, 1982, 2 [signed: Paul Shark LeWitt].
— 'Jenny Watson', *The Virgin Press*, No. 10 (February 1982), 24.
— 'Self and theatricality: Samuel Beckett and Vito Acconci', *Art & Text*, No. 5 (Autumn 1982), 2–11.
— 'Special section: Antipodality', *Art & Text*, No. 6 (Winter 1982), 49–50.
— 'Angst in my pants', *Art & Text*, No. 7 (Spring/September 1982), 48–60.
— 'Artists from Australia', *The Virgin Press*, No. 17 (September 1982), 15, 17–18 [incompletely published due to editorial errors].
— '"Vision in disbelief", 4th Biennale of Sydney', *Artforum International* [New York], Vol. 21, No. 2 (October 1982), 79.
— 'Pool talk', *Art & Text*, No. 8, subtitled: 'What is the use of intellectuals? Pool-side issue' (Summer 1982), 3–7.
— 'Rosalind Krauss (interviewed by) Paul Taylor', *Art & Text*, No. 8, subtitled: 'What is the use of intellectuals? Pool-side issue' (Summer 1982), 31–37.
— 'POPISM', *Real Life Magazine* (New York), No. 9 (1982–83), 14–20.

1983
— Letter to the editors, *Art Network*, No. 8 (Summer 1983), 48.
— 'Popism: The art of white Aborigines', *On the Beach*, No. 1 (Autumn 1983), 30–32.
— 'The men of Tom of Finland', *Stuff*, April 1983, n.p.
— 'Popism: The art of white Aborigines', *Flash Art International* [Milan], No. 112 (May 1983), 48–50.
— 'Querelle' (with Adrian Martin), *Tension*, No. 1 (May 1983), 22–24.
— 'From menswear to womenswear, a Melbourne mood: Daniel Thomas interviewed by Paul Taylor', *Tension*, No. 1 (May 1983), 30–32.
— 'Items on the menu', *Art & Text*, No. 10, subtitled: 'The art of appearance & the appearance of art' (Winter 1983), 19–25.
— 'Art news', *Vogue Australia*, October 1983, 55–57.
— 'From deserts the profits come', *Art Press* [Paris], No. 74 (October 1983), 32–33 [in French, trans. Christine Piot].
— 'Tall Poppies', *Art & Text*, Nos 12/13 (Summer 1983 – Autumn 1984), 49–53.
— 'The instrumentality of Dick Watkins', *Art & Text*, Nos 12/13 (Summer 1983 – Autumn 1984), 54–58.

1984
— 'Tall Poppies', in *Art 83/84*, ed. Jean-Louis Pradel (Paris: Chêne, 1984), 12–13 [in French, translator unidentified].
— Introduction to *Anything Goes: Art in Australia 1970–1980*, ed. Paul Taylor (Melbourne: Art & Text, 1984), 6–7.
— 'Australian "new wave" and the "second degree"', in *Anything Goes: Art in Australia 1970–1980*, ed. Paul Taylor (Melbourne: Art & Text, 1984), 158–167.
— 'Art is homosexual', *Outrage: A Magazine for Lesbians and Gay Men*, No. 13 (May 1984), 40–41.
— 'Juan Davila at the Adelaide Festival', *Studio International* [London], Vol. 197, No. 1006 (1984), 20–21.
— 'Art writing', *Artlink*, Vol. 4, Nos 2/3 (June–July 1984), 47–48 [edited transcript of Paul Taylor's contribution to Art Writing panel, Adelaide Festival Artist Week Forums].
— '3 Symposia 1983–84: Introduction', *Art & Text*, No. 14 (Winter 1984), 66–68.
— 'Knowledge is the stuff of TV quiz shows: Review: *Transavantgarde International* by

Achille Bonita Oliva (ed.)', *Art & Text*, No. 14 (Winter 1984), 96–101.
— 'Pirates and mutineers', *Express* [New York], August 1984, 14.
— 'John Nixon', *Express* [New York], August 1984, 15.
— 'Editorial: Tonight a DJ saved my life', *Art & Text*, No. 15, subtitled: 'Double trouble' (Spring 1984), joint issue with *ZG* [London], No. 11 (Summer 1984), 3.
— 'Where is love? Describing Querelle' (with Adrian Martin), *ZG* [London & New York], No. 12, subtitled: 'Religion' (Fall 1984), 19.
— 'A culture of temporary culture', *Art & Text*, No. 16, subtitled: 'Burnout' (Summer 1984), 94–106.

1985
— Introduction to *Hysterical Tears*, ed. Paul Taylor (Melbourne: Greenhouse Publications, 1985), 7–8.
— 'Ventriloquists' dummies', *The National Times*, September 13–19, 1985, 30.

C: Exhibition catalogue contributions

1980
— 'Jenny Watson', in *On Paper: Micky Allan, Mandy Martin, Sally Robinson, Jenny Watson*, Survey 12 (Melbourne: National Gallery of Victoria, June 21 – July 20, 1980), n.p.
— *Recent Tasmanian Sculpture and Three-Dimensional Art* (Hobart: The Tasmanian School of Art Gallery and the Fine Arts Gallery, University of Tasmania, September 30 – October 18, 1980; and Launceston: The Queen Victoria Museum and Art Gallery, November 3–21, 1980) [exhibition and catalogue by Paul Taylor].

1981
— 'Jenny Watson', in *Aspects of New Realism*, Travelling Art Exhibition (Melbourne: National Gallery of Victoria, 1981), 46–47.
— Introduction to *Noise & Muzak* (Melbourne: George Paton Gallery, June 1981), 4.
— 'Howard Arkley: Wall painting (Muzak mural 1981)', *Howard Arkley* (Brisbane: Institute of Modern Art, July 7–30, 1981), n.p.

1982
— Untitled essay, *Eureka! Artists from Australia* (London: Serpentine Gallery, March 13 – April 25; and London: Institute of Contemporary Art, March 24 – April 25, 1982), 61–67.
— *POPISM* (Melbourne: National Gallery of Victoria, June 16 – July 25, 1982) [exhibition and catalogue by Paul Taylor].

1983
— *Tall Poppies* (Melbourne: University Art Gallery, University of Melbourne, April 26 – June 3, 1983) [exhibition and catalogue by Paul Taylor].
— *Pirates and Mutineers* (Sydney: Roslyn Oxley9 Gallery, May 4–21, 1983), n.p.
— *John Nixon: Self-Portrait (Non-Objective Composition)* (Sydney: Roslyn Oxley9 Gallery, July 26 – August 13, 1983), n.p.
— 'Popism: The art of white Aborigines', in *Maria Kozic and Tsk-Tsk-Tsk* (Hobart: Tasmanian School of Art Gallery, September 5–19, 1983), 5.
— 'White Aborigines', *Imants Tillers* (London: Matt's Gallery, October 1983), n.p.

1984
— *Juan Davila* (Adelaide: Experimental Art Foundation, Adelaide Festival of the Arts, March 3–18, 1984).
— 'As you were', *Robert Rooney* (Sydney: Roslyn Oxley9 Gallery, March 7–24, 1984), n.p.
— 'A culture of temporary culture', *Australia: Nine Contemporary Artists* (Los Angeles: Los Angeles Institute of Contemporary Art and the Olympic Arts Festival, June–August 1984), 11–14.

- *Dale Frank* (Melbourne: University Gallery, University of Melbourne, August 1–31, 1984), n.p.
- 'On photorhetoric', *John Dunkley-Smith: Installations 1979–1984* (Melbourne: University Gallery, University of Melbourne, September–October 1984), n.p.

D: Lectures and Panels (selected)

1981

- 'Art & Text in the Australian art context' (lecture presented at Institute of Modern Art, Brisbane, July 16, 1981).
- 'Contemporary art and the role of the museum' (panel discussion at George Paton Gallery, Melbourne, September 17, 1981, transcript published as *Contemporary Art and the Role of the Gallery* [Melbourne: George Paton Gallery, Melbourne University Union, 1981]).

1983

- 'Art & Text' (lecture presented at Department of Fine Arts, University of Melbourne, Term 1).
- 'Franco-Australian round table / Table-ronde Franco-Australien' (panel presented by the Association Francaise d'Action Artistique and the Australia Council, House of Latin America / Maison de l'Amerique, Paris, October 1983).

1984

- 'Art writing' (panel presented by Adelaide Festival, South Australia, March 13, 1984, transcript published in *Artlink*, Vol. 4, Nos 2/3 [June–July 1984]).

E: Publications about Paul Taylor and/or his projects (selected)

Unless otherwise stated, all publications are Australian and/or in English.

1980

- Adrian Gemelli and Lyn Gemelli, 'Paul Taylor—Art and Text' [sic], in *A Publication from the Victorian Artworkers Union* (Melbourne, December 1980), n.p.

1981

- Patrick McCaughey, 'Well-bred spaniels', *The Age Monthly Review*, May 1981, 13–14.
- Mary Eagle, 'New journal draws the debating lines', *The Age*, May 8, 1981, 10.
- Memory Holloway, 'Riding the new wave of art criticism', *The Australian*, May 20, 1981, 10.
- Terry Smith, 'Robert Hughes merely reviews', *Sydney Morning Herald,* May 23, 1981, 44.
- Judy Annear, 'Art & Text—Autumn 1981', *Art Network*, Nos 3/4 (Winter–Spring 1981), 49.
- Richard McMillan, 'Writing about criticism', *Art Network*, Nos 3/4 (Winter–Spring 1981), 49.
- Judy Annear and Merryn Gates, 'Art & Text', *George Paton Gallery Newsletter*, No. 4 (1981).
- Ashley Crawford, 'The art of new-wave', *The Virgin Press*, No. 6 (August 1981), 12–13.

1982

- Denise McGrath, 'Contemporary art & the role of the gallery', *Art Network*, No. 5 (Summer–Autumn 1982), 66–67.
- Memory Holloway, 'Art journals: Progeny of the 1970s', in *Australian Art Review*, ed. Leon Paroissien (Sydney: Warner Associates, 1982), 148–153.
- Bernard Smith, 'Critical reformation', *The Age Monthly Review*, March 1982, 9.
- Denise McGrath, 'Australian art magazines', *Bulletin of the National Gallery Society of Victoria*, April 1982, 12.

— Judith Hoffberg, 'Australia & New Zealand: On the road with jah', *Umbrella* [Los Angeles], Vol. 5, No. 3 (May 1982), esp. 54–55.
— Denise McGrath and Vivienne Shark LeWitt, 'Art and Text No. 6' [sic], *George Paton Gallery Newsletter*, No. 3 (1982), n.p.
— Suzanne Davies, 'The Melbourne scene', *Art & Australia*, Vol. 19, No. 4 (Winter 1982), 406–407.
— Denise McGrath, 'Popism', *Bulletin of the National Gallery Society of Victoria*, June 1982, 9.
— Susan Tate, 'The mediated image. "Something in the air."', *The Virgin Press*, No. 14 (June 1982), 4–6.
— Susan McCullough, 'The National Gallery has gone pop', *The Age*, June 22, 1982, 14.
— Robert Rooney, 'Mass media images recycled in Popism', *The Age*, June 23, 1982, 14.
— Ronald Millar, 'A marriage of wood and metal', *The Herald*, Final Extra Edition, June 24, 1982, 22.
— Lee Tulloch, 'Remember pop?: Now contemporary artists swing into POPism', *Vogue Australia*, Vol. 26, No. 7 (July 1982), 40.
— Suzanne Davies, 'A certain *je ne sais quack*?', *The Australian*, Weekend Australian Magazine, July 3–4, 1982, 12.
— Martin Armiger, 'Pushing the art of pop', *The National Times*, July 11–17, 1982, 24–25.
— Jeffrey Makin, 'Gallery has class', *The Sun*, July 14, 1982, 42.
— Adrian Martin, 'Popism/Art in the Age of Mechanical Reproduction', *The Virgin Press*, No. 16 (August 1982), 9–10.
— Memory Holloway, 'Popism', *Art Network*, No. 7 (Spring 1982), 16–18.
— Pamela Waite, 'Celebrating style: Popism at the National Gallery of Victoria', *Artlink*, Vol. 2, No. 4 (September–October 1982), 16–17.
— Stuart Sayers, 'Art & Text: Seeking better criticism for Australian art', *The Age*, November 27, 1982, Saturday Extra, 11.
— Robert Rooney, 'In pursuit of popism', *The Australian*, Weekend Australian Magazine, December 11–12, 1982, 14.
— new-Australian Art a Magazine Collective (Paul Drexler et al.), *Art & a Texta* [Prahran, Melbourne], December 1982.
— Annette Blonski and Jeannette Fenelon, 'Born again pop: A discussion of the exhibition "POPISM" (16 June–25 July, 1982) at the National Gallery of Victoria', *Lip*, No. 7 (1982/3), 47–49.

1983

— Juan Davila, Letter to the editors: 'Popism transgresses', *Art Network*, No. 8 (Summer 1983), 48.
— Alison Fraser, 'Popism', in *Australian Art Review*, No. 2, ed. Leon Paroissien (Melbourne: Warner Associates, 1983), 90–94.
— Martin Armiger, 'Art & Text files writ', *The National Times*, January 9–15, 1983, 28.
— Matthew Ricketson, 'Art magazines settle out of court', *The Age*, January 17, 1983, 10.
— Martin Armiger, 'A question of aesthetics (or is it ethics?) rocks the art world', *The National Times*, January 23–29, 1983, 28.
— Announcement, 'Art & Text', *The National Times*, January 23–29, 1983, 29.
— Pierre Restany, 'I luoghi dell'arte: Australia', *Domus* [Milan], No. 636 (February 1983), 75–80.
— Paul McGillick, 'What is this thing called pop?', *Vogue Australia*, Vol. 27, No. 3 (February 1983), 120–122.
— Peter Lawrance, 'Paul Taylor: Trying to bridge the arts communication gap', *The Melbourne Times*, February 2, 1983, 9.
— Peter Lawrance, 'After Popism: Authors make a tentative return', *The Melbourne Times*, April 20, 1983, 12.
— Naomi Cass, 'Discussion evening report: Paul Taylor critic, ed. Art & Text', *Fass (Melbourne University Fine Arts Students' Society Broadsheet)*, Vol. 2, No. 2 (1983), 1–4.
— Juliana Engberg, 'Maxi crop: A review of Tall Poppies, University Gallery 27th April – 3rd June '83', *Fass (Melbourne University Fine Arts Students' Society Broadsheet)*, Vol. 2,

No. 2 (1983), 12–15.

— Robin Barden, 'Tall Poppies', *Tension*, No. 1 (May 1983), 5–6.

— Rod Carmichael, 'Artscene', *The Sun*, May 4, 1983, 32.

— Sandra McGrath, 'Mutineers learn to muddy the canvas', *The Australian,* Weekend Australian Magazine, May 7–8, 1983, 12.

— Memory Holloway, 'Tall Poppies with overseas endorsement', *The Age*, May 11, 1983, 14.

— Robert Rooney, 'Taylor-made to fit a theory', *The Australian*, Weekend Australian Magazine, May 14–15, 1983, 11.

— Terry Smith, 'Notes on art criticism now', *Art Network*, No. 10 (Winter 1983), 40–41.

— Sue Cramer, 'Tall Poppies', *Art Network*, No. 10 (Winter 1983), 44–45.

— Christina Davidson, 'Interview: Paul Taylor', *Art Network*, No. 10 (Winter 1983), 46–47.

— Stan Anson, 'On being difficult: The conservatism of Art and Text' [sic], *Meanjin*, Vol. 42, No. 2 (June 1983), 203–214.

— Tom Thompson, 'Bookwatch', *The National Times*, July 1–7, 1983, 34.

— Rainer Linz, Letter to the editors: 'Wrongly implicated', *Art Network*, No. 11 (Spring 1983), 30.

— Paul McGillick, Letter to the editors: 'Criticism or denigration—A reply to Terry Smith's "Notes"', *Art Network*, No. 11 (Spring 1983), 30–31.

— new-Australian Art a Magazine Collective, Letter to the editors, *Art Network*, No. 11 (Spring 1983), 31.

— Terry Ingram, 'The state of art in Australia', *The Financial Review*, September 16, 1983, 29–30.

— Robert Rooney, 'Tall Poppies', *Flash Art International* [Milan], No. 114 (November 1983), 74.

1984

— Gordon Bull, 'Art & Text and the second degree', in *Sex, Politics and Representation*, ed. Peter Botsman and Ross Harley (Sydney: Local Consumption, 1984), 107–116.

— Meaghan Morris, 'Identity anecdotes', *Camera Obscura* [Los Angeles], No. 12 (1984), 41–65.

— Mick Carter, 'Red centre to black hole', in *Seduced and Abandoned: The Baudrillard Scene*, ed. André Frankovits (Sydney: Stonemoss, 1984), 63–81.

— Jennifer Phipps, 'Entre deux mondes: Australians in Paris', *Age Monthly Review*, January 1984, 11–13.

— Tom Thompson, 'Bookwatch', *The National Times*, March 2–8, 1984, 34.

— Neil Chow, 'Private lives: Beverly Hills' [sic], *Harper's Bazaar Australia*, No. 1 (September 1984), 164–171 (esp. 170–171).

— Robert Thomson, 'The viruses who spread an epidemic of taste', *Sydney Morning Herald,* September 8, 1984, 45.

— Robin Barden, 'Anything Goes', *Tension*, No. 5 (October 1984), 4–5.

— John MacDonald, 'An art history Taylor-made to spark controversy', *The Australian*, October 12, 1984, 12.

— Neville Weston, 'Don't panic: It's just pluralism', *The Advertiser*, October 27, 1984, 39.

— Elizabeth Butel, 'Relieving intellectual tension', *The National Times*, November 9–15, 1984, 31.

— Tom Thompson, 'Art in the 70s: A maelstrom of ideologies', *Sydney Morning Herald*, November 24, 1984, 41.

— Jude Adams, 'Seventies art replayed', *Artlink*, Vol. 4, No. 6 (December 1984–February 1985), 20.

1985

— Paul Carter, 'Roots and seeds: Art in the directionless 70s', *The Age Monthly Review*, April 1985, 9–10.

— Leigh Astbury, 'Looking at our art of the 1970s', *Australian Book Review*, May 1985, 36.

— Judith Blackall, 'Paul Taylor', *Domus*, No. 663 (August 1985), 80.

— Annette van den Bosch, 'Anything Goes: Art in Australia 1970–1980 ed. Paul Taylor (book review)', *Art-Network*, No. 17 (Spring 1985), 60.

— Elwyn Lynn, 'Davila: The problem catalyst of our art', *The Australian*, Weekend Australian Magazine, September 28–29, 1985, 12.

— Dennis Altman, '*Hysterical Tears*', *Outrage: A Magazine for Lesbians and Gay Men*, No. 29 (October 1985), 36–37.

— Peter Blazey, 'Taylor touts Chilean art star', *The Bulletin,* October 1, 1985, 132.

1986

— Paul Carter, 'A blatant rip-off: The criticism of pornography', *The Age Monthly Review*, February 1986, 14–15.

— John McDonald, 'Davila: Modern art's critical conscience?', *Sydney Morning Herald*, March 1, 1986, 46.

— Noel Purdon, 'Tackling patriarchal super-egos', *Artlink*, Vol. 6, No. 1 (March–April 1985), 18–19.

1 Monash University Union
Daily News, September 29, 1982
collection: Adrian Martin

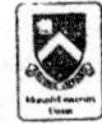

DAILY NEWS

MONASH UNIVERSITY UNION

****************************** WEDNESDAY , 29 SEPTEMBER, 1982 ******************************

MAS ACTIVITIES: Joint Function - LAST STAND BALL tickets for ANGELS CONCERT available Union Foyer today and tomorrow. Other bands are SERIOUS YOUNG INSECTS & NORTH 2 ALASKANS $11 includes glass and supper. BYO. Venue - St. Kilda.

CHONG HUA : DOUBLE FEATURE TONIGHT 7.30pm, Union Theatre. FREE for all members! Just show your membership cards at the door.

MUSICIANS CO-OP. Keep music live with a FREE JAZZ CONCERT 1pm today. ** SIMON, ANDREW & TIM ** in Music Auditorium, 8th Floor, Menzies Building, South.

THE CONNOTATIONS POST POPISM - PERFORMANCE FREE TODAY 1pm, Exhibition Gallery, Visual Arts, 7th Floor, Menzies Building. MONASH'S MUSICAL EVENT OF THE YEAR !!!!

JOHN MEDLEY LIBRARY Please return posters by 6 October - MUST be returned by this date.

Tomorrow's recital in Large Chapel features a counter-term - GEOFFREY COKER - and WILLIAM BOWER (lute) from New Zealand.

****

TODAY'S EVENTS

WOMEN'S NETWORK FREE FILM SCREENINGS - 12-1pm: Taking a part - prostitution and young women. Discussion following - Union Theatre. Then, at 1pm - film & discussion "The Power of Men is the Patience of Women" - a German feminist film.

NEWMAN SOCIETY Preparation for Friday's and Tuesday's Mass, lunchtime, Catholic Vestry.

BUSHWALKING CLUB Films, trips, great company in H4, 1pm today. ALSO .. Mems & c'tee mems formally invited to Friday's Committee meeting 1pm in Room 203. Witness decision making in its highest form. FORMAL WEAR REQUIRED. R.S.V.P.

STUDENT LIFE "A GREAT LIFE" Union Foyer 1pm.

HEALTH SERVICE ADAB Social Worker at Health Service 2-5pm to discuss any overseas student problems/queries.

CLUBS & SOCIETIES Exec Meeting 12.30pm in Committee Room. Observers welcome.

CO-REC GAMES Cricket: Swordfish v Team to Beat; Promissory Estoppel v Pirates. Volleyball: Smurfs v E. Ham Utd.; Toffs Tigers v Zoolots II.

NAVIGATORS Public Meeting R6, 1pm. "Obeying Christ: Being willing to follow Him anywhere".

TODAY'S EVENTS

CHONG HUA Committee meeting 1pm, Menzies Room 203.

EVANGELICAL UNION "Knowing God" cell group meets 1pm Arts Rms 558 & 561. Prayer mtgs in Small Chapel 8.30am, alternate Wed.

FULL GOSPEL FELLOWSHIP Prayer mtg Arts Rm 503 1pm. Come to support each other in prayer.

CRAC Committee mtg 1pm, Conference Room, Union. Affiliated groups welcome.

FILM-MAKERS COLL Meeting Arts Rm 303, 1pm.

PAC Mtg 1pm, Balcony Room.

DEPT. OF HISTORY History of the SS:TV documentary - R1, 1.05 pm. To approx. 2.30pm.

EVANGELICAL UNION Final Evangelism seminars 2.15pm, Small Chapel; 3.30 in Narthex, ON "Apologetics". Queries? See Christine.

TAE KWON DO Training 4-6pm, Games Hall.

Dr. Mary Maclean & Dr. Enid Neal - Centre for General and Comparative Literature - "Recent Developments in the Theory & Teaching of Speculative Fiction" Arts Room 310, 4.30pm.

2 *Elizabeth Gower, Howard Arkley (right) and friend*
photographer unknown

3 David Chesworth
Industry and Leisure booklet, 1982
courtesy David Chesworth
collection: Adrian Martin

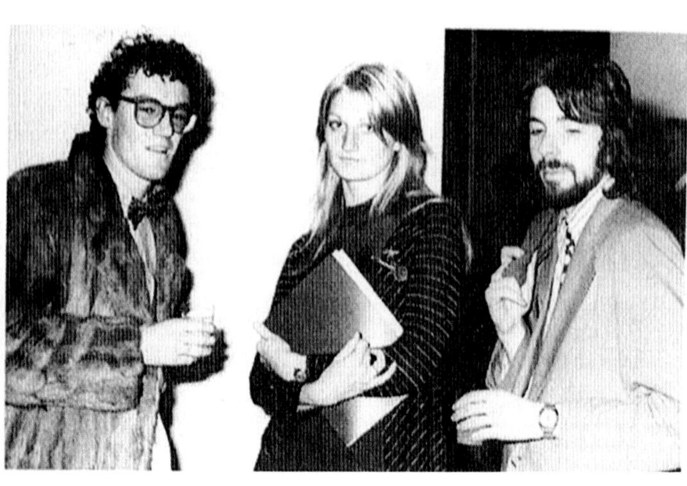

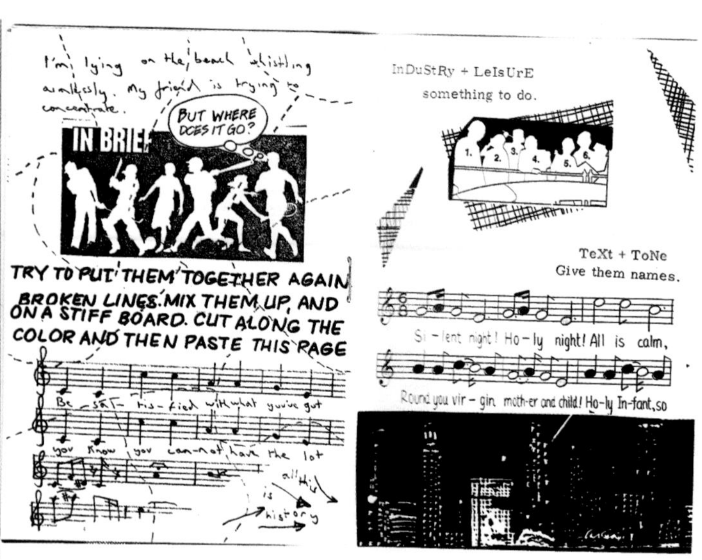

4 *Stuff*, ed. Philip Brophy, December 23, 1983, double issue
collection: Adrian Martin

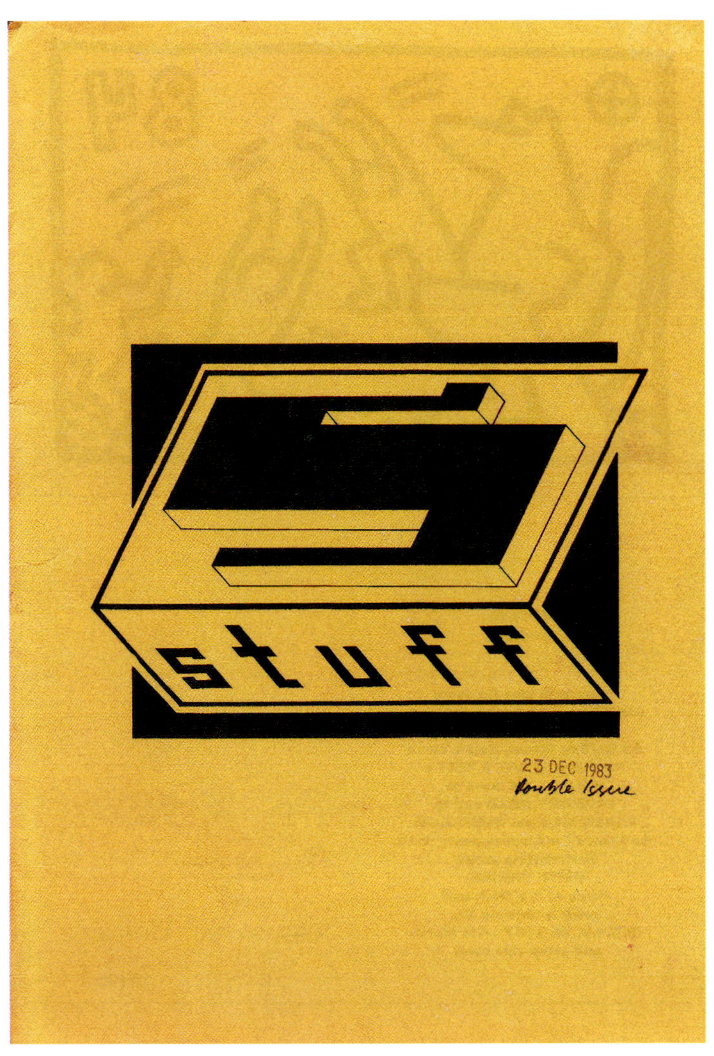

5 Invitation to Keith Haring farewell party at Beverley Hills, March 7, 1984, recto
collection: Peter Tyndall

6 As previous, verso

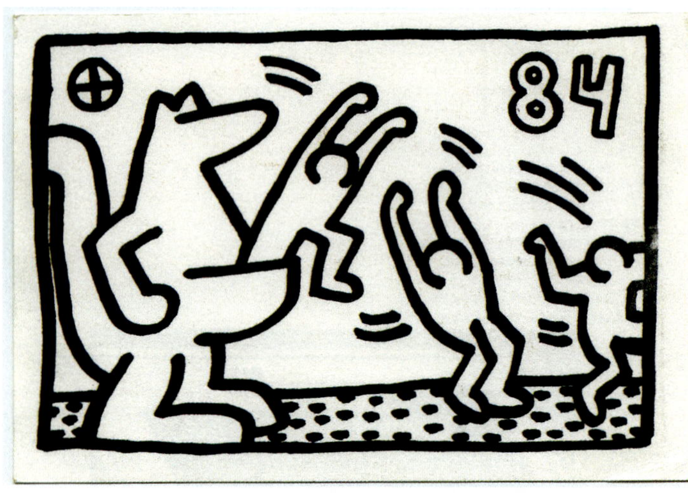

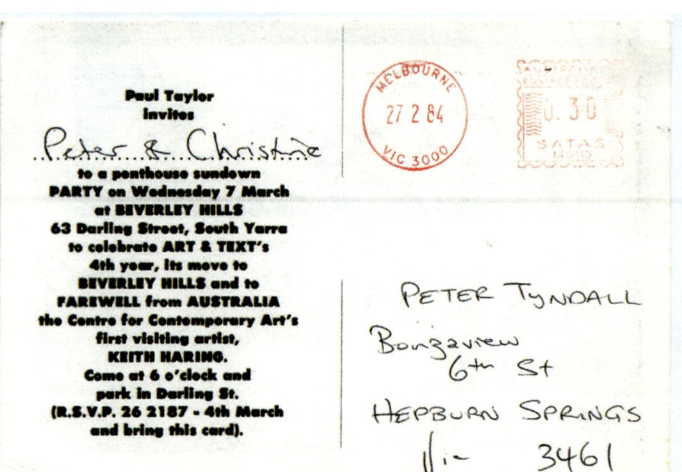

Paul Taylor
invites
Peter & Christine
to a penthouse sundown
PARTY on Wednesday 7 March
at BEVERLEY HILLS
63 Darling Street, South Yarra
to celebrate ART & TEXT's
4th year, its move to
BEVERLEY HILLS and to
FAREWELL from AUSTRALIA
the Centre for Contemporary Art's
first visiting artist,
KEITH HARING.
Come at 6 o'clock and
park in Darling St.
(R.S.V.P. 26 2187 - 4th March
and bring this card).

7 Photograph from Keith Haring farewell party at Beverley Hills, taken for *Vogue*, 1984
photograph: James Widdowson
courtesy James Widdowson

8 As previous

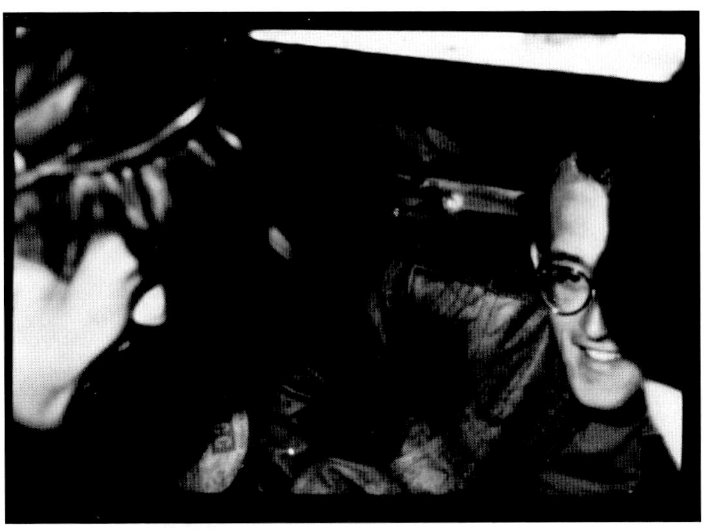

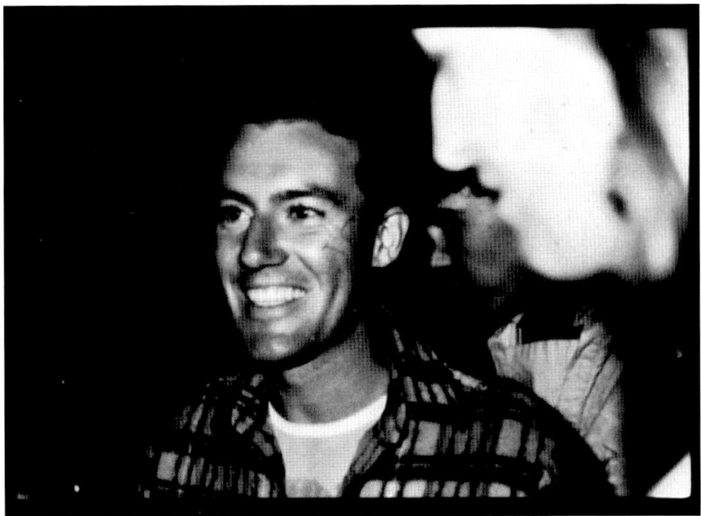

9 ‘Foreign Bodies: Semiotics in/and Australia’,
conference admittance card, 1981
collection: Adrian Martin

10 Essendon Airport, *Palimpsest* (the installation),
George Paton Gallery, Melbourne
flyer, 1981
collection: Adrian Martin

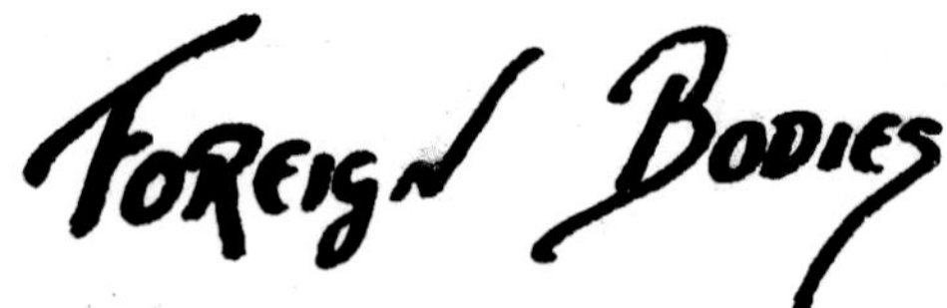

SEMIOTICS IN/AND AUSTRALIA
a conference, Feb 2-6, 1981

ADRIAN MARTIN

Admit One

No. of days 5

Signed P. Hutchings

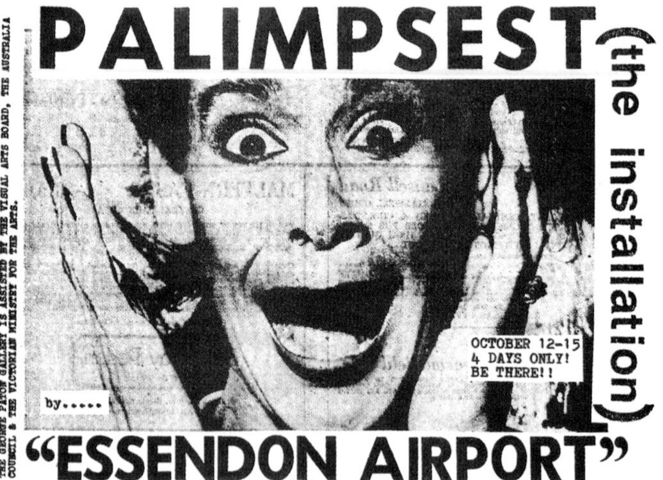

11 *Frogger*, Issue 10 (October 1984), ed. David Messer & Rex Butler collection: Adrian Martin

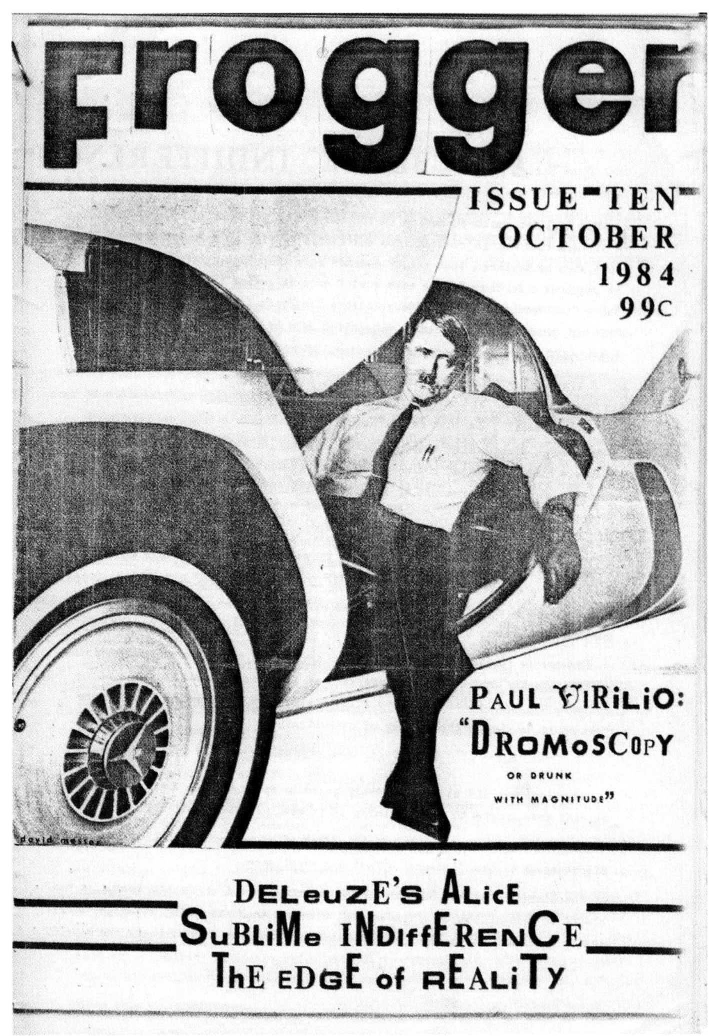

12 *Fast Forward*, Issue 10 (March 1982), ed. Bruce Milne & Andrew Maine collection: Adrian Martin

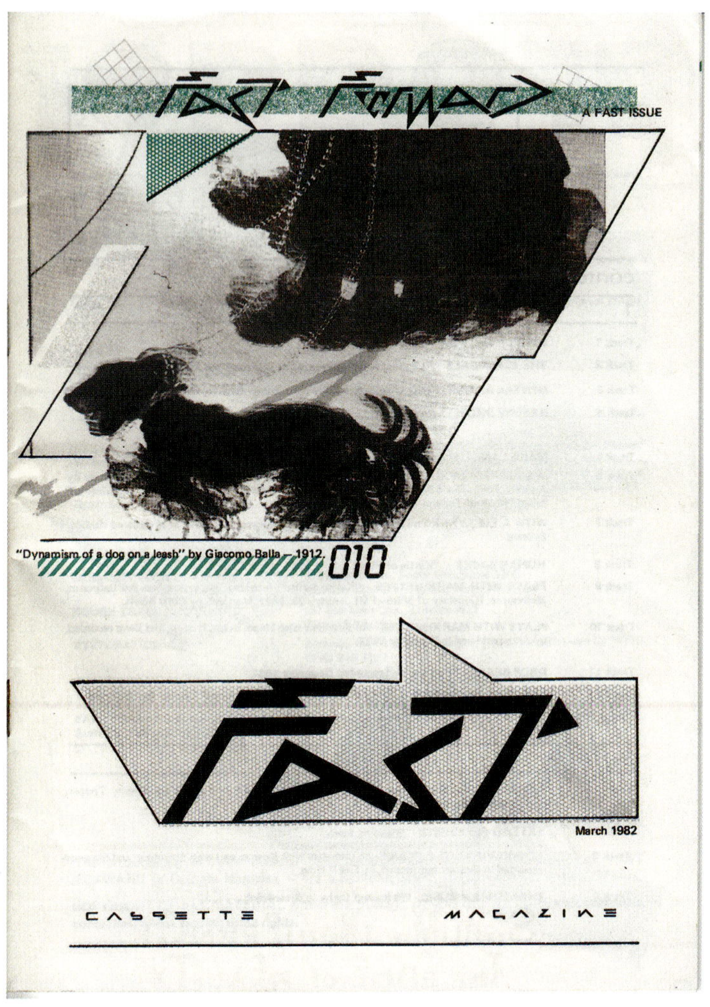

13 3RRR *Bedlam* publicity shot, 'Evening: Beverley Hills'
L–R: Philip Brophy, Peter Lawrence, Kim Beissel, Dean Richards, Merryn Gates, Julie Purvis
collection: Merryn Gates

14 *En Masse* 3RRR radio call card, 1983
collection: Merryn Gates

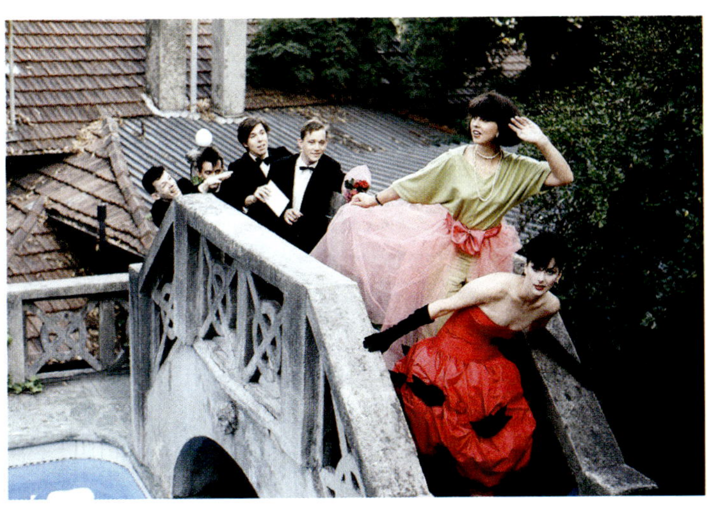

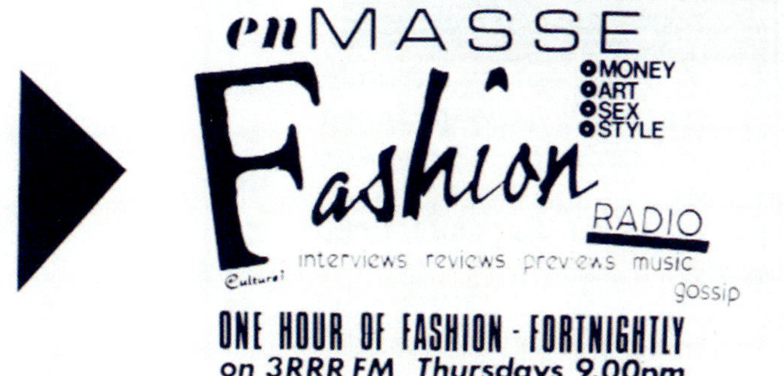

15 Mary Eagle, 'New journal draws the debating lines', *The Age*, May 8, 1981
collection: Adrian Martin

Age 8/5/81 P. 10

New journal draws the debating lines

REVIEW

Mary Eagle

THE FIRST issue of a new Australian journal, 'Art and Text', starts with the editor (Paul Taylor) calling for more considered analyses of recent art; and ends with another writer (Philip Brophy) telling us that this is what kills emerging styles.

Any journal of contemporary art faces the dilemma of whether to write about "difficult" art and thus publicise it, or to let well alone. Warring within avant-garde art since the bohemians of the 19th century have been irreconcilable impulses — on one hand, a wish to be cryptic, hermetic, a puzzle even to practitioners, and an exasperation to society at large; and on the other hand, a need to share in the vitality of society and to comment directly on it.

Taylor has committed 'Art and Text' to operating as "a healthy critical forum" on contemporary art and society. To this extent he appears to open art to public viewing.

On the contrary, Philip Brophy argues, "when the parent culture locates, identifies and names a subcultural tendency or activity, it kills the life of the subculture in one of its most productive and powerful areas — escaping naming".

(As a protagonist in a new type of art that is paraded in this issue of 'Art and Text', Brophy is himself vulnerable.)

'Art and Text' tries to position itself both within the protective subculture and outside it. Standing aside from the glossy 'Art and Australia' and the grassroots professional journal 'Art Network', it pretends to be (and sometimes is) reflective and intellectual. It is elitist. It is difficult. Nevertheless it presents avant-garde art as part of a broad spectrum of social expressions. For instance, this issue explores connections with Disco and New Wave.

There are instructive likenesses between art and these subcultures. Subcultures are fostered under a panoply of covert signs — hairstyles, earrings, cant phrases &c. Though style is not quite the subculture's substance, it certainly is its mode of communication; meanings are exchanged by indirection, through ornamentation and metaphor.

It seems jargon is indispensable after all. Need I say that this journal is full of it?

The irritating things about jargon — its obscurantism, the way it dissociates itself from ordinary speech, its clubbishness — are revealed in a new guise when we acknowledge that it is a communication which, of necessity, excludes outsiders. Jargon's potent aura is indispensable for the subculture's life and creativity.

The groupy separatism which distinguishes New Wave and avant-garde art poses a problem for 'Art and Text'. Which will it serve, the subculture or the parent culture? Through jargon it gestures towards the avant-garde, but by existing at all it threatens to destroy the conditions of creativity.

The strengths of the first issue are Brophy's book review (to my mind appallingly written but carrying a worthwhile message) and articles by two non-Australians, Giorgio Colombo and Peter Brook — who have the distinction of being the only writers to carry the burden of ideas lightly.

Its weaknesses are Suzi Gablik's sermon 'Modernism and Morality' and the off-putting didacticism of some other essays. A special journal needs new writers or else a particular approach. Janine Burke's, Ian Burns's and Memory Holloway's attitudes are already well known. Nothing distinguishes their 'Art and Text' essays from writing they do for other publications.

Brophy and Taylor are the new writers. Taylor's editorial and his other interesting essay Australian New Wave and the Second Degree suggests that he inherits more from Patrick McCaughey's mainstream teaching (Taylor is a recent graduate of Monash University) than from semiology, marxian or other schools of recent criticism. The plurality and individualism of contemporary art is obviously a puzzle to him, as is impressionistic criticism. He has the mainstream critic's urge to look for the frontrunners.

'Art and Text's ideal is a good one. If our most prolific art writers were sometimes to present their own (and to write about others') critical positions, Australian art writing would benefit.

The first issue does little more than draw the lines for what could hopefully develop into a grand ideological debate.

'Art and Text' is published quarterly and is funded by the Visual Arts Board of the Australia Council.

16 'Futur*Fall: Excursions into Post-Modernity', conference program, 1984 collection: Adrian Martin

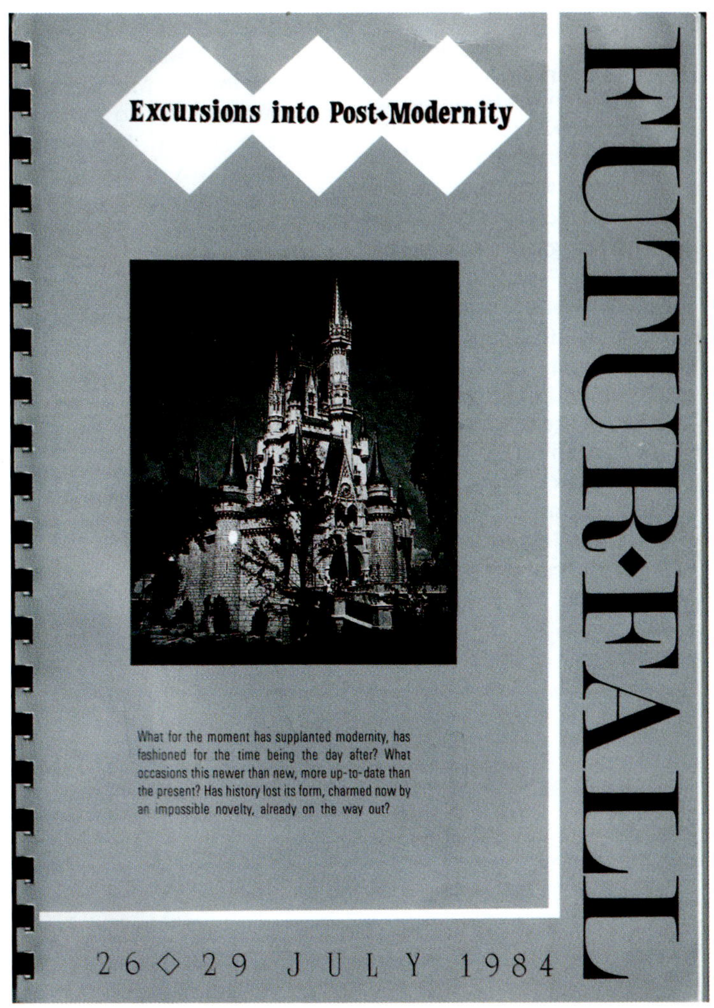

17 Review of *Art & Text*, No. 18, from *The National Times*, September 20, 1985
collection: Adrian Martin

ART & TEXT 18 ($6). Sub-titled Phantasm and Simulcra, this is a homage to the work of Pierre Klossouski, the European pornographer. It is amusing to note that in the 1980s, thanks to "the pleasure of the gaze", our many male critics can now talk seriously about semi-naked women in stockings, bound by the wrist. In the 1970s, impossible. Look what they said about the work of Geiger ("necrophiliac") or Robbe-Grillet. Now, it's just an "exorcism of the obsession", these *femmes* in underwear with males "gazing".

Edited in "New York" by Paul Taylor in Melbourne, this issue panders to current European tastes. With the absolute dearth of documentation on contemporary Australian artists, Taylor's choice of subject is peculiar, to say the least. Such choices take Taylor's reputation onward into the obsessive artistic cliques of the self-styled avant-garde, but would seem to be a blatant rip-off of the subsidy system which supports Art and Text.

☆ ☆ ☆

18 Editorial board of *The Virgin Press*, L–R: John Nixon, Ashley Crawford, Robin Barden, Paul Taylor & Peter Lawrence, 1983 photograph: Jenny Watson

19 Paul Taylor, untitled postcard, *Art Network*, No. 8 (Summer 1983), 48 collection: Adrian Martin

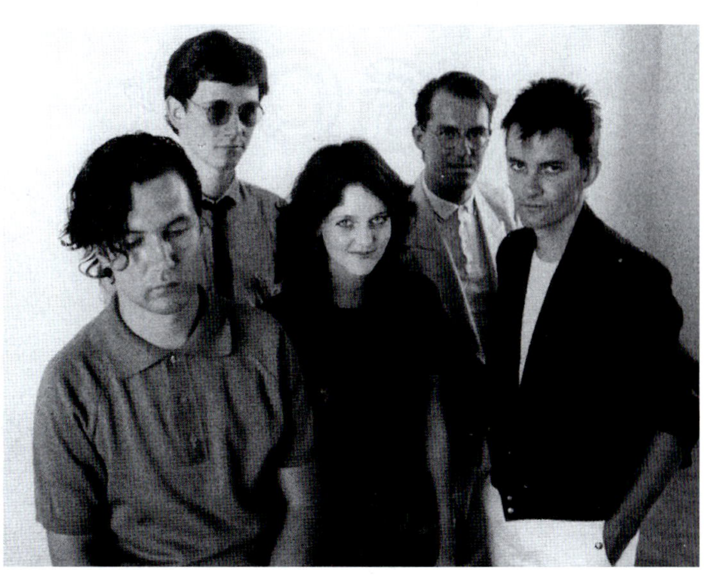

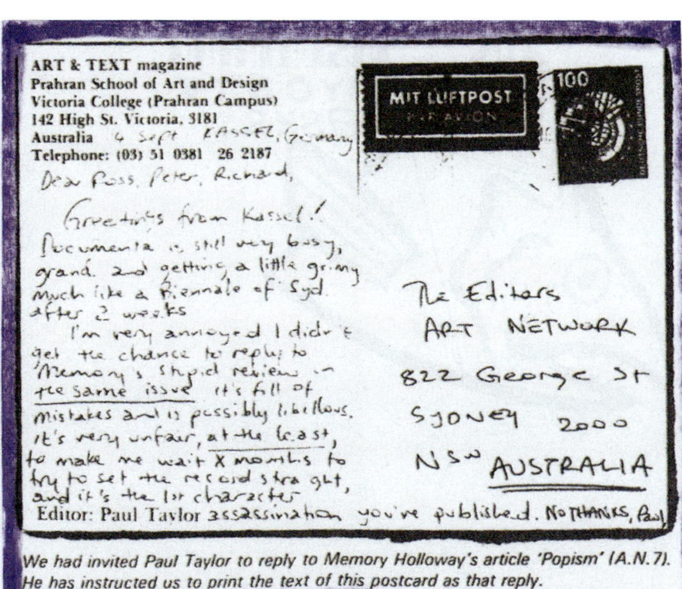

ART & TEXT magazine
Prahran School of Art and Design
Victoria College (Prahran Campus)
142 High St. Victoria, 3181
Australia 4 Sept KASSEL, Germany
Telephone: (03) 51 0381 26 2187

Dear Ross, Peter, Richard,

Greetings from Kassel!
Documenta is still very busy, grand and getting a little grimy much like a Biennale of Syd. after 2 weeks
I'm very annoyed I didn't get the chance to reply to Memory's stupid review in the same issue it's full of mistakes and is possibly libellous. It's very unfair, at the least, to make me wait X months to try to set the record straight, and it's the 1st character assassination you've published. NO THANKS, Paul

Editor: Paul Taylor

MIT LUFTPOST
PAR AVION

100

The Editors
ART NETWORK
822 George St
SYDNEY 2000
NSW AUSTRALIA

We had invited Paul Taylor to reply to Memory Holloway's article 'Popism' (A.N.7). He has instructed us to print the text of this postcard as that reply.

20 *Cargo*, Summer 1984,
a Dreamflesh production
collection: Adrian Martin

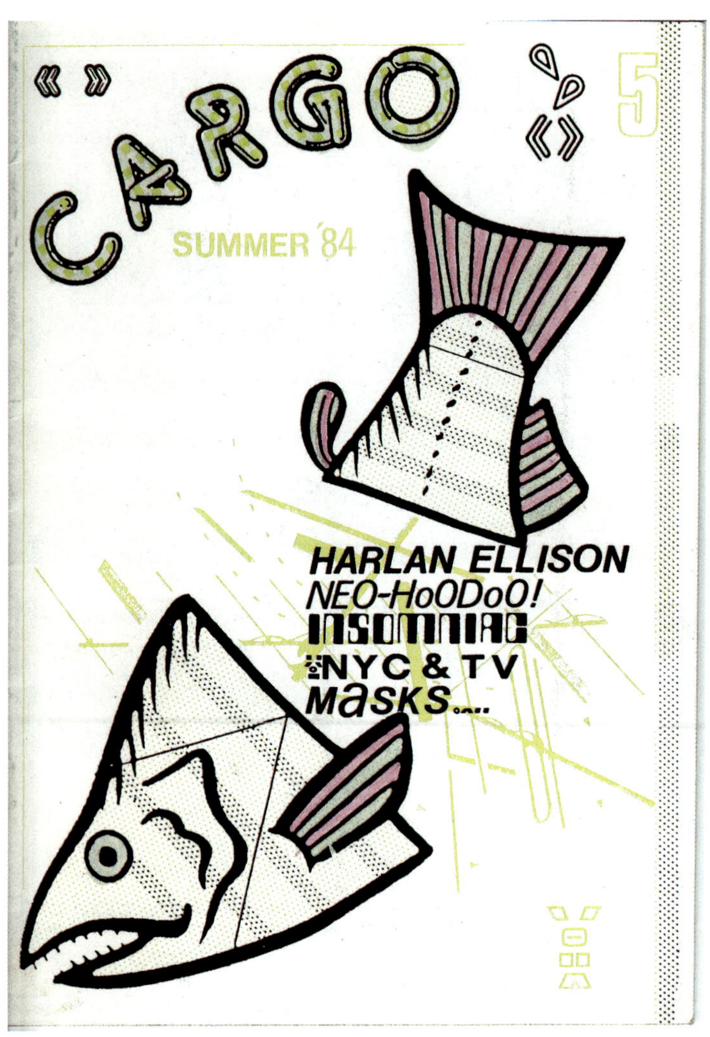

21 'Waiting for Technology', *n*-space exhibition at Yuill/Crowley Gallery, Sydney, 1983, flyer collection: Imants Tillers

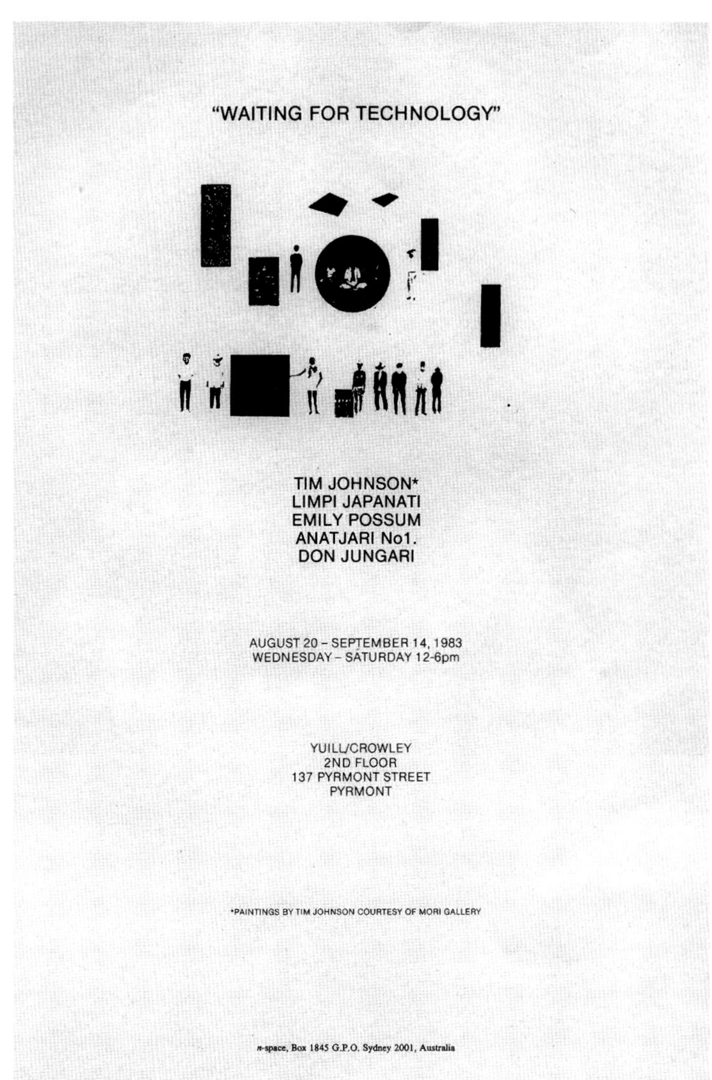

22 Paul Taylor, c. 1981
photograph: Maria Kozic
collection: Philip Brophy

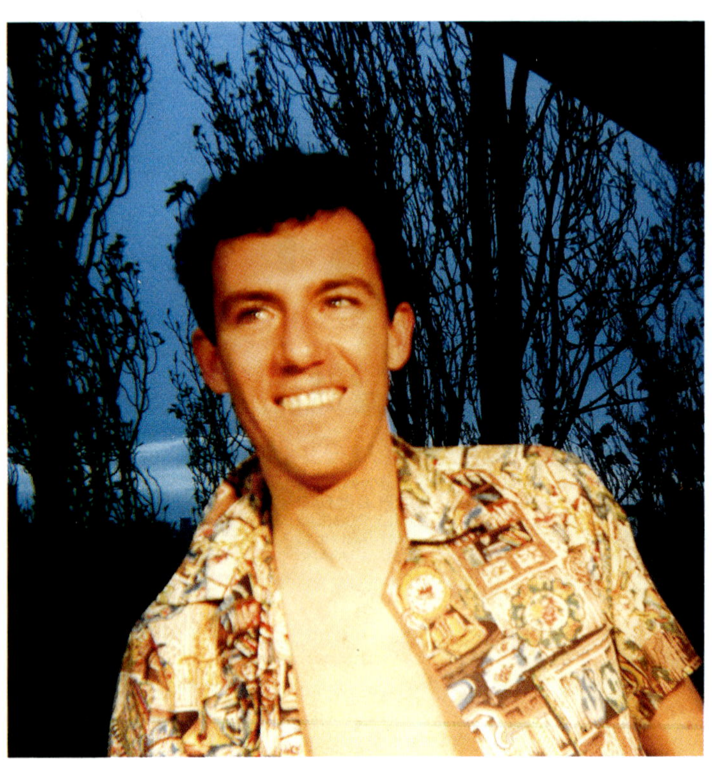

23 Illustration to Philip Brophy's paper, 'Theoretical drag and textual disco: I was a drummer in *Art & Text*', at 'Impresario: Paul Taylor / *Art & Text* / POPISM', collection: Philip Brophy

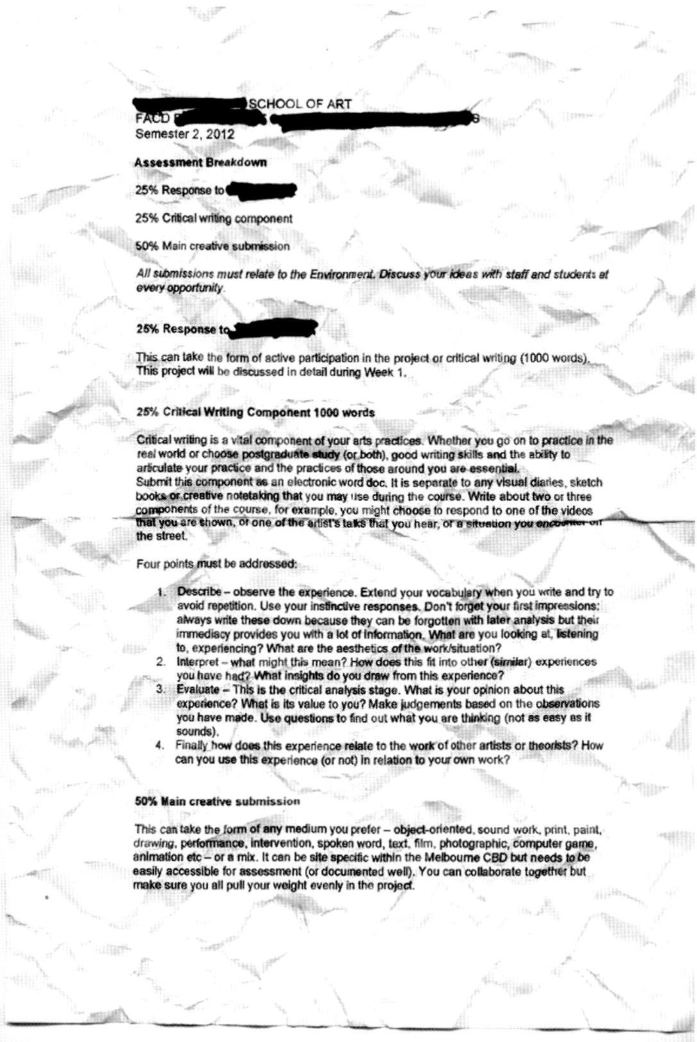

SCHOOL OF ART
FACD
Semester 2, 2012

Assessment Breakdown

25% Response to

25% Critical writing component

50% Main creative submission

All submissions must relate to the Environment. Discuss your ideas with staff and students at every opportunity.

25% Response to

This can take the form of active participation in the project or critical writing (1000 words). This project will be discussed in detail during Week 1.

25% Critical Writing Component 1000 words

Critical writing is a vital component of your arts practices. Whether you go on to practice in the real world or choose postgraduate study (or both), good writing skills and the ability to articulate your practice and the practices of those around you are essential.
Submit this component as an electronic word doc. It is separate to any visual diaries, sketch books or creative notetaking that you may use during the course. Write about two or three components of the course, for example, you might choose to respond to one of the videos that you are shown, or one of the artist's talks that you hear, or a situation you encounter on the street.

Four points must be addressed:

1. Describe – observe the experience. Extend your vocabulary when you write and try to avoid repetition. Use your instinctive responses. Don't forget your first impressions: always write these down because they can be forgotten with later analysis but their immediacy provides you with a lot of information. What are you looking at, listening to, experiencing? What are the aesthetics of the work/situation?
2. Interpret – what might this mean? How does this fit into other (similar) experiences you have had? What insights do you draw from this experience?
3. Evaluate – This is the critical analysis stage. What is your opinion about this experience? What is its value to you? Make judgements based on the observations you have made. Use questions to find out what you are thinking (not as easy as it sounds).
4. Finally how does this experience relate to the work of other artists or theorists? How can you use this experience (or not) in relation to your own work?

50% Main creative submission

This can take the form of any medium you prefer – object-oriented, sound work, print, paint, drawing, performance, intervention, spoken word, text, film, photographic, computer game, animation etc – or a mix. It can be site specific within the Melbourne CBD but needs to be easily accessible for assessment (or documented well). You can collaborate together but make sure you all pull your weight evenly in the project.

24 Paul Taylor, Hobart, 1980
silver gelatin photograph
40 × 30.5 cm
photograph: Noel Frankham

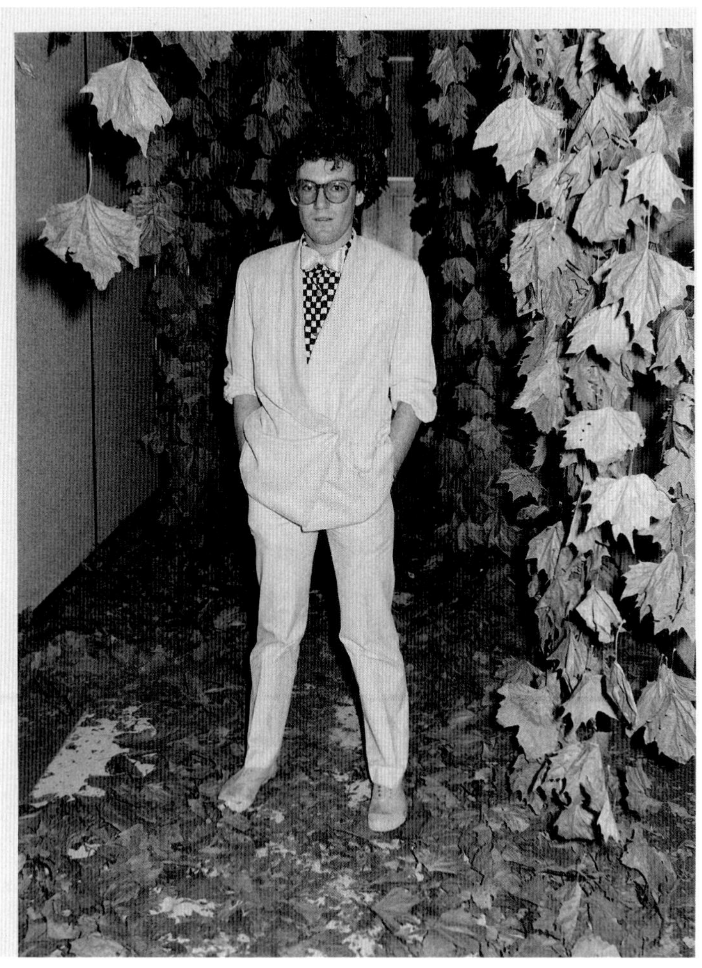

25 Linda Jackson and Paul Taylor at the 'Apparel Show', Tasmanian School of Art Gallery, Mt Nelson, Hobart, 1980
photograph: Noel Frankham

26 Denise Robinson and Paul Taylor, Paul's apartment, New York, 1988
photograph: John Williams

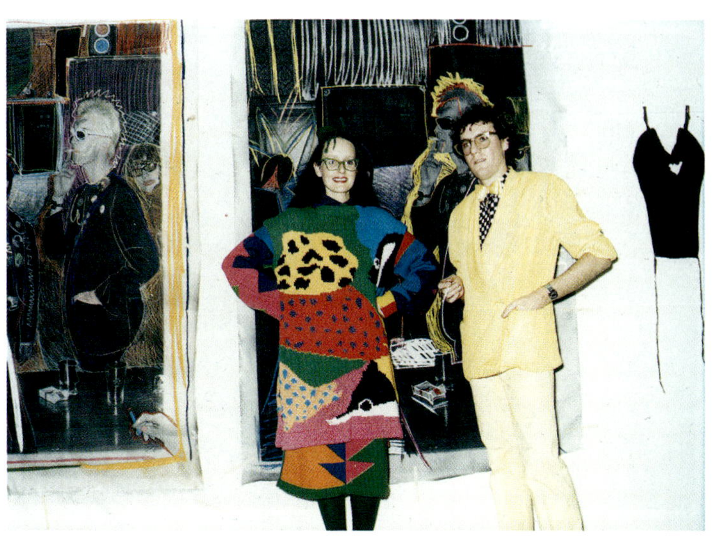

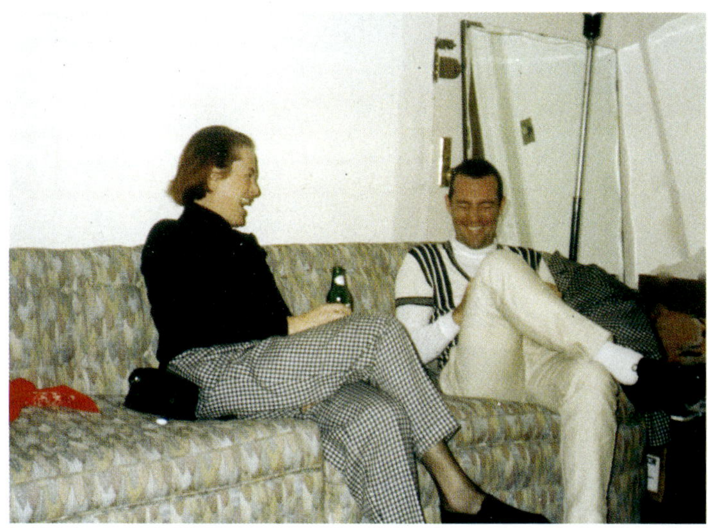

27 Ernie Althoff performing at Clifton Hill Community Music Centre, c. 1979–80
photograph: David Chesworth

28 L–R: Robert Goodge, Rainer Linz and David Chesworth performing David Chesworth's *50 Synthesizer Greats* at CHCMC, c. 1979–80
photographer unknown

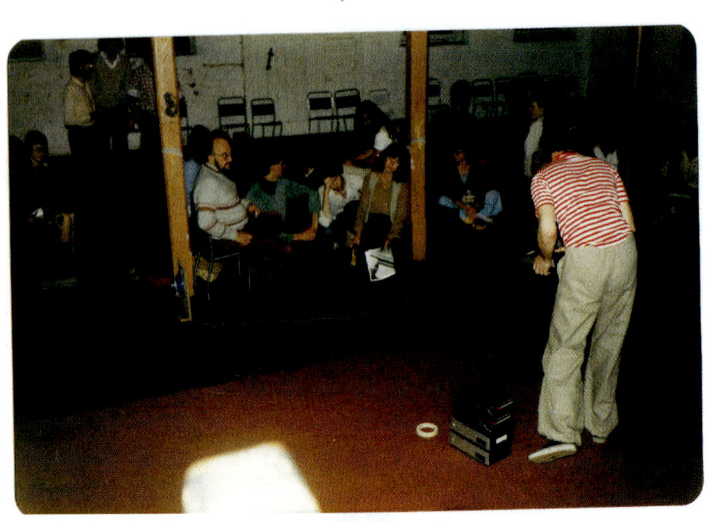

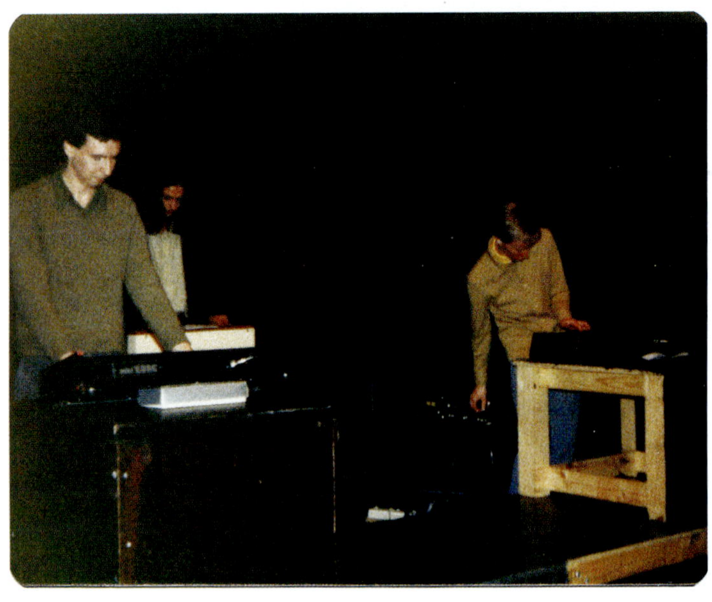

29 →↑→ performance with Jayne Stevenson and Maria Kozic at CHCMC, c. 1979–80
photograph: David Chesworth

30 Invitation to Paul Taylor's production of *Play* (1962) by Samuel Beckett, titled 'Play-Reading', at CHCMC, March 31, 1982
collection: Peter Tyndall

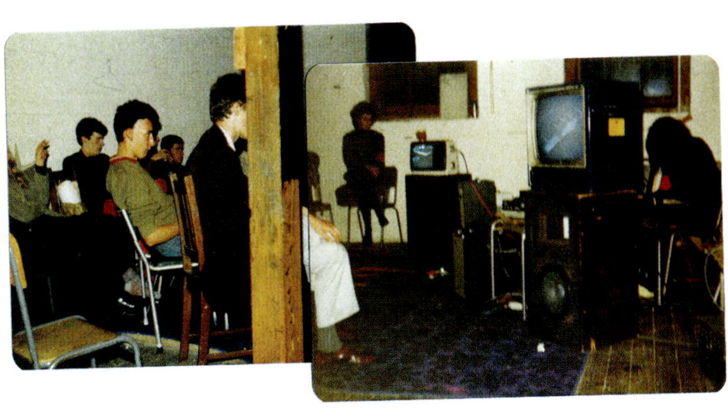

CLIFTON HILL MUSIC CENTRE **6 - 10 Page Street Clifton Hill**

admission is free
both performances commence at 8.30

MONDAY
29
March

Paul Taylor's
Production of Play (1962)
by Samuel Beckett:

PLAY-READING
(1979-82)

with

First Woman	**Lyndal Jones**
Second Woman	**Vivienne Shark LeWitt**
Man	**Philip Brophy**

One performance only

WEDNESDAY
31
March

INDUSTRY AND LEISURE
by David Chesworth

Plurality is a steady state.
The title is an element of the multiple.
Take it and use it. Create the method.
Use the things you know.
Make use of your circumstances.
Your Industry/Leisure. Give to it your own.
Isolate. Connect. Move through and beyond.
Describe discourses, regions, locations.
Work between the layers, forming patterns and pathways.
Refer to, find, and include this and that, then try again.

Cassette and booklet available. Send $5 to Praxis Inc. 46 South Terrace, Fremantle, W.A. 6160 or Innocent Records, PO Box 222 Northcote, Vic. 3070

31 Janine Burke, 1981
photograph: Sue Ford
collection: Monash Gallery of Art, Melbourne

32 'At Heide: Paul Taylor', 1982
photograph: Janine Burke
courtesy Janine Burke

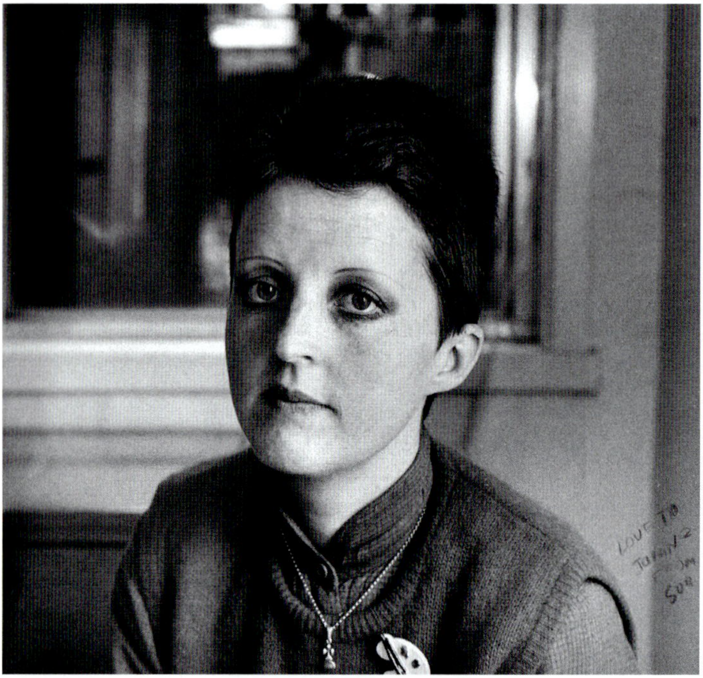

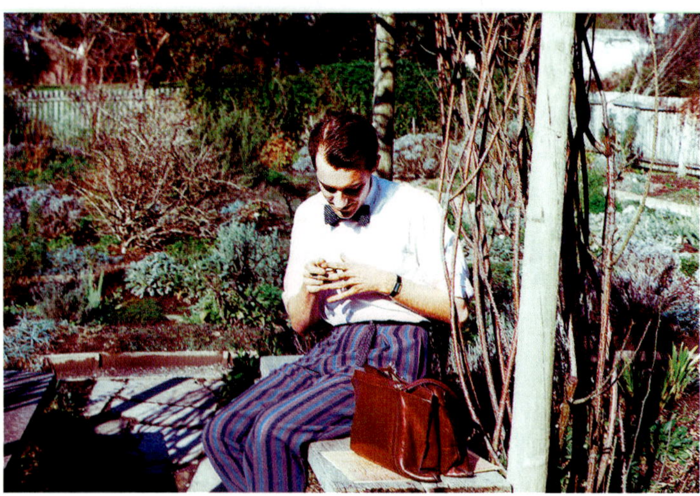

33 Paul Taylor looks at the work of Peter Tyndall, Aperto, Venice Biennale, 1988
photograph: Peter Tyndall
courtesy Peter Tyndall

34 The Society for Other Photography, *Lot 3* (detail), 1980–81
SX70 Polaroid colour photographs, installed at Pestorius Sweeney House, Brisbane, July 2012

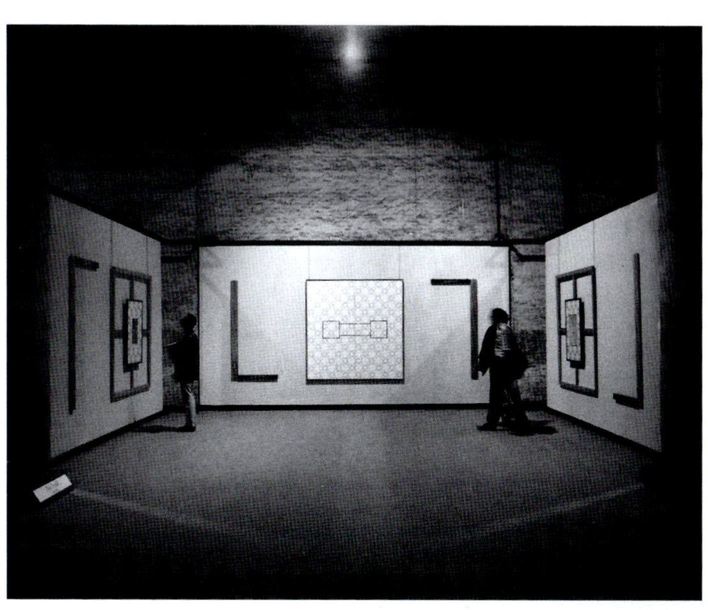

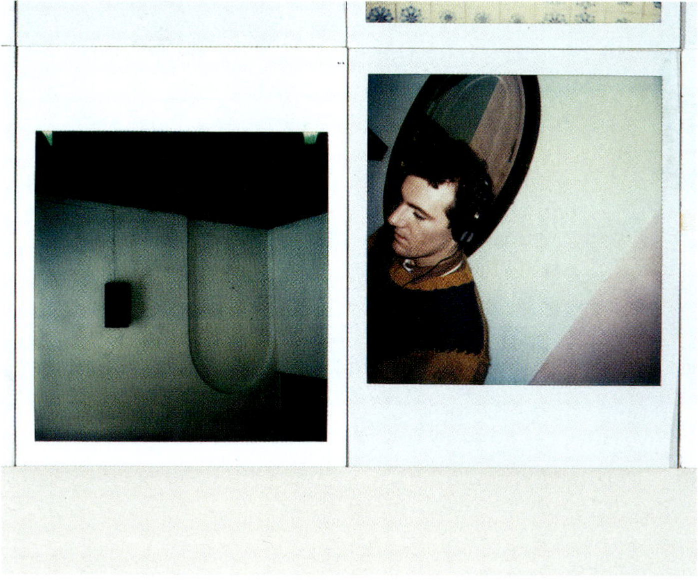

35 Vivienne Shark LeWitt and Paul Taylor, Macgeorge House, Melbourne, 1984
collection: Ian Potter Museum of Art, University of Melbourne

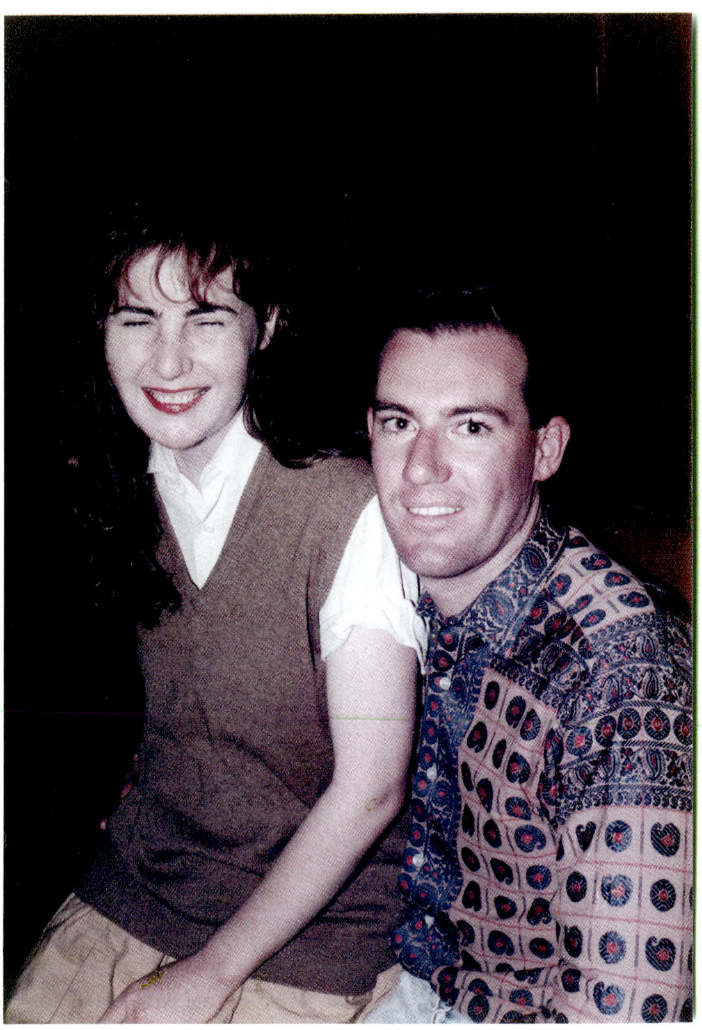

36 Back cover of *After Andy: SoHo in the Eighties* (Melbourne: Schwartz City, 1995)
collection: Helen Hughes

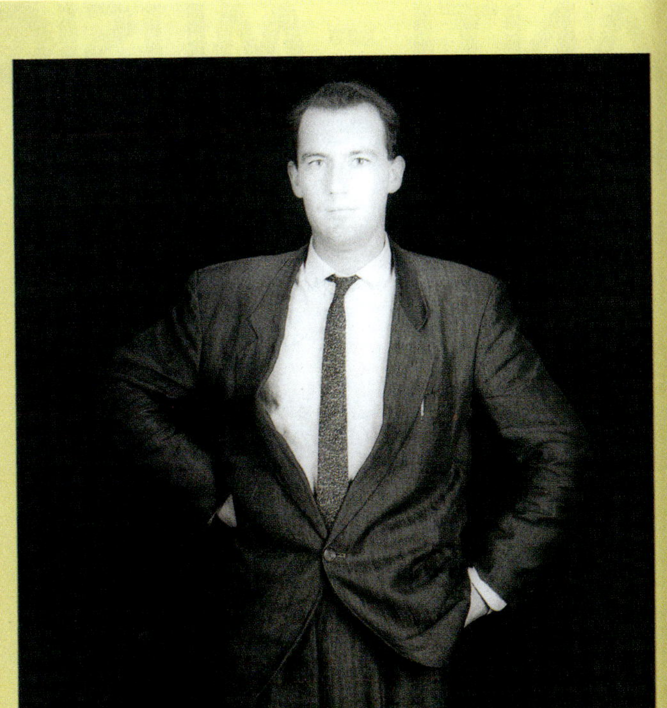

37 *Pneumatic Drill*, No. 60 (1983), subtitled: 'The Art of White Aborigines (P.T.)'
courtesy John Nixon
collection: David Pestorius

ANTI - MUSIC©

PNEUMATIC DRILL

THE ART OF WHITE ABORIGINES (P.T.)
A NEWSLETTER ON ANTI-MUSIC

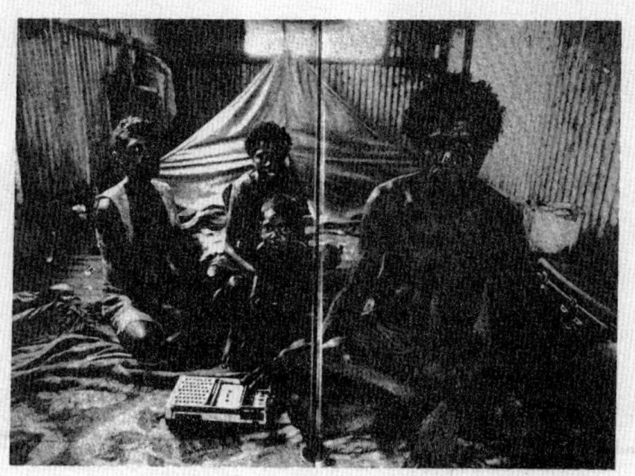

60 1983

C/- ART PROJECTS. 566 LONSDALE ST., MELBOURNE. 3000

38 Performance still from David Chesworth's *Industry and Leisure*, 1982
photographer unknown
collection: David Chesworth

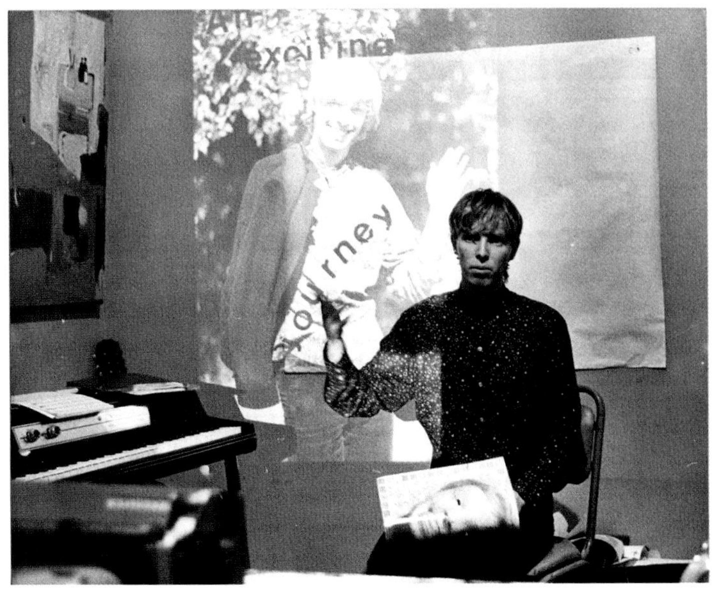

39 'POPISM' exhibition catalogue, National Gallery of Victoria, Melbourne, 1982
collection: Adrian Martin

POPISM

16 June - 25 July 1982, National Gallery of Victoria

Howard Arkley
David Chesworth
Ian Cox
Juan Davila
Richard Dunn
Paul Fletcher
Maria Kozic
Robert Rooney
Jane Stevenson
The Society for Other Photography
Imants Tillers
Peter Tyndall
Jenny Watson

The National Gallery of Victoria welcomes the opportunity of this exhibition to re-affirm its interest and concern with contemporary art and with the living artist. As a public gallery it has a responsibility to exhibit the latest developments in the visual arts so that people unfamiliar with the idiom of recent art can begin to come to terms with it. One crucial function of a public gallery is to provide a bridge between the living artist and the community which is frequently baffled by the experimental edge of art.

Discovering contemporary art can be a challenge. It requires an open mind as well as a critical one. I invite the gallery goers to this exhibition, to share the excitement and the challenge contemporary art offers.

Patrick McCaughey
Director
4.6.82

Exhibition and catalogue essay by Paul Taylor.
ISBN 0 7241 0086 5

This exhibition was made possible by a financial grant from the Victorian Ministry for the Arts

40 'Tall Poppies' exhibition catalogue, University Art Gallery, University of Melbourne, Melbourne, 1983
collection: Judy Annear

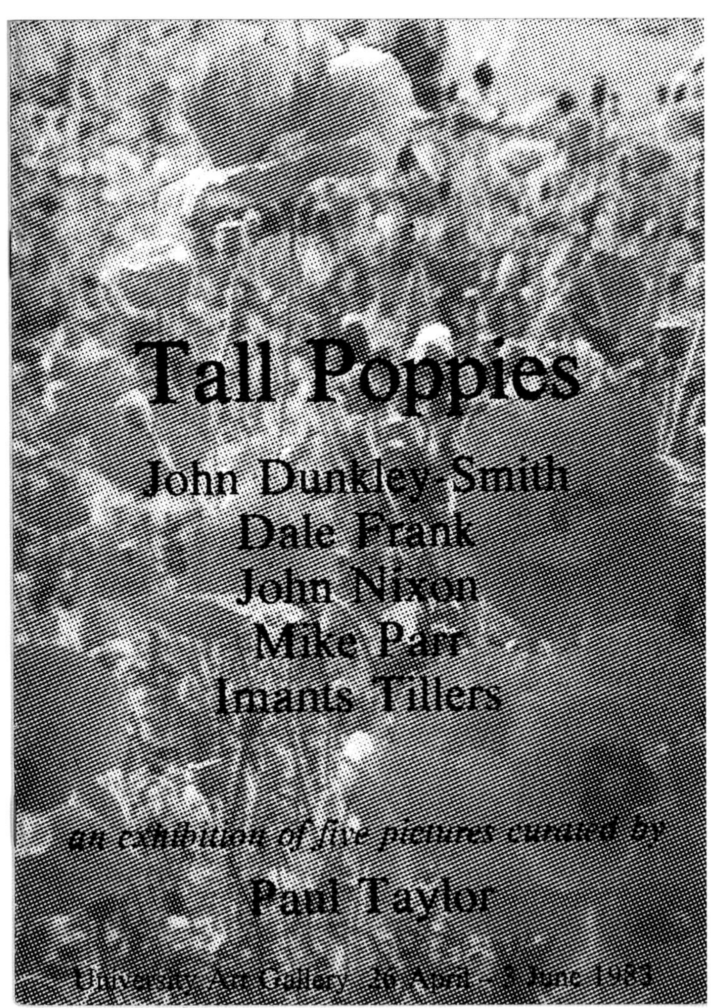

41 John Nixon, 1982
photograph: Robert Rooney
courtesy Robert Rooney

42 Jenny Watson, 1982
photograph: Robert Rooney
courtesy Robert Rooney

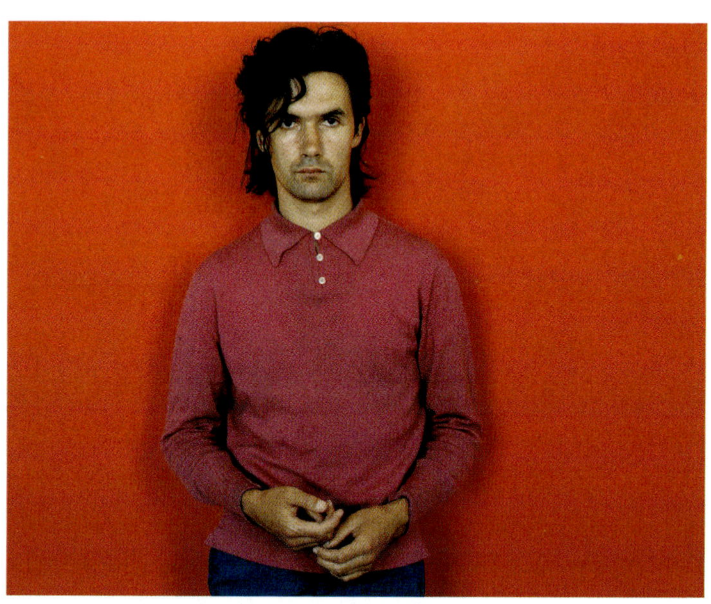

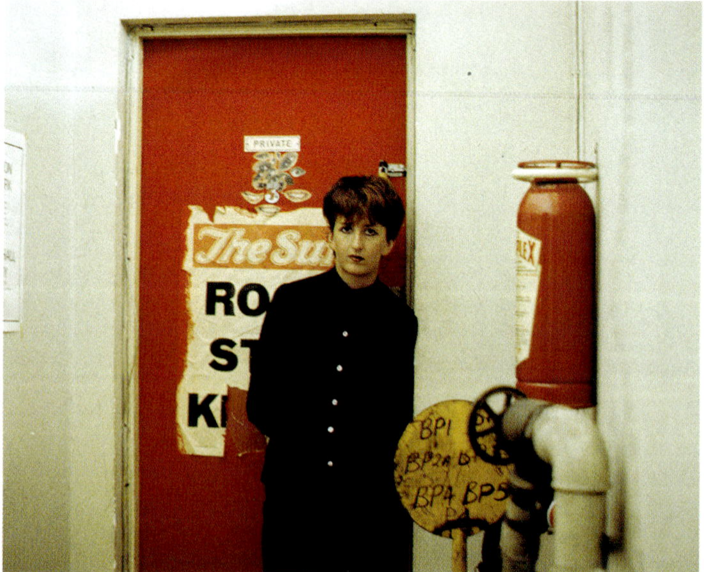

43 Howard Arkley, 1982
photograph: Robert Rooney
courtesy Robert Rooney

44 Philip Brophy & Maria Kozic, 1982
photograph: Robert Rooney
courtesy Robert Rooney

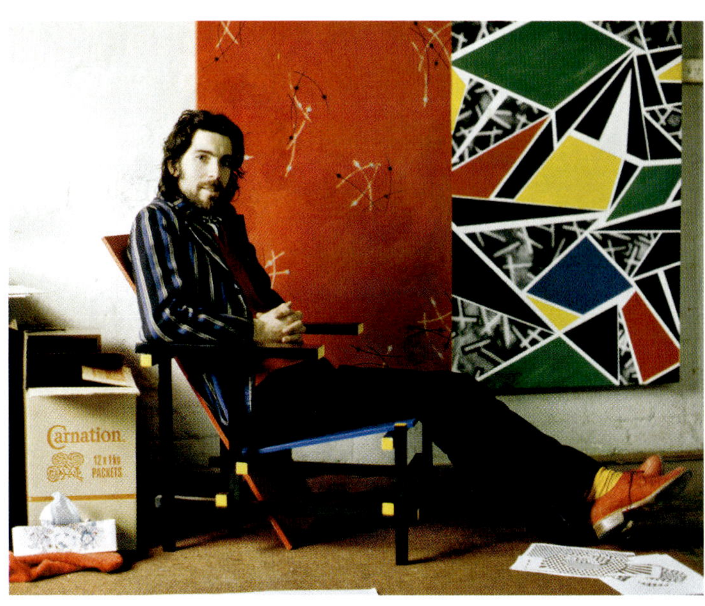

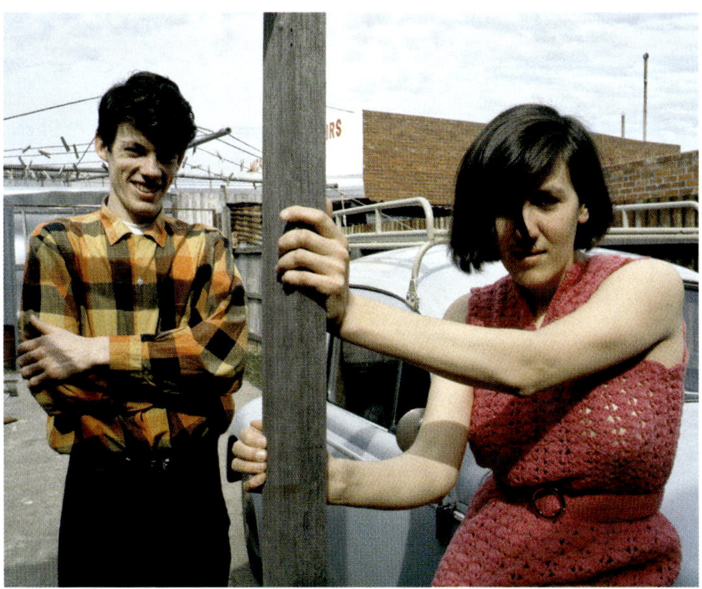

45 Paul Taylor, 1982
photograph: Robert Rooney
courtesy Robert Rooney

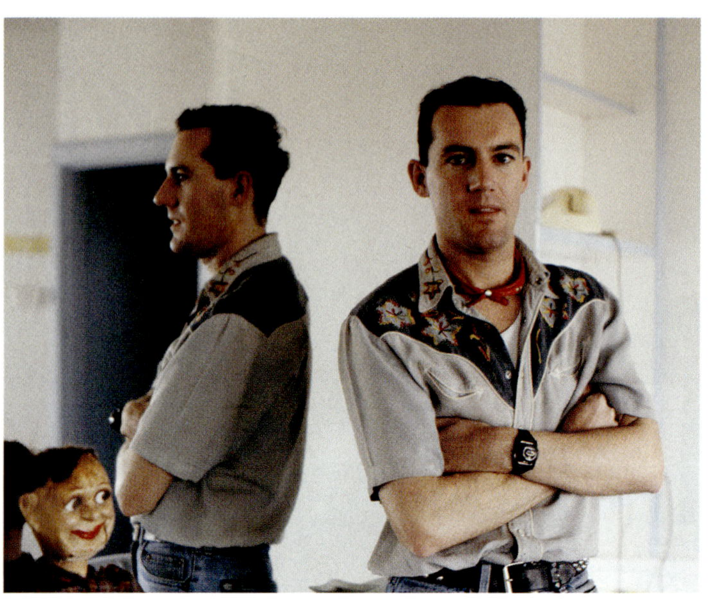

Index

Page numbers in bold refer to illustrations

Contributor biographies

Adrian Martin is Associate Professor of Film Studies at Monash University, Melbourne, Distinguished Visiting Professor at Goethe University, Frankfurt, and author of *Last Day Every Day* (Brooklyn, NY: punctum books, English, Spanish and Portuguese editions, 2012).

Ashley Crawford is a freelance cultural critic based in Melbourne. He has written on the arts for *The Age*, *The Australian*, *The Financial Review* and *The Sydney Morning Herald* newspapers and *Australian Art Collector*, *Art World*, *Art Monthly*, *Eyeline* and numerous other magazines. He is the author of a number of books on Australian art including *Spray: The Work of Howard Arkley* (Craftsman House), *Wimmera: The Work of Philip Hunter* (Thames & Hudson), *Gelderland: The Work of Stephen Bush* (Sante Fe Museum) and *First Life* (Xin Dong Cheng Art Space, Beijing/24Hour Art, Darwin). He is the former editor of *World Art*, *21.C* and *Photofile* magazines.

Professor **Charles Green** works in the art history program of the School of Culture and Communication at the University of Melbourne. He is co-authoring a book on the historiography of contemporary Australian art between 1960 and 1988 with Heather Barker.

Chris McAuliffe is an Honorary Fellow at the Australian Centre, School of Culture and Communication, the University of Melbourne. He was Director of the Ian Potter Museum of Art at the University of Melbourne from 2000–13.

David Chesworth's art practice involves several diverse areas of music and installation art. His work explores ideas about language and representation within broader cultural contexts. He regularly collaborates with Sonia Leber in the creation of large-scale installation artworks using sound, video, and architectural spaces.

David Homewood is a Melbourne-based writer and curator.

David Pestorius is a curator and gallerist based in Brisbane. His projects include 'Melbourne >< Brisbane: Punk, Art & After' (Ian Potter Museum of Art, Melbourne, 2010), and 'The Brisbane Sound' (Institute of Modern Art, Brisbane, 2008).

Denise Robinson is an independent curator and writer living in London. Major projects in recent years include Artistic Director, Arnolfini, Bristol, and Curator, Cyprus Pavilion, Venice Biennale, 2007. She was the Director of the George Paton Gallery, Melbourne, 1981–1985.

Edward Colless is Head of Critical and Theoretical Studies at the Victorian College of the Arts. He has worked in theatre, film, and architecture, been a curator and a travel writer, but mainly writes as cryptically as possible about art.

Graham Willett researches and celebrates Australian gay and lesbian history. He is a committee member of the Australian Lesbian and Gay Archives.

Dr **Heather Barker** is an independent scholar based in regional Victoria. She is co-authoring a book on the historiography of contemporary Australian art between 1960 and 1988 with Charles Green.

Helen Hughes is the co-founder and co-editor of the Australian contemporary art journal *Discipline*, and a co-editor of the online art history journal *emaj*. She is a PhD candidate in Art History at the University of Melbourne.

Ian McLean is Research Professor of Contemporary Art at the University of Wollongong. He has published extensively on Australian art and particularly Aboriginal art within a contemporary context. His books include *Arte Indigena Contemporaneo en Australien* (IVAM Institut Valencia d'Art Modern, Valencia, with Erica Izett), *How Aborigines Invented the Idea of Contemporary Art* (Institute of Modern Art), *White Aborigines Identity Politics in Australian Art* (Cambridge University Press), and *Art of Gordon Bennett* (Craftsman House, with a chapter by Gordon Bennett).

Imants Tillers is one of Australia's most internationally acclaimed contemporary artists. He has had solo survey shows at such prestigious venues as the Institute of Contemporary Arts in London (1988), the National Art Museum, Riga, Latvia (1993), and the Museum of Contemporary Art in Monterrey, Mexico (1999), and a major retrospective at the National Gallery of Australia, Canberra (2006). In 2013, he delivered his first lecture outside Australia, 'The Antipodean Dream', in the Reynolds Room at the Royal Academy in London.

Dr **Janine Burke** is an art historian, novelist and freelance curator who has published more than twenty books. She is an Adjunct Lecturer at Monash University.

Jenny Watson is a Queensland-based artist. Her work was included in 'POPISM' and was written about extensively in early *Art & Text.*

John Nixon is an artist, musician (leader of The Donkey's Tail), independent curator, publisher and lecturer in contemporary practice at Monash Art Design and Architecture, Melbourne. He exhibits regularly at Anna Schwartz Gallery in Melbourne.

Jonathan Holmes is Emeritus Professor and Honorary Fellow at the University of Tasmania's College of the Arts. He writes on recent Australian art and over the past three decades has curated many exhibitions for the University of Tasmania's Plimsoll Gallery.

Jon Dale writes for *Uncut* (UK) and teaches at the University Of Melbourne and Swinburne University Of Technology. He is currently completing a PhD on English post-punk and conceptual art practice. He is also working on his first book, dedicated to Australian post-punk and DIY.

Juan Davila is a Melbourne-based artist. His work was included in the 1982 exhibition 'POPISM', he wrote articles for *Art & Text*, and in 1985 he produced the monograph *Hysterical Tears* with Paul Taylor (Greenhouse Publications).

Judy Annear is Senior Curator of Photography at the Art Gallery of New South Wales, Sydney. She wrote for *Art & Text*'s early issues and was a member of the editorial committee 1987–94.

Kelly Fliedner is an arts writer, curator and Program Curator of West Space, Melbourne. She is also Co-editor of online publication the *West Space Journal* and part of the Next Wave Festival's Curatorial Advisory Committee.

Lyndal Jones is Professor of Contemporary Art, School of Media and Communication, RMIT University, Melbourne.

Maria Kozic is an artist known for her performance, music, film, video, painting and installation. She is currently working on a number of video installations.

Merryn Gates is researching the Melbourne post-punk milieu (fashion, art, photography, music) for a PhD at the Australian National University, Canberra. She is a curator, writer and publisher.

Nicholas Croggon is the co-editor and co-founder of the Australian contemporary art journal *Discipline*, a co-editor of the online art history journal *emaj*, and is currently undertaking a PhD in Art History at Columbia University, New York.

Patrick McCaughey is a former Professor of Visual Arts at Monash University who tried not to be too intimidated by having Paul Taylor as a student.

Paul Foss lives with his husband, the architect and designer Micah Heimlich, in downtown Los Angeles. He is currently researching the field of therianthropy in art and film.

Peter Tyndall, artist.

Philip Brophy is a drummer among other things.

Ralph Traviati is the Director of International Media Relations for the Pirelli Group. He lives in Milan, Italy, and has two teenage children.

Rex Butler teaches in the School of English, Media Studies and Art History at the University of Queensland and is currently writing a history of "UnAustralian" art with A.D.S. Donaldson.

Robert Rooney is a Melbourne-based artist. His work was included in 'POPISM', and his reviews on 'POPISM' and 'Tall Poppies' were published in *The Age*, *The Australian*, and *Flash Art*.

Russell Walsh trained in Art History at the University of Melbourne and Theatre Direction at NIDA. His doctoral dissertation 'Obscenities offstage' (Victoria University) is available online. In 2012, at the invitation of its conveners, Janine Burke and Adrian Martin, he coordinated the symposium 'Impresario: Paul Taylor / Art & Text / POPISM' at Monash University.

Sue Cramer has held curatorial positions at the Australian Centre for Contemporary Art, Melbourne, the Institute of Modern Art, Brisbane, and the Museum of Contemporary Art, Sydney. She is currently Curator at Heide Museum of Modern Art, Melbourne.

Susan Rothnie works in Access, Education and Regional Services at the Queensland Art Gallery and wrote a PhD thesis at the University of Queensland on the 1970s in Australian art.

Vivienne Shark LeWitt is an artist who sometimes writes.

Acknowledgements

We would like to thank all of the contributors to this book and everyone who supplied images, including Lisa Barmby. Greatest thanks to the Taylor family, Greg, Philip and Janice, for patronising this book and warmly encouraging its production. Thanks are also due to the Australia Research Council for Adrian Martin's 2010–12 grant, 'Intermediality and Theories of Art/Film', part of which assisted this project. Thank-you to Geraldine Barlow, Francis Parker, Charlotte Day and Rosemary Forde of Monash University Museum of Art for their hard work on the project, and to Max Delany for his major contribution to the symposium, which generated the architecture of the book. We are extremely grateful to Janine Burke and Adrian Martin, the co-convenors of the symposium, for making available their extensive knowledge, their archives, their time and patience, and for their careful guidance on the editorial process. We thank them also for the opportunity to participate in the symposium, and the privilege of editing the subsequent publication. Their support has been unerring and extraordinary; we won't forget it. An especial thanks to Russell Walsh, coordinator of the symposium, who chose to remain behind the scenes but whose research on, interest in, and commitment to the legacy of Paul Taylor and *Art & Text* was – with Janine and Adrian – the backbone of this project. Lastly, thanks to Judy Annear for digitising and sharing an interview she conducted with Paul Taylor on Arts National ABC in 1991, and Peter Tyndall for the frequent, lengthy and always-illustrated emails of support and archival documentation.

Impresario: Paul Taylor, The Melbourne Years, 1981–1984
Edited by Helen Hughes & Nicholas Croggon

First edition 2013
ISBN 978-1-922099-08-2
Edition of 1000

Editor: Helen Hughes
Assistant editor: Nicholas Croggon

Design: Brad Haylock
Print: BPA Print Group

Co-published by Surpllus and Monash University Museum of Art (MUMA)

Surpllus Pty Ltd
PO Box 418
Flinders Lane LPO
Victoria 8009
Australia

www.surpllus.com

Monash University Museum of Art
Monash University, Caulfield Campus
900 Dandenong Road
Caulfield East
Victoria 3145
Australia

Surpllus #15

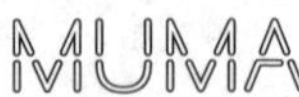